LIFE AND LABOUR IN A TWENTIETH CENTURY CITY: THE EXPERIENCE OF COVENTRY

Edited by Bill Lancaster and Tony Mason

Cryfield Press
Centre for the Study of Social History
University of Warwick
Coventry CV4 7AL

ISBN 0 9511292 0 1

CONTENTS

Illustrations

My impressions regarding Coventry after being here one month, are that it is an exceedingly difficult city in which to get things done, and that seems to be the general idea amongst the leading citizens. It lacks any real leader with a strong personality and position, and there would seem to be no old families with roots in the place. The people who have made, or who are making money, live away. The population is a very cosmopolitan one and the chief interest is what it can make for itself. The city has grown too quickly and there is little cultural side to it. (Monthly Reports from Ministry of Labour Welfare Officers Midland Region, September 1940 P.R.O. Lab 26/81).

Coventry labour has a minimum of civic sense. The peculiar employment policy of the motor industry—high wages with an hour's notice on either side—has resulted in the development of a self-conscious labouring class bargaining with the factory management on an equally ruthless basis at the highest possible price. Coventry is not, however, a communist stronghold. (Ministry of Food Special Report 3 November, 1941. P.R.O. H.O.207/1069).

At the top of my list of not-so-awful towns I would put Leeds and after that, Bradford. At the bottom I would put Birmingham, the most featureless and impersonal of all our great towns, or Coventry, which seems to me to have no civic spirit, no common consciousness, but to be just a mass of working-class people with more money to spend than they have ever had before and not the faintest idea how to spend it, no cultural interest, no concerts, no theatres, no nothing but football and dogs. (Dr. C.E.M. Joad, *Coventry Evening Telegraph*, 20 November, 1946).

Introduction

The last decade has witnessed a growing pre-occupation amongst historians with the study of individual cities. There are, however, few works which consider urban growth and development in the light of twentieth century economic and social factors. Apart from the pioneering work of Kenneth Richardson, no one has attempted a history of Coventry in the twentieth century. Coventry is a city which has occasionally seemed to embody the dominant economic and social trends of the wider society. During the 1930s, in the midst of the worst depression Britain had experienced for almost a century, Coventry was one of the centres of those new industries which would lead the British economy back to prosperity. In the early days of the war the destruction of the old city centre by German bombs gave Coventry a fame never lost as it rapidly came to symbolise the determination of Britain to resist and later, to rebuild. In the immediate post-war years life in Coventry appeared to point the way to the future for the bulk of British people. Environmentally, it meant traffic-free shopping precincts, purpose built ring roads and new housing estates. It also meant full employment and high wages. Coventry was the home of the affluent worker based largely on the success of motor manufacture and precision engineering and symbolised by above average car and home ownership of the working class. Today Coventry seems to exemplify the experience of those primarily manufacturing areas in the north, South Wales and central Scotland. The depression of the 1970s and 1980s has seriously damaged the city's manufacturing sector. Only two car assembly plants remain. Unemployment has reached levels previously unexperienced in the city. 60,000 jobs have been lost in manufacturing in eight years. School leavers have been especially hard hit.

Part of the purpose of this book is a first attempt to come to grips with these experiences. The chapters on Coventry's economic history, demographic changes, industrial relations and post-war politics focus on the city's industrial fortunes. In particular some consideration is given to the question of how far Coventry management and Coventry workers had contributed to industrial decline? How far, on the other hand, had manufacturing industry in Coventry been the victim of outside factors, most notably the policies of central government.

But this is not a book solely about the rise and decline of industry. It is also an attempt to throw some light on the experience of ordinary people, both in the home and in the wider community, at work, school and play. Although the essays have been written by professional historians an attempt has been made to allow the voices of Coventry people to be heard. This is particularly true of the essays on family life, women's work and infant welfare but it is also true to a lesser extent in the essays on the blitz, Alfred Herbert's, leisure and the rise of labour politics. In no sense is this a complete or comprehensive study. It is an early effort to grapple with what looks in the middle of the 1980s to be some of the central questions affecting Coventry this century. But plenty is left over for further work. The nature of skill among the Coventry workforce, for example; with apprenticeship opportunities falling throughout the century how was it that Coventry's industrial workers were able to maintain a reputation for being skilled? What did skill mean and how did this meaning change? The matter of what people do outside work and the obligations of family and what meaning it has for them has only been lightly touched on here. Similarly the culture of many of the newcomers to Coventry, notably the Irish and the migrants from the new Commonwealth, awaits serious historical study. In general the history of the mid-twentieth century urban family is at a very early stage although work is in progress on an oral study of the families of some Coventry car workers.

The book is by definition about Coventry's history and Coventry's people, and it is appropriate that it should come out at a time when a local history centre, based on the Herbert Museum, has been established in the city. The centre organises local history groups and publishes a thrice yearly *Bulletin*. We hope that the questions raised in this volume will stimulate local history groups both to dig out new materials and to challenge the interpretations offered in these pages. The authors also hope that the essays will make a contribution to the wider history of Britain in the twentieth century, a history which cannot be written without serious local studies of both urban and rural life.

To be sent to Coventry is a common phrase which, as every schoolboy knows, means to be ignored socially. But its origins are obscure. One explanation claims that the phrase originated amongst soldiers stationed at the local barracks during the nineteenth century. Local citizens gave the soldiers such a frosty reception that the name Coventry became another term for unfriendliness. A second locates it during the English Civil War of the seventeenth century when Royalist prisoners were locked up in the town's gaol. In the twentieth century, Coventry was not so much a place to be sentenced to as a magnet attracting workers by its expansion and prosperity for over six decades. That era seems to be over and it is therefore now an appropriate moment to see what it was like and why it has ended.

A large number of organisations and individuals have assisted the editors and contributors in the production of this volume. The University of Warwick's Research & Innovation Fund gave financial assistance with some of the research and provided a loan towards the costs of printing. Mr. David Rimmer at the Coventry Record Office proved an invaluable guide to the city archives. Debby Keene and Andrew Mealey provided much knowledgeable assistance in the Local Studies Collection. Richard Storey of the Modern Records Centre, University of Warwick, gave his usual highly professional service to all those contributors who used the Centre's important trade union and business collections. Other local librarians, especially those at the Coventry (Lanchester) Polytechnic and Warwick University Libraries gave freely their time and expertise. George Hodgkinson shared his recollections of Coventry's 'heroic period' with one of the editors. Richard Whipp read the manuscript and made constructive suggestions. The importance of Linda Tiller's help on the publishing side cannot be over-estimated. Mrs. D. Hewitt undertook with patience the difficult task of typing the manuscript. Generous contributions from Jaguar Cars Ltd., Courtaulds Ltd., the British Academy and the Coventry Co-operative Society were crucial in enabling the book to be published. Finally we wish to thank all those local people who have participated in the various oral history projects that form an important component of many of the essays in this book. It is their history but, of course, the responsibility for any inaccuracies or points of contention rests with the editors.

Chapter 1

Coventry's Industrial Economy, 1880-1980

D.W. Thoms and T. Donnelly

At the end of the nineteenth century Coventry was a city of great economic and social change. The decline of the traditional crafts of ribbon weaving and watchmaking precipitated a search for new sources of wealth and employment which, in the 1880s, was rewarded by the birth of the cycle trade, to be followed by motor cycles and cars. In addition to providing immediate relief from economic decline, these industries helped to broaden the city's engineering base to include related manufactures such as machine tools, electronics and aeronautics, which together made Coventry's name as one of the most dynamic local economies of the twentieth century. The interwar period saw the consolidation of the new staple industries and a sharp increase in the city's employment opportunities, rendering it the country's fastest growing industrial centre. From the early fifties to the mid-1960s Coventry was regarded as a 'boom town'. Part of this prosperity was attributable to the industries which emerged during the early part of the century, but increasingly the city's economic structure became dominated by motor vehicle production. Yet Coventry's proportion of national output of cars fell almost steadily from the 1950s onwards, providing an indication of what was to come in the 1970s. The seriousness of Coventry's over reliance upon motor vehicles was compounded as both the aircraft and machine tool industries experienced chronic difficulties of their own. By the 1970s the erosion of the city's engineering base was manifest in plant closures and rising unemployment, a situation exacerbated by the fact that in contrast with national and other local trends, Coventry had failed to broaden its economy by the addition of a substantial service sector. By the early 1980s Coventry was among the most badly affected areas in Britain's recession with an unemployment rate significantly above the national average. The parallels between Coventry's present difficulties and those of a century earlier are striking; in many respects the city's economic history has turned full circle.

The restructuring of Coventry's economy, 1880-1914

The Industrial Revolution was late in coming to Coventry.The city's economic structure remained long dominated by the traditional crafts of ribbon weaving and watchmaking, which in 1851 employed respectively 10,642 and 1,679 of the total population of just over 36,000. From the early 1860s, however, ribbon weaving entered a long period of decline so that by 1901 the industry's labour force had shrunk to around 2,000. For a short time during the last quarter of the nineteenth century watchmaking became Coventry's principal source of employment, though eventually it was in turn eclipsed by the new engineering products of cycles, motor vehicles and machine tools. In 1891 the Coventry watchmaking industry employed over 3,000 men and women but ten years later this had fallen by approximately one third.[1] Conversely, during the peak of the cycle boom of 1895-97 the industry employed some 6,000 workers and, although this subsequently fell away, it was compensated for by the rise of the motor vehicle industry, which by 1911 was Coventry's single most important employer with a total of almost 7,000 workers.[2] As Alfred Herbert pointed out in 1913 'We in Coventry are largely concerned with motors'.[3]

The symptoms of industrial transition also appeared in other guises. Apart from the fall in the size of the labour force employed in the ribbon industry, the value of its output declined by more than 80 per cent between 1860 and 1895. Bankruptcies multiplied, looms became idle and factories were closed, including in 1893 James Hart's Victoria Works, the largest in the Coventry industry.[4] Despite the high risk nature of ribbon manufacture, new firms regularly entered the industry, though few achieved long term success. The more stable enterprises were those which diversified into other products. Thomas Stevens, for example, developed a prosperous business in bookmarks, frillings and trimmings. Ribbon weaving also increasingly failed to attract young recruits to the industry. The apprenticeship indentures reveal that between 1850 and 1859 some 232 boys were apprenticed to ribbon weavers, while the corresponding figure for the following decade had slumped by almost a half. Similar problems were evident in watchmaking.[5] The 1890s witnessed a growing number of bankruptcies and between 1896 and 1912 the number of watch manufacturers listed in the Coventry directories fell from 106 to 35.[6] By 1914 relatively little remained of Coventry's traditional staple industries, except perhaps in the symbolic form of the artificial silk produced by Courtaulds' factory in Foleshill.

The growth of the cycle and motor vehicle industries was very rapid.

Coventry soon emerged as the principal centre of the cycle industry in Britain, with many of the leading inventors and entrepreneurs already located in the city or migrating in from elsewhere. In 1881 16 cycle manufacturers were resident in Coventry, rising to more than 70 during the boom years of the mid-1890s.[7] The importance of the local industry in national terms diminished in the early twentieth century as production increased in other parts of the country, particularly Birmingham, though by that time Coventry's economy was in any case becoming more diversified with a broad based expansion into engineering products, especially cars.

The launch of the Coventry based Daimler Motor Company in 1896 is often regarded as the genesis of the motor industry in Britain, though in practice considerable experimentation had occurred before that date. The pre-war record for the number of motor manufacturers in Coventry was reached in 1905 when 29 firms were listed in the local directories.[8] The subsequent depression in the industry removed some of the more fragile concerns, but by 1913 Coventry still boasted several of the largest and most prestigious manufacturers, such as the Rover, Singer and Daimler companies. Moreover, Coventry monopolised over 30 per cent of the West Midlands' labour force engaged in vehicle production and some 14 per cent of the national total.[9] Individually, the Coventry firms could not in 1913 rival Ford's output of their Trafford Park Works in Manchester, but collectively they were the major force in the industry at that period.

The growth of the cycle and motor vehicle industries inevitably promoted the development of component production in the city, though from the beginning many products were imported from elsewhere. For example, while Lea and Francis acquired the basic components for their high quality cycles from other Coventry firms, brakes, reflectors and bells were brought in from Birmingham, and ball bearings from as far away as Chelmsford.[10] Similarly, the early motor manufacturers found it necessary to reach beyond the city for such essential products as tyres and magnetos. However, many component manufacturers, such as Automachinery in cycles, and the specialist engine firm of White and Poppe in motor vehicles, enjoyed very considerable prosperity as the new industries expanded. Some component firms set up from scratch to take advantage of the opportunities in the industry, while others evolved from related manufacturing activities. Middlemores, for example, had their origins in the eighteenth century saddle trade but by the early 1900s were firmly entrenched in the production of cycle and motor accessories, while Rotherhams moved in the same direction after a distinguished history in watchmaking. Similarly, Alick Hill again with a background in watchmaking, set up the Coventry Chain Company in 1896 to take advantage of the expiry of Hans Renold's patent for the manufacture of roller cycle chains.[11] By 1914 Coventry's motor manufacturers had largely ceased to produce their own components. Although the Birmingham area had become the focus of this section of the industry, perhaps because of its long tradition in the small scale metal working trades, Coventry retained a special importance for particular products. For example, the Motor Manufacturing Company, one of the largest firms in Coventry in 1914, supplied 4,000 — 5,000 radiators to the trade per annum, representing some 20 per cent of the total market.[12]

Cycles and cars gave an important boost to Britain's machine tool sector. By 1914 the 17 machine tool producers in the West Midlands represented only a small proportion of the national total but among them was Alfred Herbert of Coventry whose reputation for quality products and high levels of output made the firm the outstanding manufacturer in the industry. Following its establishment in 1888, the firm's immediate growth was based upon the production of weldless steel tubes for cycles, but although this industry remained an important source of demand, production soon spread into a broad range of medium machine tools suitable for wide industrial usage.[13] The company's early success rested upon a willingness to apply best American practice and also to incorporate significant design improvements of its own. Herbert lathes, for example, came to enjoy a distinct international reputation within the industry. Yet the machine tool market was highly competitive and at the turn of the century the bulk of the equipment used by Coventry cycle firms was said to have been of American manufacture.[14] Coventry was the birth place of other machine tool manufacturers, such as Webster and Bennett (1887), Coventry Gauge and Tool (1913) and Wickmans (1925), all of which became justly famous in their own right, though none acquired the status enjoyed by Alfred Herbert.

The restructuring of Coventry's economy during this period was not wholly confined to the cycle and motor industries. The establishment in 1905 of the Courtauld and Coventry Ordnance works, together with the arrival seven years later of the electrical engine firm, British Thompson Houston, helped to channel the city's industrial activity into new directions. Courtaulds quickly emerged as one of Coventry's most important employers, with its workforce rising from a mere 200 in 1907 to around 2,200 in 1913. During the same period the firm's output of artificial silk increased more than 15 times, making it one of the outstanding industrial successes of the period.[15] The commercial progress of the Ordnance Works was retarded by difficulty in securing Government contracts, though like Courtaulds it benefited from an expansion of demand during the First World War.

The broadening of Coventry's industrial base injected fresh life into the building trades as new factories were erected and old ones extended, while housing a growing population added significantly to the demands placed upon the construction industry. By 1907 house building in Coventry was running at the rate of 800 — 1,000 units per annum, though the industry was still unable to keep pace with the demand for cheap property with the result that many workmen were obliged to take lodgings during the week and return home for Sundays.[16] Although untypical of his trade, J.G. Gray illustrates the opportunities and rewards awaiting the enterprising builder. Gray arrived in Coventry when the cycle boom was in full swing and the firm which he established soon acquired a reputation for good quality work. He became the city's most successful building contractor, his achievements including Courtaulds' Main Works, and in 1923 he was sufficiently wealthy to purchase the house and immediate grounds of the Coombe Abbey estate.[17]

The expansion of Coventry's industrial structure between 1880 and 1914 modified the geographical focus of the city's economy. While the ribbon weaving industry concentrated to the north of the city, watchmaking was to be found in the south and west. To begin with, cycle production was mainly restricted to within the city boundaries, but by the late 1890s it was spreading beyond the central areas as the accommodation problem became more acute, while much of the industrial development in the decade before the First World War centred upon Radford and Foleshill with the construction of the Courtauld and Daimler works.

Many of the Coventry cycle firms, particularly in the early days, operated on a very small scale, with perhaps just three or four employees. Movement in and out of the industry was facilitated by the limited amount of capital required by producers with modest output targets. Indeed this kind of entrepreneurial activity seems to have been a feature of late Victorian Coventry since the same practice occurred in both ribbon weaving and watchmaking. However, several of the largest firms in the industry, such as Calcott Brothers, Humber and Rudge Whitworth, were Coventry based. By 1906 Rudge Whitworth was one of the largest industrial concerns in the city with a labour force of 2,700 people and an annual output of some 75,000 cycles.[18] Despite the development of steam factory production in the textile industry during the middle decades of the nineteenth century, it was essentially the cycle industry which brought the phenomenon of large scale mass production to Coventry's industrial landscape. Yet factory employment soon reached beyond cycle manufacture. By the late 1890s Herbert had a workforce of some 500 men, while by 1913 the largest employers were to be found in the car industry.[19] The Daimler Company, for example, with an annual output of 1,000 cars and a labour force of 5,000 qualified as one of the largest engineering works in the country.[20]

In the years up to 1914 there was a considerable difference in the sexual composition of the labour force employed by the 'old' and 'new' industries. In 1901 the cycle and motor industries were dominated by men, with only ten per cent of the workforce being female. Conversely, over 74 per cent of workers in the textile industry were women, while the figure for watches and clocks was 26 per cent. Paper and printing was perhaps the industry where work was most evenly distributed between the sexes since almost 42 per cent of its employees were female.[21] This pattern of employment was largely a product of the level of skill and training which particular tasks were perceived to require, though the labour shortages of the First World War and the consequent expansion of female employment demonstrated the importance of prejudice in the traditional distribution of work. The arrival of Courtaulds made a significant difference to female employment opportunities in Coventry for by 1913 over 60 per cent of the firm's labour force were women.[22] Indeed Courtaulds attracted so many female workers that other employers found it difficult to satisfy their own requirements.

Another interesting feature of Coventry's labour force in the years before 1914 was the extreme youthfulness of males employed in the cycle and motor industries, a phenomenon which was partly related to migration patterns, a theme which is pursued later in this volume.[23] One characteristic which most production workers in the cycle and motor industries shared with their counterparts in ribbon weaving was the way employment fluctuated according to changes of season and fashion. Just as the demand for ribbons could slump as women turned to feathers or beads for decoration so the same might happen to cycles or cars as the popularity of one model eclipsed that of another, or as enthusiasm for cycling or motoring diminished during the winter months. The more general factors which caused firms to operate below capacity added to the uncertainty of employment in these industries. Some firms, Daimler, for example, were unwilling to shed skilled labour which may have been carefully recruited over a long period, but the bulk of employers were less reticent in reducing their wage bill when production levels fell.

The general explanation for the restructuring of Coventry's economy is located is broader national and international trends, though many of the specific problems and opportunities relate to the particular characteristics of the city's industrial history. The decline of ribbon weaving in Coventry is associated with the removal of tariff protection following the Cobden-Chevalier treaty of 1860. This came at a particularly sensitive time for local manufacturers since their financial position had already been weakened by serious industrial unrest in 1858-59 — trouble which flared again in the summer of 1860, only some four months after the implementation of the treaty.[24] In addition, however, the industry's prosperity was dependent upon a broad array of factors, some of which were beyond the control of individual businessmen. For example, it was always vulnerable to changes of fashion, and after 1860 there appears to have been a long-term drift away from ribbons as decoration. More fundamentally, the Coventry manufacturers were unable to compete effectively, either in design or price, with imported ribbons. French producers posed a formidable challenge with their attractive designs and quality of product, while the Swiss benefited from highly competitive pricing. Even without the strike of 1860 the Coventry manufacturers would have found it difficult to resist incursion from foreign competitors into domestic markets. The strong craft traditions of the Coventry silk ribbon industry retarded the development of efficient large scale factory production, while the more competitive environment after 1860 made entrepreneurs reluctant to invest the capital required to modernise production.

Similar problems explain the demise of the Coventry watchmaking industry. Although Rotherhams in 1843 was the first English firm to introduce centralised factory production of watches, the Coventry trade remained firmly wedded to the small scale production of relatively expensive timepieces, based upon a complex network of independent specialised craftsmen. While Rotherhams and the Coventry Watch Movement Company, founded in 1889 to produce complete movements, both introduced modern machine production, the Coventry industry was unable to match the economies of scale achieved by Swiss and American firms. Swiss manufacturers began to mass produce watches in the 1840s, closely followed in the 1850s by the American based Waltham Watch Company, with the result that output in both countries soon began to outstrip that of English producers.[25] Coventry remained important for some time in the production of pocket watches for the high class trade, but the market for cheap watches, which was growing rapidly in the 1870s, was dominated by foreign producers. By 1914 the Coventry watchmaking industry, still in the hands of relatively small firms, was shrinking rapidly, and the Coventry Watch Movement Manufacturing Company, as well as Rotherhams, had diversified into the manufacture of components for cars and cycles.

The growth of cycle, motor and science based industries was a national phenomenon, but what has to be explained is why Coventry in particular should have become such an important centre of production. Many of the major personalities in the restructuring of Coventry's economy were relative newcomers to the city. Thus few of the leading cycle manufacturers were Coventry born. The Riley family was an exception, moving from textiles to cycles, motor cycles and eventually cars, but such famous names in the industry as James Starley, William Hillman, Thomas Humber and Daniel Rudge migrated to the city from other parts of the country. Siegfried Bettman, the founder of the Triumph marque, arrived in Coventry in 1890 with Bavarian origins and experience in London as a cycle export agent.[26] Herbert, Daimler, Coventry Ordnance and Courtaulds are examples of other firms already mentioned whose presence in Coventry in 1914 was of comparatively recent origin. In addition to their capital, the entrepreneurs associated with these concerns brought technical and business skills to Coventry and a willingness to engage in relatively high risk commercial activities so that much of the city's late Victorian and Edwardian dynamism was an imported asset.

The pioneer of the cycle industry in Coventry was James Starley who in 1861 helped to form the Coventry Sewing Machine Company, originally established to exploit the local population's engineering skills. However, an indifferent market for sewing machines, coupled with a fortuitous enquiry from France for 400 cycles, saw the firm, under Starley's guidance, change its name in 1869 to the Coventry Machinists Company, and thus in effect initiate the history of cycle manufacture in Britain.[27] Several of the company's employees established their own enterprises, including George Singer and Thomas and John Bayliss, while in turn these men provided the training which enabled others to branch out as independent cycle producers. The Starley family remained important participants in the industry, and James' nephew, J.K. Starley, is credited with the invention of the first effective 'safety' bicycle.

An abundant supply of suitable labour was one of the factors which decided Courtaulds to extend their operations to Coventry with the establishment of a viscose plant in Foleshill. Women were preferred for reeling so that the decline of the ribbon industry provided a substantial pool of female workers who also had the benefit of a long tradition of employment in the textile industry. Coventry's communications network, together with plentiful supplies of coal and water, both of which were required in large quantities for the production of artificial silk, also made the city an attractive location for expansion.[28]

The availability of workshop or factory space was another way in which the decline of the traditional industries assisted the growth of the new sectors. Although some firms were located from the beginning in purpose built structures, it was common practice to rent or buy secondhand premises which could later be extended or exchanged for more spacious accommodation. This arrangement saved on capital, but it also enabled production to begin with the minimum of delay, as the Daimler operation illustrates. The Company's Chairman, Harry Lawson, informed shareholders in May 1896 that

> We did not wish to build works because it would take too long, so we visited various works in the country which were for sale. We went to Cheltenham and Birmingham, in both of which places there were motor works for sale — all old fashioned ... At last we went to Coventry, and saw what we believed to be an almost perfect place for manufacturing these machines.[29]

This was in fact a vacant textile mill on the Foleshill Road. In addition, however, Coventry was favoured because of the transferable skills of cycle workers, and because of the presence of a rapidly developing medium machine tool industry, which could be of value in supplying equipment to the works.

Once Coventry's industrial restructuring began it developed a momentum of its own, propelled by important linkages across and within different parts of the engineering sector. The experience of the Riley family of three major stages of industrial transition was perhaps unique, but many firms modified their focus of interest according to changes in the structure of demand. These changes not only provided the opportunity for diversification, but frequently made it a condition of survival. Thus in the late 1890s when many of the components used by cycle manufacturers came to be made by a pressed steel process, orders to drop-forgers fell sharply so that the Coventry stamping firm of Thomas Smith was obliged increasingly to seek business from engineering firms, coach builders and makers of agricultural equipment.[30] The presence in Coventry of firms which were prepared to react positively to the demands of the new industries helps to explain why so many cycle and motor vehicle firms should find the city an attractive venue. For example, while some car manufacturers, such as Armstrong-Siddeley and Daimler, did most of their own body work, others relied heavily upon the skills of the numerous specialist coach builders in the city.[31]

Coventry was unique in the number of motor car producers whose origins were located in the cycle industry. Riley and Humber began making cars in 1898, Swift and the Allard Cycle Company in 1899, Lea Francis in 1903, Rover in 1904 and Singer in 1906. Triumph did not enter the car market until 1923, while the giant cycle firm of Rudge-Whitworth remained aloof from the industry, though both firms were active in the production of motor cycles. The Daimler and Standard companies are two of the principal examples of car firms founded in Coventry before 1914 which did not have strong connections with the cycle trade. The transition from cycles to cars was assisted by the intermediate stage of motor cycles which provided the opportunity for technical experimentation. Capital generated by the cycle industry often provided the necessary resources to support research and initial production. In addition, however, many cycle manufacturers were forced to diversify because of the rapid influx at the end of the 1890s of cheap mass produced American products, a problem compounded by the fact that many of the leading Coventry firms, including Singer and the Premier Cycle Company, persisted with high quality/ high price machines, which represented the stagnant end of the market.[32] In the country at large, as well as in Coventry, the more flexible producers successfully adapted their manufacturing techniques and marketing strategies so that by 1913 Britain dominated world exports in cycles. Although at that time Coventry remained a powerful force in the cycle industry, many of the city's pioneering firms were fully committed to the production of motor vehicles.

Between 1880 and 1914 Coventry rapidly emerged from an industrial craft based economy to dependence upon the light engineering industries of the twentieth century. The speed and magnitude of economic change inevitably brought great social upheaval. The city's population increased from 46,563 in 1881 to 106,349 in 1911, reflecting in part boundary changes, but also the attraction to migrants of employment in the cycle and motor industries. The redistribution of people within Coventry came increasingly to favour the areas associated with the new industries. The Medical Officer of Health reported in 1887 that 'Gosford-street ward owing to its being the great centre of the cycle industry has grown from third to first place in regard to the relative number of its inhabitants: nearly one half of the total increase since 1881 has taken place within it, and last year alone there was an addition of 543 to its population'.[33] Population growth placed considerable pressure upon housing, education and other social amenities. During the first decade of the twentieth century, for example, building activity reached frenetic proportions, but the supply of houses was always in danger of being overwhelmed by the relentless growth of demand. At the same time Board of Education memoranda show Coventry's elementary and secondary school provision to have been buckling under the strain of a rapidly expanding child population.

The environment and rewards of work were also affected by the growth of the engineering industries. The spread of the factory system, aided increasingly by the application of joint stock finance, meant that many more workers than in the past were employed in relatively large units of production with less direct contact with their employer and using equipment which they themselves did not rent or own. Mechanisation increased the speed of production, particularly in the manufacture of cycles. By 1914 there was some movement towards the volume production of cars, but in many ways the industry retained its craft specialisms until well into the interwar period. In some respects the most unpleasant working environment was to be found at Courtaulds where employees could find themselves operating in conditions of very high temperatures and even in situations carrying the risk of blindness through contact with dangerous chemicals.[34] Yet Coventry, with the exception of the 1912 strikes in the bicycle trade, was not subject to the serious industrial unrest found in many parts of Britain between 1908 and 1913. To some extent this may be explained by relatively weak trade union organisation, but in addition wage rates by the early twentieth century were a substantial improvement on the traditional levels of remuneration in the textile industry.[35]

The restructuring of Coventry's economy between 1880 and 1914 radically altered the social experience of most working class people in Coventry. The middle classes also shared in these changes, reflected materially in the growth of new housing development on the city fringes and politically in the developing involvement in Coventry's local government of businessmen from the expanding industries. When George Singer became Mayor in 1891 he symbolised Coventry's transition from a craft based society to one which was shortly to become fully integrated with modern industrial capitalism.

From the beginning to the end of war, 1914-1945

Many Coventry firms were important suppliers of arms and equipment to the services during the First World War. Activity at the Ordnance Works in Red Lane was immediately boosted by a rapid increase in demand for naval and land armaments, but in addition the company expanded its aviation work, which at the beginning of 1914 was still in its infancy. Reginald Bacon, the managing director of the Works at this time, later recalled that he almost lived on the telephone taking orders for the firm's products.[36] New workshops had to be built with the 'old ones overflowing with work' and, as orders mounted, the debts that had accumulated during the company's early days soon disappeared.[37] The Ordnance Works' output during the First World War included 710 aeroplanes, 111 tanks, 92 anti-aircraft guns, nearly 400,000 cartridge cases and millions of fuses and detonators.[38]

The Ordnance Works was the obvious candidate for expansion under the stimulus of wartime conditions, but its experience was far from unique since Coventry's industrial structure by 1914 ensured that the city would be heavily committed on a broad front to the production of war materials. Courtaulds, for example, were able to sell all the artificial silk they could manufacture, while the company's Coventry laboratory was used by the Ministry of Munitions for research into explosives.[39] Yet it was the city's engineering base which made it a prime recipient of Government contracts. Alfred Herbert noted that:

> The effect of the war on the engineering industry has been to render demand, enormously and continuously, in excess of supply. It has not been a question of obtaining orders, but, on the contrary, every engineering concern has been swamped with orders in excess of its possible output and competition for the time being has practically ceased to exist.[40]

The Red Lane factory of Thomas Smith's Stamping Works became so involved in the production of engineering equipment for military purposes that in March 1916 the firm was placed under official control, with its entire output being determined by Government departments.[41]

Perhaps the motor manufacturers experienced the most significant impact of war since not only were they required to produce large numbers of military vehicles, but the practice of motoring and motor vehicle engineering received a stimulus which was to prove important to the industry in the post-war period. Although the production of cars fell away, the main War Office contractors turned to ambulances, trucks and armoured vehicles. Daimler, for example, produced more than 4,000 commercial vehicles, including a number of 3-ton lorries which were set up as travelling workshops.[42] These were used for servicing the Daimler sleeve-valve engine which was employed initially in heavy tractors for pulling 15-inch howitzers, and later in tanks.[43] The Rover company ceased production of its cars, but it became heavily involved as a contract supplier in the manufacture of parts for staff cars and ambulances.[44] It also built motor cycles for military and official use, though it was rather overshadowed by Triumph which enjoyed enormous success with its Model 'H' machines, selling some 30,000 for War Office use.[45]

In addition to providing transport for the army, the major car companies extended their production to other areas of military equipment. Thus Daimler made vast quantities of shells, while the Standard company supplied mortars, and both firms entered the market for aircraft. The Standard factory at Canley was erected in 1916 specifically for aero work and by the armistice some 1,600 aircraft had been built there.[46] Similarly, the Daimler factory was extended to meet the demand for aviation equipment and eventually the company even constructed its own airfield at Radford to test airframes.[47] Near the end of the war Daimler manufactured approximately 80 aircraft per month, more than four times the figure for Standard.[48] Siddeley-Deasy was another Coventry motor manufacturer to become involved in aircraft production, an interest which the firm retained after 1918.[49]

Under the pressure of wartime demand many Coventry firms extended their physical capacity and technical capabilities, both of which helped to facilitate the city's subsequent industrial growth. High levels of output were also sustained by the development of mass production techniques, the use of female labour and longer working hours. Labour supply was a particularly serious matter since the outbreak of war brought a rush of conscripts from among Coventry's engineering workforce. Standard recruited women shopfloor workers for the first time, mostly for the manufacture of shells, while at Daimler 'As the war progressed female labour increased by leaps and bounds'.[50] Very few women had been employed in the production of machine tools before 1914 but the exigencies of the war effort brought a dramatic change in the composition of the industry's labour force. Alfred Herbert was a rather reluctant convert to the employment of women in the engineering industry, claiming that due to 'fundamental differences in mentality it is perfectly certain that, save in the most exceptional instances, women cannot become skilled mechanics.'[51] However, he did admit that when a woman 'has become familiar with the details of a definite operation she will continue to repeat that operation satisfactorily'.[52]

Men and women were expected to work long hours in order to maintain output levels. Adults began work at the Ordnance factory at 6.00a.m. and, punctuated by meal and rest breaks, continued until

8.00p.m., when the night shift took over.[53] The relentless pace of Coventry's war effort was recaptured by an employee at Smith's Stamping Works.

> Never was a hammer allowed to stand idle! If a stamper was sick, or for any reason couldn't come to work, his hammer *had* to be kept going. Many a time, I can remember, after I'd done a hard day's work and had just gone home, there came a knock at the door. This was the foreman on the night-shift come over from the stamp shop to ask me to take another man's place on the hammer. I swallowed my tea and back I went. It meant working the full round of the clock, but many of us did it often.[54]

A Government Commission noted of the West Midlands in 1917 that 'the workmen are tired and overstrained' and no doubt the evidence of the Coventry workshops and factories contributed to this assessment.[55]

Invigorated by the experience of the First World War, Coventry's industrial development, despite suffering in the slump, recession and the unemployment that characterised the whole of the West Midlands in the early twenties, continued to follow the long-term pattern that had been evolving since the turn of the century. In particular, the growth of the motor industry quickly outstripped that of both pedal and motor cycles and more than compensated for the decline of the older watch-making and ribbon trades, though the latter's eclipse and that of textiles as a whole, was offset to a degree by the renewed growth of Courtauld's in the 1920s with its emphasis on artificial fibres. The motor industry's growth was paralleled by the rapid development of the machine tool, electrical and aeronautics industries, giving Coventry what could be described roughly as a 'development bloc' of the new staple industries that were to dominate Britain's industrial structure from the Second World War onwards. Upon these foundations was based Coventry's reputation of 'boom town prosperity' that lasted down to the 1970s when the city suffered greatly in the general slump, depression and de-industrialisation that affected the West Midlands region as a whole.

In 1919 Coventry's population stood at 136,000, dropped to 128,152 in 1921 during the slump that followed the boom years of 1919-20, recovered to 139,000 in 1927 and then expanded very rapidly to over 220,000 by the outbreak of war in 1939, making Coventry the fastest growing city in terms of population growth in Britain between the wars. Essentially, this was a relatively young population that grew primarily as a consequence of migration as people flocked from the North of England and the Celtic fringes to seek work and high earnings in the city's burgeoning industries. Indeed in 1938 the local Medical Officer of Health described the rate of population growth in the 1930s as being 'phenomenal', adding that the migrants to the city were mainly young adults and children who therefore 'fortified' the health of the population and contributed greatly to Coventry's low death rates, and healthy marriage and birth rates, the latter two being generally above the national average for England and Wales.[56]

The occupational structure of the population as shown in Table 1.1 reflected the city's industrial base over time and is indicative of how over two decades Coventry became highly dependent upon a narrow range of industries just as older towns such as Sunderland, Jarrow and the Lancashire and Yorkshire textile towns had in the previous century, and which were all experiencing economic difficulties between the wars. The difference was that at the time almost all of Coventry's industrial sectors were expanding. Between 1923 and the end of World War II the working population virtually doubled and within that figure several accompanying changes are immediately apparent. The first is the expansion of the motor vehicle and general engineering industries which included aeronautics, car components and electrical engineering. Employment in motor vehicles rose quite spectacularly, never falling below 35 per cent of the insured work force. Not quite as dynamic, but still very important, was the growth of electrical engineering, which though masked in general engineering, accounted for 4.5 per cent of the work force in 1937 and then rose to more than ten per cent during the war years, thus reflecting the development of the communications industry in the city based mainly at G.E.C. On the other hand, despite Courtauld's development programmes during the 1920s and early thirties, the percentage employed in textiles fell steadily from the beginning of the century, dropping from 11 per cent in 1901 to 8.6 per cent in 1923 and to just over three per cent in 1946.[57]

The growing importance and increasing dependency of the city on a relatively small range of industrial occupations is further illustrated by Table 1.2 which compares the percentage employed in Coventry's major industries in 1939 and 1946 in comparison with the national averages for Great Britain and Northern Ireland. Again the emphasis on vehicles and engineering is self-evident, as is the decline of textiles and the public utility industries of gas, water, electricity and transport. The low incidence of building is at first surprising, but is explained by the small scale structure of the local building industry, which was probably why

Table 1:1. Estimated Numbers of Insured Workers in Coventry 1923-46.

				Number in Each sector as a percentage of the total insured	
	1923	1937	1946	1937	1946
Vehicles/Motor Cycles	22,350	37,390	41,063	37	36.9
General Engineering	3,310	7,670	13,600	7.6	12.2
Other Metal Industries	4,960	6,610	13,131	6.5	11.6
Textiles	4,870	7,330	4,747	7.5	3.4
Coal mining	2,190	2,770	2,850	2.7	2.6
Building	2,120	6,400	5,296	6.3	4.8
Distribution	2,340	6,770	6,290	6.7	5.6
Others	14,350	25,970	25,472	25.7	22.9
Total	56,440	101,010	111,943	100	100

Source: Marson, 'Coventry: a study in urban geography' (unpublished MA thesis, Liverpool 1949),p.93.

factory and office block work was carried out by national firms. As industry grew so too did the size of unit, and the trend towards factory concentration of production, apparent from the 1890s, continued unabated. The old workshops and topshops of traditional Coventry had largely faded from the industrial scene by the end of the 1920s. By 1939

Table 1:2. Comparison of Coventry's major industries with the same in Great Britain and Northern Ireland 1939-46.

	Great Britain & Northern Ireland		*Coventry*		*Location Factor Coventry*	
		Percentage Employed				
	1939	*1946*	*1939*	*1946*	*1939*	*1946*
Engineering	6.1	7.9	11.0	21.1	1.8	2.7
Vehicles	3.5	4.3	36.1	36.9	10.3	8.6
Other Metal Industries	5.1	5.2	14.9	11.5	2.9	2.2
Textiles	7.3	4.8	7.2	3.4	.99	.7
Building	8.9	6.8	6.5	4.7	.75	.7
Gas, Water, Electric	1.4	1.5	1.1	.65	.77	.47
Transport	5.7	6.8	1.7	2.3	.3	.34

Source: Marson, *op.cit.*, p.91.

Courtaulds employed a work force nearly 5,000 strong, while British Thomson Houston and G.E.C. had nearly 10,000 on the payroll between them, and the city's main car firms averaged 5,000 each.[58]

Such industrial change led to a rather lop-sided development in occupational skills in Coventry. Table 1.3 illustrates this clearly showing the high preponderance of skilled labour in the city and a correspondingly low number of professionals, managers and administrators who earned their living there compared with the interwar figures for England and Wales as a whole. Coventry had long prided itself in being a city of skills, but in defining skill in the context of the interwar years great care is essential. It appears that the proportion of semi-skilled manual workers as a proportion of the total work force dropped from 45 per cent in 1911 to 33 per cent in 1921 and then to 24 per cent in 1931. This decline is explained by the changing nature of industry in the city in that many semi-skilled workers could be trained to do a specific task within a short space of time and so gained a local skilled status which would not necessarily be recognised as such elsewhere. According to Friedman, skilled classification in Coventry simply meant distinguishing between workers who were paid a skilled district rate for a specified job, a reward and status which were increasingly achieved as a result of bargaining power rather than by the acquisition of skill *per se*. Finally, the Table demonstrates a higher than national average proportion of women in clerical posts which in turn is indicative of the growth of large scale modern industry and perhaps also of the tightness of the labour market.[59]

The growth of the British motor industry had been inhibited during the First World War as manufacturing industry turned its attention to meeting wartime demand, but as soon as hostilities were over the production of motor vehicles was again embraced with enthusiasm as both old and new contenders entered the field once more amidst heavy competition. In 1919 and 1920 at least forty new car producing firms emerged with a further forty-six joining them between 1921 and 1925. With competition being so fierce many of the new entrants failed with over one hundred and fifty firms being eliminated from the scene over the last four mentioned years.[60] Coventry's experience in this was no exception. Listed among the vehicles which were produced and then disappeared in those heady years were the Cooper, Emms, Wigan-Barlow, Omega, Stoneleigh and Warwick. Another was the Cluley, turned out by the cycle firm of Clarke, Cluley and Company. Calcotts, an old established cycle firm tried again to move into car production in the early 1920s but failed in 1926 and were saved from extinction only by

Table 1.3. Percentage of Persons Employed in Each Occupational Group. England and Wales, Coventry C.B. 1921 and 1931.

		1921			1931		
		Male	Female	Total	Male	Female	Total
England and Wales							
Higher professionals	1A	1.36	0.17	1.01	1.51	0.30	1.15
Lower professionals	1B	2.00	7.46	3.61	1.98	7.20	3.59
Employers and proprietors	2A	6.52	5.98	6.36	5.96	4.99	5.67
Managers & administrators	2B	5.04	2.06	4.16	4.61	0.82	3.48
Clerical workers	3	5.42	8.58	6.35	6.96	10.42	7.99
Foremen, inspectors and supervisors	4	2.25	0.36	1.69	2.12	0.49	1.63
Skilled manual	5	36.21	24.14	32.65	34.10	22.64	30.69
Semi-skilled manual	6	32.61	47.39	36.97	24.77	46.10	31.11
Unskilled manual	7	8.59	3.86	7.20	17.91	7.03	14.68
		100.00	100.00	100.00	100.00	100.00	100.00
Total		*12,061,853*	*5,041,853*	*17,103,706*	*13,195,046*	*5,581,002*	*18,776,048*
Coventry C.B.							
Higher professionals	1A	0.87	0.06	0.66	0.97	0.07	0.72
Lower professionals	1B	2.04	6.28	3.15	2.31	5.83	3.27
Employers & proprietors	2A	3.79	7.58	4.78	3.73	6.19	4.40
Managers & administrators	2B	3.58	1.58	3.06	3.07	0.44	2.35
Clerical workers	3	4.76	15.65	7.61	5.94	16.03	8.71
Foremen, inspectors and supervisors	4	2.48	0.58	1.98	2.72	1.04	2.26
Skilled manual	5	53.37	32.03	47.79	53.04	34.04	47.82
Semi-skilled manual	6	24.00	32.45	26.21	14.83	28.95	18.71
Unskilled manual	7	5.11	3.79	4.76	13.39	7.40	11.74
		100.00	100.00	100.00	100.00	100.00	100.00
Total		*44,724*	*15,843*	*60,567*	*60,787*	*23,019*	*83,806*

Source: Censuses of Population.

being rescued by Singer.[61]

Despite the fluctuations of the early post-war years the long term future of the car industry was assured. After the period of heavy competition had ended the industry came to be dominated by the 'Big Six', consisting of Ford, Singer, Standard, Austin, Vauxhall and Morris. Slowly the methods of production matured with the trends towards bulk and then flow line production and output became concentrated in fewer and fewer hands. With sixty per cent of production Austin and Morris were clearly the dominant firms and their rise to prominence started the decisive move from individual bespoke to batch and finally mass production methods of a rudimentary nature which in turn led to considerable savings in costs and, along with competition, resulted in a fall in car prices of approximately 25 per cent between 1925 and 1929.[62] During the Depression of 1929-32 the motor industry appears to have suffered little in comparison with other sectors of British industry such as coal, shipbuilding, steel and textiles. This cannot, however, be attributed to the strength of the U.K. car market but rather to its lack of development in the 1920s when, for the most part, production was still mainly in the luxury class and it was not until the ensuing decade that the motoring habits and incomes of the middle class and the benefits of tariff protection permitted an expansion of this market, albeit only to a limited extent, in that the trend was towards smaller, cheaper cars of 10 H.P. or less.[63]

Turning more specifically to Coventry's role in this movement the impression is one of industrial dynamism as firms came and went leaving a residue of talent and experience from which enterprises such as Standard, Daimler, Singer, Lea Francis and Jaguar benefited, thus placing the city at the forefront of the U.K. motor industry with both mass and specialist producers functioning side by side, with two of these, Standard and Rootes (the latter replacing Singer), joining Morris and the others in the ranks of the 'Big Six' which by 1939 controlled ninety per cent of the market.[64] The headquarters of the Morris/Nuffield empire lay in Oxford, but William Morris's connections with the Coventry car industry were strong and stretched back to 1910 when he regularly spent an average of three days a week in the city where he had many contracts for supplies of component parts as well as friends. White and Poppe, for instance, which had been operating in the city since 1899 supplied him with carburettors. Though heavily dependent upon Midlands suppliers, Morris was among the first to appreciate that by 'buying out' components overhead costs could be spread, thus providing greater financial security as well as the opportunity to benefit from technical advances made in outside engineering firms, sparing the research and development costs involved. Such practices enabled Morris to minimise his own prices and maintain a high degree of cost efficiency in his own plants. In fact, Morris only acquired other firms when absolutely necessary to ensure essential supplies to maintain output. In the immediate post-war years, when White and Poppe could no longer supply him adequately with engines because of their continued involvement with government contracts, Morris approached Hotchkiss et Cie, the French armaments firm which had a branch in Coventry and secured an agreement with them to provide the firm with engines at £50 each or less. Similarly, he purchased car bodies from Hollick and Pratt, another Coventry concern, until 1922 when after a serious fire damaged their premises all Hollick & Pratt's bodywork operations were moved to Oxford. A near identical pattern evolved with the supply of radiators from the Doherty Motor Components Company which was persuaded eventually to open a branch factory adjacent to the Cowley works at Oxford under the title of Osberton Radiators. Indeed by 1923 both the Coventry and Cowley sites had been purchased by Morris and brought under direct control. A slightly different policy line was followed in dealing with Hotchkiss et Cie. Morris asked the French concern to expand and develop its Coventry interests to supply him with double the three hundred engines a week being supplied, but because of other commitments the French refused. Instead, they suggested that Morris purchase the Coventry premises which he duly did for £349,423 in 1923, changing the name to Morris Engines in the process. An investment programme of £300,000 was immediately put in train doubling capacity to over six hundred engines a week and, with further investment that followed, by 1934 all of Morris engines were produced on the Coventry site under the management of Leonard Lord.[65]

After the Great War the Standard Motor Company like others returned to car production. With a work force over two thousand strong operations were concentrated at rapidly expanding facilities at Canley on the outskirts of Coventry. After building rather large saloon cars such as the SLS and the SLO four seaters production was switched to smaller vehicles such as the Standard 7, the Standard 9 in 1927 and the Flying Standard series in the 1930s.[66] The success of this policy can be gleaned from the fact that Standard's share of total 'Big Six' production rose from 4.9 per cent in 1929 to 12.8 per cent in 1939. Much of this success may be attributed to Captain (later Sir) John Black who came to the company in 1929 after working with William Hillman for ten years. Black, like others of his ilk, who entered the industry after the war had no formal engineering training, but had a sufficient knowledge of petrol engines which coupled with a shrewd sense of management helped to mark him out as one of the most outstanding figures in the British motor industry between the wars. Under Black's direction, especially after he succeeded Maudslay as chairman in 1934, new investment at Canley in the 1930s in the form of new conveyor systems raised output to meet both rising domestic and overseas demand. Indeed, output doubled from 22,422 units in 1933 to over 54,000 in 1939.[67] The third Coventry based firm to join the 'Big Six' in the thirties was the Rootes Group. Originally, the Rootes brothers, William and Reginald had been motor distributors in Kent and it was from this that their interest in motor assembly and manufacturing grew. In 1926 the brothers took their first step in this direction when they acquired Thrupp & Maberly, a long established firm of coachbuilders, and in the following year the firm took over William Hillman & Company before completing the initial Rootes Group in 1932 when a controlling interest in the Humber Company was achieved. So the Rootes Group was born.[68]

Thus three of the 'Big Six' concerns either had all or a substantial part of their operations based in Coventry, making the city one of the most important centres of automobile production in Britain. The significance of this over the 1930s during the battle for the light car market can be seen in the strides both Rootes and Standard made in output share in that decade with their respective market shares rising from 5.6 per cent to 10.9 per cent and 5.1 per cent to 12.8 per cent between 1930 and 1939 .

Of the other car firms Singer failed to hold the momentum of the 1920s and fell out of the 'Big Six', while Riley, who were in financial difficulties in the late thirties were absorbed in the Morris empire. Rover, which had enjoyed considerable success before the First World War with its 12 h.p. four cylinder light car, failed to realise its early promise and by 1939 the company was a relative minnow in the car business. Board room disputes and poor management brought Rover to the edge of bankruptcy before the appointment of a new managing director in 1933 stimulated a modest revival based upon careful regulation of output and the introduction of a revised range of quality cars.[69] Of great long term significance was the appearance in Coventry of William Lyons, founder of Jaguar. In 1922 Lyons entered into partnership with William Walmsley and began to manufacture sidecars, but by 1927 Lyons had concluded an agreement with Herbert Austin whereby he purchased Austin chassis, took them to his premises in Blackpool, built new bodies for them and sold them as specialist cars. Business expanded rapidly and in search of new premises in close proximity to the heart of the motor industry, Lyons leased an old shell-filling factory in Lockhurst Lane, north Coventry, where he built the Austin Swallow. He also continued his practice of acquiring chassis, engines and other component parts from outside suppliers and then fitting them with his own individually designed bodies. By 1928 links had been secured with both Fiat and Swift and he displayed both theirs and his own models at Olympia that year. Over the next ten years Lyons also had close links with Standard which supplied him with engine units for his own SS cars in 1932, the name Jaguar not being adopted until just before the outbreak of World War II. Walmsley retired in 1935 leaving Lyons in sole control but by that time the firm was well established as a producer of high quality cars in a market that was contested by other Coventry firms such as Humber and Lea Francis, but space precludes a discussion of their activities.[70]

As discussed previously the expansion of the motor industry was paralleled by the growth and development of the other metal and engineering industries. These were vital not only to the motor industry but to the numerous new industries such as aeronautics and electrical engineering that generally expanded between the wars. To the motor industry, for instance, they supplied the necessary component parts such as radiators, magnetos, lights, rims, wheels, carburettors and all the other essentials that went into the construction of a car. Other firms performed the equally important functions of body pressing and drop forging and the making of machine tools, all of which eased the introduction of both batch and mass production methods in the car and other industries. Among the first group, the already mentioned firm of White & Poppe continued the progress made before 1914 while the British Piston Ring Company opened what was described as a 'model factory' in Holbrooks for the making of magnetos and carburettors. In the Calso factory in Helen Street, all-weather leather seating and roofing materials were made for twenty-two different models of British cars.[71] At the heart of this was the continued expansion of the machine tools industry whose growth is eloquently and accurately summed up in a statement by Alfred Herbert when commenting on the progress of the industry.

> For several years the position and prospects of the machine tool trade have improved steadily. The volume of work going through the shops has increased and in many instances overtime and night-shifts are running.

Indeed, the experience of Harry Harley's Gauge and Tool Company and Axel Wickman's run almost parallel to that of Herbert's. In the 1930s all three found themselves requiring factory expansion and new investment to meet rising orders. Indeed, Wickman, a Swede who had trained at Krupp's in Germany, quit his rather cramped premises in Queen Victoria Road altogether and moved to Banner Lane where he opened up over 42,000 square feet of new factory in 1937.[72]

The First World War had given a tremendous boost to the country's aircraft industry in general and during hostilities several Coventry concerns such as the Ordnance Factory, Daimler and Standard all contributed to its growth by building body frames, engines or at least parts. The nature of aircraft production both during and after the war was closely bound up with both the general and specific kinds of engineering carried out in the city and perhaps it was only natural that once experience had been gained in this field there was more than a degree of reluctance to forsake it when peacetime demand appeared promising. Though Daimler returned primarily to motor car production, as did Standard, John Siddeley did not, being well aware of the potential market for both military and civil aircraft that would follow the war. His highly successful fighter plane, the Puma, continued in high demand until well into the 1920s and in 1919 the Air Ministry adopted his Siskin plane for the R.A.F. Indeed, Siddeley has been described as probably the most dominant figure in the British aircraft industry during the twenties. In 1923 he entered into an agreement with Armstrong Whitworth, the Tyneside armaments firm, whereby all of the latter's aeronautical work was brought to Coventry where Siddeley centred his operations at Whitley, with a work force of more than three hundred and fifty men. As Richardson has argued, Siddeley's main strength lay in his financial acumen, but his lack of a formal technical training appears to have presented no barrier to his commercial success in the early days of the industry and it was not until the 'technical revolution' in aircraft design and construction occurred in the 1930s that Siddeley's began to suffer, particularly with the ascendancy of Rolls Royce. The first serious blow came in 1932 when the Atlanta aircraft of Imperial Airways had to have its Siddeley engines replaced and modified before it could function successfully. This was compounded in 1934 when the R.A.F. chose the Gloster Gauntlet with its Rolls Royce engines as its new strike aircraft in preference to Siddeley's Scimitar. Even the Whitley bomber had to have its Siddeley produced Tiger engines replaced with Rolls Royce Merlins before it could fly efficiently. Indeed, it could be argued that had it not been for the onset of rearmament then the aircraft industry in Coventry would have been in serious trouble.[73]

The emergence of the motor, aircraft and electronics industries between the wars were all part of the 'revolution in communications' and in a Coventry context this is highlighted by the rapid development of G.E.C. with its emphasis on radio and telephone equipment. Beginning with the production of magnetos in 1916, G.E.C. eventually became one of the largest employers in the city with the work force rising to approximately 7,000 just before World War Two. Between 1921 and 1938 the firm's initial site at Copsewood had doubled in size and new premises were acquired through the purchase of the old Lea Francis factory in Ford Street and also of properties in Spon Street and Queen Victoria Road which had been vacated by Rudge Whitworth and Wickman's respectively. So successful was the firm that Coventry became one of the main centres of the radio industry in the U.K.[74]

As new industries emerged the traditional ribbon weaving trades continued their decline, though as late as 1920 textiles generally gave employment to around 5,000 people, mainly women scattered around thirteen factories. Naturally, the textile industry changed markedly between the wars with the demise of cotton and wool which in turn gave rise to artificial fibres. Locally, the long-established concern of J. and J. Cash survived and adapted by producing a wide range of the new materials in the form of ribbons, tapes, stockings and underwear, but the most prominent success in this field was at Courtaulds' several factories in the city. Courtaulds had first arrived in Coventry in 1905 and during the inter-war period the firm continued its rapid pace of development in Coventry by expanding its development and output of man-made fibres with nearly 4,094 of its total Midland's work force of 11,000 being located in the Lockhurst Lane complex and a further 1,837 at Little Heath.[75]

Industrial growth and success though brought with it problems particularly in the fields of housing, education and social services generally, all of which created a great deal of activity in the building industry. Indeed, throughout the period industrialists complained bitterly of housing shortages preventing the recruitment of labour which in fact only echoed similar complaints by the local Medical Officer of Health. Yet Coventry's difficulties were in many ways unexceptional in that even without such a quick pace of economic development a great deal of new housebuilding was required, especially to clear the inner city slums such as the St. John's Street and Much Park Street areas; in the latter infant mortality alone was four times higher than the city average. Even during the Great War action had to be taken to relieve the housing crisis, mainly through the building of cottage-type houses and emergency hostels in the north of the city. Under the auspices of the 1923 Housing

Table 1:4. Housebuilding in Coventry 1920-39.

Year	*Houses*	*Year*	*Houses*
1920	277	1930	1,312
1921	361	1931	1,095
1922	223	1932	1,362
1923	122	1933	1,559
1924	324	1934	2,211
1925	536	1935	2,606
1926	871	1936	3,841
1927	1,328	1937	4,510
1928	1,128	1938	4,634
1929	1,611		

Source: *Medical Officer of Health Reports for Coventry 1920-39.*

Act the local authority began to meet the needs of the community for both private and to a lesser degree council accommodation, and the steadily upwards trend in housebuilding, most of which was of a speculative nature, is clear from Table 1:4. Indeed during the thirties Coventry enjoyed the fastest rate of growth in housebuilding in Britain and even then demand continually outstripped supply. During the 1920s new housebuilding tended to be sited in relatively close proximity to the growing factories in the north of the city with 1,024 dwellings being constructed near the Morris Engine Works, 280 near General Electric, 1,808 close by Daimler's, Cash's and Courtaulds' and a further 1,021 in the area of Alfred Herbert's, British Piston Ring and Dunlop Rim and Wheels. By 1939 some 2,500 new houses had been erected in the Radford area alone, thus helping to make the north of the city very densely populated.[76]

Similar pressures were apparent in education and Coventry's long-standing problem of overcrowding in schools was exacerbated, especially in the 1920s. In October 1925, for example, both girls' secondary schools, Barr's Hill and Stoke Park, contained approximately 650 pupils when they had places for only 434. A similar situation existed in the boys' schools. Indeed in the same year the shortage of places in secondary schools stood at 1,400. Attempts were made to overcome these by the acquisition of land for the building of the Caludon Castle School for Boys in 1938 and by the rebuilding of Stoke Park School in the following year. Equally the demands of science-based industries, with their emphasis on mathematics, engineering drawing and training in the design and use of machine tools required increased provision in technical education. By the middle thirties existing facilities were extremely inadequate and

Table 1:5. Selected Output of War Materials by Standard 1939-45.

2,800	Light armoured cars
10,000	Light vans, utilities and ambulances.
5,000	Standard 'Gwynne' foot pumps.
20,000	British Hercules engines.
54,000	Aircraft carburettors.
417,000	Cylinders for Bristol, Mercury and Pegasus aero engines.
63,000	Constant Speed Units for Aeroplanes.
250,000	Bomb release slips.

Source: Davy, *op.cit.*, p.41.

necessitated the opening of a new technical college in 1936 which by 1938 had some 4,575 students on its courses.[77]

As early as 1936, it became obvious that if Britain were to be involved in a war, then Coventry's economic strengths were precisely those that would be essential to the pursuit of modern warfare. In that year a group of the city's industrialists, including John Black, William Rootes and Alfred Herbert, became involved in planning Shadow Factories with Whitehall officials.[78] The city was to be heavily involved in aircraft engine construction, namely the Mercury and later the Pegasus for the lightweight Blenheim bomber, and consequently four Shadow Factories were built in and around Coventry between 1936 and 1937 and over the space of two years some 4,000 aircraft engines were made. Clearly insufficient to meet the R.A.F.'s needs, especially with the introduction of the Hurricane and Spitfire fighters and the Whitley, Stirling and Lancaster bombers, increased factory space to produce new and more powerful engines was imperative and so once again Daimler, Rootes and Standard became involved in the war effort in a major way. By 1944, when all the Shadow Factories were fully operational, their combined output was in the region of eight hundred engines a month, quadrupling the output target set originally in 1936. Siddeley's, or Hawker Siddeley as the firm became known, had a workforce over 10,000 strong in 1944 and had by that time turned out 550 Lancaster and 150 Stirling bombers. Other firms, though their output was not quite so spectacular in visual terms contributed all kinds of war materials.

Coventry Climax, for instance, built 25,000 trailer pumps as well as a large number of generators, Daimler produced a series of Scout cars, Dunlop made tyres, wheels and barrage balloons, anti-gas clothing and underwater swimming suits. At the nexus of much of this was the city's machine tool firms, all of whom increased output, modified existing and

Table 1:6. Population Growth in Coventry 1948-1971.

Year	*Population*
1948	250,900
1951	258,245
1961	305,521
1971	335,235

Source: Medical Officer of Health Report for Coventry 1948, Census of Population 1951-71, A. Mallier & M. Rosser, 'A Financial Profile of the Housing Activities of Coventry City Council', Draft Paper 1981, Department of Economics, Coventry (Lanchester) Polytechnic.

produced new tools to meet the ever pressing demands made upon them. Between 1939 and 1944 Herbert's produced over 68,000 machine tools, while Wickman's tripled their output. Coventry Gauge and Tool supplied seventy-five per cent of all the gauges used in the manufacture of armaments as well as a number of specialist tools. Indeed though in many ways it is invidious to distinguish between firms during a war effort, perhaps the list of products made by Standard, under the direction of Black and for which he gained his knighthood, gives some indication of the scale of operations. Clearly the impact of war on Coventry's economy can only be described as stupendous. At its peak the city's population swelled to over 250,000 for the first time as workers moved from different parts of Britain and again this put pressure on the housing stock, which in turn led to the building of some fifteen hostels under the National Service Hostels Corporation to accommodate them. Stark though these barracks may have been in terms of facilities this was perhaps compensated for by the high wages earned in the munition factories.[79]

Boom Town to Doom Town

Despite heavy bombing in the early war years Coventry's recovery from World War Two was singularly rapid. Boosted by continued government armaments orders and an orderly return to peacetime production, notably of motor cars, the city's economy was poised for yet another expansionary spurt which manifested itself in rapid population growth. Indeed, from the end of the war down to the mid-fifties population growth averaged around 3,500 per annum. More importantly, as between the wars, this was essentially a young population, many of whom had come from Wales, Ireland, Scotland and the North-East to seek employment or to join relatives and friends already settled in Coventry. The predominant group was prime aged males and in 1951 there were 14,400 of these in residence, while ten years later in the older age group covering the years 25-34 there were 21,600 males, representing an increase of roughly 50 per cent whereas the average comparable figure for England and Wales was of the order of only three per cent. Such an increase though was insufficient to satisfy the thirst for labour and this in itself explains much of the increase in the occupied population of Coventry between 1951 and 1971. Growth was most rapid over the decade 1951-61 after which it slowed up. Perhaps more significant in the following decade was that almost the total rise in the occupied population is accounted for by the increase in the numbers of working women.

Practically all of the growth in male employment from 1961 to 1966 was nullified by the subsequent drop in male employment opportunities in the latter half of the sixties, when the economy began to falter before falling into a sharp decline in the ensuing decade, which, as Table 1:8 shows, brought about radical changes in employment structures. Until 1966 and even afterwards, despite decline, metal working remained the dominant sector accounting for well over 50 per cent of all employment in the city, but when this fell off after 1966 there were no alternative growth industries to replace it as an employment generator even among the labour intensive service sectors.[80]

What emerges from the foregoing discussion is that continuing on from the trend established earlier in the century, Coventry's economic base narrowed increasingly, becoming too over reliant upon the motor, aircraft and metal engineering industries, a point put most succinctly by the *Times* in 1959 which argued convincingly on Coventry's lack of industrial diversity in comparison with Birmingham and the Black Country. This, it claimed, would render Coventry's economy highly vulnerable if such dependence continued and if ever the 'bottom fell out of the car market'.[81] Regardless of such strictures the metal based industries were extremely important to Coventry's recovery after 1945

Table 1:7. Occupied Population of Coventry 1951-71

	1951	1961	1971
Males	87,330	104,230	104,290
Females	34,918	48,490	57,670
Total	122,248	152,720	161,960

Source: Census of Population: Mallier & Rosser, 'Economic Base of Coventry', p.4.

Table 1:8. Industrial Groups of Employees in Coventry 1952, 1966 & 1977

Industry Group	1952 No.	%	1966 No.	%	1977 No.	%	
Primary	3,760	2.4	2,067	1.0	1,703	0.9	Metal
Workings	101,669	64.7	123,458	60.4	96,290	51.9	Other
Manufact'g	11,598	7.4	12,379	6.0	9,537	5.2	
Construction	6,717	4.2	9,187	4.5	4,556	2.5	
Utilities	6,067	3.9	6,307	3.1	7,365	4.0	
Services	27,429	17.5	51,110	25.0	66,007	35.6	
Total	157,140	100.0	204,508	100.0	185,458	100.0	

Source: Department of Employment Returns (1952, 1966 Card Count, 1977 Census) Mallier & Rosser, 'Economic Base of Coventry'.

because these were precisely the kinds of industries that the Labour Government was desperate to encourage as part of its overall industrial strategy to update, modernise and move Britain's economy decisively away from the traditional industries in the pursuit of economic growth. Coventry responded quickly and in addition to the Shadow Factories that fell into private ownership after the War, some 707,355 square feet of new factory space had been approved in the city by 1948. Standard motors, for instance, though continuing with the production of engines for the Mosquito fighter plane, moved back into motor cars and tried to diversity its interests by entering into an agreement with Harry Ferguson to produce tractors in newly acquired premises in Banner Lane. So successful was Coventry's recovery that in 1950 the *Financial Times* reported that at least half a dozen ministries 'were now trying to limit such expansion'.[82]

Chart 1:1 shows the distribution of employment in the metal industries from 1951 to 1976, and until the 1960s the overall trend was upwards with the exception of the aerospace industry which fell back in the early part of the decade. For the greater part of the post-war period the motor vehicle industry accounted for almost one third of Coventry's total employment and was, therefore, crucial to the city's economic welfare. Coventry is often thought of primarily as a car town, mainly because it is a car assembly centre for volume produced vehicles in particular. Though there was an indigenous components industry in the city, it is significant that few of the major British component firms with the notable exception of Dunlop established themselves there, and even their efforts were directed more at the aircraft than at the motor industry. The reasons for this have yet to be fully investigated but it is worth speculating that the excellent communications by road and rail between Coventry and Birmingham kept transport costs of components down to a minimum and this obviated the need for a physical presence in the city. Coventry, therefore, devoted its attention mainly towards one sector of the car market which made it highly susceptible to changes in model design and fashion, whereas by comparison components are very nearly universal and can be hidden either under the bonnets or dashboards of almost any vehicle regardless of alterations to its body structure.

In addition to the traditional volume producers of Rootes and Standard most of Coventry's quality producers survived at least for a time after the war before either quitting the market altogether, as in the case of Alvis, or being taken over by other concerns. During the early 1950s most British quality cars bore the Coventry imprint of Armstrong Siddeley, Alvis, Daimler, Jaguar and Rootes, through its control of the Humber marque. Their combined output was small totalling no more than 25,000 vehicles per annum and accounted for at a maximum of roughly 20-25 per cent of the city's total output of cars, and of this Rootes produced 50 per cent. By 1960 Armstrong-Siddeley had also left the market and Daimler was taken over by Jaguar which was itself eventually taken over by B.M.C. in 1966. Much of Jaguar's success in surviving so long as an independent concern lay in the sound management of its resources, careful reinvestment and dividend policy in the 1950s of keeping dividends below 12 per cent. Output tripled during this decade and so confident was Jaguar that the purchase of Daimler not only gave additional car producing capacity but allowed it to diversify into the profitable bus division.[83]

To return to the volume producers, Rootes and Standard, both were relatively small in comparison with Ford and Austin Morris and suffered eventually because of their inability to benefit from the potential economies of scale so necessary to profitability in the volume car market. Indeed, in 1959 the *Times* reported that the B.M.C., Ford and Vauxhall, none of which had any assembly presence in Coventry, had sufficient spare capacity to account for all Coventry's output and that such small firms and plants were bound to suffer abnormally in the event of a long and deep recession in the motor industry.[84] To be fair Rootes and Standard were well aware of the problem of size and spent much of the fifties negotiating with each other and with other firms on take-overs and mergers. These efforts were in the main unsuccessful even though Rootes took over the ailing Singer Company in 1956, and it was not until 1960 that Standard merged with Leyland, while later Rootes turned to Chrysler for rescue. Basically both Rootes and Standard suffered, mainly

Chart 1:1. Employment in 4 Major Manufacturing Industries in Coventry EEA, 1951–76.

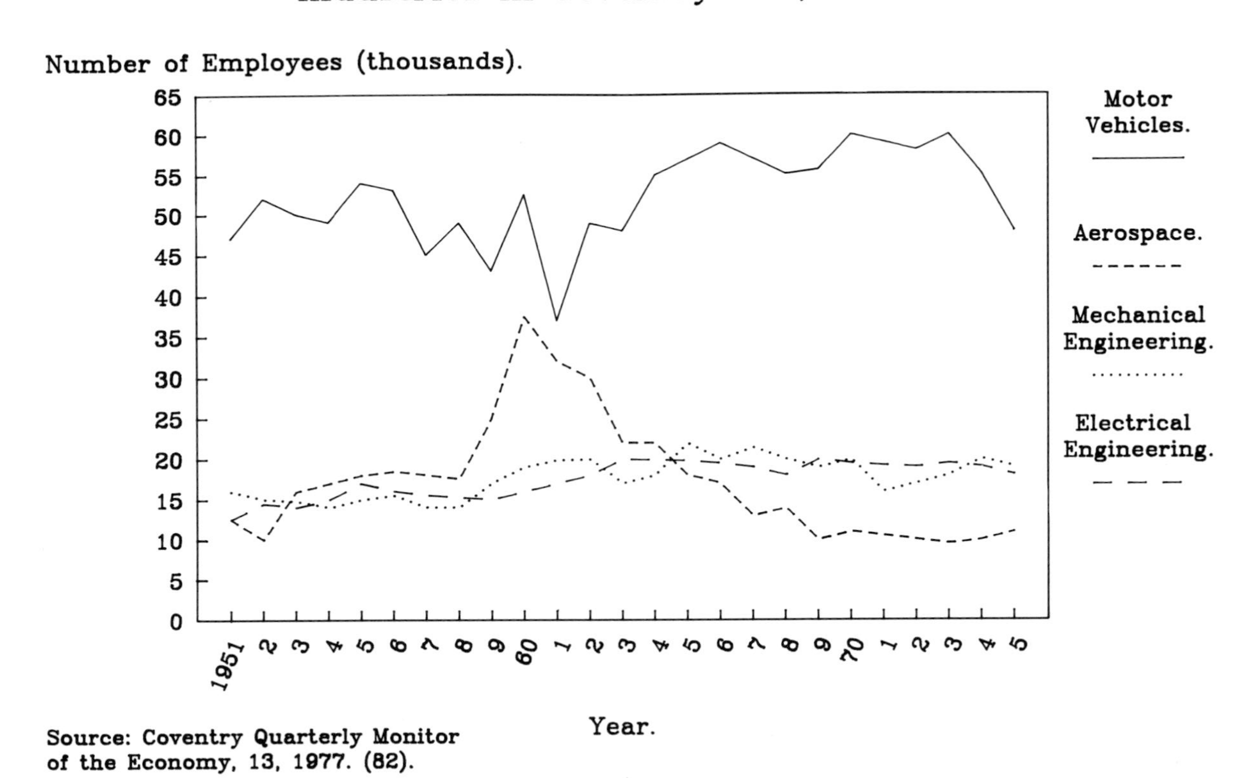

Source: Coventry Quarterly Monitor of the Economy, 13, 1977. (82).

as a result of the small scale of output, from related difficulties such as high costs, restricted prices and low investment, and for most of the fifties were obliged to follow Ford, Austin, Morris and Vauxhall in the market rather than compete with them as equals. The overall weakness of the Coventry car plants, including those of the quality producers, is summarised in Table 10 which shows that at best the total production of vehicles in the city between 1951 and 1980 was never any more than 27 per cent of total U.K. output.

It has been argued by Silberston, Rhys and Bhaskar that to gain economies of scale in passenger car production an annual output of a single model of the order of 250,000 vehicles is essential. Sadly the individual output of the Rootes and Standard plants came nowhere near that figure. Mallier and Rosser go as far as to assert that it is doubtful if Rootes entire output of cars exceeded 200,000 in any single year over the period 1951-71. Similarly, evidence suggests that Standard too fell well below that target.[85] In the *Leyland Papers* Turner points out that it was the profitable tractor side that helped it to survive independently and perhaps it is significant that it was after the sale of the tractor plant at Banner Lane to Massey Ferguson in 1959 that the firm was taken over by Leyland.[86] Rootes, however, were not quite so fortunate. During the fifties profits fell from £3.4 m. in 1951 to a loss of £600,000 in 1957, but did recover to £4.4 m. in 1961 before dropping to a loss of £960,000 the following year, and by 1970 the firm's total losses for the decade amounted to £21 m. Obviously allowances have to be made for accounting practices, depreciation, investment and research and development, but even these fail to hide the bald fact that neither of the two main Coventry volume producers was earning sufficient profits to survive independently in an ever increasingly competitive market and so Rootes were forced into the arms of the Chrysler Corporation of America for cash injections during the early sixties before being taken over completely by the American concern in 1967. Basically Coventry's car industry was experiencing considerable difficulties long before the near overall collapse of the British motor industry in the seventies when both Leyland and Chrysler had to be rescued by government intervention in the form of nationalisation in the case of the former and by heavy cash injections in that of the latter. Chrysler of America eventually sold out to Peugeot of France in 1978 after accumulating another decade of losses which peaked at £35.5 m. in 1975.[87]

If the experience of the motor industry between 1950 and 1970 was poor then the fate of the Coventry aircraft industry was even more so. Baginton's reputation after the vast experience gained in war time stood in high esteem in 1945 thus making up for the trials and tribulations of the 1930s. The government accepted that Britain would require a large aircraft industry after the war for both military and civil purposes. To investigate the requirement of the civil sector the Brabazon Committee examined two competing projects, the A.W.A. Apollo which would be designed and built in Coventry and the Vickers Viscount. Sadly the former proved disappointing. The Apollo's initial flight was a year behind the Viscount's and its engines were lacking in power and thrust

Table 1:9. Estimated output of cars in Coventry and as a percentage of total U.K. production, 1951 — 80.

Year	*Output*	*Coventry output as a % of U.K. output*
1951	133,265	27.9
1952	111,335	24.9
1953	137,830	23.1
1954	182,720	23.7
1955	205,225	23.0
1956	151,655	21.4
1957	162,600	18.8
1958	223,010	21.2
1959	256,545	21.5
1960	276,170	20.4
1961	182,100	18.1
1962	244,670	19.5
1963	294,670	18.3
1964	372,370	19.9
1965	320,351	18.6
1966	319,990	21.0
1967	325,966	21.0
1968	351,100	19.3
1969	324,850	18.9
1970	369,550	22.5
1971	390,503	22.4
1972	386,592	20.1
1973	388,825	22.2
1974	382,430	24.9
1975	321,469	25.3
1976	287,461	20.2
1977	221,314	16.6
1978	202,649	16.5
1979	160,033	11.4
1980	149,405	16.1

Source: D.W. Thoms and T. Donnelly, *The Motor Vehicle Industry in Coventry Since the 1890s* (1985).

by comparison to the Rolls Royce Dart engines of the Viscount which gave greater speed and allowed it to carry a greater payload. Consequently when the government's 'super priority' scheme for civil aircraft was made public in 1952 the Apollo was discounted. This was a cruel blow to Baginton and during the 1950s it was forced to concentrate on turning out military aircraft such as the Seahawk, Meteor and Hunter which had been designed elsewhere. After 1957 an increasing emphasis was laid upon repair and servicing rather than upon manufacturing and gradually Coventry's importance as a centre for the design and production of aircraft receded. To try to retrieve the situation the director of A.W.A. in Coventry, H.M. Woodham succeeded in obtaining the necessary finance from Hawker Siddeley, the parent company, to build both civil and military versions of a new plane, the Argosy, in an effort to keep Baginton going. But in comparison with the emergent generation of jet aircraft the Argosy proved expensive and only a dozen or so were sold; it was an initiative that came too late. The sixties proved no better and the decline of the aircraft industry continued even more rapidly, with serious job losses which, as Chart I shows, continued down to the seventies. In 1960 the Conservative government forced the British aircraft industry to amalgamate, merge and rationalise into two major groups, the British Aircraft Corporation and Hawker Siddeley and out of the engine interests of these was created Bristol Siddeley Engines to compete with Rolls Royce. 1964 was a crucial year for jobs in the aircraft industry in general with the cancellation by the Wilson government of the HS 681, TSR 2 and Hawker P1164 projects, all of which were at an advanced development stage. Such body blows again forced reorganisation in the industry and in 1966 Bristol Siddeley amalgamated with Rolls Royce and as a consequence of further rationalisation Baginton was closed in 1965, and so between 1962 and 1967, a mere five years, 11,000 jobs in the aircraft industry disappeared in Coventry. Over the same years 4,400 new jobs were found in the car industry, but again this served only to narrow the industrial base yet again. Additionally, over the same period jobs were lost at G.E.C., Smith's Stamping Works and Albion Drop Forgings to the extent that the overall level of unemployment in Coventry reached 5.6 per cent in 1968.[88]

The apparent weaknesses in both the motor and aircraft industries prompted the convocation of a series of Lord Mayor's Conferences, five in all, in 1968 to discuss the plight of the city's economy. These concluded in very general terms that Coventry was suffering from changes in defence policy over which it had no control and from the effects of regional policy which aimed at diverting industry away from the more prosperous Midlands towards the disadvantaged parts of Britain. In particular, the Conference singled out the use of Industrial Development Certificates as a device which prevented industry from either expanding in or coming to Coventry. The forcing of Rootes to open a new factory at Linwood near Glasgow and of Standard Triumph to expand at Liverpool rather than Canley are the most obvious examples of this, but others are more difficult to find. The Board of Trade denied that any firm had ever been refused permission to expand in Coventry. This was probably true, but then neither had the Board ever encouraged them to do so. Indeed, the Board's attitude seemed singularly ambivalent.

The Conferences highlighted two further problems. Firstly, Coventry's industrial structure, even allowing for the Shadow factories and immediate post-war years, was becoming dated with most of it now well over thirty years old. The age problem was correctly identified as being serious in that attempts to attract the new advanced science based industries to the area were meeting with little response often because existing premises were not readily adaptable to their needs. A second and more serious problem was the failure to attract service industries and encourage their development on any significant scale. This latter problem was due to a complexity of factors. As Chart 2 illustrates there has been considerable growth in the service sector since 1960 but this has been insufficient in scale to counterbalance the decline in manufacturing that has paralleled it. A partial reason for this lies in the fact that Coventry, albeit the ninth largest city in Britain, is neither a county town nor the main administrative centre of the West Midlands Region of which it has been part since 1964. The significance of this is that in the first instance very little employment has flowed from government administrative functions and thus the city has fewer employed in public administration than other cities of a similar size. Allied to this is Coventry's proximity to Birmingham. It is there that the regional offices of public utilities, major financial institutions and distribution organisations have tended to locate themselves. For the most part, Coventry is only a customer for their services which generates few administrative functions in the city. Furthermore, even the ownership of Coventry's major companies had become concentrated in about fifteen firms, most of which are multinationals, and again with the exception of Alfred Herbert, until it was taken over by the National Enterprise Board, none had their head offices in Coventry. So that once more the administrative posts which normally accompany large scale manufacturing benefit some other town or city.[89] The services which have expanded have been mainly in local government, educational and medical services, providing employment principally for women.

By the onset of the seventies Coventry was trying desperately to recover from the severe blows it had suffered in the previous ten years. It was recognised that the halcyon boom days of continual growth and high wages were over and that the city's industrial structure required considerable reorientation. This, however, did not take place. Britain's economy, like other Western economies, has suffered from the energy crisis and from the successive deflationary policies imposed by both Labour and Conservative governments in the pursuit of financial rectitude. All this has occurred against a background of rising unemployment taking Coventry, by 1980, above the U.K. average, and mirroring the general trend in the West Midlands as a whole. The more immediate reasons for unemployment, as distinct from the general state of recession and depression in the economy, were bound up with company rationalisation, labour shakeouts, capital substitution and demographic factors and so are not easily isolated. The genesis of unemployment lies in the late fifties rather than in the sixties and seventies, and indeed the upward surge in unemployment in recent years is really only the continuation of an earlier established trend, caused by the demise of the aircraft industry, redundancies in the motor industry and government squeezes on the economy which, at times, especially in 1957, 1964-68 and 1975-76, had a serious impact affecting employment levels in the city.[90]

The recent crisis began in 1972 when unemployment rose sharply because of redundancies at Rolls Royce with the engine plant being taken into government hands as a lame duck. This was followed three years later by the almost total collapse of the city's motor industry. Chrysler's Ryton and Stoke plants were saved from extinction only by a government loan of £162 m. whilst British Leyland plants in the city were nationalised. Similarly, Alfred Herbert which had been suffering from under investment, low productivity and mounting losses, fell into the hands of the National Enterprise Board. By the late seventies 41.5 per cent of employed people in Coventry were dependent upon the government for their livelihood. From then onwards the economic crisis deepened and all of Coventry's top fifteen firms introduced redundances, with their combined work forces falling by almost half between 1975 and 1982. In the case of British Leyland the decline in employment has been spectacular as the company has rationalised its production. The closure of the Triumph plant at Canley cost between 5,000 and 6,000 jobs with another 1,500 going with the shut down of the engines works at Courthouse Green. A further 1,600 went at Jaguar as did another 250 at

Chart 1:2. Employees in Employment by Sector. (Mid–year estimates, not seasonally adjusted).

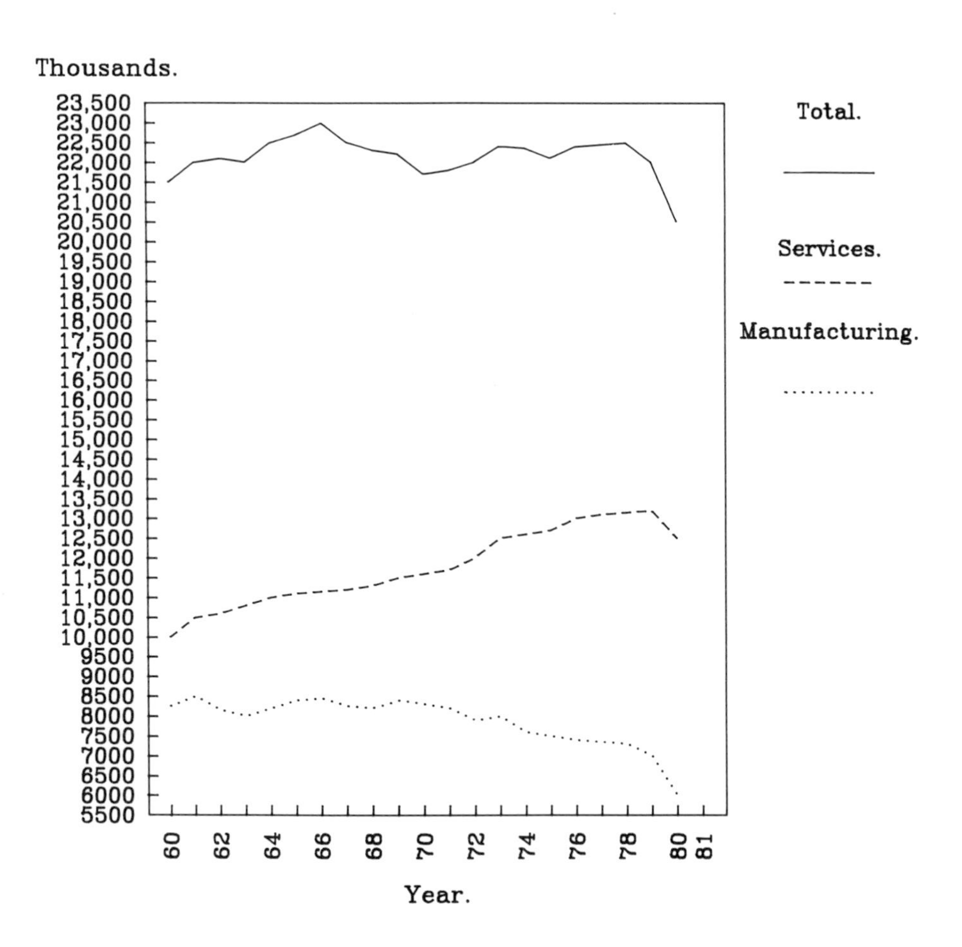

Source: Department of Employment.

Coventry Climax, both of which were part of Leyland's straggling empire. Indeed, during 1982, jobs were being lost in the city at the rate of 520 a month with 1,520 going in December alone. The loss of manufacturing jobs meant that by mid 1980 Coventry had 2.5 m. square feet of factory space on the market with seemingly no takers for it. The recession in industry eventually spread to the High Street stores, whose sales had initially been maintained by generous redundancy payments and earnings related social security benefits. Eventually in 1980 Owen Owen had to lay off staff, British Home Stores were no longer replacing staff who left and Woolworths were inviting staff to take unpaid leave.[91]

Perhaps the most depressing feature of Coventry's unemployment is that which affects the young, especially the school leaver. As the recession hit the city large numbers of teenagers joined the job market only to find that expected opportunities in the numerous factories had evaporated. By June 1980, 46 per cent of the city's 14 — 18 year olds were seeking employment and over 7,000 school leavers out of 14,000 in 1979-80 were still unemployed. To be fair to the education authority it has been pioneering in its attempts to provide even rudimentary employment and training for youngsters in cooperation with central government schemes and major firms such as G.E.C. and Courtaulds. In 1981-82, for example, some 5,270 youths were found posts in training course, work experience and community projects, but to what effect remains highly debateable.[92]

Conclusion.

Coventry's experience over the past hundred years has gone full circle, recovering from the slump of the 1880s to enjoy nearly seventy years of almost uninterrupted economic growth and prosperity only to revert to a state of deep recession in the 1970s and 1980s. The vigorous expansion of the cycle industry in the 1880s and early 1890s is indicative of a healthily resilient community willing to change, adapt and to venture its fortune in new areas of invention and innovation. Such enterprise paid off handsomely and by the middle of the 1890s Coventry was poised to break through into the motor cycle and motor vehicle industries which in turn led to the development of the aircraft industry in the city by the onset of the First World War. It was primarily through this and parallel developments in other towns such as Oxford, Luton and Bristol that the high degree of overcommitment to the traditional British 'Staple' industries of the Industrial Revolution -coal, iron, steel, shipbuilding and cotton — began to be slowly eroded. From 1914 until the Second World

Chart 1:3. Unemployment: Average percentage in Coventry Travel–to–Work Area, 1970–1982.

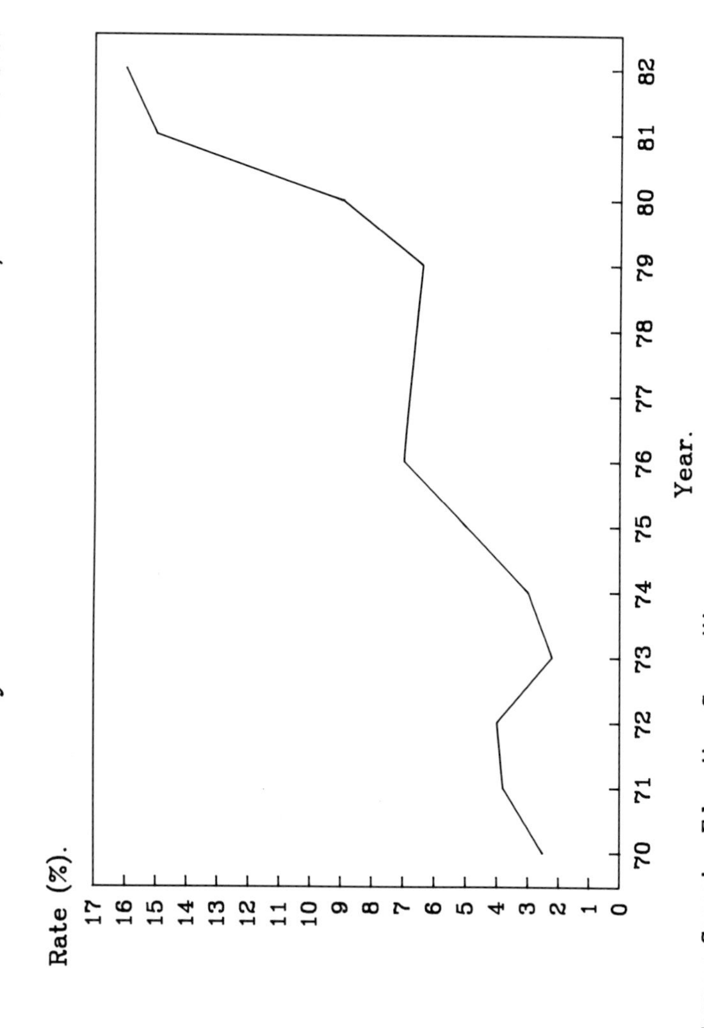

Source: Coventry Education Committee, Comprehensive Education for Life: a Consultative Document (Coventry 1982), 20.

Table 1.10. A Ranking of Coventry's Top Fifteen Manufacturing Firms.

	1975			1978			1982		
	Employees	Rank	Index	Employees	Rank	Index	Employees	Rank	Index
G.E.C.	16,166	2	100	9,700	3	60	10,464	1	65
B.L.	27,268	1	100	26,700	1	98	8,221	2	30
Rolls Royce	8,307	4	100	8,226	4	97	7,600	3	94
Talbot (Chrysler)	18,637	3	100	9,801	2	76	6,900	4	55
Massey-Ferguson	6,014	5	100	8,200	5	103	4,543	5	76
Dunlop	6,749	6	100	4,138	6	72	3,413	6	59
Courtaulds	3,766	7	100	4,000	7	106	2,773	7	73
United Scientific	—	—	—	—	—	—	1,500	8	—
Kaye Organisation	—	—	—	—	—	—	1,206	9	—
A.E.	3,679	9	100	2,286	9	85	1,036	10	39
John Brown	2,195	10	100	1,855	10	85	991	11	45
Tooling Investments	5,469	8	100	2,300	8	66	788	12	83
Ingersoll Rand	948	14	100	1,100	11	116	712	13	75
Lucas	1,010	13	100	935	14	83	671	14	57
Sandvik	839	18	100	850	15	101	561	15	67
T.I.	1,091	12	100	1,000	13	82	—	—	—
Renold	1,138	11	100	1,094	12	96	—	—	—
	93,386	—	100	80,185	—	86	51,182	—	55

Source: *Coventry Quarterly Monitor of the Economy* (various editions, 1975-1982).

War, Coventry continued to develop its new industries at an accelerated pace and in many ways epitomised the new industrial Britain, standing in stark contrast to South Wales, the North West, Merseyside and Central Scotland. But in its own way Coventry too was becoming overspecialised in its economic structure, tying up its capital resources and skills in an extremely narrow range of industries with the motor vehicle industry coming to dominate local economic activity.

Until the middle 1950s little of this seemed to matter. The motor industry continued to expand and the city acted as a magnet to labour from other parts of the U.K. in search of work and high wages in the city's burgeoning factories. It was only when the aircraft industry began to decline that there appeared a growing awareness of the narrowness of the industrial base with its increasing over-reliance on the fortunes of the motor industry. This in turn was compounded by the fact that within the British motor industry as a whole Coventry was steadily becoming of less importance as a source of output and coupled with relatively low profits and investment levels, the economy's stock was slowly ossifying and becoming increasingly immobile. It is easy with hindsight to point to the predictions of both the *Times* and the *Financial Times* in the late 1950s and ask why nothing was done to change the course of Coventry's economic development. The answer is that on the surface the economy still appeared to prosper and that the incentives to embark on a vast restructuring of local industry were indeed poor and were not aided by the efforts of successive governments to divert industry away from the area in general.

Obviously at the time of writing a very heavy price has been paid for over-commitment to the car industry and the need to regenerate the local economy is pressing. With a 16 per cent plus rate of adult unemployment Coventry is suffering more than Midland towns such as Leicester and Nottingham, both of which have broader based economies, but it is extremely doubtful if much can be achieved without a national context and government intervention both to stimulate economic growth in general and in the West Midlands in particular. It has been argued that perhaps Coventry's future growth may come from an expansion in the service industries, but the near proximity of Birmingham suggests that this is unlikely and that Coventry will continue to be a 'customer' of services based elsewhere rather than a generator of them. Similarly the claims of high technology as a means of recovery have been stressed recently, but other areas of the country, notably the axial belt running from London to Bristol, are ahead of Coventry in this field and there is a great deal of leeway to be made up if the 'sunrise' industries are to be attracted. To conclude, the local community still has a high degree of skill and large reservoir of talent to offer prospective industrialists, but these must be widened and developed across a broad range of manual, skilled, technological, communicatory, managerial and professional occupations if a long term recovery is to be effected and the pitfalls of the past avoided. The road though will be long, hard and painful.

Notes to Chapter 1

1. P. Searby, 'Watchmaking in Coventry', *Warwickshire History*, 3 (1976) 106.
2. J. Lowe, *A Guide to Sources in the History of the Cycle and Motor Industries in Coventry, 1880-1939* (1982), 10.
3. Quoted by R.F. Prosser, 'Coventry: A Study in Urban Continuity', (University of Birmingham M.A. thesis, 1955), 90.
4. J.R. Bailey, 'The Struggle for Survival in the Coventry Ribbon and Watch Trades, 1865-1914', *Midland History*, VII (1982), 135-137.
5. J. Lane, 'Technical Training of Young Persons c.1850-1914 in Coventry and the Midlands', *S.S.R.C. Report* (1979), 15.
6. Bailey, *op.cit.*, 144.
7. Lowe, *op.cit.*, 6.
8. *Ibid.*, 9.
9. Prosser, *op.cit.*, 89.
10. H. Perkin, 'The History of the Cycle Industry in Coventry, 1869-1914' (Lanchester Polytechnic B.A. Modern Studies Geography Project, 1979), 27.
11. B.H. Tripp, *Renold Chains* (1955), 41.
12. C.H. Lee, *Regional Economic Growth in the UK since the 1880s* (1971), 88.
13. R. Floud, *The British Machine Tool Industry* (1976), 53-56.
14. *Ibid.*, 72.
15. D.C. Coleman, *Courtaulds. An Economic and Social History*, vol. 2 (1969), 55, 56.
16. C.H. D'E. Leppington, 'The Evolution of an Industrial Town', Economic *Journal*, 17 (1907), 346.
17. K. Richardson, *Twentieth Century Coventry* (1972), 29.
18. S.B. Saul, 'The Engineering Industry' in D.H. Aldcroft (ed.), *The* Development of British Industry and Foreign Competition 1875-1914 (1968), 215.
19. *Ibid.*, 213.
20. S.B. Saul, 'The Motor Industry in Britain to 1914', *Business History*, (1962), 25.
21. Prosser, *op.cit.*, 111.
22. Coleman, *op.cit.*, 55.
23. See Chapter 2.
24. P. Searby, 'Lists of Prices in the Coventry Silk Industry, 1800-

1860', *Bulletin* of the Society for the Study of Labour History, 27 (1973), 48-53.
25. R.A. Church, 'Nineteenth Century Clock Technology in Britain, the United States, and Switzerland', *Economic History Review*, Second Series, XXVIII 4 (1975), 621, 622.
26. Richardson, *op.cit.*, 35, 36.
27. Saul, 'The Engineering Industry', *op.cit.*, 213.
28. Coleman, *op.cit.*, 31, 32.
29. Coventry City Record Office, Daimler Collection, Report of the Statutory General Meeting of the Daimler Motor Company, 20 May, 1896.
30. A. Muir, *75 Years. A Record of Progress* (1958), 22. See also Coventry City Record Office, Smith's Stamping, Minute Book No. 1, 18 January, 1898.
31. Richardson, *op.cit.*, 31.
32. A.E. Harrison, 'The Competitiveness of the British Cycle Industry, 1890-1914', *Economic History Review*, Second Series, XXII, 2 (1969), 302.
33. Coventry Urban District, Thirteenth Annual Report of the Medical Officer of Health, 1888, 4.
34. Coleman, *op.cit.*, 162.
35. E.H. Hunt, *Regional Wage Variations in Britain* (1973), 160, 161.
36. Sir Reginald Bacon, *From 1900 Onward* (1940), 195.
37. *Ibid.*, 188. See also, C. Trebilcock, *The Vickers Brothers. Armaments and Enterprise 1854-1914* (1977), 93, 94.
38. Bacon, *op.cit.*, 384-386.
39. Coleman, *op.cit.*, 129.
40. Committee on Women in Industry, Report, Cmd. 167 (1919), 54.
41. Muir, *op.cit.*, 47.
42. St. John C. Nixon, *Daimler, 1896-1946* (1946), 136.
43. K. Richardson, *The British Motor Industry 1896-1939* (1977), 32.
44. G. Oliver, *The Rover* (1971), 65.
45. I. Davies, *It's a Triumph* (1980), 25.
46. J.R. Davy, *The Standard Car 1903-1963, An Illustrated History* (1967), 22.
47. Nixon, *op.cit.*, 138.
48. Public Record Office, MUN 5/214, 1962/3.
49. Richardson, *Twentieth Century Coventry*, 129.
50. Davy, *op.cit.*, 22; Nixon, *op.cit.*, 139.
51 Committee on Women in Industry, *op.cit.*, 54.
52. *Ibid.*

53. *Coventry Evening Telegraph*, 7 June, 1983, 18.
54. Muir, *op.cit.*, 46, 47.
55. Committee of Enquiry into Industrial Unrest, Report of the Commissioners for the West Midlands Area, Cmd. 8665 (1917), 9.
56. Annual Reports of the Medical Officer of Health for Coventry 1918-39; G. Marson, 'Coventry: a study in urban geography' (unpublished M.A. thesis, University of Liverpool 1949), 94-108.
57. *Ibid.*, 94.
58. *Ibid.*
59. This paragraph is based heavily on A. Friedman, *Industry and Labour* (1977), 202-204.
60. G. Maxcy and A. Silberston, *The Motor Industry* (1956), 13.
61. Richardson, *op.cit.*, 45.
62. G. Rhys, *The Motor Industry: An Economic Survey* (1972), 15.
63. *Ibid.*
64. *Ibid.*, 15-17; Maxcy & Silberston, *op.cit.*, 167.
65. Richardson, *op.cit.*, 99-102.
66. Davey, *op.cit.*, 22-40.
67. Richardson, *op.cit.*, 99-102. See also Jean-Pierre Bardou, 'Labor and Industrial Relations Since 1945' in J-P. Bardou *et.al*, *The Automobile Revolution: The Impact of an Industry* (University of North Carolina Press, 1982), 245-71 for a discussion of the various stages of mass production in the manufacture of cars. The lack of records makes it difficult to be precise about the timing of these stages in the Coventry industry.
68. S. Young & N. Hood, *Chrysler U.K.: A Corporation in Transition* (1975), 73-77.
69. Richardson, *op.cit.*, 120-121.
70. Official Guide to the City of Coventry, 1918-38.
71. Richardson, *op.cit.*, 58.
72. *Ibid.*, 129-137; O. Trapper, *Armstrong Whitley Aircraft since 1913* (1973), 1-33.
73. Official Guide to the City of Coventry, 1918-38.
74. Coleman, *op.cit.*, 249-253 and 431.
75. Annual Reports of the Medical Officer of Health for Coventry, 1918-39.
76. Richardson, *op.cit.*, 246-251.
77. For a full discussion of the impact of World War II in Coventry see Chapter 11 below.
78. Davey, *op.cit.*, 22-24; Richardson, *op.cit.*, 64-97.
79. For a full discussion of the economic base of Coventry between

1951 and 1971 see A. Mallier & M. Rosser, 'The Economic Base of Coventry', Discussion Paper, Department of Economics, Coventry (Lanchester) Polytechnic, 1981.

80. *The Times*, 31 March, 1959.
81. *Financial Times*, 8 November, 1950.
82. In Chart 1:1 for 1951-8, aerospace and vehicle component manufacture are not separable. All component manufacture has been included in vehicles, therefore understating aerospace, and overstating vehicles.
83. A. Mallier & M. Rosser, 'Industrial Decline in Perspective: The Car Industry', Staff Seminar Paper, Department of Economics, Coventry (Lanchester) Polytechnic, 1982, 7-16.
84. *The Times*, 31 March, 1959.
85. Maxcy & Silberston, *op.cit.*, 75-98; Rhys, *op.cit.*, 260-300; K. Bhaskar, *The Future of the UK Motor Industry* (1979).
86. G. Turner, *The Leyland Papers* (1971), 47-54.
87. Hood & Young, *op.cit.*, 136-172; P.J.S. Dunnet, *The Decline of the British Motor Industry* (1980), 121-178.
88. This account is based heavily on Richardson, *op.cit.*, 138-139.
89. Mallier & Rosser 'The Economic Base', 19-29; 'The Ownership of Coventry's Top Fifty Firms', *Coventry Quarterly Monitor of the Economy*, No. 3 (1980).
90. 'Survey of Unemployment in Coventry since 1950', *Coventry Quarterly Monitor of the Economy*, No. 2, 1977.
91. 'Redundancies in Coventry', *Coventry Quarterly Monitor of the Economy*, No. 3, 1980; S. Taylor, 'Unemployment in the West Midlands', in B. Crick, *Unemployment* (1981), 69-71.
92. *The Coventry Report*, Manpower Services Commission, December 1977, Coventry Education Committee, *op.cit.*, 19.

Chapter 2

Who's a Real Coventry Kid? Migration into Twentieth Century Coventry

Bill Lancaster

The built environment of present day Coventry is largely the product of twentieth century economic development. The tourist who comes to wander around the ruins of the old Cathedral and view the city's few remaining ancient buildings has to search for them amongst a landscape that belongs to the second part of the twentieth century. The disappearance of old Coventry reflects four decades of unbroken economic boom. German bombs undoubtedly increased the pace of change but in the longer term economic expansion both demanded and paid for the re-creation of Coventry. The arrival of new industries and their subsequent progress is the subject of another essay in this volume; my purpose here is to examine one major aspect of urban growth: the increase and changing characteristics of the local population. It is not the intention of this chapter to explore every dimension of demographic change but rather to focus upon the role of migration in the process of expansion of the city's population and the part which it has played in shaping twentieth century Coventry. Modern Coventry is as much a city of new faces as it is of new buildings. If the tourist was to prolong his stay and turn his attention from the landscape to the people he would find that the majority, like the new buildings, were here because of fairly recent economic expansion. Boom town brought new faces as well as a new landscape.

Population growth and the influx of migrants has not, however, been a process that has continued unhindered since the introduction of new metal trades in the late nineteenth century. For much of the second half of the last century Coventry's demographic situation was the opposite to what it has been in the present century. The collapse of the old staple trade of silk weaving in the 1860s caused many Coventrians to leave the city and seek employment elsewhere. Many weavers took their skills to the Lancashire cotton textile industry or made the short trek to Leicester to find work in that town's new elastic web weaving factories.[1] Even prior to the collapse of silk weaving both Coventry's economy and population were relatively static. The census enumerators' schedules for Hillfields, for example, in 1861 show that nearly 80 per cent of

Table 2.1. Coventry 1861-1891

Year	Population	Watchmakers		Silk Ribbon Trade	
		Male	Female	Male	Female
1861	49,936	1,943	43	2,771	5,445
1871	39,474	2,368	74	1,709	3,706
1881	45,116	n.a.	n.a.	n.a.	n.a.
1891	53,004	3,032	534	753	2,505

Source: Census reports.

household heads were born in and around Coventry, while in nearby Gosford Street the number was even higher at 85 per cent.[2] Coventry was, of course, not entirely dependent upon the silk trade. The new watchmaking industry continued to expand despite the Anglo-French trade agreement. Moreover the horological industry did attract outsiders: only 65 per cent of heads of households in the watchmaking district of Chapelfields were locals, the remainder originating in centres of the trade such as Clerkenwell. But this industry was never a large source of employment with only 1,986 engaged in watchmaking in 1861, which was only 8.5 per cent of the local working population.

Table 2.1 illustrates the decline that characterised both the city's population and staple trades during the second part of the nineteenth century. Silk and watches employed 10,202 Coventrians in 1861 and only 6,824 in 1891. The slight growth in population during the years 1881-1891 signifies demographic stability rather than expansion as over 3,700 of the 7,900 extra citizens were the result of recent boundary extensions which had incorporated Earlsdon and part of Radford into the city in 1890. The remainder were the product of natural increase rather than migration. Despite this apparent stagnation of both population and traditional industry new economic developments, especially the introduction of the bicycle trade were affecting the composition of the labour force.

Table 2.2. Cycle Workers

Year	Male	Female
1881	583	10
1891	3,854	205
1901	5,541	560

Source: Census reports.

Table 2.3. Elastic Web Weaving Establishments in Coventry

1866	1
1874	7
1876	12
1880	14
1888	12

Source: Misc. directories.

This growth in the cycle industry illustrates the turnaround in the economic fortunes of late nineteenth century Coventry but there were also demographic implications with the introduction of bicycle manufacture. Local mythology has usually seen the bicycle factory as being the salvation of the unemployed weaver. But there is little evidence to suggest that local textile workers entered the new trade in large numbers. One historian has recently argued that ribbon weaving did not disappear as rapidly as previous historical accounts have claimed.[3] Table 2.1 for example shows that in 1891 there were still over 3,000 silk weavers in employment in Coventry. On the other hand in that year the trade was undoubtedly dominated by female labour. Yet there is still an element of plausibility in Bailey's argument. It was highly probable that the male ribbon weavers, who in the past had displayed an enduring hostility to the discipline of factory production, found a haven in the new sister branch of textiles, elastic web weaving, that came to Coventry in the second part of the nineteenth century. Some of these firms were substantial and although the trade declined in the 1890s the few companies that remained were employing on average 120 workers. It is extremely difficult to quantify the number of workers who were engaged in this trade locally but material in the Webb trade union collection suggests that elastic web weaving in Coventry was both substantial in size and predominantly male.[4] The evidence therefore leads to the assumption that male silk weavers in Coventry either left the city or made a sideways move into elastic weaving.

C.W. Cooper, who was Starley's foreman when the Coventry Machinist Company was pioneering the mass produced bicycle trade reinforces this point in his autobiography, while discussing the social composition of the factory workforce when sewing machines and bicycles were first produced:

> New faces were to be encountered daily. Some of the men

Table 2.4. Coventry Population 1891-1911

1891	52,742
1901	69,978
1911	106,349

Source: Census Reports.

> from Birmingham full to the brim with energy, used to hard work and capable of showing plenty for money. ... Another class of workers [quite different in their ways] from Londonwards arrived. The "come downs" they were designated. Both were superior in this: the first could boast speed, the latter better educated.

Cooper went on to point out that it was to the 'rough practical speedmakers of Brum, and the more apparently refined contingent from the South (with a few natives that managed to squeeze in) does Coventry owe her present tradition'.[5] Cooper was no doubt prone to exaggeration but it is interesting that he should still consider early migrants important in 1912 when he was writing. The point is that the new industry demanded a new type of employee, the semi-skilled metal worker, and Coventrians employed in the city's traditional trades were reluctant to seek such employment. Similarly watchmakers were equally scathing about factory work and it is not until the late 1890s when the watch trade was in serious decline that younger watchmakers sought factory employment as 'skilled mechanics'.[6]

The expansion of the new cycle industry in the 1890s attracted many workers to Coventry. The recession, however, which seriously affected the trade in the later years of the decade caused many migrants to move on and seek their future elsewhere. The census is a crude measurement of population movement. It is only carried out every ten years and offers no information on the often dramatic short term demographic fluctuations. It cannot tell us, for example, how many came and left in a particular year. All it can do is indicate the residue that remains. The 1890s were largely years of industrial expansion. Yet overall on census night in 1901 migration accounted for only 647 new Coventrians. On the other hand many important newcomers did arrive during the last two decades of the nineteenth century. These were the years, as is pointed out in another essay, which saw the arrival of a steady contingent of young middle-class men who were to perform the vital entrepreneurial functions in the establishment of new enterprises. The gloom that accompanied the

Table 2.5. The Elements in Coventry's Increase in Population 1891-1911

	Pop. Increase	*Boundary Change*	*Natural Increase*	*Migrants*
1891-1901	17,254	8,000	8,607	647
1901-1911	36,371		13,328	23,043

Source: Census Reports.

recession of the cycle trade in the late 1890s and Harry Lawson's motor empire led many locals to believe that the lean years of the 1860s had returned. Landlords were complaining of the difficulty of collecting rents and the Medical Officer of Health (MOH) was worried about possible health hazards caused by the large number of empty houses.[7] By 1905, however, prosperity had returned and the MOH, concerned that the registrar general's population estimate for Coventry was inaccurate and therefore overestimating the local death rate, persuaded the council to carry out an unofficial census. This claimed that the population was 83,000 compared to the official estimate of 76,000. The findings of the local census were confirmed by the official one of 1911 which showed that an increase of 50 per cent had taken place over the ten year period. Table 2.5 demonstrates the importance of migration to this expansion. Where did the migrants come from, and what did they do when they arrived? These are questions which can only be answered in the broadest of terms.

The most notable features of Table 2.6 and Map 2.1 is the diversity of source areas. There is no distinct North to South movement. Indeed London is as important as the North West and Londoners far exceed migrants from the five northern counties. Another important dimension, somewhat clouded by these large geographical divisions, is that there was no distinct rural-urban pattern. For example Sussex, one of the South Eastern counties was the birthplace of 304 Coventrians in 1911, 175 of whom came from Brighton, most of the others coming from Hastings and Eastbourne. Similarly Devonshire was the birthplace of 160 Coventrians, but 121 of these came from Plymouth, Exeter and Devonport. There is also little evidence of movement from mining areas. Migrants from Northumberland numbered 506 in 1911 but 432 of these came from the manufacturing districts of Newcastle. Thus most migrants to Coventry came from a diversity of urban areas. There were few rustics. The majority that came were probably familiar with a manufacturing environment which may partly explain the comparative ease of Coventry's industrial transition from small scale production units to large factories.

Map 2.1

COVENTRY 1911:
BIRTHPLACES OF RESIDENTS BORN ELSEWHERE IN ENGLAND & WALES

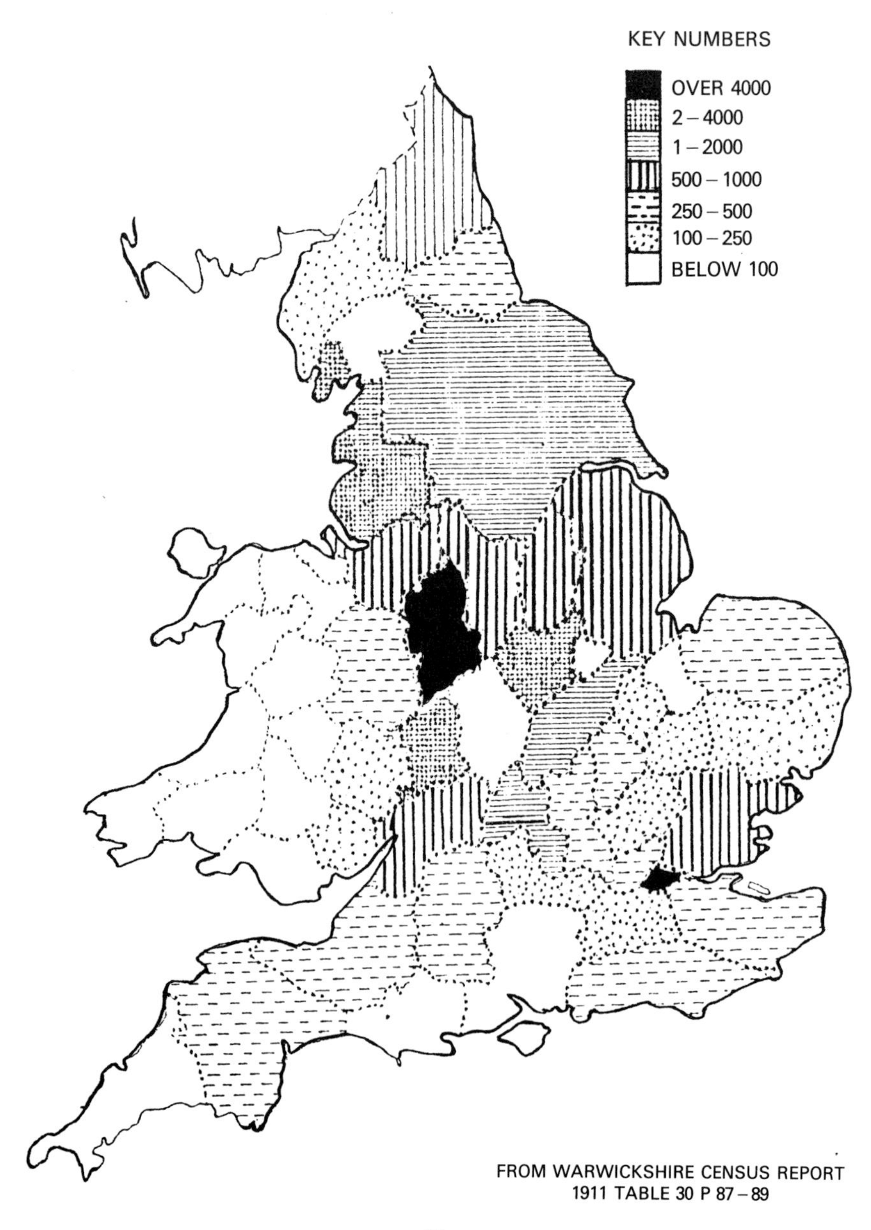

Table 2.6. Birthplace of Coventry Citizens

	1901	*1911*
London	1,483	2,846
South East	687	1,184
South West	512	1,168
South Midlands	2,220	4,268
Eastern Counties	418	1,186
West Midlands*	59,152	81,097
North Midlands	1,908	4,796
North West	1,137	2,977
Yorks	697	1,607
Northern Counties	179	1,161
Wales	357	525
Scotland	298	702
Ireland	416	620
Foreign	274	465

* including Coventry

Source: Census reports.

The second question, what did the migrants do when they arrived in Coventry, is largely answered by reference to the city's remarkable economic growth during this decade. In particular the cycle and new motor industry displayed an insatiable appetite for labour. There were 6,001 cycle and motor workers in Coventry in 1901 compared with just under 13,000 in 1911. This growth is even more remarkable if the age structure of the workforce is examined. In 1911, 10,188 workers in these trades were aged under 35 and over 5,000 of these were under 25. The rate of natural increase in Coventry could not meet such a demand for labour and it was this increase in young workers which accounts for much of the migration during this decade. Table 2.7 illustrates the contribution of migration to the youthfulness of Coventry. The below average number of 10 — 15 year olds and the above average of under fives highlights just how recent the migratory surge had been. Conversely the excess of Coventry over the national figures in the 20 -35 year old range points to the age structure of the majority of migrants. The larger number of 55+ to 75 year olds in the national figures suggests that in this period it was unusual for migrants to be joined by older members of their family.

Another important question posed by this early migratory surge concerns the sexual composition of the newcomers. The predominant pattern of migration during these years was for the young adult male to arrive first, find employment and accommodation and then send for his

Table 2.7. Distribution of Population According to Ages. Per 1,000 Pop. 1907.

	England & Wales	Coventry
Under 5	114.2	122.0
5 — 10	107.2	106.0
10 — 15	102.7	98.7
15 — 20	99.7	100.9
20 — 25	95.9	99.4
25 — 35	161.5	190.0
35 — 45	122.8	119.9
45 — 55	89.2	82.2
55 — 65	59.7	54.4
65 — 75	33.0	32.6
75 — 85	12.0	12.1
85 and over	1.5	1.4

wife and family if he had one. The needs of the dynamic local economy was mainly for young male labour. The percentage increase in female labour in the cycle and motor trades between 1901 and 1911 was the same as the rise in male employment. But numerically there were only 1,116 women workers in these industries in 1911. Moreover, Coventry, apart from the declining silk trade, did not have a tradition of extensive female factory employment. In particular there appears to have been a prejudice, held by both employers and workers, against married women working in factories. In 1907 it was reported that only 388 out of 5,149 women engaged in sixtyfive local factories were married. The percentage of married women and widows in employment between the ages of 25 and 35 was only 9.9 per cent for Coventry compared to 21.2 per cent in Nottingham and 53.5 per cent in Blackburn.[8] Overall in 1911 the Coventry workforce consisted of 37,322 males and 13,060 females. Males were, as would be expected, more numerous than female migrants, women accounting for only fifteen and a half of thirtyfour and a half thousand newcomers in 1911. This gave the city a marked imbalance in the sexual composition of its population even when compared to surrounding districts as Table 2.8 demonstrates.

Leppington in his 1907 article singled out for comment the predominance of young male workers in the metal, machine and cycle making industries, 'For these [trades] lads and young men below the age of twentyfive make up more than two fifths of the army of employees. Even in the older industry of engineering, the use of high speed machinery demands the keen sight and nimbleness of youth'. During his visit to Coventry Leppington spent some time observing the activities of

Table 2.8. Warwickshire Population by Sex, 1907

	Males	*Females*
Administrative County	197,756	210,471
Birmingham C.B.	245,789	263,780
Coventry C.B.	52,464	50,589

Source: Leppington, *op.cit.*

the newly established Labour Bureau outside the market. He noted that

> Applications are made in person by quite a decent number of young men of not at all the unemployable class, some of them cycling in from ten or fifteen miles round. In a list of applications just received the present writer noticed that Birmingham, Rugby [where a big engineering firm was slack at the time] London, and Leicester contributed the greater part.

The growth in population continued unchecked up until 1914. During the first world war with the rapid build up of the local munitions industry and the influx of armaments workers, particularly women, the number of inhabitants climbed to 130,000. In 1918, at the end of hostilities, Coventry did not immediately return to the pre-war pattern of economic and demographic expansion. What evidence that is available suggests that the majority of female munition workers returned home and the post-war economic crisis forced many males to move elsewhere. By 1921 the population had dropped to 128,000 and the city began to experience a much slower rate of growth.

The twenties started against a backcloth of economic uncertainty. The majority of factories were operating on short time, many new firms failed, and local labour relations were soured by the 1922 engineering lock out.[9] These factors, together with the recent trauma of war, were expressed in a marked decline in the local birth rate. Since the 1880s the Coventry birth rate had been a few points higher than the national average. In the early 1920s, however, the number of live births in Coventry fell below the national figure, a pattern which continued until 1925.

Such a trend, particularly in the early 1920s when local unemployment was much higher than the national average, is not surprising. But the continuation of a lower than national birth rate well into the 1930s raises many interesting questions. Why, for example, should prosperous

Coventry, as it was after 1925, have a lower birth rate than the rest of England and Wales? Historical demographers are in broad agreement that the decline in the birth rate nationally between the wars was caused by a complexity of factors. The recession in the economy made many couples hesitant in starting a family; while the more prosperous middle classes were increasingly using contraceptive methods. The latter in particular were opting for smaller families and a more materialistic life style.[10] It may have been the case that Coventry's prosperous working class were emulating this middle class trend.

Another possible explanation of Coventry's low inter-war birth rate is the high level of migrants within the community. The argument here would be that a large number of newcomers perceived their stay in Coventry as short term. They came to make as much money as they could as quickly as possible with the aim of returning to their families and communities. This type of migrant may have been married but would have been apprehensive about starting a family, seeing children as a potential obstacle to his short stay plans. It is also highly likely that such migrants would seek out cheaper, smaller types of accommodation, unsuitable for child rearing, in order to maximise savings. It is difficult to find solid evidence to back up such explanations. On the other hand the supply of housing during this period does suggest a close relationship between accommodation and the birth rate. The population of Coventry grew from 167,083 in 1931 to 224,247 in 1939. More than 42,000 of these new citizens were migrant. Pressure upon the local housing stock was undoubtedly acute and was a continual source of alarm to the MOH. House building increased only slowly in the late 1920s and early 1930s but a major leap in the supply of housing occurred in the mid 1930s notably with the development of land previously owned by the Stoneleigh estate. It is surely more than coincidental that the birth rate should rise in Coventry during 1934, a year which witnessed a nearly 50 per cent growth in local house building. Indeed from 1931-39 the rate of birth increased by one point with each increase of a thousand houses built. When 1,300 houses were built in 1930 Coventry's birth rate stood at 14.5 per thousand population. By 1939 when 4,600 new houses were erected the birth rate had risen to 17.7.[11]

Overall the growth of Coventry in the 1930s exceeded even the boom pre-war years. The turn around from the stagnant early 1920s was dramatic. Coventry was one of the few communities to have an excess of males in the late 1930s. The proliferation of jobs in the rapidly expanding motor and engineering industry and the post 1935 growth of armament production was the attraction. Table 2.9 clearly indicates the

Table 2.9. Population 1921-39

	Male	*Female*	*Total*	*Migrants*	
1931	82,816	84,313	167,083	1921-31	3,459
1939	114,023	110,224	224,267	1931-39	42,148

Source: Census Report 1931 and Registrar General's 1939 Report.

importance of migration, but where did these new inhabitants come from? This is difficult to answer with the precision that is possible for the pre-1914 period. Post first world war government expenditure cuts reduced the scope of the 1921 census and no information was published relating to place of birth. As often happens, one generation's economy produces difficulties for another. Thus by the 1930s, when parts of the national economy were expanding rapidly, government departments lacked vital information on population movements. To fill this gap, a series of surveys was undertaken, using the place of issue of workers' national insurance books to identify the migrant's place of origin. They were only concerned with insured workers and therefore reveal nothing about children, many women and non-insured workers such as Irish building employees. Despite these qualifications, the major trends in migration to Coventry can be discerned.

It is difficult to compare Table 2.10 with Table 2.4 as the census regions differ from the Labour exchange areas. Nevertheless some important new trends in migration are apparent. The high number of Welsh males who came to Coventry during the inter-war period from the Cardiff/Newport mining area is one. Indeed, Table 2.10 represents the slowing down of this particular stream. In 1937, for example, it was estimated that 21.5 per cent of all migrants into Coventry were Welsh.[12] The contraction of the South Wales coalfield in the 1920s was the major reason for this influx. But it is interesting that other coalfields were under-represented. Geordie and Scottish miners were equally capable of performing the semi-skilled factory jobs that were filled by Welshmen.

The larger numbers of Welshmen probably reflected the social structure of the Welsh mining towns. The South Wales coalfield had expanded rapidly in the two decades prior to 1914. These booming pits relied heavily on migrant labour, much of which was recruited from England. When depression arrived in the 1920s it is likely that many Welsh miners had yet to establish deep roots in the valley communities.[13] Many families had only been there for one generation and this lack of roots, together with recent memories of migration made the Welsh far more mobile than miners from older communities such as

Table 2.10. 'Foreign Insurance Books' 1920-39 by Percentage

		Male	*Female*
Leicester	...	2.5	3.7
Birmingham	...	1.7*	2.1*
Black Country	...	4.2	3.7
Northants	...	2.3	2.2
Potteries	...	1.6	2.2
Notts/Derby	...	2.0	2.3
London	...	5.6	9.6
Sheffield	...	2.1	1.2
Manchester	...	10.7	23.0
Merseyside	...	3.7	4.3
Cardiff & Newport	...	14.7	3.8
Yorks/textiles	...	1.9	3.0
Swansea	...	1.5	0.7
Tyneside	...	4.3	3.7
Teeside	...	1.2	0.7
Clydeside	...	6.4	6.6
other coal areas	...	4.5	1.6
Rest of U.K. (including Warwickshire)	...	31.7	27.5

*1941 figure

Based on a 16 per cent sample of all books exchanged.
Source: A. Shenfield, P. Sargant Florence, *Review of Economic Studies* 12(1) 1944.

those in the North East. Table 2.10 also illustrates that migrants from coal areas generally and the Welsh in particular either did not bring their womenfolk with them or if they did these women rarely worked. The opposite tendency was present amongst migrants from the Manchester cotton area. More than twice the number of females came from this region than men. One reason, of course, was the slump in the cotton industry which released a large pool of women workers who had a tradition of factory work. As we noted earlier, Coventry women tended to either shun factory work or leave upon marriage. This latter point undoubtedly aggravated the much commented upon shortage of female labour in Coventry during the 1930s.[14] Finally, the arrival and expansion of GEC in Coventry during this period provided employment for many women workers who came south from the company's Manchester factory.

Blue collar rather than white collar workers continued to dominate the migrant streams that flowed into Coventry. Inter-war economic growth demanded workers rather than managers and professionals. The 1931 census shows that the middle classes accounted for 22 per cent of the national population but only 19 per cent of Coventry's. The top three occupational groups which in 1931 nationally accounted for 10.4 per cent of the workforce provided employment for only eight per cent in Coventry. In contrast skilled workers represented almost 48 per cent of employed Coventrians compared to the national figure of 30.6 per cent.

Certain reservations must, however, be registered against the above census data. As previously mentioned the Census gives no indication of often dramatic short term movements. Moreover it is concerned with residents, not workers. Thus the low number of professionals may be an under-representation given the phenomena, discussed in another essay, of the middle-class to reside outside Coventry.[15] Similarly there is some evidence which highlights the large number of workers who commuted into Coventry. An unofficial survey undertaken in 1927 estimated that 27,000 workers entered Coventry daily from the surrounding area and Birmingham.[16] The dovetailing of Midland seasonal employment trends could also alter the composition of the local workforce. For example, during the 1930s it was a common practice for railway carriage builders and wood workers to come to Coventry to work in the motor trade's peak period during the winter months, which coincided with the railway carriage works slack season.[17]

When war began in 1939 the local population stood at 224,247. The rapid influx of labour during the arms build-up of the late thirties created tremendous problems for local society. Education and housing provisions were strained. Evacuation in the early stages of the war eased the situation slightly but bomb damage and the increasing growth of the labour force resulted in notorious overcrowding. The government, whose ministry of labour was reported to be sending 300 new workers to Coventry every week, was forced to take action. The National Service Hostels Corporation was formed in May 1941 and this body built fifteen hostels in and around Coventry to house over 8,000 workers.[18] Even this rudimentary form of accommodation was luxurious compared to the lot of many other migrants. Beds were shared by shift workers in lodgings, derelict buildings became occupied and the less fortunate were forced to live in makeshift shelters, tents and caravans.

Life for the majority of migrant workers in wartime Coventry was undoubtedly uncomfortable. Accommodation problems apart, there were frequent complaints about the lack of social and leisure amenities. One wartime study of Coventry expressed fears that local industry could suffer a loss of labour unless facilities were quickly improved.[19] The fear grew that once state controls of labour were lifted, workers would leave, but despite many privations, Coventry was paying high wages and providing regular employment to a large number of workers, many of whom had not previously enjoyed such prosperity.

Other new workers did not have such a choice. Coventry, like so many other manufacturing centres, attracted a sizeable number of European wartime refugees. In 1931 less than 1,100 foreigners, mainly from the old Commonwealth, lived in Coventry. By 1951 there were over 5,400 foreigners in the city, just under two per cent of the local population. The largest group came from Europe during and immediately after the war. The most notable of these newcomers were the 1,046 Poles and 953 Russians, the latter group largely originating from the Ukraine. Another important group came from India. it was estimated that one thousand Indians were recruited as unskilled textile workers during the war. By 1951 this group numbered 1,100.

The impact of migration on local politics during the second and third quarter of the present century is dealt with in another essay in this volume.[20] A lively debate, however, has taken place in recent years concerning the role of migrant workers in local industrial relations.[21] Jonathan Zeitlin has argued that the influx of skilled workers into Coventry from areas with strong trade union traditions was crucial to the growth of unions in the local motor industry. Dave Lyddon on the other hand has raised two major objections. First, Lyddon questions Zeitlin's claim that migrants significantly strengthened the trade union movement during the 1930s. He argues that it was not until the 1950s that trade unionism took hold amongst the majority of car workers. Second, Lyddon draws attention to the fact that in many factories migrants formed only a small minority of the workforce. Lyddon's comments suggest that Zeitlin's conclusions need refining. He may be wrong on the timing of trade unionism. We need only think of Messrs. Park, McGarry, Healey and Griffiths to understand this point. However, it is not a debate which can be resolved until detailed work has been carried out on the backgrounds of Coventry's trade union activists during the 1940s and 1950s.

Coventry during the 1930s was often described as a cosmopolitan city. This, however, was somewhat misleading. The population in the 1930s was certainly mixed. The proportion of migrants rose to 40 per cent in 1935, but the majority of newcomers were from other UK regions. This remained the dominant trend throughout the war and the immediate post-war period. In 1951 the overwhelming majority of citizens were of UK origin. Table 2.11 illustrates both continuity and change in the geographical origin of Coventry's population. The regional categories

Table 2.11. Birth Place 1951

Northern	10,532
Yorks	5,250
North West	10,938
North Midlands	11,678
West Midlands	160,750
Eastern	4,087
London & South East	10,034
Southern	5,087
South West	5,059
Wales	10,558
Scotland	7,747
Ireland	9,993
Commonwealth	1,831
Foreign*	4,471

* 2,608 aliens
Source: Census reports.

used in the 1951 census are not precisely comparable to either the earlier insurance books surveys or the pre-1921 censuses. But in broad terms the major trends are clear. The London area continued to send just under ten per cent of the city's migrants, a pattern that had remained constant since 1911. A similar trend is noticeable for North West England. One major new development is the somewhat sudden arrival of over ten and a half thousand people from the Northern area. This census category largely consists of Northumberland and Durham, two counties which had been under-represented amongst Coventry migrants since the turn of the century. As recently as 1940, insurance book analysis highlighted a dearth of migrants from coalfields other than Wales. Clearly the war years had a major impact upon the mining communities of the North East. Perhaps war time experience helped to increase the Geordie's willingness to move while the high wages of Coventry helped to keep him there once he had arrived.

The 9,993 Irish who were present in Coventry on census night 1951 represent the second new major migrant stream of the post war period. Despite the frequent stationing of Irish regiments in Coventry Barracks, and labour demand during the early twentieth century, the local Irish population remained quite small. In 1931 there were only 2,057 Irish in Coventry but this number may have expanded rapidly during the building boom of the 1930s. At the close of the second world war the streets surrounding St. Osburg's and St. Mary's churches had a distinctive Irish atmosphere. These two inner-city areas were well

Map 2.2

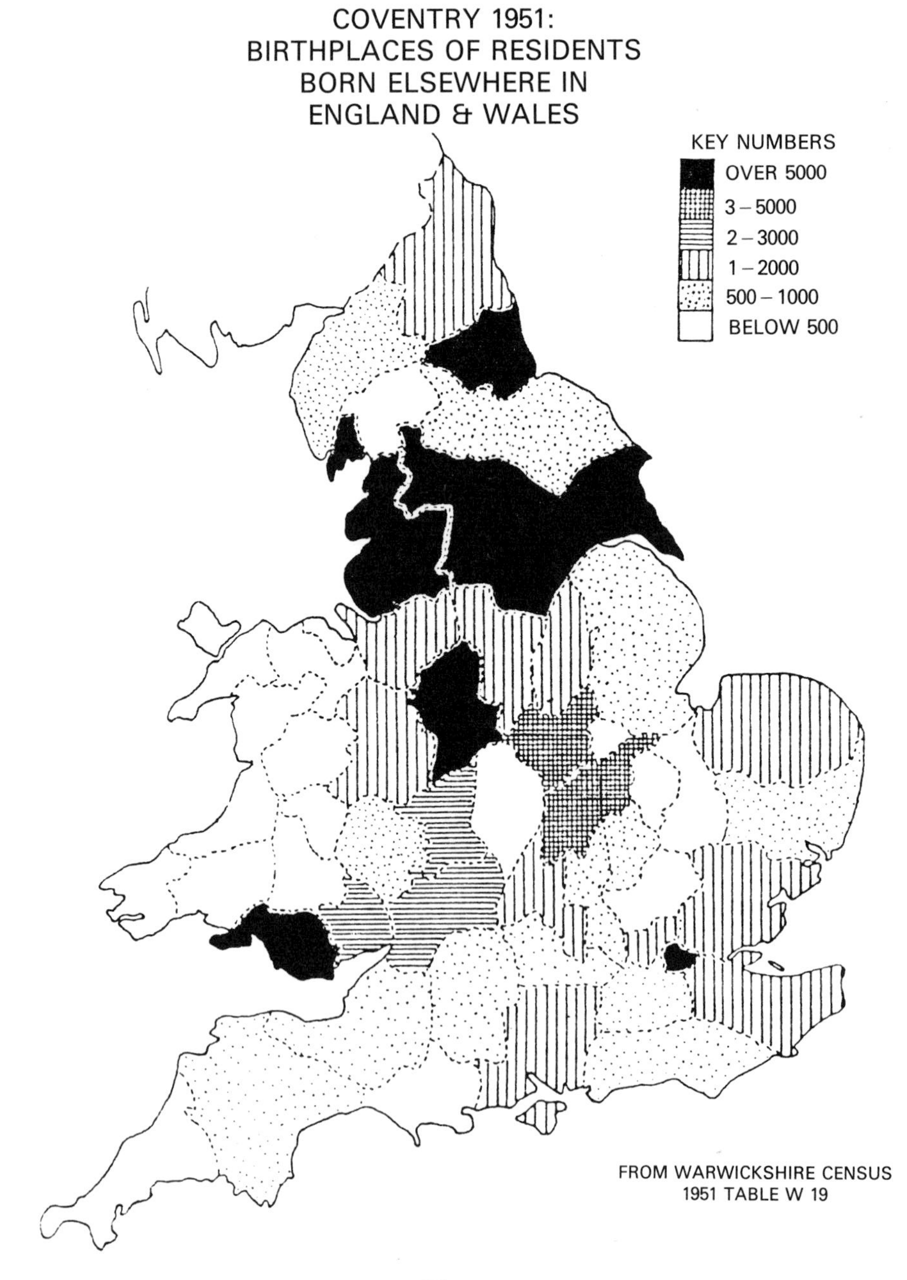
COVENTRY 1951:
BIRTHPLACES OF RESIDENTS
BORN ELSEWHERE IN
ENGLAND & WALES
KEY NUMBERS
OVER 5000
3 – 5000
2 – 3000
1 – 2000
500 – 1000
BELOW 500
FROM WARWICKSHIRE CENSUS
1951 TABLE W 19

Table 2.12. Catholic Churches in Coventry

Year	*Number*
1913	2
1939	6
1984	17

Source: Misc. directories.

supplied with lodging houses and multi-tenanted buildings whilst their proximity to Roman Catholic churches made them both an ideal port of call for itinerant building workers or those 'after a start' in local factories. Although casual building workers formed an important part of the Coventry Irish community many more settled permanently. The expansion of catholicism in Coventry in the twentieth century illustrates both the growth of the Irish and their desire to retain their religious identity. It also needs mentioning that two of the present day Catholic churches serve specifically European congregations. St. Stanislas Kosta in Springfield Road supports a Polish congregation while St. Wladimir the Great in Broad Street is a major institution of the Ukrainian community. Six Lutheran churches with mainly central European protestant congregations are also present in Coventry. In contrast there are only three local chapels with a distinctive Welsh identity. This may indicate the thinness of the Welshness of those migrants who came to Coventry in the 1930s.

The small wartime Indian community had expanded to an estimated 4,000 by 1954. This quiet, peaceloving ethnic minority soon colonised some of the more rundown housing stock in the Foleshill Road area. Like other migrants in Coventry the Indians were anxious to protect their own culture and identity. In October 1952 Muslim members of the Indian community applied to the Planning and Redevelopment Committee for separate burial facilities and land for the building of a Mosque.[22] Although relatively few in number, Coventry's Indian community was not immune from racial prejudice that was already beginning to disfigure Britain nationally. In October 1954 it was reported that local estate agents were operating a colour bar.[23] In the previous week the *Coventry Standard* reported:

> The presence of so many coloured people in Coventry is becoming a menace. Hundreds of black people are pouring into the larger cities of Britain including Coventry and are lowering the standard of life. They live on public assistance

> and occupy common lodging houses to the detriment of suburban areas. ... They frequently are the worse for liquor — many of them addicted to methylated spirits — and live in overcrowded conditions sometimes six to a room'.[24]

This article was not the juvenile outpourings of a bigoted cub reporter but the major editorial. Indeed racism appears to have infected a wide spectrum of Coventry society in the early 1950s. The *Standard* article also mentioned that a branch of the AEU had 'approached Miss Burton, M.P. on this subject'.[25] Such hostility is all the more remarkable when it is borne in mind that the coloured minority during this period represented less than 1.5 per cent of the city's population and as Stephen Tolliday has shown in another essay in this volume, coloured workers were never a threat to the jobs of those employed in local factories.

By 1951 Coventry was predominantly a city of newcomers. It has been estimated that in that year only 30 — 35 per cent of the city's population of 258,000 were born in Coventry. Of the thousands who came to the city many soon left, having failed to find accommodation or work. One study claimed that in 1949 18,000 newcomers entered Coventry and 17,000 left.[26] Moreover, reports suggest that Coventry was hardly a melting pot. Besides racial prejudice Coventrians were reputed to be anything but welcoming to newcomers generally.[27] Thus friendship and social networks typically followed regional and ethnic lines. Clubs, pubs and religious institutions often catered for particular migrant groups. In some ways the status of Coventry as a migrant city since early this century probably mitigated against the standoffishness of the indigenous population. In 1912 for example, migrants had established their own clubs and societies. The 'Caledonian Corks' had branches in 17 pubs, 'The Association of Lancastrians' met regularly in the King's Head Hotel, the 'Society of Yorkshiremen' in the White Lion, and the local 'Society of Londoners' was also active.[28] Sargant Florence's 1949-51 survey confirms that migrants continued to socialise inside their own regional or ethnic networks which could produce a lack of interest in establishing neighbourhood friendships.[29]

The census of 1961 showed the 1954 estimate of Asians living in Coventry to be an exaggeration. Table 2.13 illustrates that immigrants from the new Commonwealth over the previous ten years had been a trickle rather than a stream. New Commonwealth immigrants in 1961 accounted for only 1.5 per cent of the population compared with 6.1 per cent from Eire and Northern Ireland. Between the census of 1961 and the so-called mini-census of 1966 some major shifts in the pattern of

Table 2.13. Commonwealth and Irish Residents in Coventry 1961

Country	*Number*
India	2,843
Pakistan	596
Jamaica	789
Rest of Caribbean	413
Eire	14,802
N. Ireland	4,020

Source: Census reports.

Table 2.14. Birthplace of Coventry Residents, 1966

Place	*Number*
Not stated	460
British Isles	311,880
England	266,370
Northern Region	11,580
York & Humberside	6,630
North West	11,220
East Midlands	10,310
West Midlands	201,550
East Anglia	2,450
South East	17,140
South West	5,280
England not stated	210
Wales	11,410
Scotland	12,320
N. Ireland	4,080
Eire	16,790
Isle of Man & Channel Islands	240
Commonwealth Countries, Colonies and Protectorates	11,340
Foreigners	5,130

Source: Census report 1966.

migration into Coventry did take place. Table 2.14, which is taken from the 1966 survey, a survey based upon a ten per cent sample of local households, illustrates these changes. Although the category Commonwealth Countries, Colonies and Protectorates is not the same as 'New Commonwealth', a substantial increase in coloured immigration had taken place during the previous five years. This expansion however

*Table 2.15. Coventry Population 1951-1971**

1951	265,765
1961	316,629
1971	335,240

*NOTE: All figures relate to the city area as constituted in 1971.

Source: Census reports.

needs to be kept in perspective. Nearly two thirds of the local population were born in the West Midlands. There were also nearly twice as many migrants from Ireland as from the Commonwealth and Colonies. Indeed in 1966 only 3.5 per cent of Coventry's population were born outside Britain compared to the national figure of five per cent. Again these census regional categories are not directly comparable to previous ones but some patterns can be identified. For example, when we compare Table 2.14 with Table 2.11 it is noticeable that the Welsh stream had slowed down. The number coming into the city from Wales had increased by only eight per cent in the previous fifteen years. Similar small increases had taken place amongst migrants from the various parts of Northern England. On the other hand the Scots had increased by nearly 60 per cent and London and the South East by over 70 per cent. Foreigners, mainly European registered a small increase of 659 which indicates that this group was essentially the product of immediate post-war factors.

The rate of migration into Coventry was undoubtedly slowing down by the mid-1960s. Between 1961 and 1971 the population rose by 5.8 per cent compared with a rise of 19 per cent between 1951 and 1961. The failure of Coventry's manufacturing industry to maintain immediate post-war growth rates was providing fewer opportunities for migrant manual workers, while the completion of the central area redevelopment programme and the large housing schemes reduced the number of itinerant building workers. Between 1951 and 1966 the local population increased by approximately 4,000 per year; in the following five years the net annual increase fell to approximately 1,000. Moreover, the proportion of this expansion attributable to migration had dramatically declined. Between 1951 and 1961 a Department of the Environment survey estimated that migration accounted for 44.5 per cent of population growth in the Coventry belt. In the five years 1961-66 migrants only made up 17.6 per cent of the rise. In the following three years the survey noted that the Coventry belt had reversed its demographic position and had lost 0.1 per cent of its population through out migration.[30]

Despite these indications of impending change in the structure of the local population the authorities continued to view Coventry as a major area of demographic expansion. In October 1970 a Ministry of Housing representative predicted a 33 per cent rise in Coventry's population over the next 20 years.[31] The economic boom during Anthony Barber's Chancellorship, which greatly benefitted the local motor industry, briefly reversed the slowdown in population growth. It was estimated, for example, that the population was rising by 2,000 per year in 1974, twice the rate of the late 1960s.[32] By 1976, however, important signs of demographic change were again apparent. The local social services department were the first to notice. In 1976 the proportion of over 65's rose above the national average to 11.5 per cent of the population.[33] Coventry by the mid-seventies was faced with a new situation. Not only was local industry experiencing major problems, but the city was also having to come to terms with the difficulties brought about by demographic change. Between the 1920s and the 1960s, migration had given Coventry a youthful character. This necessitated that housing and education were given priority in the allocation of resources. A youthful population on the other hand is generally more healthy and requires less resources to be invested in health services. Moreover migrants tended to leave their families, particularly their parents, behind. Many Coventry children were deprived of regular contact with their grandparents but the city escaped the cost of having to care for the elderly, a cost that is now proving hard to bear given the city's declining economy.

Intuition suggests that Coventry, with its large migrant element, would rapidly lose population in a period of economic decline. The loss of 7.5 per cent of the population, from 335,238 to 310,216, between 1971 and 1981 in part confirms this prediction. What seems surprising is that this loss has not been greater. Nearly 60,000 jobs have disappeared during the present recession.[34] Given the shallowness of the family structure of many Coventrians this lack of roots should result in a sizeable proportion of locals being all too willing to seek their fortune elsewhere. The problem is, of course, that the recession has hit manufacturing industry throughout the UK. For most there is nowhere to go. There is a cruel irony in the present recession. What economic growth that is taking place is in such areas as the service sector or the so called 'high-tech' industries. This growth is not being realised in Coventry, nor are Coventrians well suited for such work. Coventry's under-representation in categories I, II

Table 2.16 Coventry and the UK Employed Population by Social Class. 1981

Class		*Coventry Percentage*	*UK Percentage*
I	Professional	4.4	4.5
II	Intermediate	12.7	18.8
IIIa	Skilled Non-Manual	7.8	9.1
IIIb	Skilled Manual	28.9	26.2
IV	Semi-skilled	17.5	12.2
V	Unskilled	5.0	4.1

Source: Census reports.

and IIIa needs no explanation. Moreover their numbers are unlikely to increase. What evidence that is available suggests that the skilled non-manual workers are proving the more mobile. Nissan is reputedly recruiting 250 foremen in Coventry for its new Sunderland plant, while Talbot in 1983 removed its Whitley research and development facility along with personnel to Paris.

The recession is also generational in its impact. The thousands of workers who streamed into Coventry between the 1930s and 1950s enjoyed working lives that were largely uninterrupted. By the time local manufacturing declined they had retired or faced the prospect of early retirement cushioned by redundancy payments. It is the children and grandchildren of those fortunate two generations whose future is bleakest. Another essay in this volume makes the point that Coventry has come full circle. The city now faces a crisis of similar proportions to that of the 1860s. There is, however, one major difference. The 1860s recession was local. The skilled weaver could take his craft to more prosperous manufacturing districts. Coventry's redundant engineers, car workers and their families do not have such an option.

Notes to Chapter 2

1. Census Report for Leicester 1871.
2. 'Mid Victorian Coventry', University of Birmingham Department of Extra Mural Studies (Coventry, 1975).
3. J.R. Bailey, 'The Struggle for Survival in the Coventry Ribbon and Watch Trades 1865-1914', *Midland History* VII, 1982.
4. Webb Trade Union Collection, Section A, vol. 34.
5. C.W. Cooper, 'Fifty Years Reminiscences of a Coventry Working Man', (Coventry 1912).
6. *Coventry Herald*, 25 June, 1897.
7. M.O.H. Report 1900.
8. C.H. D'E. Leppington, 'The Evolution of an Industrial Town', *The Economic Journal*, 17, 1907.
9. See Chapter 6.
10. J. Walker, *British Economic and Social History 1700-1967* (1968), 317-319.
11. M.O.H. Reports 1930-39.
12. B. Thomas, 'The Influx of Labour into the Midlands 1920-37', *Economica*, 1938.
13. G. Williams, 'From Grand Slam to Great Slump', *Welsh History Review*, Vol. 11, No. 3, June 1983.
14. M.O.H. Report 1937. See also Chapter 5.
15. See Chapter 12.
16. C. Saunders, *Seasonal Variations in Employment* (1936), 98.
17. *Ibid.*, 99.
18. K. Richardson, *Twentieth Century Coventry* (1972), 93-4.
19. A. Shenfield & P. Sargant Florence, 'The Experience of Coventry', *Review of Economic Studies*, 12 (1), 1944-45.
20. See Chapter 12.
21. Jonathan Zeitlin, 'The Emergence of Shop Steward Organisation and Job Control in the British Car Industry: a Review Essay', *History Workshop Journal*, 10, 1980. See also Dave Lyddon's criticism in *HWJ*, 15, 1983 and Zeitlin's reply *HWJ*, 16, 1983.
22. City of Coventry Planning and Redevelopment Committee Minute Book, 8 October, 1952.
23. *Coventry Standard*, 15 October, 1954.
24. *Ibid.* 8 October, 1954. Mr. Edgar Letts was the editor.
25. *Ibid.*

26. *City of Coventry Development Plan* (1951).
27. P. Sargant Florence, *et.al.*, *The Coventry Sociological Survey 1949-51*; see also L. Kuper (ed.), *Living in Towns*, (1953), Chapter I passim.
28. Miscellaneous Directories 1910-14.
29. P. Sargant Florence, *et.al.*, *op.cit.*
30. Department of the Environment, *Long Term Population Distribution in Great Britain* (1971).
31. *Coventry Evening Telegraph*, 13 October, 1970.
32. *Ibid.*, 17 June, 1976.
33. *Ibid.*, 21 September, 1976.
34. *Coventry Quarterly Monitor of the Economy*, No. 4, November 1984.

Chapter 3

Aspects of Infant Welfare in Coventry 1900–40

Marjorie Lodge

This essay is about the growth of the infant welfare movement in Coventry and in particular the part played in it by the voluntary activity of working class women in the years between the wars.[1] In a sense it is a study which looks at attempts to cope with the darker side of Coventry's rapid economic progress and development. High infant mortality rates disfigured most industrial districts in Britain and Government concern both with these and the high level of unfitness among volunteers for the Boer War prompted the anxious Conservative administration to appoint the famous inter-departmental Committee on Physical Deterioration to see if anything could be done to improve the nation's human stock. But in spite of a recommendation from the Committee supporting the introduction of a nationally co-ordinated scheme of health visiting, nothing was done.

However, the publicity surrounding the work of the Physical Deterioration Committee did apparently prompt the Coventry Medical Officer of Health, Dr. Hugh Snell, to take his first tentative steps towards doing something about the problem of infant mortality in the city. In 1904 he issued leaflets to local mothers advising them to breast feed their infants if at all possible and listing the hygienic precautions they needed to take if 'hand feeding' was necessary. Dr. Snell was concerned not to encroach on the prerogative of the general practitioner. Although the circular was issued to all mothers of newly-born children it was accompanied by a letter which asked them to ignore the leaflet if they were already receiving advice from a medical man. He also wanted the Sanitary Committee to appoint a health visitor who could advise nursing mothers about how to look after their babies. The Committee, worried about the cost as much as the novelty, refused. But the next year, 1905, they changed their minds and in February 1906 Miss Strover took up her position.[2]

Between 1906 and 1914 Coventry slowly expanded infant welfare provision and two more health visitors were added to the establishment by 1914. Between them these women managed to visit at least once over two-thirds of the babies born in the city. There were revisits if the baby was not considered to be in a satisfactory condition or if the mother was having difficulties. The next important local initiative was again, however, prompted by Government action.[3]

In July 1914 the Local Government Board (the central government department responsible for health) issued a memo which laid down a comprehensive scheme for Maternal and Child Welfare. Grants of 50% were made available for the introduction or expansion of health visiting schemes to cover all pre-school children and expectant or nursing mothers and for the establishment and maintenance of ante-natal clinics, maternity hospitals, and baby clinics or infant dispensaries where both advice and treatment could be given. The response of Coventry City Council to this offer of financial aid was not to broaden their service and begin new ventures but only to apply for a grant towards the existing health visitor scheme.

At this point the debate was opened up to a wider circle of participants. In October 1914 the local branch of the Women's Cooperative Guild held a public meeting to discuss the issue. The national care of maternity had for several years been a major concern of the Guild at national level. It had been instrumental both in having maternity benefit included in the 1911 National Insurance Act and in securing the amendment to that Act which laid down that the benefit should be the property of the mother. Some writers have claimed that the W.C.G. initiative of July 1914 largely embodied suggestions which the Guild had put to the Board.[4] At any event after the memo's publication the Guild directed its energies through its local branches into pressurising local authorities to implement the Board's recommendations. Public meetings were organised throughout the country. Following a lively debate, the Coventry meeting passed a resolution that there was in the city a need for the further care of maternity. The city council was urged to take advantage of the L.G.B.'s grant and to establish a municipal maternity centre as soon as possible. This demand was in line with the Guild's national policy.[5]

Not everyone who participated in the meeting supported the resolution. Nurse Pitt of the Midwives Union feared that midwives would lose work if women went to free clinics but she was reassured by Mrs. Annie Corrie, a prominent member of the local W.C.G. and the Women's Labour League that there was 'no intention of sweating either doctors or midwives' and that they would be paid a 'proper fee' for work performed at a clinic. Opposition also came ironically from the M.O.H. Hugh Snell informed the gathering that there was no need for a maternity centre in Coventry because of the low death rate, high wages and absence of poverty.[6] Coventry's health statistics were certainly better than the figures for other industrial cities in the Midlands.

Table 3:1.

1913	*Death Rate per 1000 Population*	*Infant Mortality Rate per 1000 births*
Coventry	11.7	92
Leicester	13.3	120
Birmingham	14.7	129
Nottingham	14.1	130
Wolverhampton	15.6	130
West Bromwich	17.6	140
Stoke-on-Trent	18.6	180

Although it is strange that the man who had done so much to begin an infant welfare scheme in Coventry should be so discouraging of further action, the women viewed the question from quite a different angle. They were not concerned with comparing statistics. They were concerned with what infant and maternal mortality meant to the individual families involved. In such a light a rate of infant deaths of 92 per 1000 was far too high. The immediate outcome of the public meeting was the establishment of a Care of Maternity Committee composed of an alliance of working class women's groups, feminists and middle class philanthropists. The organisations represented on the Committee were the W.C.G., the Women's Labour League, Railwaywomen's Guild, Freedom of Women Workers, Federation of Women Workers, Women's Auxiliary of the Free Church Council, Women's Adult Schools, Women's Suffrage Society and the Coventry District Nursing Association. The first three organisations drew their membership from working class housewives. The W.L.L. had already shown concern nationally over child welfare. In 1911 it had opened a free baby clinic in Kensington in memory of Margaret MacDonald and Mary Middleton, the first leaders of the movement and in 1913 it also had launched a national campaign for the spread of clinics on the Kensington model. At Kensington children under five were admitted free of charge to receive medical advice and treatment; dental treatment, minor operations and medicine were also available.[7]

The Freedom of Women Workers and the Federation of Women Workers were female trade unions concerned principally with improving the conditions of employed women. The main aim of the Women's Suffrage Society was, of course, the achievement of the female franchise but for the duration of the war it suspended its ordinary political work and instead used its entire organisation to help 'those who suffered from the economic and industrial dislocation caused by the war'.[8] The

Women's Adult Schools and the Women's Auxiliary of the Free Church Council, as their names imply, were committed to the intellectual and spiritual needs of women. The District Nursing Association was a charitable body organised by middle class citizens to provide nursing care both for the poor and for those who could afford to make a small donation or contribution to the scheme. Wives of some of the town's leading industrialists such as Mrs. Alfred Kirby and Mrs. Kevitt Rotherham also sat on the Care of Maternity Committee. With such a mixture of social class and experience, aims and attitudes, it is not surprising that the Committee could not contain all the values and aims of its original members.

Nonetheless, the Committee was dominated by Guild members and Guild policy. The president was Mrs. M.A. Keene who was also president of the W.C.G. One of the secretaries was Mrs. Chalder, another Guild official, whilst the other was Miss Avril Wilkes of the Women's Suffrage Society. The main aim of the committee, in line with the nationally agreed policy of the W.C.G. was 'that of persuading the municipal authorities of the urgent need of their running a municipal maternity and infant welfare centre as is already being done by other municipal authorities in the country'.[9] The W.C.G. was strongly opposed to charity. In 1915 their General Secretary wrote 'It is not charity but the united action of the community of citizens which will remove a widespread social evil. The community is performing a duty, not bestowing a charity...'. The aim was that 'the mothers of the country shall find themselves as free to use a municipal maternity centre as they are to use a Council School or a Public Library'.[10]

This was probably the cause of the early division of the committee. The middle class philanthropists favoured charitable provision with control in the hands of the providers. They soon broke away to form the Coventry Voluntary Infant Welfare Committee and opened their first clinic in the summer of 1915. It was held each Wednesday afternoon in Lord Street school. It was based on the School for Mothers model after the well known one at St. Pancras. In addition to offering individual advice on infant feeding it also, in its early days, ran lectures for mothers. During 1915 Mrs. Olorenshaw, a certificated nurse, spoke on home nursing and Mrs. Alfred Kirby, one of the committee members, spoke on economical cooking.

The Voluntary Infant Welfare Committee were able to expand their activities steadily. By 1922 it was holding a fortnightly ante-natal clinic. In 1924 it was recorded that 466 mothers had attended simple lectures on health matters and housecraft. By this time the Voluntary Infant Welfare

Committee had acquired the premises 'Dunsmoor' formerly used by the Care of Maternity Committee. In addition to running clinics at its headquarters in 'Dunsmoor' it also held one afternoon session each week in premises in Leicester Causeway and Brays Lane. By 1930, when the local authority took over responsibility for providing the medical and nursing staff, the committee employed two paid full-time health visitors and a part-time woman doctor and also had the voluntary part-time services of a female gynaecologist. A further service developed as an adjunct with the establishment in 1924 of the Coventry Crippled Children's Guild. This began on the 'Dunsmoor' premises and then later acquired what was to become the Paybody Children's Hospital. These two bodies, the Voluntary Infant Welfare Committee and the Crippled Children's Guild continued to play a large part in Coventry child health care facilities right until the inception of the N.H.S.

Meanwhile the Care of Maternity Committee was running its own clinic and continuing to press for a municipal service. This clinic was established in June 1915 in Palace Yard, off Earl Street. The clinic was an offshoot of a social institute established a few months earlier by the Local Women's Suffrage Society in accordance with their aims of alleviating suffering caused by the war. The 'Tipperary Club' had been established in Palace Yard in February 1915 with the aim of being 'the medium by which women relatives of Coventry soldiers and sailors might meet together and offer mutual comfort and assistance to each other'.[11] Reading and writing facilities were provided and there was a nursery where babies could be cared for whilst their mothers were resting.

The baby clinic which was open each Saturday afternoon in one of the rooms of the Tipperary Club was not, however, exclusively for the use of the relatives of soldiers and sailors. It was available for anyone who cared to use it. But as in previous official council ventures in the city concerned with infant welfare, such as the educational leaflets and the health visiting scheme, the service offered at the clinic was restricted because of the desire not to compete with existing medical facilities.[12] The Palace Yard centre was not modelled on the lines of the W.L.L. clinic at Kensington. Its aims were strictly limited to giving advice and checking minor ailments. The Care of Maternity Committee secured the professional services of Miss Crabbe, superintendent of the district nurses and Dr. Power, a local G.P., but if an infant was found to be ill no treatment was given and instead the mother was instructed to take it either to her own doctor or the local hospital. The work at the clinic consisted mainly of weighing the children and giving advice on diet, clothing and management, again avoiding encroachment on the work of

G.P.s.[13]

Given that nationally they were opposed to the problem being dealt with by charitable provision it may seem contradictory that the Guild-dominated committee themselves established a voluntary clinic. But it would have been short-sighted of the Guild to have opposed voluntary provision altogether. Indeed, some of the earliest centres in the country had been established through the efforts of Guild members after visits to France and Belgium in 1905 and 1906 where they saw the 'Consultations de Nourisons' and 'Goultes de Lait' which had been established there.[14] The key was the attitude of the voluntary worker herself and in their own clinics the Guild could take steps to avoid the patronising overtones of middle class workers in some other voluntary clinics. And while in 1915 it was supporting voluntary initiative it was also insisting that such measures were only temporary and that the ultimate goal was municipal schemes.[15]

In the Spring of 1916 the Care of Maternity Committee in Coventry expanded its activities. At 'Dunsmoor' in Lower Holyhead Road it established both a hostel for working girls and a day nursery for the children of women employed in munitions factories. The hostel side of the activities was very soon abandoned and instead became a maternity home, as this was more in keeping with the committee's aims. In an appeal for funds in February 1916 in order to continue the work at Palace Yard and at 'Dunsmoor' the committee used the rhetoric of war-time to move the citizens of Coventry to dip into their pockets.

> ... with the terrible wastage that is going on upon the battlefields of the world, where will be the men and women of tomorrow ... Depletion of the present manhood of the city by the shot and shell of an enemy; depletion among the men and women of tomorrow by an enemy at home—ignorance and neglect.[16]

Meanwhile the Care of Maternity Committee was still working for its main objective of a free municipal centre. A public meeting was held in September 1915 at which the speaker was another leading member of the W.C.T. national campaign. Margaret Bondfield, trade union official and an honorary member of the Guild, had in 1914 written a pamphlet published by the Guild on the aims of the movement in the Maternity and Child Welfare field and she spoke at many of the public meetings organised up and down the country.[17] At this second meeting in Coventry the local authority was urged to take an active part in the Care of Maternity Committee and to increase its own provision by extending the health visiting service.

In December 1915 it was the turn of the Women's Auxiliary of the Free Church Council to put pressure on the local authority when it presented the city council with a resolution regarding the desirability of a maternity centre. In March 1916 there was further pressure when a petition signed by 984 women demanding a municipal Maternity and Child Welfare Centre was presented to the Council. This was followed by a deputation of four women from the Care of Maternity Committee to a meeting of the Sanitary Committee: Miss Pridmore, niece of the mayor, in her capacity as mayoress; Miss Wilkes of the Women's Suffrage Society, Mrs. Corrie of the W.C.G and W.L.L. and Mrs. Briggs of the W.C.G. Their request was that the council should take over the Palace Yard clinic and use it for the development of municipal facilities.

The local authority declined to do this, deciding that the system of health visiting was a more effective solution to the problem of infant welfare. But if we look at Dr. Snell's comments in a report he made to the Carnegie United Kingdom Trustees about Maternity and Child Welfare provision in his area we get more clues about why a municipal centre was not thought necessary at this time. Dr. Snell's view was that as there was 'very little poverty in the city at present, no reason is apparent for the health visitors to refer cases for advice to a general practitioner attending at one of the Baby Clinics in preference to any other general practitioner who may be consulted at his surgery'.[18] The encroachment issue remained a live one.

Nevertheless once the idea of baby clinics had been introduced to the city by the two voluntary bodies and with the continued pressure from the women's organisations it was not long before a municipal clinic gradually emerged. It began in an indirect way with, at first, only a minority of mothers being asked to take their babies to be weighed at the office of the health department. Those singled out for attention were the ones whom the health visitor considered not to be thriving. By 1917, after some difficulty finding space in council premises, the facility for weighing babies and offering advice on feeding was extended to all when a municipal centre began opening on three afternoons each week. This clinic was staffed by the health visitors with the M.O.H. himself sometimes being in attendance. When the municipal clinic opened the Care of Maternity Committee clinic at Palace Yard ceased. However, the committee continued their work with the 'Dunsmoor' day nursery and the maternity home which succeeded the working girls' hostel.[19]

It was again the initiative of the national Government which precipitated the third phase in the movement for infant welfare in Coventry. After the passing of the 1918 Maternity and Child Welfare Act, Coventry women were able to play a direct part in the decision-making process affecting public provision of Maternity and Child Welfare services. Whilst this Act did not make local government provision of Maternity and Child Welfare facilities mandatory, it did lay down that every local authority which made such provision should appoint a Maternity and Child Welfare committee which was to include at least two women. There were in fact four women appointed to Coventry City Council's first such committee:

Mrs. Pitt, the president of the Coventry Midwives Union.

Mrs. Griffiths, a socialist member of the Board of Guardians from 1907 and a member of the W.C.G.

Mrs. Keene, another member of the Board of Guardians and president of the W.C.G. and

Mrs. Biggs, another W.C.G. committee member.

As the W.C.G. had been involved in infant welfare work for some time it is not surprising to find the guild so well represented and Jean Gaffin has pointed out that a thorough education in cooperative principles and the practical experience of participating in a democratically organised movement like the Guild enabled working class women to take public office with confidence.[20] 92 year old Mrs. Essex, in an interview with the author, remembered the training given to her by guildswoman Mrs. Annie Corrie, one of the women who took part in the deputation to the Sanitary Committee in March 1915.

> Mrs. Corrie was one of the finest women to train another woman there is. She made us do things. She taught me everything I know. How to sit at the table, if I was president, on the committee, if I was chairwoman ... And you were taught even to sit, even as you sat at the table, you should never have your handbag, you should never fiddle about, you should never have your legs open. We were taught all the little things you see'.

Emily Smith, Mrs. Gant, Sally Griffiths, Annie Corrie, Mrs. H.E. Givens and Pearl Hyde were all W.C.G. members elected to the Coventry City Council between the wars.

Cooperative guildswomen carried on as voluntary workers in the field of Maternity and Child Welfare as clinics were established by independent voluntary committees in various locations in the expanding

Table 3:2. Number of Children Attending Clinics

	a) *Municipal Clinic*	b) *Voluntary Clinics*
1933	1886	2407
1934	1859	2685
1935	1930	3066
1936	1980	3400
1937	1825	4139
1938	1960	4916

Source: M.O.H. Reports City of Coventry.

city. Mrs. Davies had memories of her mother's work in a voluntary clinic. She recalled that as a child of about 12 years of age she had helped tear old sheets into strips to make the 'belly bindings' which had formed part of the contents of maternity bags issued to mothers in need. Both Mrs. Essex and another elderly guildswoman, Mrs. Mosely, recalled how they had heard guildswomen speak at meetings of their voluntary work in baby clinics. Evidence of the guild's involvement is also to be found in their minute books. In 1935 Alderman Mrs. Hughes, as she was then, spoke to Lower Stoke Branch 'of the wonderful way our guildswomen have taken to the Maternity and Child Welfare work', a new clinic having been opened at Radford, staffed with guild women.

From the days of the Palace Yard clinic in 1915 right until the 1948 reorganisation of the health services voluntary workers played a large part in Maternity and Child Welfare work in the city. During this period there was only one clinic administered by the city council although after the 1929 local Government Act they did provide medical and nursing staff for the voluntary clinics. Statistics showing the number of children attending clinics evidence the extent of the voluntary commitment. Proximity was probably the biggest factor in the popularity of the voluntary clinics for they were held in church halls and similar buildings in residential areas, whereas the municipal clinic was held in the city centre. The attitude of the volunteers at the voluntary clinics may also have been important. In 1941 the Women's Group on Public Welfare reported that as well as being deterred by personal difficulties such as the inability to afford to pay the fare to a centre or to attend at awkward hours 'poor people' may also have been put off by 'harsh or wooden administration' or 'unacceptable personnel'. These problems could be overcome by the use of voluntary workers who had both a genuine concern for the mothers and a thorough understanding of their problems.

Mrs. Ivy Cowdrill was involved both in the establishment and in the day to day administration of a clinic which was opened in Tile Hill in 1937. Her account of her work shows that when voluntary workers were part of the community in which a clinic was established they had a shared experience which helped them to understand the mother's problems. She begins with an explanation of the circumstances in which her local clinic was opened.

> Well they were starting to build up here and Tile Hill North and the people used to come along the lane here 'Course it was all fields then, all round here, that was a golf course over there. They [i.e. the mothers] used to go down with the prams all the way to Gulson Road [the municipal clinic] to get the cheap food. And I used to feel so sorry for them. Well, we all had. And Pearl Hyde talked to us about it and asked us if we'd help her. We certainly would! ... Pearl Hyde started it. There were several of us in the Guild, on the Coop Guild and some of our neighbours. We talked about it at the Guild but it was when Pearl started to come round that we got to talk about it more!.[21]

Mrs. Pearl Hyde was at this time the Labour Party candidate for the ward and it could be argued that she had an ulterior motive in working to establish an infant welfare clinic, especially as the election canvassing and enquiries about potential users of the clinic were carried out within a short time of each other. Although she did not, in fact, win the seat she was successful shortly afterwards in a by-election in another ward. Because of her local government commitments and her work with the Women's Royal Voluntary Service, Mrs. Hyde's practical involvement with the clinic soon ceased but the enthusiasm of her followers remained and many of those originally involved were inspired to carry on until 1941 when in Mrs. Cowdrill's words 'the Health took over'.

The minutes of the City Council corroborate Mrs. Cowdrill's account of the establishment of the Tile Hill clinic but a few lines in a minute book cannot portray the enthusiasm and energy of the women involved, the way an oral account can. Mrs. Cowdrill:

> We got talking about it and they all said they'd help. And we used to go out every day. My daughter used to go with me, knocking on doors, enquiring. We all done our share. To see how many babies and who would come.

With the approval of the Ministry of Health and with professional personnel provided by the city council the clinic was opened in October 1937. Mrs. Cowdrill went on to give her view of activities at the clinic by telling of the duties of voluntary workers.

> We bought aluminium bowls and we used to put a clean piece of tissue paper in the bowl for to put the babies' clothes in, by the side of every chair. We used to go early and do that before the clinic opened. And put everything ready and the scales ... One would be weighing the toddlers this side and one the other side weighing the tiny babies. And we had a couple of nurses from the council [health visitors] and a doctor. We had a doctor's room. We took it in turns to do the jobs we done. But I don't think there's one besides me still alive. We used to weigh the babies. We used to take it in turns or it wouldn't be fair or someone would have the dirty jobs all the while, washing the aluminium bowls out, washing the cups and saucers.

From evidence in the M.O.H. Reports it appears that the majority of voluntary clinics were organised in this way. The volunteers administered the clinic and were the ancilliary workers whilst the city council provided the health visitors and the doctor. A criticism of voluntary clinics of this era was that voluntary helpers were inclined to usurp the duties of the health visitor but there is no evidence either written or oral that Coventry volunteers overtly took over any of the health visitors' educational or advisory duties. Indeed, they did not receive training on such matters. What many of them did have, though, was the experience of being mothers and this would qualify them as experts on baby care in the eyes of many of the young mothers who attended the clinic. In this capacity they may have passed on common sense advice or words of encouragement as they handled the babies and exchanged small talk with the mothers.

Not only were many of the volunteers experienced mothers, most of them had experienced a life style similar to the women who attended the clinic, and they spoke the same language. The usual image of a voluntary worker is of a middle class 'lady bountiful' but at this time working class helpers were fairly common in Coventry baby clinics. While working voluntarily at the clinic Mrs. Cowdrill had a part-time job supervising the cleaners in a car factory. One of her voluntary colleagues also worked there. Mrs. Gerrard, another volunteer who was interviewed had been a millhand in Lancashire in her youth. The woman mentioned earlier as making the 'belly bindings' acquired the discarded sheets through her job as a hospital laundry worker. Although Mrs. Cowdrill's work at the clinic occurred in a period of her life when she was financially more secure than many of the young mothers using the clinic, she had in her younger days known hardship.

> When my husband came back from the first war there was the means test and they were digging the roads for a shilling a day. He was out of work and I'd got the baby. And my brother was in Coventry and he said 'Come over and try your luck' and the Standard [car factory] had just started up and he came over and got a job there. And we was living in a bedroom, further up the street here, in one of these houses. And I lived and slept and cooked and everything in a bedroom. But then we got this house and I've been here ever since.

Apart from the weighing of babies the main tasks of a voluntary worker at a child welfare clinic centred around the sale of baby food and food supplements. Here too their knowledge of working class life was useful -the volunteers were aware that some of the mothers needed flexible arrangements regarding payment.

> We used to sell Bemax, Marmite, Ovaltine and every food there was until the National Food came out; orange juice, vitamin pills, the lot. ... It was a very big welfare. You can tell by the money we took 'cause the food was cheap, very, very cheap. We used to sell the food cheap and there used to be a big tin of Virol, about 28 lbs and we used to fill them little cream cartons and they was sixpence. And the Ovaltine was only about a shilling, elevenpence-halfpenny. ... If anyone said "I've no money" I'd say "Well get it". I'd lend them the money and they'd bring it back here. ... And I've come home here like a packed mule 'cause the soldiers' wives used to have their money on a Monday and the clinic wasn't till Thursday, so you see they'd no money come Thursday come round. I used to bring the food home and they used to come for it here. My husband used to shout "Shop!"

As well as being aware of the financial problems the volunteers at the particular clinic where Mrs. Cowdrill was active were also aware of other needs of their clients. The concept of 'welfare' was extended and clinic attendance made into a social occasion by the provision of tea and biscuits. Special social events were also organised.

> All the year we was involved, looking for Christmas, looking for the summer holiday ... we took them to London once, to Bourton on the Water, to Tewkesbury. I had a red dressing gown, a scarlet dressing gown. One of us would have it on to be Father Christmas and every time they'd have a present off the tree. We used to get Cadbury's chocolate cheaper. And when we were having the Christmas parties and the summer parties we used to write to Mackintosh's and Cadbury's and Fry's to see if they'd help us out and they used to send us little bars of chocolate and little packets of sweets for the children.

This clinic seems to have been the sort of centre which could have developed into the type of women's club advocated in 1939 by Margery Spring-Rice of the Women's Health Enquiry Committee. Such a centre would enable women to 'meet their fellows', 'form social ties', 'talk and laugh', and 'eat food which they had not cooked themselves'. The efforts made in this direction by the Tile Hill volunteers were appreciated by the women of the district as evidenced by this extract from an interview with a woman who had been a regular attender in the early 1940s.[22]
M.L. Was there any difference between the two Clinics?
Mrs. Frost. Yes, this one [Tile Hill] had a little more go about it. They arranged days out, for the mothers to take the babies like, afternoon out I suppose it was. And there was a lovely party at Christmas and all that sort of thing. And I must have taken my son until he was about four.
M.L. Just because it was so enjoyable?
Mrs. Frost. Yes, it was an afternoon out.
This idea of 'an afternoon out' was given as one of their reasons for attending clinics by many of the women interviewed about their role as mothers in this era. As Margery Spring-Rice appreciated this is a factor not to be overlooked when considering the health of women and young children.

Towards the end of the second world war there were plans in Coventry to emulate or even surpass the health ideals of the 'Peckham Experiment'. In Peckham, a working class district of London, there had been established in 1934 a health centre which not only included doctors' consulting rooms but also a theatre, gymnasium and a swimming pool. In the more ambitious scheme for Coventry it was planned to create an entirely new community with its own farms and based on a health centre. Land was purchased but unfortunately the scheme did not get the approval of the city council and had to be abandoned.[23] But, in their own way, although they were probably unaware of it, the voluntary workers at the Tile Hill Maternity and Child Welfare Clinic were also carrying out the ideals of Williamson and Pierce, the instigators of the Peckham experiment—not only to improve the health but also to improve the quality of life of local inhabitants.

In the course of the interview with Mrs. Cowdrill it became obvious that not only was she deeply committed to the work but also that she gained a great deal of satisfaction from what was, in effect, an extension of the traditional female role of nurturer within the private domain of the family.

> It was great. I loved it. Thursday was my day out ... and I just lived for Thursday every week. You know it was so great to be involved in it. ... It wasn't only working at the welfare, we was interested in the life of the children altogether. You seem to live for them really. You got so interested in it, it seemed to occupy your mind all the while.

The evidence presented earlier showed how some women were equipped through their membership of the W.C.G. to venture out from their role in the private domain and to influence the development of Maternity and Child welfare services by becoming public women. Others, like Mrs. Cowdrill, made their mark by transferring the caring values of the private domain into the public domain of the clinic, and putting a humane face on what had been an impersonal service. Though taking diverse paths and using different talents both sets of women played an important role within the city. Coventry in this period was an industrially buoyant and expanding city. The people who flooded in attracted by jobs in the new factories were mainly young people. As Bill Lancaster's essay has shown, the proportion of the population aged over 45 was less in Coventry than almost anywhere else in Britain. The people had more consistent and better remunerated work than in many other places and yet infant mortality remained unacceptably high and old vested interests resisted the modernisation of medical services. The women of the Coop Guild, with a little encouragement from the State, set about tackling this problem and confronted it with zest and enjoyment until the war and then the National Health Service prepared the way for bureaucracy. Many of the 'clinic activists' gave up their positions with reluctance.

They would have liked to have seen a clearly established role for the voluntary worker within the health care schemes designed by the State. Unfortunately not enough people felt like them at the time.

Notes to Chapter 3

1. I should like to thank Celia Davies, Tony Mason and Margaret Stacey for their comments on earlier drafts of this chapter.
2. The reason for the change was the need to appoint an officer to enforce the Shop Hours Acts. Dr. Snell persuaded the Committee that the two posts could be combined. In the event the new position also involved inspecting midwives as required by the Act of 1902, visiting homes suspected of being insanitary and advising on how to isolate infectious diseases being treated at home. They were obviously determined to get their money's worth out of Miss Strover.
3. See J. Lewis, 'The Social History of Social Policy', *Journal of Social Policy*, 1980, Vol. 9 for a lucid discussion of the national campaign for improved maternal and child welfare provisions.
4. Gloden Dallas, Introduction,M.L. Davies (ed.), *Maternity: Letters from Working Women* (1978 ed.). See also Jean Gaffin and David Thoms, *Caring and Sharing. The Centenary History of the Co-operative Women's Guild* (1983).
5. Its leaders had by this time not only recognised the health of the mother as being an important factor in the producing of healthy offspring but were also acutely aware of the demands which childbirth and child-rearing made on the health of women.
6. *Coventry Herald*, 30, 31 October, 1914.
7. Lucy Middleton, 'Women in Labour Politics' in Lucy Middleton, (ed.), *Women in the Labour Movement* (1978), 27 and Sheila Ferguson, 'Labour Women and the Social Services in *ibid.*, 44, 46.
8. *Coventry Herald*, 14 August, 1914.
9. *Ibid.*, 5, 6 November, 1915.
10. M.L. Davies (ed.), *op.cit.*
11. *Coventry Herald*, 25, 26 December, 1914.
12. Lewis, *op.cit.*, p.483 argues that the early 'welfare centres' fear of encroaching upon the GP's territory and thereby concentrating upon advice rather than treatment has been a major factor in the development of the schism between preventive and curative medicine. *Coventry Herald*, 5, 6 November, 1915.
13. *Ibid.*, 2, 3 July, 5, 6 November, 1915.
14. Catherine Webb, *The Woman with the Basket* (1927), 124.
15. M.L. Davies (ed.), *op.cit.*, 212.

16. *Midland Daily Telegraph*, 12 February, 1916.
17. *Margaret Bondfield,* A Life's Work (1949).
18. *Coventry Herald*, 18, 19 May, 1917.
19. The day nursery closed at the end of the 1914-18 war when women were no longer needed to work in the munitions factories but the maternity home continued to be run by the committee until 1922, when because of shortage of funds it was taken over by the city council who soon disposed of it to the Voluntary Infant Welfare Committee and the Crippled Childrens Guild.
20. Jean Gaffin, 'Women and Co-operation' in Lucy Middleton (ed.), *op.cit.* (1978) 113-42.
21. Mrs. Cowdrill's evidence has appeared at length in *Health Visitor*, 56, July 1983. The interview took place on 10 June, 1981.
22. Mrs. Frost was interviewed 14 May, 1981.
23. Kenneth Richardson, *Twentieth Century Coventry* (1972), 275-76.

Chapter 4

A Twentieth Century Paternalist: Alfred Herbert and the Skilled Coventry Workman

John McG. Davies

During the early years of the twentieth century, Coventry's engineering industries gained a reputation for uneasy industrial relations. Militancy on the assembly line was a frequent occurrence at the Royal Ordnance Factory, and car factories like Maudslay Motor Company, Motor Manufacturing Company, Deasy and Company (nicknamed Diddlum-easy) and the Daimler. At these and similar firms, workers were frequently in dispute with management over such things as the introduction of complex wage systems and what they considered to be excessive supervision by management. In 1901 for example, the manager of the Motor Manufacturing Company told the workforce that they were all to start piecework and 'if any man didn't like the terms they'd be paid off at once'. In 1907 the Amalgamated Society of Engineers' District Committee heard from workers at the Royal Ordnance Factory that 'things were unbearable. They were being sweated and bullied, and as soon as their jobs were finished, out they had to go 'til fresh jobs were ready'. Six months later, the Daimler management were reducing the time taken to produce work without altering the method of manufacture. A works notice stating that all men failing to make the bonus on the job would be discharged, led to an instant stoppage of work, and the notice was eventually withdrawn.

Tension grew during the First World War, as workers were often asked to operate several machines at once. Over such an issue a strike occurred at the Coventry Ordnance Works, and only intervention by Admiral Bacon got the men back to work. Dilution also caused problems in many Coventry firms. At the Rudge Cycle Company in 1915, the Amalgamated Society of Engineers were opposing the introduction of girls working on fuses and being paid 2.1/2d per fuse, when the work had previously been done by an A.S.E. member at 11.1/2d per piece.[1] In 1917, the *Midland Daily Telegraph* reported that 35 to 40,000 workers were idle over the issue of shop steward recognition. The dispute began at the White and Poppe factory with a sit-in strike, and rapidly spread across the city.[2] Five years later, Coventry employers were in the vanguard of the 'Engineers Lock Out' dispute with the Amalgamated

Engineering Union, over the employers' right to manage.[3]

The problems at some firms however, have to be set against the paternalistic quietude of others, such as Courtaulds and Herberts. As suppliers of machine tools, the fortunes of Alfred Herbert Ltd. were closely linked to the manufacture of bicycles then cars, and like the car manufacturers, Herberts rapidly expanded both plant and workforce during the early decades of this century. Yet in terms of employer/employee relationships the firm appears to have been troubled less than the car factories with disputes and militancy. Many employees have explained this stability in terms of the 'Herbert Spirit', a concept carefully constructed by management through speeches, newspapers and the house magazines, promoting the image of a happy, caring, family atmosphere, the consequences of which were loyalty and quality workmanship.

This image building developed randomly at first, based loosely on the social and labour relations style practised by Herberts' own entrepreneurial family in the nineteenth century. Paternalism was not consciously adopted as a management style until the 1920s however, when it came to be located within the wider industrial welfare movement which emerged from World War One, and with which Herbert, as Head of Machine Tools at the Ministry of Munitions, was very familiar. The 'caring' image was actively promoted through articles in the monthly journal, the *A.H. News*. In 1927, for example, Herbert can be found expressing his concern to provide improved ventilation for the offices, and a nutritious diet for workers by personally supervising food preparations in the canteen.[4] In the same year, a fully equipped accident clinic was opened at Edgwick, and workers were being encouraged to make suggestions for other environmental improvements. In 1926, in an article for the house journal, Herbert noted that 'many hundreds of boys have learned useful trades under our roof. Many have risen to positions of responsibility and good pay ... all by happy cooperation'.[5] His son-in-law, Captain Hollick, also told members of the A.H. Cycling Club at their annual dinner that they numbered among 'the world's luckiest people', and he praised 'the sportsmanship and good fellowship connected with the name of Alfred Herbert Ltd.'[6] On the entrepreneur's death, the Bishop of Coventry, Cuthbert Bardsley, told the congregation that 'he [Herbert] did not regard the men as employees but friends'.[7] This image has been carried through to the present day by Ian Hollick, the grandson of Sir Alfred Herbert, and an ex-director of the firm. In a letter to the *Coventry Evening Telegraph*, shortly after the firm's collapse in October 1983, he wrote:

> Anyone who has worked for Alfred Herbert Ltd. will know what is meant by the Herbert Spirit ... To one visiting the works for the first time in a quarter of a century, there was exactly the same strength of comradeship, warmth, pride, loyalty and goodwill that has existed since the foundation of the firm.[8]

And many Herbert employees believed the firm was unique in this respect. One declared 'If the gaffer told us to jump in the river we'd do it, you know what I mean'.[9]

As this essay will argue, the major factor contributing to this attitude, was without doubt the paternalistic management strategy and style practised by the employer and his family. Yet how accurate is this picture of complete harmony and cooperation? The early decades of the twentieth century, which provide the focus for this essay, saw rapid changes in workshop technology and conditions. Job security for the so-called 'aristocrats of labour' — the skilled engineers, was, as they saw it, being eroded by the arrival of automatic machinery which could be operated by unskilled or semi-skilled workers. With the new machinery and the influence of American techniques, came a greater emphasis on reducing production times by increasing feeds and speeds, and the implementation of the premium bonus and gang systems. In 1911 the District Committee of the Amalgamated Society of Engineers felt it necessary to record in their minute book that 'the conditions of the workshops [of Coventry] were being got up to a fine state of supervision, being equivalent to the American hustle'.[10]

Such policies were not excluded from Herberts and as a result industrial relations problems did occur. Pressure for changes in workshop practice, employment of cheap unskilled labour and low wages have been recurring features of the firm's management policies and often resulted in industrial militancy. Moreover, rather than smoothing the path of industrial relations, there is evidence that during periods of crisis in the engineering industry, Herbert management sometimes led the employers' offensive.

In summary, the claims for harmony and cooperation appear to have been exaggerated, but a number of factors, such as the firm's reputation for quality products, the reputation of Herbert himself and his right-hand men, the notion of job security, and the active pursuance of paternalism by management and the Herbert family, brought a relative stability to Herberts that has enabled the myth to be maintained. Alfred Herbert has long been popularly regarded as a 'rags to riches' entrepreneur. However, the evidence reveals striking similarities to an American study by Gregory, Neu and Miller who, after examining the backgrounds of American businessmen, challenged the 'rags to riches' notion and concluded that, overwhelmingly, they were from middle or upper class families, with fathers who were also businessmen. 'Their actual social origins were, in fact, precisely the opposite of the prevailing myth'.[11]

In his writings in the firm's house journal and through speeches at social gatherings, the idea that success for Alfred Herbert came purely through personal thrift, self discipline and hard work was frequently suggested. In an article written in 1929 for example, entitled 'Thoughts for Young Engineers' he urged his workforce to remember that 'the world is full of men who started life with no chance at all except their own courage and determination'. Elsewhere, he declared rich parents to be 'an absolute handicap' for young people with ambition.[12] Thirty years later, and one year after Sir Alfred Herbert's death, Lady Herbert told apprentices that they were setting out on the same road that her husband had taken, sixty-two years earlier.[13] Thus the image of the self made man was promoted, for employees to admire, respect and attempt to emulate.

Alfred Herbert's circumstances however were somewhat different to those of the majority of his workforce. He was born in 1866, the son of a wealthy landowner. The extent of the Herbert family fortune was considerable. His father, in addition to owning a town house in a salubrious area of Leicester, was the largest landowner in the parish of Whetstone south of Leicester, with a 250 acre farm, which in 1871 employed ten men, five boys and two domestic servants.[14] The young Herbert was educated at Stoneygate, a private school, and was destined for University and a parsonage, until he went to see an old school friend, William Hubbard, working on a lathe at Joseph Jessop's engineering company in Leicester. 'He was running a small lathe and I was spellbound to see the curly chips he was producing ... Hubbard's achievements were too much for me and I persuaded my father to let me follow his example'.

Herbert subsequently became an apprentice at Jessops, but not before his father had secured for him a type of training suitable to his rank. His indentures, he says, 'were of the traditional kind, stipulating that in consideration of a modest premium I was to be instructed in the arts of a turner, fitter and draughtsman'.[15]

Much as he might wish to give the impression that his training or status was no different to anyone elses, there is no doubt that this was not entirely the case. 'Premium' apprenticeships in fact emerged as a response to the need for more efficient organisation and increased technological knowledge as industrial units grew larger. They were 'a special type in which (unlike a typical engineering apprenticeship) an all round training was given, designed to fit the apprentice for management'.[16]

In 1887, with his apprenticeship nearing completion, Alfred Herbert sought a position at his brother William's highly successful Premier Cycle Company in Coventry, but there was 'no opening at my brother's concern'.[17] With the firm doing well however (by 1894 it was producing over 20,000 bicycles a year, with factories in Coventry, Nuremberg and Bohemia)[18] it is difficult to imagine that there would have been a problem in finding Alfred a job there. It seems likely that his brother already had something else in mind, namely the firm of Coles and Mathews at the Butts. Though Alfred Herbert never spells out this connection, as the extract below indicates, all the evidence points to the instrumentality of his brother in establishing Herbert junior in an engineering career in Coventry.

> Coles and Mathews disagreed and Mathews bought Coles out. Mathews then became associated with the Sparkbrook Company of which my brother was one of the directors, and wished to get rid of the Coles and Mathews business. I was asked to manage this business for a year to see if I'd care to take it over. I was released from my apprenticeship just before its termination and took on the job of Works Manager for Mr. Mathews. At the end of twelve months Mathews, off to Germany for Premier, offered to sell me the business for a relatively small amount.[19]

In going to work for two companies in which William Herbert was involved, Mathews was releasing his own business for a takeover. The theory that Alfred's move from Leicester had been planned for him is consolidated by his own admission that he never completed his apprenticeship. To leave before 'serving your time' was an act not to be undertaken lightly, and according to Charles More, writing of the period 1870-1914 'all the evidence suggests that this (premature termination of apprenticeship) was rare'.[20] The only feasible explanation is that Mathews was ready to leave his firm in Coventry and William Herbert had offered Alfred the job as manager there, with the major incentive that he could ultimately take over lock, stock and barrel, and begin producing machinery for the cycle trade, with guaranteed orders from the Premier

Cycle Company.

On Mathews' departure in 1888, Herbert bought the business in partnership with his old school friend and fellow apprentice, William Hubbard. For this purpose their fathers provided them with £2,000 each. With the help of Hubbard's 'considerable inventive capacity' they began making drilling machines, rim bending machines, spoke screwing machines, and hand lathes, which 'sold very freely at about £28 a piece'.[21]

The firm was given a further boost when Herbert's brother introduced him to Monsieur Scretan, the president of a French company making weldless steel tubing, much in demand by midland cycle makers. 'Alfred Herbert secured the sole selling rights in the U.K. and thereby not only greatly profited himself, but also laid the foundations of the agency side of the business which was later to become so important'.[22] Indisputably the firm was now on the road to success, yet Hubbard chose this moment to return to Leicester. The reason remains unclear, and Herbert deals with it only very briefly: 'After a time Mr. Hubbard and I came to the conclusion that although our personal friendship was unimpaired we were not suitable as business partners. It was arranged that I buy his share, which was done'.[23]

One explanation for the conclusion of the partnership may be related to what has been described by Alfred Herbert's step-granddaughter as his 'autocratic' behaviour at home and at work'. Hubbard may also have felt overpowered by the influence of the Herbert family. Alfred Herbert tells us that in 1894 'a small, limited liability company was formed, in which I took a majority of the shares, but a certain number were held by my late brother, Marston (works manager) and others interested'.[24] A closer look at the 'others interested' reveals the grip the Herbert family had on the business. On 17 July, 1894 a meeting took place regarding the purchase of shares. Attending the meeting for this purpose were, significantly, its chairman William Henry Herbert, Fannie Millicent Herbert, Ellen Adela Herbert, William Herbert, Sarah Ann Herbert, Alfred Edward Herbert, Frank Floyd (in charge of accounts at the firm) and J.M. Marston.[25] For decades after this, the firm's expansion was almost continual. In 1887 it employed twelve men and one clerk; ten years later there were 500 employees, and in 1926 the workforce totalled 2,600.

Throughout this period of expansion however, the management's approach to industrial relations appears to have changed little. Herbert believed in the right of management to manage, and carried out this policy decisively. This led inevitably to conflict with the unions, against whom his firm frequently led the employers' offensive. Even before the turn of the century the development of automatic machinery was facilitating the introduction of cheap labour for machine manning. This was anathema to the A.S.E. (Amalgamated Society of Engineers) whose members feared for their jobs, and the management activities at Alfred Herbert Ltd. could only consolidate their fears. In 1901, for example, the A.S.E. District Committee declared that 'the conditions at that firm regarding boy labour is scandalous'. In addition, cheap labour was being used to run machinery that had traditionally been the preserve of the time served engineer. In July 1901 the District Committee heard evidence from members working at Herberts of handymen boys and youths running lathes, planers and horizontal borers. The youths and handymen were earning approximately £1 per week, and according to the A.S.E. Minutes the district rate at that time for skilled men averaged 9.1/2d. per hour for a 54 hour week, making an average wage of £2 per week. In the Auto and Capstan Department

> one man and one boy run ten of these but lately they have been given another man to help. He was paid 24 shillings per week. Another man turns cones to pulleys and has four youths helping. On the horizontal borers there was one fully paid up man and the rest handymen.[26]

This obvious headache for the A.S.E. must at least in part have been a consequence of their defeat at the hands of the engineering employers in 1897. The issue had been the limit of union involvement or 'interference' with managerial decisions, and thus the selection, training, and employment of machine operatives. The unions had maintained that if any machine were to be used for work previously classified as skilled then that machine should be operated by a skilled man. Employers on the other hand had argued that, as owners of the machines, with responsibility for the work produced, they should have the freedom to employ whoever they thought fit. The unions therefore tried to enforce the skilled rates while employers maintained that they should be free to set the rate for any employee.[27]

The years prior to the First World War brought considerable friction with regard to industrial relations nationally, and this was reflected at Herberts, with trade unionists finding themselves barred from certain departments, and having to state any union affiliation when applying for a job there. The policy of employing cheap labour seemed more widespread than ever. Machine manning tactics at Herberts involved the employment of 'improvers' who, after a short while were replaced by labourers. The skilled men protested because 'they have to finish the unskilled men's work'. Bowing to the inevitability of the 'machine men' the A.S.E. had in one case attempted to get a youth at Herberts to join their union as a machinist but 'always objections were raised' by management. The District Committee concluded that 'such action of the management is causing much friction amongst ours and other members and having a tendency to bring the wages down'.[28]

If keeping wage bills to a minimum was an active policy of Herbert management, the years of the First World War provided the ideal conditions. In April 1915, Alfred Herbert took up his post as Head of Machine Tools at the Ministry of Munitions, and soon began campaigning vigorously for the introduction of women workers into the industry as dilutees. His own firm led the way. On 6 July, 1915, the A.S.E. District Committee received a report stating that Alfred Herbert Ltd. were 'about to introduce girls on centre lathes doing cock and pipe connections for capstan pumps'. The committee were informed that the management had 'given notice to those members who were asked to put the girls right when introduced'. Subsequently the union's Organising District Delegate (O.D.D.) wrote to the Employers Association, demanding that the same rates be paid to the women as the men. But the issue dragged on until the autumn, when an attempt was made to arrange a local conference between the A.S.E. District Committee and the Coventry and District Engineering Employers Association (C.D.E.E.A.). The A.S.E. Executive Council 'strongly urged' that the District Committee should 'refuse to countenance in any way the introduction of female labour in the shops which are confined to the production of machine tools'. The Executive Council 'repudiated the whole question of female labour in machine tool shops'.

The employers were of course hoping for success simply by delaying their reply to the ASE's request for a meeting, as witness the report received by the ASE District Committee on November 2, 1915. Herberts, it said, had been 'introducing girls in their fitting shop' and the secretary was instructed to ask Brother Ryder (the O.D.D.) 'if the Employers Association had replied to the D.C.'s application for a local conference regarding female labour in machine tool shops'.[29]

The A.S.E. appeared impotent before the continuous pressure of the employers and the Ministry of Munitions, and in March 1916, just two weeks after dilution had been given statutory force, a shop steward at Herberts reported girls being introduced on slotting, milling and gear cutting and one week later the District Committee were told that 'there were now at least seventy females employed by Herberts at the Butts'.[30]

The A.S.E. had made some attempts to protect their position however. They were represented on the government appointed Central Munitions Labour Supply Committee which in the autumn of 1915 approved Circular L2 which laid down that women on time work usually performed by skilled men should be paid the district rate, and established a basic minimum of twenty shillings per week for women on work usually done by non-skilled workers. But as Hinton points out, 'L2 had a number of crucial flaws as a guarantee against cheap labour ... it made no provision for the payment of equal time rates to women replacing semi-skilled men and the twenty shilling minimum was far below the rates earned by the semi-skilled. Moreover, the crucial battle was fought over the wages to be paid to a woman doing work previously performed by a fully skilled tradesman'. The employers could argue that the nature of the work had changed, that the dilutee was not on work customarily done by a fully skilled tradesman and therefore need not be paid the skilled rate for the job.[31]

Even so, there was some employer resistance to the introduction of L2, led by Alfred Herbert. At his suggestion a meeting took place in December 1915, between representatives of the Central Munitions Labour Supply Committee and four employers representatives (including a representative from Herberts), to lay before the Committee 'the difficulties as to the construction and application of the recommendations of Form L2 dealing with rates for women workers'.[32]

The reduction in labour costs was without doubt one of the principal motives behind the employment of females at Alfred Herbert Ltd., as the A.S.E. Minutes reveal. In August 1916 the District Committee received a letter from the National Federation of Women Workers asking for 'A.S.E. assistance and witnesses in the Arbitration Case over Payment of Women at Herberts'. Further, when in 1918 an arbitration award gave women examiners 46s. 6d. per week the firm 'gave a week's notice to a woman and introduced a probationary woman'. When the man she worked with refused to help the probationer, he was also given a week's notice.[33]

Herbert appears to have maintained double standards over the issue of women in industry. In an article for the *Machine Tool Review* he waxed eloquent on their ability to cope with the work.

> In some tasks women show exceptional skills, particularly where fine perception and manual dexterity are required; notable instances of this are an inspection of the filaments used in incandescent lamps and in the inspection of ball

> bearing races. In the latter they seem to be able to detect shadow marks far more readily than men. I have come across instances where even in original thought and in the higher branches of mathematics they have excelled.

He further cites the case of a factory in the north where large calibre shells were being produced on heavy turret lathes: 'The results attained by the men were deplorable. The manager cleared them all out and replaced them with hefty women, who produced about twice the output'.[34]

But if the entrepreneur valued their services so highly why did he not pay them accordingly? When in 1917 the government attempted to clarify the issue of wages for women by circulating among employers Order 49, which laid down that women on work hitherto done by skilled men should receive the skilled rate, irrespective of whether the work required skilled labour or not, Alfred Herbert apparently felt the situation demanded a united response from the employers. He convened a meeting of twenty-five principle machine tool manufacturers who resolved 'not to employ women on the terms of the Order'. The employers agreed emphatically that the terms of the Order and especially its insistence on the full rates of pay for split jobs, made the employment of women 'expensive and unremunerative. Skilled men, said the Secretary of the Employers Federation, are going to make the employment of women as expensive as possible so as to make it unattractive. If that is the case the Department will not get dilution'.[35]

The problems for the skilled workers were made worse by the firm's persistent policy throughout the period under discussion, of paying below the district rate. In 1898 for example, the A.S.E. District Committee received a letter from Herberts stating that the firm 'could not see fit to adhere to the rates laid down in our District Rules and the men are satisfied with the rate they are receiving'. The company also complained that 'in the past our members have been a source of trouble in the shop, and that they did not do as much work as non-society men'. The Committee's only answer was to censure A.S.E. members at Herberts for working contrary to district rules.[36]

Wage rises were often hard won, as witness the case of the patternmakers in 1911-12. The firm's profits had increased steadily annually from £3,012 3s.6d. in 1896 to £89,400 14s.10.1/2d for the year ending in April 1914 and the available figures reveal that during this period Alfred Herbert had increased his salary from £500 per annum in 1896 to £2,500 per annum in 1907. For machine tool manufacturers who supplied machines to the motor industry, trade was good. In June 1912, for example, the *Midland Daily Telegraph* noted that 'the motor industry in Coventry is certainly in a very buoyant state'. However, when the Coventry patternmakers applied for 1/2d. per hour in the autumn of 1911, a conference in December, at which Herbert's management was represented by Mr. J. Milburn, resulted in the offer of 1/4d. per hour, which the men turned down.[37] By 1912, relations had deteriorated to such an extent that a strike took place in Coventry, and the matter was important enough for the Mayor to intervene by inviting the protagonists to a meeting over which he presided. Representing the employers were

> Messrs. Herbert, Craig and Henson, with Mr. Martin, Secretary, Employers Association. Mr. Herbert stated the case for the employers and held no hope of meeting the (union) request. In fact having got over the temporary inconvenience which the strike had originally caused them, they objected to the idea that they should now pay more than before the strike, and they'd be willing to open the shops for a fortnight for any men who liked to apply and for whom jobs could be found at the rate of 9.1/2d as prior to the dispute.

The union representatives declared that they could not go back to the men with a reply like that.

After another meeting a few weeks later, the *Midland Daily Telegraph* reported that the strike, which had lasted nearly six months, was over. The patternmakers accepted 1/4d per hour, which they had earlier rejected, and the employers insisted that the new rate should be binding for five years from the date of the agreement.[38]

Herbert management also played a leading role in the imposition of wage cuts locally and nationally during the trade depression of the early 1920s. In the autumn of 1920, in an effort to save jobs, the unions had pressed for reductions in overtime and the establishment of two-shift systems. The employers promised, publicly, to consider these ideas, but did little of substance. Then in December 1920 John Milburn, a director of Alfred Herbert Ltd. and a member of the national negotiating Committee of the Employers' Federation, proposed to the Coventry and District Engineering Employers Association a motion in favour of a reduction in wages. This received the Committee's unanimous approval, and from then on pressure for wage reductions was maintained or increased. Pressure for reductions was recorded as having come from firms such as Herberts, Humber, Lea and Francis, Swift, Triumph,

Rover, Rudge-Whitworth and Albion Drop Forgings. During the Engineers' Lock Out that followed in March 1922, when employers claimed that the unions were usurping their right to manage, Alfred Herbert played a prominent part at the C.D.E.E.A., reminding the Committee of the importance of the wages issue and arguing that the Lock Out should be forced on the question of a wage reduction of 26s.6d. a week.[39]

The actual reduction when it came was 16s.6d. One ex-employee recalled the occasion well. 'They took 16s.6d. off. That was a terrific blow to us lads of about twenty. They did that because things were so bad, you were almost willing to accept anything. This 16s.6d. was a hell of a lot of money in those days. It was a massive reduction'. With factory wages in Coventry at the time ranging between £3 and £4 per week according to grade, the reduction proposed by Alfred Herbert eventually resulted in a drop in earnings of approximately 25 per cent.[40]

In June 1922 with their funds rapidly diminishing, owing to the large number of members requiring benefit, the A.E.U. was finally forced to concede defeat, and the members went back to work. The unions were forced to accept the employers 'right to manage' terms and further wage cuts followed. In Coventry the Executive Committee of the C.D.E.E.A. felt that the results were 'exceedingly good'. A vote of thanks was proposed to the Coventry representatives of the National Negotiating Committee of the Federation. These included Colonel Cole of Humber and J. Milburn, esquire of Alfred Herberts. 'These gentlemen had for the past six months devoted a large amount of time and energy for the benefit of all members of this organisation'.[41]

As well as problems over wages, Herbert employees often found working conditions less than adequate, although their employer took a different view. In an article with an historical emphasis written for his firm's magazine, he declared that 'Coventry manufacturers are alive to the advantages of giving workers good conditions and allowing and encouraging workers to earn high wages'.[42] But the claims did not always match the reality. Working conditions may have improved after 1928, when the firm's new factory was built at Edgwick, but there is evidence to suggest that conditions in the preceding years were less than adequate. Some employees recall working by candlelight around the turn of the century. Another employee recalled conditions in the offices. W.L. Jackson went to Herberts in 1903 and found a slow burning combination stove in the centre of the office. 'The staff would cough and choke at the thick smoke that shrouded the office in gloom'.[43] Toilet facilities were also poor. Harry Greenhill, who began an apprenticeship in 1920 recalled the situation:

> When you went to the toilet it was just a trough and you sat on a plank ... open to the elements, and when it flushed it was just like a brook ... a slight gradient for it to run down. The blokes used to light a piece of paper and send it down to make you get off.

There was, however, a 'toilet for staff marked "gentlemen" and "men" on the other'. It is interesting to note that the wife of the latter respondent when interviewed, after declaring herself to be an ex-employee of the firm, was quick to defend the entrepreneur remarking that Herbert 'hadn't the money to put fancy toilets in'.

Washing facilities were also crude, and ensured that time spent washing prior to the midday break was kept to a minimum. At the Butts, 'when you wanted to wash your hands the labourer brought a bucket of hot water and put it in the gangway ... and if you weren't one of the first it wasn't any good washing your hands'. Smoking was forbidden: 'only the old man [Herbert] used to smoke' and there were restrictions on refreshments. Drinks or sandwiches were not allowed during the morning, even while work continued. In one other Coventry factory at least, the rules were less strict. At Coventry Chain, workers could get a cup of cocoa and could smoke all day if they wished.

There were attempts by workers at Herberts to improve such conditions, as Harry Greenhill's statement testifies:

> some who were termed agitators, they weren't agitators they were idealists. They knew that wasn't right for a human being. They had to fight for things like toilets and a cup of tea.

Time spent at the toilet was also monitored, and this led to objections by the workforce: 'Nippy Parsons used to argue that some people naturally took longer than others'. The problem was not confined to Herberts. At Renold Chain for example 'there was a chap in there with an alarm clock. He put your name down and if you were in there too long you lost money'. At the Daimler, objections were raised by workers to the installation of a turnstile for entry to the toilet block, and 'they broke that down in the end'.[44] Tom Mann had outlined the role of the A.E.U. in this respect when it came into being on 1 July, 1920:

> May it ever be found ready ... a pioneer force for changed

> conditions of society ... when as a result of the effective organisation of industry, poverty shall be eliminated from human society, and the conditions of life became worthy of an intelligent, dignified people.[45]

At a time when the concern of the factory workers centred around the new and difficult conditions being imposed upon them, Alfred Herbert's thoughts were at least partially turned to the more pleasant problems of choosing an estate. The first specification was that it should if possible be within a fifty mile radius of Coventry, but 'north and east of Coventry was considered too cold; west somewhat too wet, and the south therefore remained the most hopeful hunting ground'. Other considerations besides climate however were important for Alfred Herbert, for 'the possibilities of sport, both with rod and gun, must have due weight'. Eventually he and his wife 'stumbled' on the 1800 acre estate of Dunley Manor in Hampshire, which Herbert assures his employee readers, 'by no means realised our ideals for the distance from Coventry was greater than we wished ... and the house was both small and inconvenient'. (From a photo there appears to be a minimum of seven bedrooms). In spite of its 'drawbacks' however, Herbert acknowledges that Dunley possessed 'a certain quality of homeliness, and many happy hours have been spent here by ourselves and our friends'.[46]

The more leisurely pace of life in Hampshire was not reflected on the shop floor in Coventry. Throughout the period under discussion, the development of automatic machinery and new tool steels, allowed manufacturers to increase machine feeds and speeds, and employees found the workrate constantly being increased, with greater emphasis being placed on timekeeping. In June 1901, for example, the A.S.E. District Committee were discussing Herberts and the 'grievances' of fortyeight men who had stayed out in protest at the rule that if a man were one minute late he would be fined a quarter of an hour, and locked out if he was three minutes late. With the men under threat of being discharged, an A.S.E. deputation went to see the manager, Arthur Marston, next day. Marston told them he was 'surprised the men had grievances'. He would have the men back, but had decided to 'punish the ringleaders to make an example of them'. According to the deputation, 'this was the best terms to be obtained'.[47]

The First World War period, according to one historian, ushered in a revolution in workshop conditions, as time and motion study men, operation inspectors and the complex premium bonus systems appeared. All were designed 'to extract the maximum of work from each worker'.[48]

Alfred Herbert had long been enthusiastic about such techniques, and the war period offered ideal conditions. In the Spring of 1916, the A.S.E. District Committee were receiving reports from Herbert chargehands of 'changes in workshop conditions'. The workrate on the gang system had been increased, without a corresponding increase in piece-work prices. This the manager proposed to remedy by increasing the number of machines under the supervision of the chargehands. One chargehand said that he had thirteen semi-autos already and had 'as much as he could possibly do to keep that number running. The men resent this method, and have held a meeting to consider the position, but find they are being given away by ... a member of the Foremen's Mutual Aid Association, working in the shop'.[49]

Ratefixers' attempts to reduce component production times also met with resistance. Harry Greenhill referred to the rate fixer as 'an obnoxious kind of a being', and Grace his wife recalled how her father, brought from Tangyes in Birmingham to Herbert's Butts factory because he was a good engineer, smashed the ratefixer's gold watch. The firm sought to present the workforce with a *fait accompli*, by introducing the 'speeds and feeds' men during a dispute which had brought about a closure of some parts of the works. In January 1920 for example, the A.S.E. shop stewards at Herberts noted that 'altered conditions' were being implemented while the firm was partly closed 'owing to the moulders' dispute', a national strike over a five shillings a week advance, which had lasted sixteen weeks and caused great hardship for Coventry workers. The stewards' report to the A.S.E. District Committee noted 'a great increase in the number of foremen and ratefixers'.[50]

We have seen that Alfred Herbert and his management did not shun conflict, if they did not necessarily seek it. And they were certainly not keen on trade unions. The house magazine though, has always done its best, with considerable success, to minimise the reality of worker-management divisions. Occasionally, however, the journal testified unwittingly to the fact that industrial relations problems did arise. In 1931, for example, Alfred Herbert was the main speaker at the Ex-Servicemen's Annual Dinner. The *News* declared Sir Alfred to be, together with the directors '"one of us" who shares the same spirit of comradeship which pervades the gathering'. The entrepreneur noted that it was 'the fashion perhaps to harp on what I think is foolishly called "class warfare" — to assume that because a company is employing labour it is their enemy. I flatter myself that that feeling does not exist to any large extent among my friends here tonight'.[51]

It has been suggested elsewhere that Herbert prided himself on his relationship with the unions. He may well have done so; he certainly prided himself on his relationship with his workforce. But as we have seen the reality may have been somewhat different. With regard to the unions the evidence suggests that they were not welcome. Ernie Digger, for example, who started at Herberts as an apprentice in 1925, said that Herbert was 'a self-made man, not a lover of unions. He paid for the work to be done; that was his attitude'. Harry Greenhill has consolidated this view. 'It was almost, well I wouldn't say a crime, but you'd be ostracised almost if you were in the union'. Another ex-employee, Harry Earnshaw, pointed out that in order to get a job at Herberts you did not reveal that you were in the union. 'You had to keep it dark if you was in the union'. Mr. Earnshaw was speaking from personal experience. In 1912, when the patternmakers were on strike he worked at the Deasy Company, and went to meet a friend who was working at the Edgwick plant. He was early, having made a mistake over the works finishing time, and he was spotted by Edward Broughall, the foundry manager. Nothing was said, but years later when working at Herberts, he was asked by his boss whether he had ever been mixed up in a strike, and whether he had ever 'touted' for the patternmakers. On replying that he had not, he was told: 'Mr. Broughall has entered you in the book as touting, and that's what's barred you from many a job'. 'The book' was a reference to Herbert's Black Book in which the names of those involved in union or strike-related activities were entered, and 'it would go against you anywhere'.[52]

Alfred Herbert's opinion of unions is revealed in an article written by him some years later. Monopolies, he argued, were distasteful because they sought to insure themselves against the annoyance of private competition and thus to have the consumer at their mercy. This was 'quite in harmony with trade union policy, which seems to create a monopoly in labour in the hope of having the employer at their mercy as well'.[53] It is interesting to note that at first, interviewees found it difficult to recall some of the industrial relations problems at Herberts. Jack Barnsley for example, a retired machine tool fitter, who started at Herberts in 1920 said he could not recall strikes. 'Unions wasn't prominent. They had a little say about matters. It was a damn fine firm to work for'. The available figures from the A.S.E. Minute Book in fact indicate that in 1907 there were approximately 900 trade union members at Herberts, which at the time accounted for almost half the workforce. Despite the evidence of grievances, militancy and union activities, these have not been recognised as significant features of the relationship between management and workers. A number of factors perhaps account for this. Herberts has been described as a firm that employed 'best practice' techniques, and there is evidence to suggest that this promoted a sense of pride in the work and loyalty to the company, especially among skilled workers, which became known as the 'Herbert Spirit'. Jack Barnsley said that workers were

> rather proud to be working for the firm which produced the best machine tools in the world. That was the Herbert Spirit. They was proud to work for a firm as stood number one ... and everybody gave of the best.

Harry Greenhill, a retired toolmaker, also recognised the importance of quality in the work, and what it meant for employees. The Herbert Spirit was in his opinion, dedication to the job: 'I couldn't do a shoddy job; it'd gotta be right. The machines were accurate and robust. They didn't break down so much as our competitors'.

The fact that most of the management team were as capable of producing as high quality work as the men themselves, fostered respect for each other and provided a shared interest, obscuring to some extent the division between workers and management. Jack Barnsley recalled how the manager at Edgwick, Edward Broughall, always set a good example. 'He was there at 6 a.m. ... a very very strict man ... very very strict ... but he knew his job'.

George Troughton noted the ability by management to converse knowledgeably with workers about the job. 'Kelway [a director] asked me something about electrics, and he knew what he was talking about'. With reference to an apparent lack of militancy at Herberts, Mr. Troughton explained: 'It's the type of work ... because they're interested in it they don't think of these little problems'.[54]

Herbert's ability as an entrepreneur no doubt consolidated the relationship between workers and management. Unlike some of his more conservative contemporaries, Herbert welcomed the new American machine tool techniques that were geared to interchangeable mass production methods. He ordered several American lathes, planers, shapers and drills, and 'soon began to sell these machines very freely throughout the country and this was the beginning of our importing business'.[55] Recognising the conservatism of British customers, who were used to having machines built specifically to their requirements instead of adapting standard machine tools, Herbert compromised, catering for individual customers, and building large numbers of standard machines, as witness the production of machines such as the famous Herbert Capstan Lathe and Herbert Turret Lathe.

Floud in fact has noted that Alfred Herbert 'was regarded as one of the most advanced engineers in the country'.[56] Others, however, point to the contribution of the Irish-American Oscar Harmer as the most influential figure in the firm's success story. He joined Alfred Herbert in 1897 after managing the Capewell Horse Nail Company in Millwall, and 'it became no unusual occurrence for conferences between him and Mr. Herbert to last from early in the evening to the small hours. At these conferences, design, manufacture, and sales policy were discussed, and decisions made which were to exert a great influence on the future progress of the firm'. He encouraged the entrepreneur to look for customers outside the cycle industry and to 'take advantages of the opportunities among other branches of engineering which were rapidly expanding and demanding more and better machine tools, and this led to further developments in the design and scope of machines'.[57]

Employees also appreciated his abilities. According to Harry Earnshaw, Oscar Harmer was '*the* man'. He told Alfred Herbert, 'look here Herbert, I've come to make machines not these ploughing implements. He was a grand old chap. He could swear for ten minutes without repeating himself'. Harmer is remembered with affection by employees, and his personality perhaps did much to maintain cohesion within the factory. Ernie Digger remembered him as 'a grand old fellow. When he was eighty they rapped him all the way round, as if he was an apprentice coming out'.[58]

Alfred Herbert does not appear to have evoked a similar response. Ernie Digger referred to him as 'a sterner sort'. Prior to a works outing, an employee had approached him for a donation: 'What he gave him wouldn't a bought a packet of Woodbines and they were twopence a packet'. Harry Earnshaw said that Herbert 'hardly ever spoke to the man in the shop ... he was not one of the lads ... it was as much as he could do to speak to the watchman, "Fetch Earnshaw"'. George Troughton vividly recalls his encounter with the entrepreneur. As an apprentice, he had gone with a skilled man to repair Herbert's telephone: 'He [Herbert] wanted to know why two electricians had been sent to mend one telephone. The skilled man started to explain "Well er ... the lad's an appren..." "Shut up! Get on with the job". When we told the foreman he said "Oh dear". He was quaking in his boots to think what might be said to him'.[59]

Alfred Herbert would of course, attend some social events, such as an apprentice's prize giving, and annual sports or departmental dinners. This formal, more distanced type of communication with his workforce was perhaps one that he felt most comfortable with, given his upbringing. He could make a speech, include references to the 'Herbert Spirit', make presentations, and withdraw. Thus the men saw Herbert, and he was 'real' to them.

Although the entrepreneur was not on the friendliest of terms with the men on the shop floor, there were other factors which buttressed workforce loyalty. There is no doubt for example, that workers perceived certain benefits accruing to them because of the firm's reputation. Croucher has noted that in the early part of the twentieth century, the skill of the British craftsmen allowed them to travel all over the world, and for some sectors of the workforce, this was the case at Herberts. Unlike most engineering firms Herberts had from the turn of the century adopted efficient, progressive sales techniques. In 1900, branch offices were opened in London, Birmingham, Manchester and Newcastle; in 1903 Paris and Glasgow; 1905 Milan and Leeds; 1906 Yokohama; 1909 Calcutta and Berlin; 1913 Bristol and New York. In the inter-war years also, 'an extensive network of sales offices and agencies' were established.

This policy opened up careers abroad for both office and shop floor workers. Harry Earnshaw recalled that Oscar Harmer used to place men all over the world. He was offered a job in India, but was unable to accept because his wife was expecting a baby. The house magazine indicates what was possible for employees in this respect, although it seems that in some cases they had little time to consider the matter. Mr. E.D. Mitchell, for example, started as a shorthand typist at the Butts in 1906 and in 1913 he was asked to go to Japan to reorganise the branch office: 'Sir Alfred gave me fortyfive minutes to go home, consult my wife, and give my answer'. After the First World War he became a manager of Alfred Herbert Ltd. in the United States, and in 1922 went to India, where he eventually became managing director of A.H. India Ltd. After starting as a shop floor apprentice at the Butts in 1910, Mr. Sidney Poole was sent to Scotland in 1919 as a demonstrator. Six months later he was sent to the India branch and after twentytwo years there was posted to the Herbert offices in Australia.[60] Employees were also allowed to remain at work long after retirement and, perhaps aided by the publicity this received in the house journal, the length of service devoted by workers to the company became a source of personal pride and interdepartmental rivalry. Patrick Joyce has noted how for the mill operatives in Lancashire,

> Work got under the skin of everyday life. There is evidence of a willing acceptance of both the rigours of authority and of increased workloads. Ill and injured weavers would work flat

> out to avoid the stigma of incompetence.[61]

A similar situation can be found at Herberts. In 1939 Mr. Fred Ince retired aged eighty and the *A.H. News* reported his work record with enthusiasm. 'In the past few years he had had his hand badly crushed in a door, he had been knocked down by a charabanc, and fallen from his bike ... but he refused to stay away from work any longer than absolutely necessary'.[62]

One employee when interviewed, recalled his grandfather being taken off crane driving at Herberts when he reached retirement age: 'It hurt him that much that nobody knew at home for a long while. But they gave him a job in the stores greasing components, and he died aged eightyfour. Came home one day and keeled over. Herberts was a job for life, provided you toed the line'. In 1937, the house journal focussed on the long service of Mr. T.H. Goddard and his family:

> Mr. Goddard's three sons are at Herberts, his father was at the Butts for over fifteen years, and his own unbroken service of thirtytwo years is a record of which his family can justifiably be proud. He says he will not be satisfied until he has equalled the feat of his workmate Mr. G. Wilson.[63]

Though the journal does not provide details of Mr. Wilson's feat, the Goddard family's allegiance to the firm, consolidated over the generations, is clear. Moreover, despite the fact that wages were generally lower than the district rate, employees felt that Herberts provided more regular work than the high paying car factories, thereby compensating for their lower weekly earnings. George Troughton, for example, recalled the attitude of Herbert workers: 'They used to say "I've worked at Herberts for the last twelve months, but car factories were only doing six months. So although my wages are not quite so high, I've come off better"'. Another commented:

> Alfred Herberts was always known for low pay. But in the car factories, it was three months on and three months off. But at Herberts it was steady work.[64]

Another factor consolidating stability in worker management relationships at Herberts has been the active pursuance of paternalism as a management strategy and style. Paternalism has been identified as a significant factor in the evolution of British industrial society, though there is disagreement about when it began to decline in importance. Roberts for example argues that after the mid-nineteenth century, it 'increasingly failed to meet the problems of an urban and industrial age', while Joyce declares that paternalism brought social stability to the industrialisation process, thriving on the shared sense of community that emerged from the urban and industrial conditions of the later nineteenth century. Even so he regards it as being in decline and in its 'latest and weakest stages' between 1890 and 1905.[65]

Using the definition of paternalism proposed by Roberts, however, it seems that with regard to Alfred Herbert Ltd., the policy was actively practised from the firm's inception in the late nineteenth century, through to the mid-twentieth century and beyond. Authoritarianism for example, has been identified as an active element in Victorian paternalism. This involved a belief in strict laws and punishment for wrongdoers, and with this Alfred Herbert would surely concur. Writing in the *Machine Tool Review* in 1954, he recalled an incident involving Arthur Marston (d. 1903) his Works Manager, and an apprentice:

> He [Marston] had an impulsive temper. I remember him whacking a lad who was caught breaking up our packing cases and stealing the wood. After exercising great patience with a very troublesome apprentice and finding it impossible to do anything with him, Marston threatened to cancel his indentures. "You can't do that" said the boy. 'Can't I by jove" said Marston, and without more ado he took the lad's indentures out of the safe, tore them into the street and threw the fragments after him. I never heard any more of the boy but I have no doubt that he became a reformed character and probably a distinguished citizen.[66]

Ex-employees have testified to the importance of discipline at Herberts, and this included Alfred Herbert's insistence on some uniformity of dress. Grace Greenhill remembers male employees being sent home for not wearing a tie. 'He [Herbert] wouldn't do it himself. He would contact his staff to deal with it. They would never come to work again without a tie'. Shoes had to be polished too, and these rules applied to everybody, 'labourers, apprentices, all the lot of 'em'. Alfred Herbert reinforced this policy through the house journal. Writing on 'manners' he praised the 'scrupulous care' office workers were taking with regard to clothes, but found other employee characteristics displeasing. 'I like to see my people neatly and becomingly attired, ... I wish the same attention were paid to manners'. There was 'a regrettable tendency for juniors to use such words as "righto, cheerio, ta-ta" — expressions which simply must *not* be used'.[67]

Paternalists, says Roberts, also believed in an hierarchical society and, 'at the heart of a paternalist's hierarchical outlook is a strong sense of the value of dependency'. Herbert certainly appears to have believed in an hierarchical system. In his writings, he frequently refers to employees as 'my people', and the first of his series of articles entitled 'Memories' reveals an awareness of his position as the creator of jobs and consequent moulder of lifestyles, from which flow employee dependency.

> If I had not decided to be a mechanic, ... the lives of many thousands of people would have been different and some who are now living would not have existed at all.[68]

This dependency was mirrored when whole families became employed at the works, like the Goddard family mentioned earlier. Ernie Digger went to Herberts 'to be a fitter like me dad'. His two brothers and his wife also worked there. Jack Barnsley's family were even more heavily involved with the firm. In addition to himself, there was his father, brother, cousin and son; and his wife's father, uncle and brother-in-law.

Many lived within easy walking distance of the works. Ernie Digger again lived in the short Canal Road, at one end of which were the gates of the factory. Jack Barnsley lived in Cromwell Street at first, about twenty minutes walk from Edgwick. He moved twice after that, each time closer to the works. The close proximity of employees to the factory meant that they could be summoned to work collectively in the mornings. One ex-employee recalled starting work at Herbert's Edgwick works in 1903 when he was thirteen years old. The works' hooter would awaken the inhabitants of Foleshill at 5.30 a.m. for the commencement of work at 6 a.m. It was, he says, 'a kind of communal alarm clock. But unlike a clock which could be shut off, the hooter would blow for ten or more minutes'.[69] The length of time the hooter would blow may be an exaggeration, but it is significant that when the Chief Constable moved into the Foleshill area, the hooter was no longer used.

Employees were tied ever closer to the factory when recreational and educational facilities became available at the Alfred Herbert Club and Institute, which was opened around 1901. Apprentices could attend evening classes where they were taught 'machine drawing and elementary mechanics at a time when there was no technical school in Coventry'. Employees who started work for the company in the 1890s have testified to considerable recreational involvement by the workforce. Mr. A.J. McLardy, writing in 1928, recalled the 'early days' at the Butts where there was keen support for boxing, rifle shooting, cycling and football. Mr. McLardy himself played in the 'Married vs. Singles football matches'. By the 1920s recreational facilities catered for a wide variety of interests. The house journal included a section entitled 'Social and Sports News', and in addition to printing announcements about presentations, lectures, dances and outings, they published details about the activities of, for example, the A.H. Male Voice Choir, the Angling Club, Hockey Club, Table Tennis Club, Cycling Club, Air Rifle Club, Rugby Football Club, Motor Club, Golf, the Horticultural Society, the Gymnastics class, and the Bowling Club. Ernie Digger met his wife at the Gymnastics class and was actively involved with the Bowls Club. Herberts was for him more than just a job. 'I never wanted to leave. I liked my job, and my bowling as well'.[70]

The paternalist's third assumption, according to Roberts, was that of the organic nature of society. Everyone of whatever rank, had their place in the body politic. If the factory can be seen as the 'body politic' in microcosm, then there is a distinct 'organic' flavour about the way Herbert saw the various roles of his workforce:

> Even the simplest and dullest job is essential to the finished result. The stoker has a hard, dull job, but without him where would we be? Even the floor sweeper and charwoman do their bit ... I believe many an order has come because a clean works makes customers realise we do take pride in our work and are therefore likely to do it well. The other day I watched a bright little chap filling containers with cast-iron chips for remelting ... and we see his little hand in the finished machine, like fitters, if we look for it. When we look at a finished machine tool let us take our hats off to it as representing the united efforts of every department and every helper from the designer who first conceived a picture of it in his brain, to the painter who covers up the last rough spot on the castings.[71]

Roberts also suggests that paternalists placed considerable emphasis on three principal sets of duties. First there was the duty to rule, firmly and resolutely, to suppress crime and disorder, to put to work the idle, to reprimand servants, and to tell bailiffs how to manage. In the case of Alfred Herbert Ltd., its figurehead could be said to have ruled via the printed word (house magazine), frequent visits to the factory and office floor, and through his managers and foremen. Disapproving of noise in the offices, he reminded people that he had already spoken of this when the offices were first opened, he declared that 'somehow or other we must learn to do our work more quietly'. He went on to suggest that people should walk and talk more quietly, and should not shout when using the telephone'. Shop floor workers were reprimanded for carelessness with machine tools. In an article entitled 'Brutality to Machine Tools' Herbert declared:

> When I see, as I have just seen, one of our newest and up to date machines which has only been at work for about six months looking as though it were twenty years old, I get really angry. Everyone who ill-treats a machine is sacrificing his own self-respect, injuring the goodwill of the Company, indulging in waste of the most reckless description and will in future be looked upon as a promising candidate for promotion to some other sphere of activity.[72]

Herbert would frequently tell junior management how to manage. Harry Earnshaw, a fitter who rose to become Works Manager, recalled that he saw too much of the entrepreneur, probably on the occasions when he was at his flat at the works, from which he could easily visit the night shift on the shop floor. On one occasion, the Works Manager was reprimanded by Herbert for leaving lights on in a bay where men had to clock on. The story is best told in Mr. Earnshaw's own words:

> I said "good evening Sir Alfred". He said "Earnshaw, you've got too many lights on" ... I let him go on, and I said "I've kept them on because I don't want men to fall over in the dark and hurt themselves ... He said "Well, it's a waste of money Earnshaw... If I was a millionaire I'd still deplore waste. No doubt you're fond of figures, find out how much this is costing me per night". I worked it out and sent him a memo ... he never answered ... it came to 3s.6d. a week.

A second major duty of the paternalist was to guide the poor morally. A good paternalist is 'one who is convinced he knows what is good for his dependents, and has the power to insist that his ideas be carried out'.[73] In a speech to the Coventry Engineering Society in 1927, entitled 'Some Thoughts for Young Engineers', Herbert spelled out what he considered were the qualities an engineer should possess in order to get on. First, a man needed character. 'If a man has character he will get all the necessary education somehow'. The 'fundamentals' of character he described as reliability and a sense of responsibility. Other qualities he listed as desirable were energy, courage, judgement, pride, a sense of humour, politeness and tact. With regard to education he was 'a firm believer in its advantages', but it could not take the place of fundamental qualities. I've seen boys with no education do well and vice versa, but some with a good education have also done very badly'. However, the idea that upward mobility was desirable and that it could be achieved by, among other things, education, was frequently stressed by Herbert.

> Nothing pleases me so much as to see our boys rising from the ranks ... to fill important posts ... Excellent opportunities exist at Technical College for learning English and languages. I strongly advise young people who wish to improve their chances of advancement to consider this very seriously.[74]

Moral guidance extended even to such 'coal face' topics as wages. In the 1880s at Jessops of Leicester where Herbert was apprenticed, good work says Herbert was turned out at competitive prices, partly because of the low wages (30 shillings for a 54 hour week for skilled men and 20 shillings for labourers) and the low cost of office work and general expenses. The main message for employees however, followed on from the need for the firm to be competitive: 'although their wages sound appallingly low the men were a cheery lot, well fed and comfortably clothed'. The cost of living was 'at a correspondingly low level' and 'it was amazing what could be bought for sixpence on Saturday nights when the market stalls were packing up'. The passage is especially significant when it is realised that Herbert never paid high wages to his workers. The implication that there was something virtuous about accepting a low wage is clear. One retired ex-employee who actually knew Herbert socially through the A.H. club system, suggested that he could have afforded to pay more but would not because he believed workers should not be spoiled. 'Give them too much and they become greedy'.[75]

An example of how to live on a modest wage yet still be successful, is provided by Herbert, who, in relating his early days at Coles and Mathews recalled that, though his wages were only £2 per week, his nearby board and lodgings were just under £1 per week, thus leaving 'a small margin for saving'. Again the implication appears to be that there is always room at the top for the independent and determined worker, and to some extent this may have been true, but in the case of Herbert a little more than these factors was involved. The role of his father and brother has already been discussed, and the close proximity of his brother's house 'The Grange' in Davenport Road, Earlsdon, to the area in which Herbert lived and worked in the early days (Spencer Road and The Butts, Earlsdon) must have been a great source of personal, social and financial support and comfort to a 'struggling' young entrepreneur.

In addition to ruling and guidance, says Roberts, the third set of duties incumbent on a model paternalist was that of 'helping the poor in their afflictions and sufferings'. This policy was actively promoted by the Herbert family. Alfred Herbert's wife frequently visited sick employees at home and in hospital. The *Midland Daily Telegraph*, in reporting her death in 1930 declared that 'the deceased lady took a great interest in the welfare of all employees and the sick and needy always had in her a kind and sympathetic friend and helper'. This is supported by the statements of ex-employees who spoke warmly and with reference of her visits to the sick. Ernie Digger for example, recalled an occasion when as an apprentice in the 1920s he fell ill. 'Lady Herbert came to see me when I was off with pneumonia and pleurisy. She brought me a sliced Madeira cake'.[76]

When she died, the *Coventry Standard* referred to her as 'the mother of the firm, for the welfare of the employees was always in her thoughts and it was her custom to obtain once a week a list of those who were absent, and she would personally call on the sick and assist any financially distressed'.[77] Such incidents when the Herbert family were in personal contact with the workforce were remembered vividly by employees, and the importance of this policy with regard to the maintenance of a good relationship between workers and employer was recognised by the entrepreneur. In an article 'Lady Herbert's Work Among Us', written not long after she died, Herbert declared that his daughter, Mrs. Hollick 'had already begun to take up the threads, and it is my earnest wish that in some measure she may be enabled to continue the tradition which Lady Herbert established, and to maintain at least to some extent the spirit of personal contact and human understanding between you and me'.[78] Five months later at a staff Christmas dinner, a toast was proposed to Mrs. Hollick 'and the splendid work she was doing for the firm in visiting those who had the misfortune to be sick'. In the same month, Captain and Mrs. Hollick also attended the children's Christmas Party, where they 'kindly assisted in the distribution of presents'.

Many cups were donated by the management for various sporting activities, so that for example, workers were competing for the Alfred Herbert or the Oscar Harmer Challenge Cup. Thus, as Joyce has noted with regard to employers' gifts, the giver, being possessed by fortune, 'put the recipient in the shadow of his name. For the poor, that shadow could be lifted only by hard work and good faith'.[79]

The Herbert family also consolidated the relationship of factory and community through involvement with the local church. The *Coventry Herald* in May 1930 noted the comment of the vicar of St. Paul's church in Foleshill, that the name of Herbert would 'go down among the list of civic benefactors of Coventry'. Sir Alfred and Lady Herbert were 'great benefactors of St. Luke's Foleshill', and that Lady Herbert had on occasion opened bazaars there. When Herbert remarried, his new wife, a hospital matron, continued this tradition well into the mid-twentieth century. This policy bears a striking resemblance to that described elsewhere by Joyce as 'the rule of authority by industrial deference'. With regard to paternalist control over the factory community he refers to the Lancashire mill owner's wife, who would visit the millhands at home and knew half the operatives in a very large mill by name. The success of this policy depended on the delicate balance between the aloof and the familiar; the ingredients and correct proportions being provided by the employer and his wife respectively, as was the case with the mill-owning Cloughs of Keighley.[80]

The duty to help the poor manifested itself in many ways. Interviewees have reported that Herbert was 'good to the city'. He had a children's home built at Easenhall, contributed to hospital funds, cathedral reconstruction, and paid for a public garden to be built in the centre of the city. There is no doubting his generosity on these and other projects, though equally there is no doubt that his name was becoming indelibly etched on the face of the city. In 1930, on the death of his wife, Herbert informed the Mayor that the public garden being built with his money was now to be named Lady Herbert's Garden.[81]

A decade later, Herbert made a gift of £100,000 to the city, to provide for an Art Gallery and Museum. According to George Hodgkinson, this project was an 'embarrassment' because 'the city council did not like the strings attached'. The Planning Committee for example, contested the conditions that Herbert nominate the architect 'who happened to be a member of the family', and that the building be constructed in Portland Stone.[82] Despite these differences of opinion, agreement was finally reached, and on 20 May, 1954, Sir Alfred Herbert laid the foundation stone of what was to become the Herbert Art Gallery and Museum.

Many people have publicly praised the 'farmer's son' from Leicestershire who provided work for thousands of Coventry citizens, and the extent of the praise is itself testimony to the importance of the man who has been referred to as 'one of the last great princes of industry'.[83] And the inaccuracies are perpetuated. Richard Crossman for example remarked that 'Sir Alfred Herbert, head of the famous machine tool firm, was among the rare exceptions to the rule that once anyone became a leading industrialist he would, if he hadn't done so before, move his town residence to London and acquire an estate far removed from Coventry'. At Alfred Herbert's funeral on 5 June, 1957, the lesson was read by D. Pugh, the son of Lady Herbert. Cuthbert Bardsley, Bishop of Coventry, told the 'hundreds of workers' who attended, that 'Sir Alfred could have ceased to take any interest in the men in the factory. He'd plenty of money to live in luxury. But no ... he didn't regard men as employees, but friends. He didn't throw away money. He used it as a good steward'.[84]

Many of the elements in Roberts' model of nineteenth century paternalism are evident in the Herbert management style. These included authoritarianism, an emphasis on discipline, and a belief in a hierarchical system that involved interdependence between employer and employee. Employers, Herbert also believed, had responsibilities and duties with regard to the workforce, and he and his family saw to it that these obligations were carried out. A central feature of Roberts' 'model' however, was religion, a factor not evident at Alfred Herbert Ltd. While some captains of industry might read sermons to their workforce, the competitive world of machine tool manufacturing led progressive entrepreneurs to preach lessons on efficiency and craftsmanship.[85] The lathe held a greater attraction than the lectern.

The story of the firm since the entrepreneur's death has largely been one of decline. Some employees have directly related this to the diminishing influence of the Herbert family. As George Troughton explained: 'Things deteriorated rapidly after Sir Alfred died ... because he had had control, his word was law'.

Several members of the Herbert family continued as management at the firm and officiated at various events such as prize giving ceremonies, parties and dinner and dances, but in 1967, almost exactly ten years after Alfred Herbert died, his grandson, W.D.A.H. Allen, retired because of ill health. With his resignation, the last link with the founder of the company was severed.

Paternalism no longer figured in the firm's policies as new men such as R.D. Young and Neil Raine arrived from other firms to take the helm. Pointing to a fall in orders for the firm's products, they clinically presided over redundancies. Many workers resented the new style of professional management who, they felt, had no intimate knowledge of Herbert products. Further, the management consultancy firm that was introduced to increase productivity was regarded by long serving skilled engineers as something of a joke, although, unfortunately, an expensive one.

Interestingly, some policies remained unchanged, such as low pay and the forced pace on the shop floor. In August 1968, for example, three thousand workers came out in support of two hundred fitters who were on strike because their pay was two shillings and five pence per hour below the district average. The management offered them another one shilling per hour provided concessions were made over time allowed for clocking in, washing up and making tea.[86] When W.D.A.H. Allen resigned the company was still a major employer of labour in Coventry. The workforce in 1967 for example was 7,300 strong, while in the same year Wickman's, another machine tool firm, whose founder had been a Herbert apprentice, employed 5,000.[87]

By the early 1970s the firm's total workforce was around 12,000 nationally, but the redundancies had begun. On 5 February, 1971, the *Coventry Evening Telegraph* carried a headline '810 Axed at Herbert Plants' which, the paper declared, together with other recent cuts brought the total reduction in the Herbert labour force to 1,100. From then on, despite government cash injections through the National Enterprise Board, redundancies and the selling of plant became frequent occurrences.[88]

Although there were hopes for a recovery when Tooling Investments took over the firm in 1980, debts three years later of some £17 million led to the firm's collapse, and the sale by auction in October 1983 of the entire stock, from sophisticated machine tools to office furniture. At the time of the auction the workforce numbered 400, approximately the same as when Alfred Herbert declared it a private limited company in 1894, and many highly skilled workers with immense product knowledge had been irretrievably dispersed. News of the collapse led the *Coventry Evening Telegraph* to publish a centre page article outlining the history of the firm and describing it as having once been the world's largest machine tool manufacturer, with a name comparable to Rolls Royce.[89]

Redundancies in Coventry of course, have not been confined to Herberts. In 1982 for example, Massey Ferguson shed 800 workers, G.E.C. 1,200, Coventry Climax 350, Brico 350, Lucas 40, Automotive Products 900, Talbot 400, and the machine tool firms Webster and Bennetts and Wickmans together announced 240 redundancies. Against this background, George Park, Labour M.P. for Coventry North-East described the collapse as 'particularly unfortunate. It all marks the continued drifting of skills out of Coventry. We are seeing the progressive de-skilling of the city'. Councillor Edge, Chairman of the

West Midlands County Council's Economic Development Committee placed Herberts in a wider context, declaring that 'everyone in the West Midlands must regret the collapse of Alfred Herbert Ltd. It is another indication of the collapse of the machine tool industry in Britain'.[90]

Clearly these statements indicate that Herberts was more than just a major employer of labour. For many the company was a symbol of Coventry's engineering skill and virility, with the craftsmanship of Herbert employees regarded as second to none. Upon taking up employment at the firm, skilled men did have to prove their competence by reading a micrometer and a vernier gauge under the supervision of a foreman. But to what extent were Herbert men superior to workers in other Coventry firms? Many were highly skilled, and were attracted or brought to the firm for that reason. Equally however, many time-served men elsewhere could list among their skills the ability to read a micrometer and a vernier. Moreover, there was a large number of unskilled and semi-skilled workers employed throughout the factory, who, according to one ex-employee 'didn't know how many 32nds there were in an inch'.[91]

Statements like those of Councillor Edge, however, help to maintain the myth of Alfred Herbert Ltd. as the place of excellence, a myth that perhaps had its origins in the fact that, relative to other firms, especially the car factories, Herberts was a place where skill was still used. Whatever the case, status certainly went with a job at Herberts, and this fostered a pride that promoted stability, and the emergence of the 'Herbert Spirit'. The strong sense of identity was further consolidated by the fact that the firm provided regular work, perhaps thereby attracting the more conservative employee, willing to accept Alfred Herbert's authoritarian style of management. Thus was presented an image of solidity and permanence of relations, in contrast to the car factories of Coventry, which tempted the less skilled and perhaps more volatile worker.

In return for their loyalty of course, some Herbert employees did rise through the ranks to positions of prominence within the firm. For the workforce the sight of such men with proven engineering skills at the managerial helm, provided a constant reminder that upward mobility was possible, and did much to foster and maintain good social relations. While the claims for harmony and cooperation have been exaggerated, many workers did experience a sense of comradeship that has helped give Alfred Herbert Ltd. a unique place in the history of Coventry's industrial society.

Notes to Chapter 4

1. Amalgamated Society of Engineers District Committee Minutes, 3 October, 1901, 24 September, 1907, 8 March, 1908, 11 October, 1914, 18 June, 1915.
2. *Midland Daily Telegraph*, 28, 29 November, 1917.
3. Coventry and District Engineering Employers Association, Minute books for 1922.
4. *Alfred Herbert News*, April 1927, hereafter *A.H. News*.
5. A. Herbert, quoted in *A.H. News*, December 1926, 2.
6. Capt. Hollick, quoted in *A.H. News*, January-February, 1932, 10.
7. Cuthbert Bardsley, quoted in *A.H. News*, May-June, 1957.
8. Ian Hollick, letter to *Coventry Evening Telegraph*, 1 November, 1983.
9. J. Barnsley, interview, 11 February, 1981.
10. A.S.E., District Committee Minute Book, January 23, 1911.
11. F.W. Gregory and I.D. Neu, 'The American Industrial Elite of the 1870s: Their Social Origins', and W. Miller, 'Men in Business' in J.N. Ingham (ed.), *The Iron Barons* (1978) 14.
12. *A.H. News*, June 1929 and February 1928 respectively.
13. Lady Herbert, in *A.H. News*, May-June 1958, 90.
14. Leicester Record Office, 1871 Census for Whetstone Parish.
15. A. Herbert, 'Memories' in *Herbert Machine Tool Review*, September-October, 1953, 97.
16. Charles More, *Skill and the English Working Class* (1980) 104.
17. A. Herbert, 'The Business of Alfred Herbert, Early Days' in *A.H. News*, February 1927, 41.
18. R. Prosser, 'Coventry — A Study in Urban Continuity', (unpublished M.A. thesis, University of Birmingham, 1955,) 131. S.B. Saul, 'The Engineering Industry' in D.H. Aldcroft (ed.), *The Development of British Industry and Foreign Competition 1875-1914* (1968), 214.
19. A. Herbert, 'The Business of Alfred Herbert, Early Days', *op.cit.*, 41.
20. Charles More, *op.cit.*, 76.
21. A. Herbert, 'Memories 4', in *Herbert Machine Tool Review*, March-April 1954, 26.
22. *Herbert News*, January-February 1967, 4.
23. A. Herbert, 'The Business of Alfred Herbert, Early Days', *op.cit.*, 41.
24. Ann Mytton, interview, September 1982. A. Herbert, 'The

Business of Alfred Herbert, Early Days', *op.cit.*, 42.

25. Directors Minute Book, Alfred Herbert Ltd., ACC 586, Coventry and Warwickshire Collection.
26. See A.S.E. District Committee Minutes, 3 April, 9 July, 1901.
27. R.O. Clark, 'The Dispute in the British Engineering Industry 1897-8 — an Evaluation' in *Economica*, May 1957, 130-31.
28. A.S.E. District Committee Minutes, 6 December, 1901 and Joint Committee Meeting 20 May, 1913, recorded in A.S.E. Minute Book of above date. A.S.E. District Committee Minutes, 24 April, 1912.
29. A.S.E. District Committee Minutes, 6, 21 July, 12 September, 2 November, 1915.
30. A.S.E. District Committee Minutes, 14, 21 March, 1916.
31. James Hinton, *The First Shop Stewards Movement* (1973), 67.
32. Coventry and District Engineering Employers Association, Executive Committee Minutes, 8 December, 1915.
33. A.S.E. District Committee Minutes, 15 August 1916 and 12 March, 1918.
34. A. Herbert, 'Memories 12' in *Herbert Machine Tool Review*, July-August, 1955, 74.
35. *History of the Ministry of Munitions*, Vol. V, part II, 40-41.
36. A.S.E. District Committee Minutes, 28 April, 1898.
37. General Minute Book, Alfred Herbert Ltd., ACC 586, Coventry and Warwickshire Collection. *Midland Daily Telegraph*, 8, 20 June, 1912. A.S.E. District Committee Minutes, 5 June, 1912.
38. *Midland Daily Telegraph*, 20 June, 1912.
39. C.D.E.E.A. Executive Committee Minutes, 6 December, 1920. A.E.U. District Committee Minutes, January-July, 1921. C.D.E.E.A., Executive Committee Minutes, 27 February, 1922.
40. H. Greenhill, interview, 12 January, 1981 and 10 January 1983. Visits to the Herbert Recreation Club on pensioners afternoons, and a letter in the *Coventry Evening Telegraph*, produced a number of volunteers who were subsequently interviewed at home. Occupationally their experiences were very varied, including for example, office workers, machinists, fitters, foremen and a works manager. A.S.E. District Committee Minutes, 24 May, 1921 and A.E.U. Complaints Sub-Committee, 11 July, 1921.
41. C.D.E.E.A. Executive Committee Minutes, 12 June, 1922.
42. A. Herbert, 'The Machine Tool Trade of Coventry' in *A.H. News*, June 1927, 153.
43. W.L. Jackson, 'Personal Column' in *A.H. News*, April 1930, 62.

44. H. and G. Greenhill, *op.cit.*
45. J.B. Jefferys, *The Story of the Engineers* (1945), 194.
46. A. Herbert, 'Memories 15' in *Machine Tool Review*, January-February 1956, 1.
47. A.S.E. District Committee Minutes, 7 June, 1901.
48. J.B. Jefferys, *op.cit.*, 132. S. Pollard, *The Development of the British Economy 1914-67* (1969), 80.
49. A.S.E. District Committee Minutes, 2, 9 May, 1916 and 27 March, 1917. The gang system had been implemented at Herberts at least as early as 1899 (see A.S.E. District Committee Minutes, 30 November, 1899) and possibly earlier (see George Dowell, 'Personal Column' in *A.H. News*, February 1927, 37).
50. *Midland Daily Telegraph*, 22 January, 1920; *Coventry Herald*, 9, 10, 16, 17 January, 1920. A.S.E. District Committee Minutes, 27 January, 1920.
51. *A.H. News*, November-December 1931, 340.
52. 'Touting' meant a worker who was checking to see if any employees were working when they should have been on strike. Interviews: E. Digger, 27 January, 1981, H. Greenhill, *op.cit.*, H. Earnshaw, *op.cit.*
53. A. Herbert in *Herbert Machine Tool Review*, July-August, 1953, 73.
54. J. Barnsley, interview, 11 February, 1981. A.S.E. District Committee Minutes, 4 July, 1907. D.H. Aldcroft, 'The Performance of the British Machine Tool Industry in the Interwar Years' in *Business History Review*, Vol. XL, 3, (1966), 295; R. Floud, *op.cit.*, 89.
55. Interviews; J. Barnsley, *op.cit.*, H. Greenhill, *op.cit.*, and G. Troughton, *op.cit.*
56. A. Herbert, 'Memories 6' in *Herbert Machine Tool Review*, July-August, 1954, 74.
57. R. Floud, *op.cit.*, 53.
58. Oscar Harmer, 'Personal Column' in *A.H. News*, October 1927, 315. A. Herbert, 'Memories 6' in *Machine Tool Review*, July-August, 1954, 73.
59. H. Earnshaw, *op.cit.* This is a reference to the ritual 'banging in' or 'rapping in' ceremony performed in the workshop on the day the apprentice comes out of his time. Hand tools are rattled against tin drums or swarf guards etc. The noise is deafening and often continues for several minutes.
60. Interviews; E. Digger, *op.cit.*, H. Earnshaw, *op.cit.*, G. Troughton, *op.cit.*

61. R. Croucher, *Engineers at War 1939-45* (1982), 1. D.H. Aldcroft, *op.cit.*, 295; R. Floud, *op.cit.*, 89. 'Early Days at Alfred Herbert Ltd.', in *Herbert News*, January-February, 1967, 4.
62. E.D. Mitchell, 'Personal Column' in *A.H. News*, May-June, 1934, 55, and S. Poole, in *A.H. News*, November-December, 1960, 133.
63. P. Joyce, *Work, Society and Politics* (1980), 97.
64. *A.H. News*, May 1939, 135.
65. G. Troughton, *op.cit. A.H. News*, November-December, 1937, 130.
66. G. Troughton, *op.cit.*, and E. Digger, *op.cit.*
67. D. Roberts, *Paternalism in Early Victorian England* (1979) 278. P. Joyce, *op.cit.*, 163.
68. A. Herbert, 'Memories 5' in *Machine Tool Review*, May-June, 1954, 50.
69. H. and G. Greenhill, *op.cit.* A. Herbert, 'Manners' in *A.H. News*, October 1928, 299.
70. D. Roberts, *op.cit.*, 3. A. Herbert, 'Memories 1' in *Machine Tool Review*, September-October, 1953, 97.
71. W.L. Jackson, 'Personal Column' in *A.H. News*, May 1930, 62.
72. A. Herbert, 'Memories 5', *op.cit.*, 50. A.J. McLardy, 'Personal Column' in *A.H. News*, June 1928, 172. *A.H. News*, September-October, 1931, 306 (and others).
73. D. Roberts, *op.cit.*, 3. A. Herbert, 'Craftsmanship' in *A.H. News*, March 1927, 64.
74. A. Herbert in *A.H. News*, January 1931, 5, 34.
75. D. Roberts, *op.cit.*, 5.
76. A. Herbert, in *A.H. News*, February 1928, and June 1929, 187-88.
77. A. Herbert, 'Memories 2' in *Machine Tool Review*, November-December 1953, 122. W. Britten, interview.
78. D. Roberts, *op.cit.*, 6. *Midland Daily Telegraph*, 26 May, 1930.
79. *Coventry Standard*, 30 May, 1930.
80. A. Herbert, 'Lady Herbert's Work Among Us' in *A.H. News*, July 1930, 235.
81. P. Joyce, *op.cit.*, 170.
82. *Coventry Herald*, 30 May, 1930. P. Joyce, *op.cit.*, 164.
83. *Midland Daily Telegraph*, 27 May, 1930.
84. G. Hodgkinson, *Sent to Coventry* (1970), 193.
85. C. Bardsley, Bishop of Coventry, in *A.H. News*, May-June, 1957. R. Crossman, Introduction, p.XVII in G. Hodgkinson, *op.cit. A.H. News*, May-June, 1957.
86. *Coventry Evening Telegraph*, 2 May, 1968.
87. K. Richardson, *Twentieth Century Coventry* (1972) 41. The G.E.C.

employed 18,000 in three factories, the Standard Motor Co. 14,000 and Massey Ferguson 10,000.

88. *Coventry Evening Telegraph*, 5 February, 1971; 2 December, 4 July, 1975, 4 July, 1978, 3 December, 1982, 11 March, 6 April, 27 May, 1983.
89. *Coventry Evening Telegraph*, 7 April, 1983.
90. *Coventry Evening Telegraph*, 2 December, 1982, 6 April, 1983.
91. H. Greenhill, *op.cit.*

Chapter 5

Factory Work for Women: Courtaulds & GEC between the Wars

Josie Castle

The history of Coventry is largely a story of masculine energy and enterprise. The industries which identify Coventry in the popular mind are overwhelmingly male — cycles, machine tools, cars and aircraft. So powerful is this image that it has obscured the tradition of women's work which grew up in the home based textile industries of the eighteenth and nineteenth centuries and was transmuted into the factory based industries of the twentieth.

The focus of this chapter is the experience of working women in two major Coventry industries in the inter-war period, Courtauld's rayon factory on the Foleshill Road and the General Electric Company's telephone and wireless factory at Stoke. Both firms developed manufacturing processes which offered unskilled females opportunities to participate in Coventry's industrial boom, similar to those enjoyed by male workers in cars and aircraft. Female opportunities were narrower and the pay more limited, but for women they were better at GEC and Courtaulds than elsewhere in Coventry. These two firms together employed one-fifth of the city's occupied females, concentrating them in a factory setting which was in many ways unique.

The place of women in the Coventry workforce of the inter-war years has important links with their role in industrial developments at the turn of the century. In the late 1890s and 1900s, the cycle, ribbon and watch trades were transformed by the adoption of semi-mass production methods based on the large scale employment of cheap unskilled labour, both male and female.[1] For the first time, female, and indeed, male, Coventrians began working in large numbers in factories. It was in these trades that factories were first established in Coventry after a long resistance by skilled male artisans. Now, process production for a large market reduced the need for skilled labour and the industries came to depend on semi-skilled and unskilled workers. By 1901 26% of the workforce in watchmaking were unskilled females; the figure for cycles was 10%.[2]

In 1891, 2,505 women still worked in the silk trade making up 80% of the workforce. They were sweated labour employed in cottage factories

Table 5:1. Distribution of Female Employment by Major Occupational Groups 1911, 1921, 1931. (Percentage)*

*(*Coventry C.B. Only) Coventry C.B. and Foleshill Rural Dist.*

%	1911	1921	1931
Metal Workers	11.54	11.10	10.54
Electrical Apparatus	—	1.6	4.99
Textile Workers	23.49	19.70	15.00
Makers of Textile Goods	10.22	6.28	3.75
Commercial & Financial Occ.	—	10.38	10.87
Professional Occ.	5.61	5.27	3.33
Personal Service	19.51 (13.34)	18.85 (0.77)	21.14 (15.88)
Clerks & Typists	7.31	14.01	16.06

Source: Census of England and Wales, 1911, 1921, 1931.

dominated by a few skilled men. In the next two decades the textile industry underwent a restructuring at least as radical as that in watches and cycles. In silk alone the workforce shrank to 1,671 in 1907, but the advent of Courtaulds had created jobs for 833 women between 1904 and 1907.[3] In this new textile industry the majority of workers, as in the old, were female, some 80% of the total, but in all other ways Courtaulds broke sharply with Coventry traditions, replacing numerous small workshops and employers with one factory and a single employer and inaugurating a new style of work for women in Coventry.

The continuity of factory employment for women, begun in the 1890s, is clearly apparent in censal data for 1911, 1921 and 1931. The above table shows the percentage of female workers in major occupational groupings for these years. The 1911 figures must be treated with caution as the categories used here do not always coincide with the later ones. Table 5.1 shows the continuing importance of textiles, but also its relative decline by 1931. In 1911 one third of all female workers were employed in the textile group, one quarter in 1921 and just under one fifth in 1931. Metal work employed a remarkably stable 10% of female workers over the whole period.

The growth area is electrical apparatus. This goes from nothing in 1911 to employing 5% of female workers by 1931 and nearly treble this percentage by 1939 (see Table 5.3). This industry expanded rapidly in the thirties as a source of employment for unskilled women at a time when employment in rayon began to stagnate and eventually to decline. By 1939 GEC had become the largest single employer of women in Coventry, a position which it holds post-1945, thus repeating the

Table 5.2. Female Participation in the Workforce.
(14+) Coventry 1911, 1921, 1931*
(Figures in brackets are G.B. rates)

	1911	*1921*	*1931*
Total Occupied	13,049	19,555	25,009(inc. 2,343 out of work)
Total Unoccupied	23,710	42,355	47,447
Total Female Pop'n, 14+	36,764	61,910	72,456
Total Participation Rate	35.49 (35.32)	31.59 (33.71)	34.51 (34.20)
Unmarried Females	81.25 (69.32)	69.96 (68.14)	N/A (71.62)
Married Females	8.93 (9.63)	7.26 (8.69)	N/A (10.04)
Widowed/Divorced	29.58 (29.43)	28.31 (25.62)	N/A(21.24)

G.B. Figures: Source: W.H. Halsey, *Trends in British Society*, p.61.
Figures on the marital status of workers in Coventry were not calculated in the 1931 census.
* Coventry C.B. only - 1921 and 1931 includes Foleshill.

performance of Courtaulds post-1914.

In all three censal years personal service accounted for about one-fifth of women workers. This category included cleaning and serving in hotels, lodgings, restaurants, hospitals and forms of laundry work, together with private domestic service. This latter area actually employed more women in 1931 than in 1911; after a sharp decline in 1921 it occupied about 15% of women in 1931. It was growth here which was largely responsible for the fact that personal service supplanted textiles as the largest single occupation for females in Coventry by 1931.

The proportion of female clerks and typists appeared to double from 7% to 14% of all female workers between 1911 and 1921, but was only slightly higher in 1931. The national figures for these years showed the same trend. Tertiary occupations for women, including shops, expanded only slowly in Coventry between 1911 and 1931, but again this was the national trend. The professional group actually declined from 5% in 1911 to 3% in 1931.[4]

How many women of working age, living in Coventry, actually worked over the same period? Table 5:2 shows participation rates for Coventry and Great Britain. It is clear from this table that up to 1931, one third of all women of working age were at work in Coventry and that this figure was close to the national average. Further, most of these working women were single. Indeed, in Coventry, the participation rate for this group was higher than the national average, while that for married women was lower.

The 1911 figure for Coventry of 81% of single women in employment is very much higher than the national figure of 69%. It is reasonable to assume that most of these single females were young. Leppington, writing in 1907, commented on the youthfulness of Coventry's workers, noting that 62% of girls aged 15 were already earning. This high participation rate for young females arose partly from the fact that Coventry had far more people under the age of 45 than the country as a whole. But it also arose from the peculiarities of Coventry's class structure; being a city of artisans and the smaller middle class, it had no wealthy residential class whose children would remain economically inactive until adulthood.

In 1911 very few of Coventry's female workers were married. Of all those married only 9% were at work, slightly lower than the national figure of 9.6%. Leppington in 1907 found the proportion much higher in Nottingham and Birmingham than in Coventry. These towns differed from Coventry not only in their local traditions and type of industry, but also demographically; in 1907 Coventry was the least feminine of all major towns in the U.K. with just on 49% of its population female.[5]

The participation rate for all females dropped in 1921, more sharply in Coventry than nationally and probably because of Coventry's unusually high rate of unemployment in that year. By 1931 the rate had returned to 1911 levels and matched the national figures. It is impossible to get details on the marital status of the local workforce from the 1931 census, but from other evidence it continued low and still presented problems to wartime authorities seeking female labour for Coventry industries. It is difficult to explain this apparent reluctance of married female Coventrians to participate in paid employment. Could it be the operation of an absolute marriage bar by one major employer (Courtaulds) and a *de facto* marriage bar in a very large occupational grouping — private domestic service? Or was it the result of a mix of social prejudice against married women working outside the home and/or rational decision by female workers to use marriage as an escape from boring and monotonous jobs? Coventry's female workers were heavily concentrated in secondary industries which were industries organised for large scale production based on process and assembly work. Some of these women workers reminiscing in the 1980s said they were glad to leave such grinding monotonous work.

Between 1931 and 1939 the fastest growing source of employment for females was the electrical apparatus group, followed by the metal industries. Textiles and textile goods increased slowly but employment in rayon fell (this was especially evident in 1939). It is clear that

Table 5.3. Employment at Courtauld's, Coventy, 1913-47*

	Women	*Men*	*Total*	*% Female*
1913	1,320+	880+	1,200	60
1919	1,470+	1,530+	3,000	49
1925	2,300+	2,421+	4,721	49+
1935	3,050	3,250	6,300	49 (insured workers only)
1937	2,597	3,736	6,333	41
1939	2,100	4,000	6,100	
1944	245	865	1,010	24
1947	2,400	4,200	6,600	36

+ estimates derived from known percentage of female workers.
* includes Little Heath.

Source: Coleman, the Courtaulds archive, Table 3, and the Draper's Record, 1947.

rearmament and the actual onset of war brought labour shortages to the engineering sector which filled them by using women. But the reluctance of married women to work continued through the war years as a recent study by Nakamura shows.[6] Thus, although we have no precise statistical information on marital status and participation rates for the 1930s, it seems reasonable to assume that the trend first noted by Leppington and confirmed by the 1911 and 1921 censal data, continued, i.e. few married women worked in Coventry. The quantitative picture of female employment in Coventry shows a very high proportion of women workers in secondary industries, with fewer in tertiary industries than in Britain as a whole, or as Leppington noted, in other similar towns, e.g. Birmingham.

Within the range of secondary industries in 1921, group XII, textiles, employed the largest number of females, 3,852. From other sources, it is possible to establish that 40% of this number worked for one firm, Courtaulds on the Foleshill Road. Such concentration of female workers made Courtaulds unique as early as 1907. Other industries employed women, but in smaller numbers and distributed amongst numerous employers in textiles or engineering. Large groups of women in a factory setting was something new to Coventry in 1907, but Courtaulds quickly assumed a qualitative significance beyond its sheer numbers and was by 1920 the yardstick by which female work in Coventry was judged. The explanation for this lies in the conditions under which Courtaulds laboured to establish itself before the first World War. Of the two firms which offered employment to large numbers of females Courtaulds arrived first in Coventry. The reasons for this choice of city cannot be precisely determined, according to Coleman, the firm's official historian. He lists a number of theoretically valid reasons, including the most plausible, the abundance of female labour. Richardson suggests that the Courtauld family wanted a site quite separate from their Essex silk factories. If this be the case a move north to the Midlands seems a good compromise and Coventry as an old centre for silk a logical choice for a big silk firm to make. Moreover in Coventry, apart from larger concerns like Cash's and Stevens, the silk trade was at a low ebb and the labour movement weak, which factors augured well for a new business needing labour. In 1904 Courtaulds followed the city's established textile traditions in siting their factory on the Foleshill Road, the centre of the silk trade. The long rows of the old top shops stretched to the very edge of the new site, an objective reminder of the point at which a new textile tradition took over from the old.

By 1920 Courtaulds was the largest artificial silk producer in the world. The Coventry works was producing half of the company's total British output and had become the base for an empire of yarn mills reaching across the Atlantic. Although output at Coventry was overtaken during the twenties by output at Courtaulds' other plants, Coventry remained the firm's nerve centre. The research laboratories moved there in 1925 and thenceforth a wide range of new developments, including the acetate process in 1928, were originated and tested at Coventry.[7]

The firm's economic performance between the wars was impressive. In the 1920s their profits were staggering; in the thirties they were pleasing. Two factors were mainly responsible for their success. First, in the twenties they consolidated an overwhelming market dominance in a product enjoying a world boom. Between 1920 and 1941 world output of rayon increased by 8,700%. British output rose 500% between 1921 and 1928 and 60% of it was Courtauld's. High levels of profitability made possible the adoption of a high wage policy and welfare benefits during the 1920s. Increased profits came in part from technical improvements and innovation which greatly improved output. In 1928 Courtauld's cash trading profits and total income reached a high point not again attained until after 1945. Courtaulds weathered the depression better than most and never ceased to pay a dividend, while most other rayon companies never succeeded in paying one.[8] But the super profits of the 1910s and 1920s were over. Courtaulds had to settle for more moderate returns in the thirties, although it adjusted uneasily against the splendour of the past decade.

Such was the framework of profit and loss within which managerial practices developed. But old achievements and solutions to problems of a past era remained as powerful determinants and were largely summed up in the person of Harry Johnson, Managing Director of Courtaulds from 1917-1935. He it was, as manager at Coventry after 1907 who shaped workforce and production methods to make rayon the outstanding commercial success of the textile world of the early twentieth century.

The process of rayon production had important implications for the disposition and status of workers and the sexual division of labour on the shop floor. All work involving heavy machinery and potent chemicals was allocated to males. The process begins with wood pulp since rayon is a cellulosic fibre obtained by chemically treating cellulose extracted from wood pulp (or cotton linters).[9] At the Coventry works men began by cutting wood pulp into sheets and immersing them in caustic soda. They next fed damp sheets into a kneader to be turned into crumbs. The crumbs were churned with more chemicals to produce cellulose xanthate, which after further mixing became the viscose spinning solution. During spinning the viscose was forced through spinnerettes of varying deniers into an acid bath where it became a strong pliable thread. Male spinners then plucked the thread from the acid bath and looped it over godets. It ran from there into a box where it was spun into a cake of pure unbleached rayon (originally called artificial silk until 1925 in the U.S., 1929 in the U.K.). The spinner then 'doffed' the cake and handed it on to women for reeling.

After reeling, the skeins were returned to male workers for bleaching, washing and machine drying. Women looked after the final drying and then women sorted and checked skeins for defects, despatched to customers or to other women for winding on to cones, pirns or bobbins or for making into warps or wefts, before final despatch. Women played no part in the actual production of the yarn and were therefore not strategically placed to disrupt the process. Cakes, once doffed, could be left for an indefinite period before reeling. Women could only hold up delivery to customers and not even then, if stocks were high.

Men, on the other hand, were strategically placed not only to hold up production, but to damage costly equipment. If spinners ceased to draw threads over the godets, machines jammed and required days of cleaning and repair and not doffing the cakes had similar consequences. One implication of this division of the work process meant that successful industrial action for women depended on the support of the men, though the reverse was not true.

This arrangement of production meant also that women workers need not work with men. For women contact with the opposite sex was restricted to their supervision by foremen. Finally, it meant that all women's work was clean and safe. Nearly half required no machinery at all and where machines were operated by women, as in reeling, they were light and relatively simple, posing no danger to stray limbs or hair. All work was clean by the very nature of the product as both shop and workers were kept spotless for the sake of the rayon.

Building on these advantages management at Courtaulds made determined efforts to create a special moral atmosphere for its women workers. By contrast the work process and the nature of the product at G.E.C. did not lend itself to the exclusive reservation of dirty and dangerous work to men, nor to segregation of the sexes on the shop floor. If either of these conditions obtained, the occurrence was entirely adventitious and not the result of any special managerial policy for women workers. The local image of G.E.C. was much like that of any engineering factory — dirty and noisy but with the sole exception that there were plenty of jobs for women.

G.E.C. was the other important factory employer of female labour in the inter- war period. Overshadowed by Courtaulds in the twenties, its rapid growth in the thirties made it by 1939 the biggest employer of women workers in the town. G.E.C. came to Coventry in 1916, 12 years after Courtaulds, building a small factory on the Copsewood Estate at Stoke called the Conner Magneto and Ignition Works.[10] Presumably, the existence of Coventry's car industry as potential consumers, heavily influenced the choice of city. One of the company's historians suggests that Coventry was chosen because of ready supplies of female labour and also because 'the workpeople there were more or less accustomed to the fine precision operations necessary in magneto manufacture...'. The former were more compelling, at least *post facto*. Inter-war developments which were on wireless and telephone required large numbers of unskilled females.

After the war G.E.C. built a much larger factory at Copsewood and in 1921 transferred from Manchester its Peel Conner Telephone Works. At the end of 1921 it had 2,000 employees, about 60% of them female. Profits were at first low, but by 1925 were handsome and increased thereafter to 1929. The decision taken in 1922 to produce wireless receiving sets paid off. Telephone and wireless enjoyed a boom in the twenties, not on the scale of rayon, but a boom nonetheless, and one which lasted through the thirties. In 1930 500,000 radios were sold in Great Britain — in 1937 the figure was two million.[11] Profits fell between 1929 and 1931, but, like Courtaulds, G.E.C. weathered the depression better than most British manufacturers. Short time working obviated the need for large scale sacking and shutdowns and by 1936 the works had expanded so greatly that G.E.C. was buying or leasing extra factory space from other Coventry firms including sites obtained from Triumph, Lea Francis and the Coventry Stamping Co.[12] From insurance figures G.E.C. was one of Coventry's fastest growing industries. By 1939 G.E.C. had as many employees as Courtaulds, and more females — 3,450 compared with 2,100 at Courtaulds.[13] The following Table is a guide to total employment at G.E.C. and the proportion of women workers there. The second Table is a useful check on the probable sexual composition of the workforce. There were more female than male members of the G.E.C. sick fund in every year except 1938. If we assume that men and women had an equal rate of joining then the workforce is never less than 50% female over the whole period. It is possible, however, that the female workforce, being younger and less stable and earning less, had a lower rate of joining in which case the workforce was more feminised than these figures indicate. Insurance figures show the percentage of females at 60, a figure confirmed by the company archivist.

At Coventry G.E.C. manufactured automatic and manual telephone exchanges, telephone instruments and telephone repeater equipment as well as wireless receiving sets, loud speakers and all kinds of wireless accessories. It catered for a very large home market as well as a substantial export trade mainly to the Empire.[14] The production of this telephone and wireless equipment was organised on mass production process and bench assembly methods. Manufacturing was distributed amongst 21 sections and shops. Heavier production work was left to men; the Frame Shop, and Ebonite Moulding shops were 100% male. But women operated presses set up for them by skilled males in the Press Shop and in Cable Making. Adjusting, Coilwinding, Polishing, Buffing, Lacquering, Testing and Finishing, Wiring and Wireless Assembly were left almost entirely to unskilled women. Most of this work involved the production of thousands of identical small parts, requiring close attention to detail and considerable manual dexterity.[15]

From *The Loudspeaker* (the house magazine) from old photographs and oral reminiscences it is possible to build up a picture of G.E.C.'s operations. Photographs show the 140 acre Copsewood site in 1930 with perhaps 20 acres of sheds, single storied, with glass or tin roofs and galvanised iron walls. Interior views show expanses of floor with bank after bank of presses and lathes often beneath a tangle of wiring, pulleys, blocks and tackles. Many shops were noisy and dirty. All were pervaded by the mingled smell of oil, hot metal and dust so characteristic of engineering works. Both exterior and interior views of G.E.C. contrasted

Table 5.4. Employment at G.E.C., 1921-1939

Year	*Total M. & F.*	*Estimated Numbers Female*	*% Female*
1921	2,000	1,000	50
1924	2,850		
1934	4,300	2,600	60
1935	5,000+		
1939	6,100	3,450	57

Source: A. Ensley (Company Archivist) and Insurance Figures.

markedly with the four storeyed red brick solidity of Courtauld's dignified Edwardian buildings with large windows, high chimney stacks and clock tower fronting the Foleshill Road; they are reminiscent of the solid Victorian textile mills of the North. G.E.C. on the other hand was unmistakably an engineering factory.

Some of the work was very dirty. R.T., who worked on Shop Detail from 1921-1924 said the smell of hot oil turned him sick every Monday morning. He moved all over the factory recording the workers' production rates and became familiar with all the shops. He found most women workers at G.E.C. very different from the assistants in the ladies and childrens millinery section of Watts, the Manchester clothing retailers who had formerly employed him. Some sections were cleaner and the girls more ladylike (e.g. in coilwinding) but

> the girls on the bumper presses ... worked like horses ... big girls ... some Scotties. They wore rubber aprons and they were a mass of oil ... rough and ready types. Some of them gave the ratefixers a fair mouthful ... and their presses ... came down so heavy the floor fair shuddered ... they called a spade a spade and could give you merry hell.[16]

Table 5.5. Membership: G.E.C. Sick and Benevolent Fund

Year	*Total*	*Males*	*Females*	*% Female*
1924	1,619	444	725	62
1927	905	393	512	57
1930	1,258	539	719	57
1933	1,185	548	637	54
1936	2,456	1,018	1,438	59
1938	3,453	1,755	1,698	49

Source: *The Loudspeaker*, December 1938.

Some of this work was dangerous as well. W.C. remembers one girl on the big presses who lost her thumb. Another lost only the top of a finger, but died later in hospital of septicaemia resulting from the injury. W.C. later moved from the press shop to coil winding, which ' ... was much cleaner and lighter, but very eye straining and frustrating...'.[17]

Thus some female workers at G.E.C. worked under very much more dirty and dangerous conditions than girls at Courtaulds, where, if the oral evidence is sound, there were few, if any accidents with machines. Not one of the Courtauld's workers interviewed could remember accidents involving women workers. There are in the archives records of accidents to males involving machines and chemicals and in the mid-1930s Courtaulds made a fetish of safety precautions. One of the few references to the health of female workers is in 1927 when the local Medical Officer of Health was concerned about sulphur on the girls' hands; but it seems reasonable to conclude that for women workers Courtaulds was safer.[18]

The two firms, largely because of the nature of their product, provided very different working conditions for females and the contrasts quickly found their way into local mythology. The ingredients of local myth were the recruitment policies, wages, pay systems, work discipline, welfare, sporting and social activities operated by the two firms and these now require detailed investigation.

Both firms offered factory work, but at Courtaulds cleanliness and safety freed it from the most undesirable material features inevitably associated with factories since their nineteenth century beginnings. Courtaulds was aided by the nature of its production process which allowed a division of labour so as to reserve dirt and danger for males. But management did not rest here. Segregation extended to meal breaks, by means of staggered dinner hours and later, the provision of separate canteens. In 1911, Nurse Gaskin took charge of Courtaulds' surgery, but quickly extended her medical province to embrace the morality of women workers as well.[19] An aura of respectability quickly developed recommending Courtaulds as a suitable place of employment for the daughters of the local working class and overcoming the remnants of local hostility to factories as immoral places for women.

By 1920 a management strategy, designed initially to overcome the establishment problems of the Edwardian years was firmly in place. It reposed securely in the persons of Harry Johnson and Nurse Gaskin and its persistence to 1939 owes more to their presence than to the material realities of the local scene. So the efforts to maintain cleanliness, safety and respectability, originally devised to overcome the reluctance of the local working class to enter the rayon factory, remained in place even when the problems of recruitment lessened. Instead, these operated in the twenties to give a certain cachet to being, or having been, a Courtauld's girl, not only amongst employees, but also local employers. (E.M.).

This superior image was still useful to a firm employing large numbers of female juveniles. In the twenties and thirties a constant one-third of the firm's female workforce was under 18. Courtaulds took girls as soon as they were eligible for work at 14. The operation of a marriage bar kept up the numbers of juveniles; as senior girls left their places were filled by new 14 year old recruits. Their reputation for respectability was a relief to parents fearful for the physical and moral safety of such youthful offspring.

By the mid-twenties girls seeking factory employment in Coventry thought at once of Courtaulds and G.E.C. The choice was guided by family and friends who had worked for the two firms and also by the policy of local schools. Each year representatives from Courtaulds (and other firms) gave lectures on employment to school leavers. Geographical imperatives also played a part — transport was a big consideration and a girl living in Keresley was almost bound to seek work at Courtaulds rather than at G.E.C. on the other side of the city at Stoke. But other things being equal, the decision was based on considerations of what was clean and suitable work for girls and upon wages. Here Courtaulds had the edge. Its rates in the twenties for unskilled female juveniles were well above all other district employers, whatever the industry. In Coventry, Courtaulds' wages atoned for a multitude of other sins — the occasional smells, the strict discipline, the lack of unions. Was their high wage reputation deserved? To answer this question we need to look at the actual level of wages in the firm between 1922 and 1940 and at wages in other 'female' occupations in Coventry. It seems, in fact, that Courtaulds did offer its unskilled female labour higher wages than elsewhere at least until 1937. In the company archive there is a complete list of wage rates for women dated October 1922. The starting rate for a 14 year old was 16s.0d. for a 48.1/2 hour week (4d per hour). E.L. started sorting in 1924 on 16s.1d. per week -perhaps the extra 1d. was for warehouse work, the most desirable. After 12 months and three increments a 15 year old could earn 20s.0d. a week. Thereafter she advanced by thrice or twice yearly increments to a top rate of 40s. 0d. after 5.1/2 years service. Foremistresses earned 1s.8d. a week extra on the top rate.[20]

In 1921 G.E.C. paid 18s.0d. for a 48 hour week to W.C. as a 15 year old starter and the pay did not increase until she turned 21 when it was

Table 5.6. Industrial Court Awards: Coventry

Age	*Average Earnings per week*		
Day Rates	*Time Workers*	*Piece Workers*	*Courtaulds*
15	12s	14s	20s
15-16	16s	19s	22 - 26s
16-17	20s	24s	26 - 30s
17-18	25s	29s	32 - 34s
18 +	31s	36s	34 - 40s

Source: *Coventry Graphic*, 20 February, 1920, p.15.

24s. 0d. (Compare 40s.0d. at Courtaulds). However, G.E.C. operated a bonus system and these amounts are probably the basic rate. Workers could improve their earnings with piecework bonuses and overtime. By the mid-thirties when G.E.C. was expanding, bonuses were more regular and workers could expect to earn close to the Courtaulds top rate which by this time had been cut to 34s.0d.[21]

Yet G.E.C. paid more than other local employers. In 1919, at the age of 14, W.C. started as a messenger girl with Rudge Whitworth on 8s.6d. a week. In 1922 she regretfully turned down a telephonist's job with the Coventry post office at £1 per week since she already had a job at G.E.C. which was paying more. Rates for young girls in domestic service were lower, even allowing for the keep.[22] At G.E.C. W.C. never earned more than £2 in a week before she left in 1929 (aged 23) and that was only with overtime and was rare. Her pay was usually 24s.0d. weekly for the two years she stayed on after reaching 21. (At Courtaulds 16 year olds were on 24s.0d. a week at this time and 19.1/2 year olds on £2 at time rates). And E.J. left G.E.C. in 1937 as a chargehand on 30s.0d. a week. Even within the textile group, Courtaulds' rates were exceptional, especially for juniors, as the comparison with some Industrial Court awards for the silk industry indicates.

Wages in the local silk industry were very poor and declined in the twenties. E.J. started at Perkins Weaving on 9s.0d. a week in 1926 when she was 14. Management told her that the rate was low because she was in training. Later her uncle persuaded her to take a job at G.E.C. where his daughter was earning 'good money'. E.J., at 17, started at 22s. 0d. a week. She knew Courtaulds paid more, but her mother forbade Courtaulds to all four daughters 'because of the fumes'. The whole family had weak chests; mother died of T.B. in 1926. Courtaulds' wages continued high throughout the twenties. At the time profits were very high with dividends as much as 50 per cent. But profits peaked in 1928 and thereafter declined. Henry L. Johnson, director of yarn mills during his father's absence, wrote to father Harry (in America) in September 1930:

> Trade is still very uncertain. We are making 15 shifts at all factories and trade is just about balancing production ... Prices are very low. Competitors keep quoting lower prices and we keep following them down with any stock lots we have ...[23]

Short time working meant that a girl earning, for example, 31s. 6.1/2d. in February 1930 was reduced to 27s. 3d. per week. There was some compensation to be had by signing on at the Labour Exchange and E.L. and E.J. (Courtaulds, G.E.C.) remember doing so.

In April 1931 Courtaulds announced wage cuts of about 20 per cent for female workers. These followed an interim arrangement for 1930, whereby the top rate of 1922 was cut to 34s. 0d. and the rate of increments slowed but only after the first 16 months. Now the starting rate was also cut. New girls would begin on 13s. 0d. weekly instead of 16s. 0d. Girls who had started up to 16 months before April 1931, were not affected, i.e. having started at 16s. 0d. their increments were at the old rate up to 16 months service. After 5.1/2 years with Courtaulds a girl would earn 34s. 0d. (40s. 0d. in the 1920s).[24] Yet the cuts were high. At almost 20 per cent they compare unfavourably with the 10 per cent cut imposed on civil servants and indeed with the 10 per cent cut which Courtaulds imposed on male workers at the same time (see below, p. 164).

Despite these cuts E.J., who at 21 in 1932, earned 30s. 0d. a week at G.E.C., still concedes that Courtaulds paid more to girls of her age. There is, therefore, justification for the company's place in local mythology as a high wage firm (at least until 1937). Courtaulds assiduously promoted this image of themselves as high wage employers and in 1931 made this claim a matter of public record.[25] They certainly paid better, in Coventry at least, than other textile firms and certainly more than the textile industry as a whole. They also paid better than competing rayon firms like British Celanese as evidence from the Workers' Union shows. In 1928 this union negotiated agreements with British Celanese for its Spondon works near Derby. Female workers on two shifts, averaging 40 hours, were paid as follows. Courtaulds' rates are included in brackets for purposes of comparison.

British Celanese cut wages 10 per cent in 1931, but even with cuts

Table 5.7. British Celanese: Female Wages 1928

	Age	*Weekly Wage*	*Courtaulds*
	16	16s. 4d.	(28s. 0d.)
Grade III	17	19s. 9d.	(30s. 0d.)
Grade II	18-21	22s. 7d.	(34 - 40s.0d.)
Grade I	21 +	25s. 2d.	(40s. 0d.)

Source: *Workers' Union Record*, No. 177, August 1928, pp. 6-7.

Courtaulds' wages for males and females remained higher than their competitors, which Harry Johnson stressed in a press statement announcing the cuts:

> New rates are appreciably more than the wages paid for adult labour in any of the towns where we have factories ... It should be noted that in other branches of the Textile trade ... the wages for a male 21 and over are 49s. 3d. for a 48 hour week.[26]

Courtaulds' new (cut) rate for semi-skilled male spinners was £4 a week. According to Carr, the Coventry District Rate for skilled men was £2. 16s. 0d., which means that Courtaulds' rates were indeed high.

The dual effects of recovery and rearmament tightened up the Coventry labour market after 1935. Employers, especially in engineering, began to compete for any available labour. Courtaulds' reputation as a high payer for women was severely threatened. One of the directors, J.E. Redder, wrote privately to Henry Johnson that 'we were too slow off the mark on women's wages' and that the new jobs in Coventry were paying wages to females which Courtaulds could not match. Nonetheless there were no rises until November 1939, despite industrial disputes in 1937.[27]

The operation of a marriage bar meant that older female workers left regularly at about age 20 or so. Their places were filled by girls straight from school, thus ensuring a steady supply of new labour which was not only cheap but docile by virtue of its extreme youth. The nature of the work — unskilled processing — easily 'picked up' by new recruits meant that not much premium was attached to experience. The oral and written evidence suggests that Courtaulds pursued this policy from 1907. High wages for unskilled females at Courtaulds were a 'fact of life' in Coventry at least until 1937. They go a considerable part of the way in explaining the company's ability to attract and hold large numbers of female

Table 5.8. Juvenile Employment at Courtaulds, 1937.

	Under 18 Yrs.	*Males*	*18 Yrs. & Over*	*Males*
Main Works	414	103	631	1,049
Matlock Road	142	23	309	77
Lockhurst Lane	57	10	75	14
Little Heath	33	48	58	916
Yarn Processing	210	46	483	119
TOTAL	856	230	1,705	3,175
(Weekly Staff)	36	28	149	303
TOTAL	892	258	1,854	3,478
Total Males:	3,736			
Total Females:	2,597			
Total Employed:	6,333			
% Female: 41				

Source: Courtauld Archive CLR2. Returns. December 1937.

workers. But there are other important reasons.

First, the state of the labour market. In 1921 the general rate of unemployment in Coventry was very high and dropped only slowly during the twenties. The market did not pick up again until 1935, which meant that at least until this date women were thankful to get any relatively well paid job and that they hung on to it when they got it. Ex-workers from G.E.C. and Courtaulds all stressed that in those days you were glad to have a job and they put up with almost anything to keep the money coming in.

The second reason for Courtaulds' facility in attracting female labour was its emphasis on juveniles. For female school leavers of 14, Courtaulds was an employer of surpassing importance and 33 per cent of women workers there were under 18 compared with only six per cent of males. G.E.C. has kept no precise records but the available evidence suggests that although they took juveniles in the 1920s, there was certainly a preponderance of older workers in the thirties. The insurance figures also show that only 14.5 per cent of G.E.C.'s insured female workers were under 18 in 1935, a much smaller proportion than at Courtaulds.

Though slight, the evidence from these figures and oral sources suggests division in the local female labour market with Courtaulds concentrating on juveniles. After 1936 G.E.C. expanded very fast. There was overtime and earnings increased, though not wage rates. In times of prosperity this was an advantage. But a greater advantage in the thirties was the ease with which a job could be had there. 'Everyone knew if you couldn't get a job anywhere else you could get a job at G.E.C.' said E.M. Even married women, were they so inclined, could get jobs at G.E.C. E.M., barred from Courtaulds by marriage in 1932, went straight to G.E.C. and signed on. There are no figures on the marital status of workers, but oral testimony and the evidence of the house journal suggest that a significant, if minor proportion of female workers, were married. Women workers at Courtaulds worked mainly in reeling and sorting. In 1935, 35 per cent of women worked as reelers, 20 per cent as sorters and the remaining 45 per cent were divided between pirning, coning, cheesing, warping, sizing and despatching.[28] None of this work, some of it complex, was classed as skilled by management, nor on questioning, deemed to be so by the women themselves. 'You spent a day or so learning and then you got on with it' said J.H., and E.L. said 'You just picked it up as you went along'. Wages increments were for age rather than experience, which after a certain level of proficiency, ceased to pay dividends. The pay scale was very definitely for unskilled labour. Within the range of women's jobs at Courtaulds there developed a hierarchy based not on skill, but niceness — a genteel criterion, stemming from the workers' own assessment of cleanliness, quiet and the absence of chemical odours. E.L., D.A. and others said that sorting in the warehouse was the nicest job, reeling the worst, because of the smell. In between came warping, pirning, coning, winding and sizing.

In the warehouse's two sorting rooms there were distributed about 400 girls. The girls sat in rows stretching the full length of the very big rooms. Between the rows were wide gangways where the foreman patrolled. Each row was divided into sections of 30 or so with a female chargehand. Talking was forbidden. If you were caught talking too often your name went in 'the book' and you did get caught because 'you were watched all the time' (E.L.). The first stint lasted from 8 a.m. to 12 noon and there was no tea break. Girls wishing to use the lavatory took a check from the chargehand and hurried out. Any absence longer than five minutes was also noted in the foreman's conduct book. Each girl had a daily quota of skeins for checking and sorting. E.L. remembers a few girls, who persistently failed to make the daily quotas, getting the sack. The work had to be up to standard as well. Each skein sorted was marked with a girl's own number and the checkers reported faulty work to the foreman. If the work failed to improve the next pay increment was stopped.

The work they did was monotonous and tough on the eyes. Even management acknowledged that sorting required good eyesight. Sorters took the skeins of rayon ('silk' they called it) from the drying room. Each skein had to be shaken out and hung on a peg where the worker spread it to look for imperfections — broken threads. You needed good eyesight for this work and the only 'aid' the girls had were the compulsory black overalls worn by all sorters and against which the white silk stood out. E.M. remembers the routine: if there were too many broken ends the skein went on the reject peg; if fewer on to the peg for C quality; fewer still to B and none, A. E.M. remembers that some of the skeins when shaken released clouds of acrid dust: 'and it was like peeling onions. Your eyes would be streaming'. Often her eyes hurt so much that she had to go to the surgery and have drops for them. 'Now they wouldn't stand for it; you'd have to wear special glasses'.

Before World War I Courtaulds had much trouble with workers' health, especially sore eyes (reported in the *Coventry Sentinel* in 1909), but by the twenties most of these difficulties had been overcome or procedures developed to cope with them in such a way as to allay workers' fears. Anyone with sore eyes had to report immediately to the surgery and, if necessary, go home. Such cases were still paid for the whole shift.[29]

Apart from the occasional visits to the surgery the only breaks to the daily working stints in the sorting rooms were trips upstairs to the drying rooms to collect the next quota of skeins. On the way up the girls talked and larked. E.M. remembers doing the Charleston on the way up the stone stairs. But no one lingered in the drying room. The heat was unbearable. 'I don't know how they stood it', said E.L. of the few girls working in there.

All ex-workers stressed the cleanliness of Courtaulds: 'you could eat off the floor there', several of them observed. And workers had to be spotless, too, keeping soft hands and manicured nails so as not to snag the 'silk'. In fact, shop floor discipline was carried home, because girls spent some of their leisure time manicuring their nails. E.M.'s brothers teased her because she spent so much time at it.

E.L. liked the work despite its monotony. She enjoyed the company of other girls and friendships developed in the dinner hours and in snatches of fun on the way to the drying room. Some girls helped friends on the shop floor. 'If you'd finished your skeins and your friend was having trouble you'd do a few for her, when the foreman wasn't looking', said E.M. Some of the women interviewed still had friends made at work forty years before.

E.L., who started in the twenties, was quite firm that working at Courtaulds gave her a certain prestige. She liked her work, but D.A., who hated hers, acknowledged also that Courtaulds had prestige. And

E.J., who worked at G.E.C., also acknowledged the primacy of Courtaulds in the social ranking of Coventry's female workers. E.L. is quite definite, not only about Courtaulds, but about the warehouse: 'it was something to work there ... only very nice girls where I worked ... the others thought you were toffee nosed if you worked in the warehouse...'. The least pleasant, though most common job for women at Courtaulds, was in the reeling. One-third of the women employees worked in this department. Sorters, like E.L., thought it an awful job mainly because of the fumes, and 'some of them, in reeling, were a bit common'.

The reeling department was attached to the spinning and reelers came closest of all the women workers to the chemical processes of production. Finished cakes were doffed on to stacks with slide through trays to the reeling section (the other half of a long building housing the spinning workers). The girls got the cakes still smelling of sulphur, fresh from their baths of acid.

> The smell was terrible. After a few days one did get used to it, but the odour would cling to your clothes; even laundering did not remove it ... Courtaulds employees were well known in Coventry, because of the aroma surrounding them ...[30]

But in the warehouse and other places where women worked the smell was not obvious and never permeated clothing. Reeling was more physically taxing than sorting. Instead of rows of seated girls quietly grading silk skeins, there were rows of reeling machines, 18 or 20 to one girl, who hurried endlessly between them. B.G. recalls

> Sometimes you ran ... you were never cold, the sweat poured off you. I had 18 machines, as one stopped, I laced it, then the next one would be stopped and I had to lace that. By the time you got to the end the other end would be stopped and you'd start again.

But B.G. liked it — she liked the company of the other girls (at dinner time for there was no time to chat in the shed and there were no scheduled breaks). She even liked the work though 'it was a sweatshop, I suppose'. But after twelve years she was glad to give it up in 1940 on marriage, even though wartime exigency had forced Courtaulds to drop its marriage bar by then and she could have stayed on.

Others of a less philosophic temperament stress the unpleasant aspects. D.A. still recalls her terror lest the foreman find her with half her machines stopped. With a poor quality batch of rayon, stoppages were frequent because of broken threads. 'You dreaded the bad cakes' she said. 'The foreman made no allowances, even when he knew my father was working a few yards away in the spinning'.

D.A.'s legs and feet ached from standing all day on the bare concrete floor. She always hated the work even though, by 15, she was so proficient she was one of four reelers selected by the firm to travel to Canada and demonstrate the job in the new factory opening there in 1925.[31] J.H. is another worker with bad memories of reeling:

> the amount of work done each day was recorded on a card which hung above the machines ... The charge hand would check the cards every day and woe betide any girl who was 'down' on the amount of work produced or had too much waste. No allowance was made for anyone who had been off colour and therefore not worked so hard and workers daren't lose time otherwise it was the sack – you went to work if you were half dead.[32]

J.H. was happier at Little Heath where she was transferred in 1938. Here, rayon was made by the acetate process and conditions were different from those prevailing at the main works.

> [they] were far less strict and the work was more interesting. I worked on warp sizing, a process of coating the warp with size to prepare the yarn for weaving. The sizing machines were huge things, containing large hot cylinders over which the warp passed to be dried after having been through a bath of size ...[33]

The women workers had to stretch the warps evenly over the cylinders and make sure they stayed that way.

E.M. transferred from sorting at Main Works to warping at Little Heath in 1928 when Courtaulds first started to manufacture acetate rayon and found the work more enjoyable. It was more active and varied than sorting. She had to gather up threads from 100 to 200 bobbins and thread them on to a frame and thence on to a wheel which produced rolls of silk.

> It was lovely ... you had to watch the rolls and get them even, but it was fun. You could talk ... and the foreman didn't

bother you ... you just did what you could.

At Little Heath she never got sore eyes which had troubled her at Main Works, and she earned more because Little Heath was on shifts and there was a loading for two shift workers.

All Courtaulds workers were paid a fixed weekly wage — either for a 48.1/2 hour week for most women, or after 1936 for two shifts at Main Works. Most men worked on three shift rates. There was no piece work, nor a bonus system. This strict adherence to day rates made Courtaulds an unusual employer in Coventry where the major engineering firms all used forms of piece work. Courtaulds' main competitors in rayon also used piece work; indeed three rayon firms enthusiastically adopted Bedaux schemes of management after 1926. Henry Johnson, after reading a glowing report on Bedaux in the trade journal, wrote to his father in America, suggesting its adoption. Harry's reply was prompt and negative. 'I have no interest in either Bedoux [sic] or his system'.[34] There, apparently, the matter rested. Harry's word was law.

Courtaulds workers such as E.T. often comment that Harry Johnson was 'one of the old school', a tough, North country businessman who called a spade a spade. The style is reminiscent of another local employer, Alfred Herbert. The system of factory management Johnson favoured was intensely personal; he believed in driving the workers by sheer force of personality. At the beginning he hand picked his foremen in his own hard driving image and many of them were still working for the firm in the twenties. They were known as his favourites and usually disliked as a result.[35] Not even his own son escaped censure. If Henry appeared at the works a little late, the whole section, including quite junior under-managers like R.T., heard about it. Harry would open his door and bellow 'Henery, where have you been till now?' Thus it was the foremen that the workers resented. They were real 'nigger drivers' said E.L.

Henry continued at least some of his father's methods. He knew many foremen and foremistresses by name and was prompt to place those who had earned his approval in charge of slacking workers. One favourite, Flora Jones, was moved to the film cutting room in 1932 because she was 'just the person we need to keep those girls working. They are getting very slack'.[36]

At Courtaulds, slackness was severely punished. Women workers arriving just after starting time were not 'docked a quarter' as at G.E.C. They were sent home and thus deprived of a whole day's pay. Absences were excused only on production of a doctor's note or by proving bereavement or other family crisis. All other excuses were unacceptable and earned punishment. One weekend E.L. took Saturday morning off and went to Skegness. On Monday morning the foreman asked 'Where were you, Saturday?' She replied truthfully and was sent home for the week 'to have a real holiday at Skegness'.

But foremen and foremistresses like this were essential to the production system developed at Main Works. With process workers on day rates the discipline almost inevitably had to be imposed by management using threats and punishments like the deprivation of increments. It is not surprising therefore that Courtaulds had a reputation for toughness.

Why did the women workers put up with it? High wages were crucial both for the girls and their parents. Most families, especially large ones, depended on more than one wage earner to tide them over periods of unemployment and the seasonality so characteristic of the Coventry labour market. For example, E.L. was one of eight children. Her father worked at the Daimler and his earnings were seasonal. When she started work in 1924, the family was still recovering from the 1922 lockout and needed her wage. She remembers girls from better off homes who left Courtaulds because of the discipline and hard work. This option was not open to her.

But there are other explanatory factors. Almost as important as wages to the acceptance of work discipline at Courtaulds is the way in which working class girls were brought up. Their experiences within the family bred low expectations for themselves and a sense of responsibility towards siblings and parents. This was a harsh discipline in itself and it began at an early age.[37] The regime at school was just as tough and so, for a 14 year old who started work at Courtaulds in the twenties, the discipline was familiar, though worse. 'More like a concentration camp', said E.L., with feeling. There is much implicit and explicit evidence from oral sources which underlines the importance of home discipline. E.L., who apparently felt the need to explain her quiescence, said:

> You weren't brought up to answer back ... you were seen and not heard in them days ... at meals ... we daren't talk or put elbows on the table ... it lives with you ...

Family or friends working at Courtaulds would arrange a job for a girl as soon as she turned 14. They spoke to the foreman and 'booked' an impending vacancy. The new worker began therefore with a sense of both familial involvement and an obligation to the foreman which helped to weaken any rejection of working conditions. Moreover, girls were brought up in an environment where early marriage and a lifetime of domesticity were the norm for women. Thus work was an interlude before marriage and perhaps monotony and harshness were more easily borne because they were not perceived as a life time sentence.

But parental control did not always breed passivity. B.G. remembers her father, a strong Labour man, ordering her to strike with her fellow workers in October 1937. She was loath to strike but being marginally more frightened of him than her foreman, went out. This incident underlines the strength of parental authority for many working class girls. B.G. was 24 at the time.

The stern Victorian paterfamilias seemed to be the model for work discipline at Courtaulds. E.L. and E.M. still remember their foreman with dislike, as do D.A. and J.H. In sorting there was Alf Bartlett, 'a really nasty man' who stood at the back 'where you couldn't see him and watched all the time to put your name in the book so you lost your rise' and Alf could reduce a worker to tears if her work came back too often from the checkers as unsatisfactory.

But work discipline at Courtaulds was something more than hard driving on the shop floor or pass outs for the lavatories. The firm took on itself responsibility for both the inner and outer cleanliness of its female workers in a most thoroughgoing way. For Courtaulds cleanliness became godliness and in the person of Nurse Gaskin, management assumed responsibility for an astonishing degree of 'personal hygiene' in its workers.

Miss Edith Gaskin was appointed Nurse at Main Works in 1911. By 1931 she had become the Lady Superintendent.[38] At some time in the years between, Harry Johnson, with whom she had a close personal relationship, delivered the fate of his female employees into her sole charge. As the works expanded the surgery's medical duties were shared with others, and she devoted herself almost wholly to the morality and cleanliness of the works. 'She was a Tartar', recalls R.T. and 'no one dared cross her ... she had the ear of management ... she could do what she liked really'.

Nurse Gaskin interviewed all new recruits and directed them as to the pattern of overall to wear. These differed according to section so that reelers were instantly distinguishable from sorters and so on. She also subjected all of the recruits to an intense medical scrutiny, requiring them to strip while asking searching questions about skin trouble or menstrual irregularity. Popular myth held that it was she who instituted the monthly supervised bath mandatory for all female workers together with an inspection of the hair for nits. Sarah Parker, warehouse foremistress used to make a joke of bath day. 'You're *it* tomorrow – don't forget your towel' she would warn as she handed out the discs to the 'chosen few'. During working hours next day the worker and her disc reported to the surgery. Here the nurse gave out some rather nasty soap and inspected the hair before directing the 'patient' to the bathroom. E.M. said she would reappear to check up that 'you were in the bath and actually washing. But 'at least the water was hot'. This concern for outward cleanliness was matched by an equal effort to preserve inner moral health.

> [Nurse Gaskin] ... ruled the female staff with a rod of iron. She toured the factory twice a day and any girl wearing too short a dress or a sleeveless garment would be sent home and told to dress respectably for the next day. The nurse would be round early next morning to make sure that the girl was dressed in what she deemed suitable. Anyone caught chatting to a member of the opposite sex was "on the carpet". Even the canteen had separate rooms for men and girls.[39]

These efforts to maintain sex segregation apparently met with the approval of parents. E.L.'s mother was anxious that she should not work with men and this was for her a powerful recommendation of the work at Courtaulds. E.L. was even forbidden to attend the mixed dances in the firm's ballroom.

Segregation was strictly enforced too at the company Convalescent Home near Cheltenham where the relaxed atmosphere might presumably have encouraged a corresponding degree of sexual license. The male and female sections were divided by a high wall and Matron so arranged the daily (and compulsory) country walks, that male and female moved in opposite directions, preventing any chance encounters in a rural setting. Despite this, evidence from *The Rayoneer*'s engagement columns suggests that many marriages were made at work.[40]

Dental health was not neglected either. Women workers had compulsory dental checkups at least once a year during working hours, but they were not always grateful for the privilege. E.L. recalls that one of her checkups disclosed a cavity. She lived in fear of having it filled on the next call up, but somehow this never came and she left Courtaulds in 1933, cavity intact.

Such concern for dental health *may* have been an attempt to cut down absenteeism; since the war dental appointments have been a common excuse for absenteeism.[41] But dentists were a middle class luxury in the thirties, so this is unlikely. More likely, it was part of a general welfarist policy popular with responsible firms at the time and certainly with the Chairman, Samuel Courtauld. He was known in business circles for his advanced 'leftist' views apparently because of his espousal of such organisations as the Industrial Welfare Society and, during the war, mild utterances in favour of state intervention.[42]

From this mix of directorial influences, managerial style, welfare provisions, work process, wages and the structure of the labour market, there emerged a distinctive environment for Courtaulds workers. At G.E.C. the same factors interacted to give a different environment. Wages as we have seen, were lower, the work process was entirely different owing to the nature of the product and so were workers' attitudes to their jobs. For example, the job hierarchy which developed at Courtaulds as between sorting and reeling has no counterpart at G.E.C. From oral evidence (W.C.) jobs where earnings were higher were more desirable, though they often involved dirty work with dangerous machines.

W.C. remembers being, at first, overwhelmed by the noisy machinery and 'all those men' in the press shop. But she soon got used to it. She was glad to be put on the lighter kick presses, because they were less dangerous than the big bumper presses, but also because she felt the girls on those presses were a bit 'crude'. She found their language shocking and avoided dealings with them, keeping to her end of the shop. There is here a suggestion of an internal job hierarchy based on respectability (and R.T. spoke in similar vein) but it is only a faint echo of the Courtaulds system.

Work in coil winding was lighter and all female, but for W.C. it was less desirable because she earned less:

> We only got paid for coils that registered properly on the ampmeter, if not they had to be stripped and started over again ... everything was piecework so you could actually be in debt ...

Oral evidence suggests that in the early years G.E.C. operated an individual bonus system as described above. This was altered about 1924 to a group bonus system with a base rate. In the shops, chargehands supervised groups of workers. The group's total output was averaged and the bonus for those workers and the chargehand paid on that basis. Each week the rate of bonus for every shop was posted in a central hallway. Everyone could see what rates other shops had achieved and workers in one area were inclined to think that others were doing better and to wish that they worked elsewhere, according to both E.J. and W.C. W.C. remembers the introduction of the group bonus system:

> They brought a new system in that they reckoned they'd imported from America, from the Kodak workers ... the Kodak we always called it. Instead of your individual job, the whole section all put in together. ... we didn't like it because people who didn't work so much got the same as you ... At the end of the week the secretary who did all the booking of the jobs, would put the bonus up on the blackboard ... e.g. a rate of 0.4 would bring your wages up 2s. 0d.

In 1935 the company's attempts to return to an individual bonus system provoked the first major strike since its arrival in Coventry. 3,000 workers came out, the T. & G.W.U. was called in and eventually the strike was settled on terms more favourable to management.[43]

This payment system produced a form of factory discipline quite different from that at Courtaulds. The bonus scheme meant that the workers disciplined themselves very largely, and the focus of resentment was rarely the foreman: it became instead, the rate fixer. W.C. remembers the short plump figure of Mr. Stephens, glowering behind her, stop watch in hand and 'swearing you could do more than that ... talk about being brought to tears ... He'd set the basic at so much for 1000 and you'd always be racing to do more'. Mr. Stephens, fortunately, visited only intermittently and the hard driving bullying frequently mentioned by the Courtaulds workers is absent from accounts of the G.E.C.

There were the same officially unbroken stints of work. Workers visiting the lavatories slipped away when no one was looking, though W.C. remembers 'nine times out of ten the foreman would be watching ... watch in hand and his eyes on the big clock ... AND black looks'. There were no official tea breaks either, but whereas all ex-Courtaulds workers insist that this rule was strictly enforced, girls at G.E.C. could 'sneak' a bit under the bench and E.J. even remembers an old man who came round the shop selling biscuits and milk. She worked in the adjusting and always took a snack. The snack could be anything except fruit or similar acid foodstuffs which may have marred the finish on the selectors. When she became charge hand she used to turn a blind eye to 'her' girls having a snack.

Perhaps because discipline was less obviously imposed by

management, thus producing a more relaxed atmosphere, G.E.C. was a 'homely' sort of firm. The style of its house journal is informal and chatty. Its editor could conceivably be speaking from the shop floor, whereas the editor of *The Rayoneer* speaks very differently, *de haut en bas*. Even his name, Geoffrey Steele-Morgan, is distinctly managerial.[44]

Management showed itself at the G.E.C. not by cleanliness and compulsory baths, but by its presence at section get togethers or by honouring its long serving workers. Anyone who served five years or more was dubbed a 'dependable' and got a badge which said so. Larger badges were awarded after 10, 15, 20 and 25 years service. Dependables who left kept their badges and received an extra token of the company's appreciation such as E.J.'s gold plated pencil for nine years service. The *Loudspeaker* ran a regular Dependables page, featuring new qualifiers. There was no similar scheme at Courtaulds, although *The Rayoneer* occasionally mentioned workers with outstanding long service. In the late thirties women workers of ten or more years' service got leaving gratuities of 10s. 0d. for each year of service. B.G. got £6 in 1940. In earlier years girls leaving to be married were honoured by a speech from the foreman and a presentation gift paid for by workmates. E.L. got a clock in 1933.

But Courtaulds was more generous than G.E.C. and this went beyond wages. Each year employees received New Year gifts ranging from 5s. 0d. for the under 18s to hundreds of pounds for higher management. B.G. remembers her delight in turning 18 to find the New Year gift doubled to ten shillings.[45] W.C. and E.J. never received gifts of this nature at G.E.C.

Management at G.E.C. did not share Courtaulds' concern for respectability. During the twenties recruitment at G.E.C. was far more casual. Those wanting work could present themselves directly at the firm without having another worker speak for them, as at Courtaulds. In part this policy reflects the state of the Coventry labour market in the twenties, when unemployment made female labour easier to come by than in the period 1905 to 1914 when Courtaulds established their hiring practices. It reflects, too, changed attitudes to women's work in factories produced by more than 20 years activity and the extraordinary experiences of wartime armaments work.

Women workers at G.E.C. escaped the intense personal scrutiny of a Nurse Gaskin. The efforts of the G.E.C. nurses were much less ambitious. The Ambulance Department dealt with minor accidents and provided a couch for those afflicted with headaches or faintness. Attendance at the surgery was voluntary and since workers were either docked or put on waiting time if they left the shop floor for medical attention, they kept the visits to a bare minimum. (W.C.). The nurses did not double as moral vigilantes, either. Pregnancies went for long undetected. W.C. remembers a girl working on the heavy presses, who came into labour on the job, set off for home and gave birth on the way in a hedge up by Stoke Aldermoor. At Courtaulds, Nurse Gaskin was daily on the lookout for symptoms of immorality and had at least one girl dismissed on suspicion of pregnancy, unjustly as it turned out. (J.H.).

Managerial styles also differed in the operation of broadly similar welfarist policies like pensions and convalescent homes. From 1920 G.E.C. operated a Contributory Pension Fund, open to all employees who paid yearly four per cent of wages or salary with the company contributing an equal amount. There was also a benevolent Pension Fund for those not in the other scheme.[46] Courtaulds operated a similar fund but it seems (from oral evidence and from the House magazine) that their women workers rarely contributed. Both funds were in theory open to females, but in practice female employees were regarded and so regarded themselves as 'temporary' workers for a term fixed by a marriage bar, real or self imposed. A 14 year old recruit might work for six, even ten years. During their later working years most were courting. E.L., W.C. and E.J. were engaged for two or three years during which time they saved to buy a house or other appurtenances of married life. Such goals made time at work seem an interlude before the real business of life.

G.E.C. employees had a Sick Benefit Fund.[47] About two-thirds of all employees belonged, more females than males. E.J. remembers joining and paying her 6d. a week. At Courtaulds all medical arrangements were made by the firm which operated a convalescent home near Cheltenham, where ailing workers stayed free of charge. Transport to and fro was provided by Courtaulds. E.L. suffered from nervous debility in 1932 and was sent for a two week break. Though treatment was free, Matron had her own system of charges; the women patients did a daily stint of light housework, under supervision. E.L. remembers to this day being upbraided for some imperfect dusting.

Employees at both firms had sporting clubs using buildings and grounds supplied by the firms, and where necessary, company transport to away fixtures. In this both G.E.C. and Courtaulds conformed with other district employers and were in tune with the company welfare movement which stressed sport as promoting the workers' physical and mental health. Much copy in *The Rayoneer* and the *Loudspeaker* was generated by the activities of various sporting clubs. Coventry newspapers, too, were tireless in reporting fixtures between teams from the major local firms like Standard, Daimler, Rudge Whitworth, G.E.C. and Courtaulds, as well as teams from firms in London, Manchester and other industrial centres.[48] G.E.C. had football fields, cricket pitches and even a golf course at Copsewood and Courtaulds had a sports ground in Lockhurst Lane. There were swimming clubs at both firms. A Courtaulds director had this to say: 'Recreations were encouraged ... and the firm did everything possible to keep the workers healthy, because it was good business to do so ...'.[49]

On the social side both firms had ballrooms which achieved considerable local popularity. Courtaulds' ballroom had high status in the twenties. In 1937, G.E.C. built a new one of palatial proportions which quickly eclipsed Courtaulds' in local estimation.[50]

There were works outings. B.G. remembers going to a London theatre in the late thirties. They filled a whole train and the engine pulled out of Coventry station with the Courtaulds crest above its buffers. E.J., from G.E.C., remembers a trip to see Jack Buchanan and Elsie Randolph in a London musical. Oral evidence indicates that these outings were arranged by workers and they therefore differ from practices at the Standard where Colonel Black annually entertained his girls to afternoon tea at his own home.[51]

For Courtaulds workers balls and outings were presumably the chief opportunity for men and women to socialise and some apparently led to marriage. In February 1938 out of 21 marriages announced at Main Works and Little Heath, nine were between couples where both worked at Courtaulds.[52]

Both companies had canteens which provided cheap meals. Most women brought their own dinner and perhaps bought a cup of tea for a halfpenny at Courtaulds. At G.E.C., hot water was free and the canteen would warm dinners for nothing. E.J. often took baked beans to be warmed in a metal basin. Fish and chips were standard Friday fare at both factories and most women workers treated themselves once a week to this ninepenny meal.

There were incidental benefits. Courtaulds workers whose bikes got punctures on the way to work had them mended free, by the bike shed attendant. (D.A.). There was no such service at G.E.C., but despite this and other superior benefits at Courtaulds, the G.E.C. employees felt more at home. Homely is not an adjective which springs readily to mind when summing up the feelings of Courtaulds workers about that firm.

What was the pay off in their industrial relations for the different regimes? Both firms seem, on the archival, press and oral evidence, to have avoided confrontations with their workers throughout the twenties, but in the thirties recession and recovery generated unrest. Courtaulds had strikes over wages in 1931 and again in 1937. G.E.C. had a strike in 1935, but it is difficult to tell what was most responsible for industrial peace — worker apathy or contentment, welfarism or wages.

Courtaulds did not officially recognise the T. & G.W.U. until 1937, though its few skilled employees like maintenance men belonged to the A.E.U.[53] Some skilled workers at G.E.C. belonged to craft unions. R.T.'s father, foreman of the Ebonite Moulding Shop, belonged to the Iron Moulders. But the bulk of the workers in both firms were unskilled and semi-skilled process workers, both male and female. The obvious union for them was the Workers Union, but this was decimated in Coventry after 1922 and was in no position to organise for the rest of the twenties. In 1929 it merged with the T. & G.W.U., which inherited the agreement between the Workers Union and the Textile Workers, leaving workers in 'artificial silk' to the Workers Union.[54] But the T. & G.W.U. remained curiously inactive in Coventry though it used the 1931 strike to recruit workers from Courtaulds. (E.J. joined in 1931). But it was always an undercover operation and did not gain significant numbers until the 1937 strike, when it signed enough members to warrant the firm's recognition.[55] By 1937 the attitude of management was softer. Harry Johnson had retired in 1935; the chairman, Samuel Courtauld had always argued in favour of union recognition — indeed had negotiated agreements with the Workers Union for his Essex factories. It was Harry, given to dubbing all unionists 'Reds' who had kept unions out of his Coventry fiefdom for almost 30 years, despite worsening labour relations in the final decade. His removal was the key to a new policy increasingly dictated by changed circumstances. It is likely that Courtaulds' high wage policy was, in the first instance, partly designed to keep unions out. Management alluded to this when explaining their change of heart in 1937. '... Our employees at Coventry have not previously sought trade union assistance by very reason of the high standard of wages which this company set itself to pay some 17 years ago ...'.[56] Local unionists were of the same opinion. For example, Billy Buxton, organiser for the Workers Union and then the T. & G.W.U. wrote:

> At Courtaulds Coventry factory there were no Trade Union recognition of any trade union [*sic*]. They paid 3d. per hour above a trade union rate of competitors or ancillary trades ...[57]

Frank Carr has demonstrated the interest of some Coventry employers in 'buying off' worker unrest with high wages. In 1954, Morris, reviewing 30 years of business success for the *Journal of Industrial Economics*, wrote that 'a low wage is the most expensive method of producing. A moderately high wage is the cheapest'.[58] In this, Courtaulds seems at one with local engineering employers. G.E.C. is more difficult to place though it belonged to the Coventry Engineering Employers Federation, its wages were not as high as those at Courtaulds, though workers' earnings, in the thirties, did approach Courtaulds'.

However, neither firm was immune to the pressures of a labour market invigorated by rearmament after 1936. Worker unrest created opportunities for the T. & G.W.U. which in the late thirties at both Courtaulds and G.E.C. came into the factories on the basis of existing strikes by organised women, recruited heavily, and then settled the strike over the heads of the strikers in such a way as to suit management rather than workers.[59]

The T. & G.W.U. organised amongst males at Courtaulds factories in Flint and Wolverhampton, but made little effort to recruit women workers there or at Coventry. Tolliday argues that Bevin was cautious about over-reaching in the early thirties, that women workers were peripheral to his concerns and that he left T. & G.W.U. business in Coventry to a small autonomous enclave of ex-Workers' Union officials like Buxton and Nelson (who were not textile workers). The 'easing' out of Alice Arnold meant that the enclave of ex-Workers' Union organisers was entirely male and less likely to be interested in women workers. Oral testimony is clear on this point. No one ever came round recruiting and both E.L. and J.H. on their way home one day joined themselves up at the Union shop in Lockhurst Lane. Tolliday found amongst car workers a pattern of passive acceptance of intensive working conditions, interrupted by spontaneous 'wildcat' patches of resistance. E.L. describes such an incident in the Courtaulds warehouse in 1931. Workloads were arbitrarily increased one Monday morning. This followed on a previous intensification of their rate of sorting about 18 months before. During the dinner hour the women talked amongst themselves and decided not to return that day. Instead they stood outside in the yard beneath the warehouse. Eventually the foremistress appeared and told them not to be so silly or they'd lose wages and they all returned. Nothing came of this incident and the increased workloads remained. But after this E.L. joined the T. & G.W.U. to the amusement of her fiance (a member of the Vehicle Builders) who said the T. & G. was not a 'real union'. She never saw any results from joining before her departure from Courtaulds in 1933.

E.J. recounted an incident in Section 20 at G.E.C. in 1935. Management introduced a conveyor track for the girls to shunt part-assembled selectors from one to the other. At the same time management docked the bonus arguing that the track alone increased production. The girls struck work, refusing to use the track unless the bonus was restored. It was and they resumed work. 'We didn't need a union, we did it ourselves', said E.J. She never belonged to a union and cannot remember anyone else in her section belonging either. 'You didn't have unions in them days'.

W.C. said it wasn't allowed. 'You'd have got the sack' and the Courtaulds workers were even firmer on this point. J.H. joined in 1937 but when she found she didn't get strike pay, dropped out — she couldn't justify the expense of the dues, especially when there was nothing to show for it.[60]

In 1931 because of stagnating production and falling profits, Courtaulds cut wages. This was a last resort for management. Since 1929 it had followed common practice in the textile industry in trying to reduce costs by speed up and intensification. All workers complained of the increased loads (E.L. sorting and D.A. reeling). H.H. Scott, officially charged with responsibility for 'labour planning and safety', but who seems to have been a time and motion man, precipitated the strike. He planned the speed up in routines which preceded the announcement of wage cuts. The ensuing strike which began on April 30, 1931, was about these as much as about wages. But it was the men, not the women who started the strike. The *MDT* reported the strike meeting:

> curiously enough the wage reduction which is the apparent *causus belli* did not appear to be the main concern ... speakers ... were, however, very critical of the conditions of labour which they allege to have existed at the Foleshill works for some two years now. ... Speakers contended ... that wages have also been reduced indirectly by increasing the responsibilities of the spinners, one man now controlling two machines where he formerly only looked after one. Criticisms were also directed to the speeding up of operations.[61]

Nonetheless, the spinners had to return to work on the company's terms accepting a ten per cent cut in their wages from £4.10s.0d. to £4 a week, much less however than the near 20 per cent cut in women's wages which we have already discussed. The only concession was the temporary removal of Scott, whom Harry Johnson recognised as the source of trouble. 'There is more talk of conditions of work and bullying than about wages reductions and I have sent Scott for a fortnight's holiday...'.[62]

In 1937 trouble began among the women and spread to the men. No one is quite sure of the precise *causus belli* — one theory is that management lifted its marriage bar in favour of one worker (this was denied by H.L.J. in the press). A more plausible suggestion was put forward by the company's own Labour Department that it was unrest over higher wages being paid in the shadow factories. (One director, Pedder, also inclined to this view). There were girls leaving both G.E.C. and Courtaulds for jobs in the shadow factories. E.J. knew two girls who left in 1937 for higher wages at the Armstrong. She herself did not leave G.E.C. because her impending marriage meant that she would shortly be giving up work altogether. J.H. remembers people leaving Courtaulds; there was an atmosphere of general unrest and the strike started for no apparent reason:

> A crowd of girls came running into the reeling department and shouted, come on we're all out on strike. Everything was a muddle, no one knew what was happening ... someone switched the machines off and we were more or less forced out. Quite frankly to me it was all a great adventure and a break from a boring job. I never really knew the why's and wherefores of the strike, rumours were rife. 1. a girl had been sacked unfairly; 2. our pay was to be cut; 3. we were on strike for more money. I can't remember how long it lasted, but we started back in dribs and drabs ... but things hadn't altered except that we were on short time for a long time...[63]

These experiences of women workers at Courtaulds and G.E.C. are similar to those identified for car workers by Tolliday, i.e. long periods of passive acceptance broken only rarely by spontaneous unorganised and thoroughgoing strikes. But these episodes were few and did little to relieve harsh and monotonous work regimes. G.E.C. workers had a small victory and a larger defeat; at Courtaulds, workers lost on each occasion.

Generally, despite differences in pay systems, discipline and welfare arrangements, female workers at both firms showed little opposition to either ordinary working practices, or to speed up and intensification. But they did indicate a willingness to organise which the T. & G.W.U. failed to exploit. Oral evidence shows that some women took the initiative in seeking out and joining a union which evinced remarkably little interest in women workers. Other women would probably have joined if any effort had been made to recruit them; none expressed hostility to the concept of organisation. The majority simply believed that management 'would not have allowed it' and that, for them, closed the matter.

In Coventry between the wars factory work for women was dominated by Courtaulds and G.E.C. They offered women's work, paid at women's rates, and unskilled by definition, even when demanding considerable manual dexterity. The pay, though generous by local and national yardsticks, was low by masculine standards. But this comparison was rarely made because women's work was *women*'s work and never done by men.

At both firms the elaborate division of the work process meant that the work experiences of men and women were entirely different. In addition, women workers were at the bottom of a line of authority stretching from male foremen to male managers and thence to male directors and the chairmen at each pinnacle. Women's subordination to men was underlined by lower rates of pay and by their youth which, especially at Courtaulds, prompted paternalistic management practices. At both factories the female workforce was young and juxtaposed with a male work force which was overwhelmingly adult and largely semi-skilled or skilled. Thus male workers had a superior status conferred by age and skill as well as by their gender. On the shop floor women were controlled and directed by males; even the foremistresses and female chargehands exercised only a delegated masculine authority.

In many ways women at Courtaulds and G.E.C. are classic examples of the female worker stereotype: young, cheap, docile and ephemeral. But there are qualifications. They were cheap, but not as cheap as female labour in other occupations, owing to the peculiarities of the local labour market and/or the idiosyncrasies of a particular firm. Docile they were, in the main, but at times exhibiting a spontaneous militancy more thoroughgoing than any of their male co-workers. Unorganised, too, but not always from their apathy; unions made little effort to recruit them and had even less to offer them when they did.

It is true though that women workers were ephemeral. Most worked ten years at a maximum and during most of their working life their sights were fixed on marriage and escape from monotonous work and harsh discipline. But these were rational responses to their material circumstances, to shop floor conditions which largely reproduced the social relations of the working class family and exploited their limited expectations of life. The factory, consciously or not, stood in *loco parentis*, building on and reinforcing the discipline of the family and a daughter's place in it. Courtaulds which derived such benefit from family discipline reciprocated by operating a marriage bar, thus implicitly upholding the notion that women's rightful place was in the home.

Two decades is a short period by historical standards and though it was for Coventry and the nation as a whole a period of many short term fluctuations and some long term changes, these are more fairly reflected in the world of women's work. Though Coventry was a little island of prosperity offering opportunities for men and women which did not exist elsewhere, the nature of women's work was unchanged. It remained the province of the young, unskilled and temporary. For women in Coventry the major change was the relative decline of Courtaulds during the thirties when it ceased to be the largest employer of women, yielding first place to G.E.C. after 1935. The rise of G.E.C. was a portent of female factory work in the post war world which relied on married, part time females, still cheap and docile but no longer so juvenile. War brought to an end an era in Coventry in which factory work for girls 'meant G.E.C. and Courtaulds'.

Notes to Chapter 5

1. A.E. Harrison, 'The competitiveness of the British cycle industry, 1890-1914', *Economic History Review*, 2nd Series, XXII, 2 (1969); J.R. Bailey, 'The struggle for survival in the Coventry ribbon and watch trades 1865-1914', *Midland History*, VII, (1982).
2. See Chapter 2.
3. Bailey, *op.cit.*, 142 and K. Richardson, *Twentieth Century Coventry* (1972), 39.
4. W.H. Halsey, *Trends in British Society since 1900* (1972), 114; K.E. Gales and P.H. Marks, 'Trends in the work of women', *Journal of the Royal Statistical Society* (1974) A, Table 3, 64 shows a national decline in teaching from 3.8% to 3.2% in the same time.
5. C.H. D'E Leppington, 'The Evolution of an Industrial Town', *Economic Journal*, 17 (1907) 348-49.
6. Nobuko Nakamura, 'War, Work and Women. Industrial Mobilisation and Demobilisation during the Second World War with special reference to Coventry and Bolton', (Ph.D. thesis, University of Warwick, 1984).
7. D.C. Coleman, *Courtaulds. An Economic History* (2 vols. 1969), 243-325; Richardson, *op.cit.*, 152.
8. Coleman, *op.cit.*, 245-64.
9. The description which follows is adapted from 'How Rayon is Made' in *The Rayoneer* (Wolverhampton, November 1931), 63-66.
10. Letter to J. Castle from A.E. Ensley, Company Archivist, 4 January, 1984.
11. B.W.E. Alford, *Depression and Recovery?* (1984), 45.
12. Ensley, *op.cit.*
13. A. Shenfield and P. Sargant Florence, 'Labour for the War Industries: the experience of Coventry', *Review of Economic Studies*, XII (1944), Table V, 36.
14. *The Loudspeaker*, I (December 1924), 3.
15. *Ibid.*, see also numbers 36-38, 42-43.
16. All material referred to in the text by the undermentioned initials is taken from the following series of interviews with the author during March 1984 or from letters written by some interviewees to the author at the same time. Tapes of the interviews, with transcripts, and the letters, are in the Modern Records Centre at the University of Warwick (M.R.C.).

Interviews:

R.T.: Richard Teers, b.1901; G.E.C. Shop Detail 1921-24; Courtaulds Production and Sales 1924-62.

E.L.: Elsie Lee, b.1910; Courtaulds 1924-33. Sorting.

W.C.: Winifred Cotterill, b.1906; G.E.C. 1921-29. Press Shop, Coil Winding.

E.J.: Elizabeth Johnson, b.1911; G.E.C. 1928-37.

Section 21, Adjusting.

E.M.: Eva Mullis, b.1910; Courtaulds 1924-32. Sorting, Warping; G.E.C. 1932, Coil Winding.

D.A.: Doris Addicot, b.1910; Courtaulds 1924-34. Reeling.

B.G.: Bobbie Garner, b.1913; Courtaulds 1928-40. Reeling.

Note:

J.H.: Joyce Hampson, b.1921; Courtaulds 1935-40. Reeling. Letter April 1984. There is no taped interview. She also published an account of her work at Courtaulds in *Equity Life*, Summer 1980.

17. W.C. letter to J.C., March 1984.
18. Courtaulds Archive, HLJ1, H.J. letter to H.L.J., May 1927; see also HLJ2 and CLR1. A file on Welfare, which is on closed access, may contain references to other incidents.
19. Coleman, *op.cit.*, 170.
20. Courtaulds' Archive, CLR2. Courtaulds made efforts to recruit school leavers. Company representatives addressed those in their last term at Coventry elementary schools, throughout the twenties and thirties. See M.O.H. Annual Reports. HLJ2. Girls' Wage Rates: October 1922.
21. Courtaulds Archive, HLJ2; Girls Rates, 22 April, 1931.
22. P. Taylor, 'Daughters and mothers, maids and mistresses: domestic service between the wars' in *Working Class Culture*, J. Clarke, *et.al.* *Working Class Culture* (1980) 6.
23. Courtaulds' Archive HLJ1b. H.L.J. to H.J., 5 September, 1930.
24. *Midland Daily Telegraph*, 2 May, 1931. (Hereafter *MDT*). Courtaulds' Archive, HLJ2; Girls Rates, 22 April, 1931.
25. *MDT*, 2 May, 1931.
26. *Ibid.*
27. Courtaulds' Archive, HLJ4. *Daily Express*, 18 November, 1939, and see note in Courtaulds' Archive, JHW69.
28. Courtaulds' Archive, CLR2, 1935.
29. *Ibid.*, CLR1, 29 February, 1936.
30. Joyce Hampson, *op.cit.*, 27-28.
31. 'Memory Lane', *The Rayoneer*, February 1940, 36.

32. Joyce Hampson, *op.cit.*, 27-28.
33. *Ibid.*
34. *The Rayon Record*, 1 July, 1932. Courtaulds' Archive, HLJ1g letter October 1932. In the same file as a cutting of the article.
35. Coleman, *op.cit.*, Chapter XIV.
36. Courtaulds' Archive, HLJ1f. H.L.J. to H.J., 24 June, 1932.
37. P. Taylor, *op.cit.*, recounts similar experiences for girls going into service.
38. *The Rayoneer* (November 1931), 69. George V visited the Wolverhampton works in October. The official luncheon party consisted of Nurse Gaskin, two senior directors, Samuel Courtauld (chairman) and the Chief Constable of the County.
39. Joyce Hampson, *op.cit.*, p.28.
40. *The Rayoneer* (January 1937) no. 67. Four couples announced their betrothal; in two cases *both* partners worked at Courtaulds.
41. A member of Courtaulds' library staff had dental appointments arranged by the firm in the late fifties.
42. Courtaulds' Archive SAM 43-44; see file marked Industrial Welfare. The society was founded by Robert Hyde in 1918. Seebohm Rowntree and Jimmy Clynes also belonged. *Daily Herald*, obituary, 3 December, 1947. 'Millionaire who loved Unions'.
43. *MDT*, 22, 23, 24 July, 1935.
44. *The Rayoneer*, (December 1937), Vol. 1, No. 1, 16.
45. Courtaulds' Archive, CLR 1 & 2.
46. A.G. Whyte, *Forty Years of Electrical Progress* (1930) 114-16.
47. *The Loudspeaker*, December 1938.
48. e.g. *Coventry Graphic*, 14 May, 1920.
49. *The Artificial Silk World*, 21 September, 1928, 380.
50. *MDT*, 27 October, 1937, 5.
51. S. Tolliday, 'Militancy and Organisation: Women Workers and Trade Unions in the Motor Trades in the 1930s', *Oral History*, Vol. 11, 2, 44.
52. *The Rayoneer*, February 1938, 130-33.
53. Courtaulds' Archive, CLR2 and HLJ3.
54. *Workers' Union Record*, no. 187.
55. Courtaulds' Archive, CLR2, October 1937.
56. *Ibid.*
57. Letter to R. Hyman, 9 October, 1965 (M.R.C.).
58. Cited in F. Carr, 'Engineering Workers and the rise of Labour in Coventry 1914-39', University of Warwick Ph.D., 1978.
59. Tolliday, *op.cit.*, 48.

60. Letter to J.C., April 1984.
61. *MDT*, 1 May, 1931.
62. Courtaulds' Archive, HLJ1g, H.L.J. to H.J., 4 May, 1931.
63. Letter to J.C., April 1984.

Chapter 6

Municipal Socialism: Labour's Rise to Power

Frank Carr

This chapter deals with the rise of the Labour Party in Coventry before the Second World War. It concentrates in particular on Labour's relations with the other political parties in the city, including the Communist Party, and its relations with the trade union movement. The aim is to put Labour's municipal victory in 1937 into a political and social context. Why, in such a strongly working class city did it take Labour so long to win office? We shall look at the way the older parties hung on to power and how they set the ground rules for local politics. How did Labour change in its long march to power? We shall contrast its fortunes at key points, such as the period of the engineers' lockout, with the fortunes of the Communist Party, which sought to build a different political movement. Finally we shall look at the way Labour developed while unions were in retreat, and see the impact of this. In this way it is hoped to measure the significance of Labour's taking office, and assess what this meant in terms of changing consciousness of working people before the War.

Labour and the Coalition

In 1837 the Chartist candidate in the General Election in Coventry was heavily defeated by a middle class Radical, and left the city denouncing the freeman's franchise as a 'shopocracy'.[1] One hundred years later, the shopocracy was eventually overthrown, not by Chartists, but by the Labour Party.

In 1837 Coventry had been a town of small trades, where weavers and watchmakers could reasonably hope to become masters and employ a handful of other skilled workers. Class boundaries could be breached; all were united in opposition to factory working. In 1857 Coventry home workers in the silk industry were able, after a strike, to prevent the new factory owners paying their workers by wages instead of by the piece, an achievement 'without parallel in nineteenth century England'.[2]

In 1937 Coventry was a city of large factories, a national centre for motor vehicles, electrical engineering and aircraft. The factories were controlled by large companies, the city was divided into a tiny class of owners and managers, a small group of retailers, businessmen, professionals and small manufacturers, and a huge army of workers.

Presiding over the city's industrial and social revolution was the 'shopocracy' which survived as a major force in the political life of the city long after its social base had ceased to be dominant. The 'shopocracy' was an uneasy coalition of different social forces, lacking in resources, seldom able to achieve united and disciplined action. Yet it succeeded in holding up the Labour advance for decades. In fighting against it, and in its drive for municipal power, Labour was in a fight, not with the big companies that controlled the economic life of the city and the life of the workers, but with a political anachronism that remained in power until it was virtually exhausted. In 1937 Labour gained power almost by default.

The political expression of the 'shopocracy' were the Liberal and Conservative Parties. In the late 1920s they came together to form the Coalition, and this is a useful title for the social group that was so tenacious in staying in control of the city. A study of the social background of Coalition councillors and aldermen shows its base. Of all of these people whose occupations can be identified in the inter-war period, one third were dealers or retailers, mostly shop keepers. Over one fifth were manufacturers, mostly associated with old established trades such as watches, silk, clothing. A similar sized group was from the professions, particularly lawyers and doctors. Builders, publicans and commercial agents were also well represented. Only a very small number were associated with the big engineering companies, and this included a few senior managers that were politically active for only a brief period; in general the managers of the engineering industries were under-represented.

In terms of riches and resources, the manufacturers of the city were more powerful than the Coalition. But they were concerned with achieving profitable returns from their factories, and were content to leave the running of the city to the Coalition. The two groups shared a broadly similar ideology, and this enabled them to operate on a day to day basis with little contact. A few key individuals helped to ensure harmony between the groups. John Varley, a local solicitor who moved in Coalition circles was the full time secretary of the Coventry and District Engineering Employers' Association (C.D.E.E.A.); Edward Iliffe, Conservative politician and owner of the *Midland Daily Telegraph*, seldom involved himself in local affairs directly, but used his paper to create a link between the Coalition, from which he came, and the engineering employers.

While manufacturers might contribute prestige to the Coalition, it survived for so long because it was able to hold the support of a large number of working people. It did this through its leadership in the social as well as the political life of the city. Besides having a sympathetic local press it had many supporters in the Chamber of Commerce and in trade organisations. It administered the funds from various charities such as Sir Thomas White's, and the Freeman's Trustees funds. Many of these funds were used for loans for small businesses.

The list of trustees and managers of the Coventry Savings Bank and the Coventry Permanent Economic Building Society shows that many Coalition councillors and aldermen were interested in the work of these institutions. Both aimed at attracting working class savings. The building society had as its aim 'to promote habits of thrift and independence amongst the industrial classes, and especially to encourage and assist every man to become his own landlord'.[3]

The society expanded its business throughout the first three decades of the century. In 1939 some 40 per cent of the families in Coventry had an account with it, and of course, there were many other building societies in the city as well. The number of people with mortgages from the Society grew rapidly in the 1930s, as Coventry was a boom town for private sector builders. By the outbreak of the second world war a significant minority of working class people had their own homes. There is no evidence to suggest that this meant that they were more likely to vote for the Coalition, but it is clear that this is what the Coalition expected, and the Building Society was one of a network of institutions used by the Coalition to encourage others to accept their values.

As in many other cities, the Liberal Party had a strong tradition of working class support. In Coventry this did not lead to a Lib-Lab alliance; the Labour Party was fairly late to develop and chose to grow on its own. This may have contributed to the decline of the Liberal Party in the city, but it also brought working class votes to the Coalition, as the Liberal Party won every Parliamentary election up to 1918. It might well have won then but for the fact that the sitting M.P. was a pacifist and had taken a strongly anti-war stand that had made him unpopular, and opposed by an official Liberal candidate. When he refused to stand down the split in the Liberal ranks let in the Conservative.

In the Municipal elections of 1919, Labour did well and one of the results was closer cooperation between the Liberal Party and the Conservative Party. After 1919, they divided up seats and jobs on the Council. By 1923 they had reached an agreement on seats and aldermen that effectively meant they were acting as two wings of one party, although they did not formally come together until 1928. The divisions that existed within the Coalition were not primarily between Liberal and

Conservative. The main division was between those who wished to keep public spending to a minimum and those who were prepared to see some public development of an expanding city that badly needed modernising. Right up to 1937 there was a strong 'economy' group in the Coalition that was opposed to most forms of public expenditure. Even on the question of a town hall, where most authorities tend to be a bit expansive, the economy group held schemes up for years, on the ground that the city could not afford it. A compromise was reached within the ruling circles to go for a modest building that would be funded by having shops on the ground floor, but this was turned down by the Local Government Board as being unworthy of the city, and the original scheme was eventually put in hand just before the first war.[4]

In the aftermath of the war it was clear that public intervention was needed in providing working class housing, and the Government made plans for local authority spending. In Coventry, the Coalition members resigned en masse from the Housing Committee, and for the next three years, until they lost their seats, Labour Councillors, in a minority on the Council, were able to run the Housing Committee and establish a modest programme of council house building. It may be that the Coalition members of the Housing Committee had been demoralised by the recent rent strike on the Stoke Heath estate, the first council estate in the city, when amongst other facts, it emerged that several Councillors who were builders had done very well out of putting up expensive but shoddy houses.[5] Whatever the reasons it was a remarkable example of the Coalition's lack of enthusiasm for public spending.

Throughout the inter-war years, almost all the figures on comparative expenditure by county boroughs show Coventry lagging behind the majority, in particular on libraries, houses, schools and poor relief. Coventry therefore, was low in the list of rates levied per head. Speaking at a Rotary meeting in 1925, the City Treasurer claimed that 'Coventry, at the present moment, may be described as a ratepayers' paradise'.[6] It is not known if this favourable aspect encouraged more concerns to move into the city, but the extension of the city and lower than average rates of unemployment allowed a policy of inactivity to survive, and presumably won some political support for the Coalition.

A good example of the way the Coalition managed the city can be seen in expenditure on education in the inter-war period. The city was fortunate in having the funds of several charities at its disposal. The Chairman of the Education Committee spelt out this happy position:

> ... the cost of secondary education of boys in the City to the

> ratepayers was nil. They had never had to bear the cost of a Council secondary school for boys. The secondary education of boys had been defrayed by past benefactors. They were unique in any city of their size and importance ... Supplementary to that, in fifty years of technical education in the City the only capital expenditure on technical education had been £6,000. They sent annually to the Universities 12 to 15 boys and girls from monies left by benefactors.[7]

The benefits of past generosity were used to justify parsimony at the expense of educational standards. Coventry was faced by a rapid rise in the number of school children in the War and immediate post-war years and a steady increase in the late 1930s. The city lagged behind in the provision of new primary schools, and the result was severe overcrowding throughout the city in the 1920s and in the new suburbs in the 1930s. Old and inadequate schools remained open long after they had been condemned. While the charities funded boys' secondary education, girls had to rely on the Education Committee; in the inter-war period there were only two small secondary schools for girls in the city, both underfunded and overcrowded. Barrs Hill School had originally been the home of J.K. Starley, the cycle maker; by the 1930s it housed 436 in cramped conditions.[8]

The independence of the boys secondary schools was something of a myth. Bablake School depended on charities controlled effectively by the Council. Most of its Governing Board were members of the city Education Committee, including the Director of Education. Both it and the Grammar School were given money when they ran into trouble, but neither were owned by the city, and could determine their own policy. The result was that in many years even when children passed the tests applied by the Education Committee they were not sure of a place, as the schools reserved a number of places for fee payers and kept the number of places for scholarship holders to a very low number indeed. Even those lucky enough to get a scholarship received less money than was given in nearby rural areas. It was more difficult for a working class boy to get a secondary education in Coventry than almost anywhere else in the country. It is interesting to note that the sons of the Coalition were much more likely to be sent to Bablake School, with its lower fees, than to the more prestigious Grammar school.

Elementary education also suffered from a programme of extreme economy. During the national reorganisation of elementary organisation, Coventry's Director of Education was summoned to London to explain why the city hoped to carry its programme through without requiring any new schools. The record of the meeting notes

> One gathered from Mr. Harrod's general remarks that industrially the position at Coventry was far from unsatisfactory. There was, however, an 'economist' element on the Council headed by the deputy Mayor.[9]

In contrast to an underfunded school system was the pattern of technical education in the city, which by the 1930s was seen as a model for the rest of the country. Technical education preserved the social leadership of the Coalition while ensuring a supply of skilled workers to the local factories. One of the few monuments of one hundred years of the Coalition was the Technical College, built in 1933. Its grandiose facade contrasts with shabby schools and overcrowded classes. Even here the 'economy' element hesitated; plans had been drawn up in 1920 but there were always good reasons for delay, and in 1933 the Coalition split on the issue of whether the College could be afforded. The project was agreed only because Labour also supported it.

A more detailed study of the development of education in the inter-war period would reveal a lot about Coalition values and assumptions, about how Coalition policy reinforced Coalition values and ensured cohesiveness in the 'shopocracy' and how in the long term the failure to spend money condemned the Coalition. Extreme economy, besides creating tensions within the ruling group itself was clearly an inadequate philosophy for a changing city. Some developments, such as new roads, new services to the new private housing estates, renovation and slum clearance in the City centre, had to be undertaken, but a spirit of meanness and a lack of expertise hindered what work was put in hand. One of the very few schemes to improve the city centre was the building of Hertford Street. The council ended up paying high prices for land and the scheme took much longer to complete than was expected. Labour, suspicious of profiteering, was able to make various criticisms about the Council's ability to plan and carry out work.

By the 1930s Coventry, a modern industrial city, had a ramshackle administration and a congested city centre. It was not without charm, as J.B. Priestley discovered on his visit to the city:

> You peep round a corner and see half-timbered and gabled houses that would do for the second act of the "Meistersinger". In fact you could stage the

> "Meistersinger"—or film it—in Coventry. I knew it was an old place—for wasn't there Lady Godiva?— but I was surprised to find how much of the past, in soaring stone, and carved wood, still remained in the city.[10]

A less romantic view was presented by an editorial in the *Midland Daily Telegraph*:

> Coventry is now emerging from the shackles of a purely utilitarian era, stretching back for a hundred years or more. It has been an era of commercial revolution allied with civic stagnation during which the city has been so intent upon servicing the machine that it has given little thought to the service of its people. There are vast arrears to be overtaken, for succeeding generations have contented themselves in seeking solutions to the problem of the moment, and have given little thought to the future in any other sphere than those of mechanics and invention. Generations of bad planning—or a complete absence of planning—slums, narrow streets, overcrowding, sewers, all the trouble saved up for the present from an unimaginative past, must be tackled.[11]

This indictment of the Coalition only appeared in the paper as it was attacking Labour for complaining about the Hertford Street scheme; nevertheless it shows that the dead weight of the Coalition past was bearing down heavily on it by the 1930s.

With a gradual improvement in the Labour vote in the 1930s, it was clear to the Coalition that its days were numbered unless drastic action was taken. Labour had hopes of taking power in the 1936 local elections, but although it advanced, it failed to do so. It was clear that it only had to retain its vote to win in 1937. The Coalition decided on a new initiative, and launched a new Party, called the Progressive Party. There were two reasons for this change; one was to improve organisation, the other was to draw in support, in particular, from Coventry industrialists.

For years the Coalition had won elections because of the weakness of the Labour Party rather than because of its own strength. An editorial in the *Midland Daily Telegraph* complained of the fact that the Labour Party had a central organisation, did political work throughout the year, and had developed a policy for the city. The Coalition, it disarmingly revealed, had done none of this:

> In recent years the Coalition has attempted to meet this

> Socialist organisation by placing in the field candidates whose names have been unknown to their constituents until a few days prior to nomination day. Elections have been fought on hastily-recruited ward committees, their organisation dependent upon the varying enthusiasm of individual candidates, and the degree of support they have been able to command among their personal friends.[12]

In order to win support from industrialists, the new Progressive Party claimed that its establishment 'would remove any suggestion of political interest'.[13] This was part of its approach of trying to portray Labour as dogmatic, and its candidates controlled by the Labour Party, but more specifically it was intended to make possible closer links with the C.D.E.E.A. This body had as public policy a determination to avoid any form of party politics. By claiming to have broken from the Liberal and Conservative parties (despite the fact that its Chairman was the leader of the Conservatives and its Vice-Chairman was the leader of the Liberals) the Progressive Party hoped to get support. It needed money, organisation and candidates. It had lost several seats in the 1930s simply because of its failure to find candidates.

The Progressive Party had some success in getting money. The C.D.E.E.A. did hold meetings to discuss how to boost its fortunes to stave off the Socialist threat. One of its members acted as treasurer, and no doubt because of this the money was found to pay for a full-time agent. Few industrialists, however, were prepared to put any time into building up the new Party. In the elections in November 1937 the Party was able to contest every seat for the first time for some years, but Labour won control of the Council. The *Midland Daily Telegraph* admitted the lack of progress that the new Party had made. The Progressives had

> a dearth of that type of candidate for municipal honour which is truly representative of the commercial and industrial life of the city. It has not been necessary to penetrate far "behind the scenes" to become aware of the almost frenzied search for candidates that has taken place during the months of September and October ... The work of the City Council has been carefully shunned by many of our outstanding business men.[14]

Although the C.D.E.E.A. continued to monitor the work of the Progressive Party, and to fund it, in 1938, it was unable to halt its decline. In the 1938 elections of the nine Labour councillors who were elected, five were unopposed.

With no common ideals other than opposition to socialism, no policies other than curbs on public spending, no electoral machinery, and a declining social base, it was clear that in the 1930s the Coalition remained in power by default. It had been able to project itself as the social leadership of the city and use its powers to look after its social base, but had lacked the will and ability to develop policies that could have encouraged industry to have supported it, or working people to be attracted to it. Its inability to plan to meet the needs of the city and develop a modern infrastructure meant that its removal ended an obstacle to progress, not just to working people, but to a wide range of commercial and industrial interests. It had outlived its usefulness, and Labour's victory, besides making possible the application of progressive policies, also provided an opportunity to make the city more responsive to the needs of modern manufacturers.

George Hodgkinson, one of the leaders of the Labour Party, not unnaturally saw Labour's victory in November 1937 as the start of a new age:

> To us the clouds had lifted, the people had responded to the appeal "England arise, the long long night is over". Our dreams had become a reality, we had escaped from history and saw the dawn of a new day.[15]

His exuberance can be excused by the fact that over a period of fifteen years he and a small group of Labour leaders had succeeded in taking the Party from a situation where it had ill-defined policies and no clear political practice to one where it concentrated all its energies into the drive for municipal power. The result of a victory over an ailing if not senile opposition, meant that Labour, far from having stormed the citadel of Capital, had to preside over the renewal of the city, and make up for several decades of neglect. Though many of Labour's policies were aimed at improving the lot of working people, they were bound to improve services to capital as well. The taking of municipal power by Labour had no impact on class relations within the city, nor industrial relations within the workplace; an obvious point, but one not always grasped by a Party dedicated to municipal socialism.

Almost inevitably, a Party that so dedicates itself will tend to overemphasise the importance of local power both to its supporters and to its activists. As we shall see, the failure of the trade unions in the industrial struggle pushed the Coventry Labour Party into seeking its salvation in the municipal strategy. Initially it hoped to achieve through the electoral system what it could not achieve in the factories; a defeat of the capitalist system. However, instead of the reality of the Coalition pushing Labour into a broader strategy with an industrial element to it, it tended to fix Labour firmly into the field of municipal politics.

Labour projected itself as the party of planning. Municipal enterprise and cooperative ideals would be linked in a planned way to create socialism. Many of Labour's leaders were active in the cooperative movement, and their vision of socialism—large, generous, and undefined—was that of a cooperative movement that embraced the whole city. Public ownership, properly handled, was the key to socialism. As the Labour Party's election newspaper pointed out to its readers:

> The safeguards of municipal health and sanitation, the facilities of municipal recreation, the opportunities of municipal education—all these are so much a part of our lives that we rarely stop to think: "Why, this is pure socialism!"[16]

In 1935, when the City Council agreed to promote a Parliamentary Bill to extend its powers, Labour saw this as a victory for socialism. The Bill was necessary in particular to deal with the new lands that the City had taken over in view of its expansion. It sought to acquire powers to drill water wells, acquire land for roads, close private slaughterhouses, and set out an airport and parks. It was not controversial, yet Hodgkinson at the Council meeting declared 'We are all socialists now' and Labour made it clear they supported the Bill as a socialist measure. Certainly their opponents, having had an extreme policy of non-intervention, tended to look uneasy when presiding over the inevitable growth in the authority of city departments. Coalition parsimony tended to encourage Labour to overemphasise the socialist aspect of extending Council services.

These services had to be planned. The worst charge that Labour could throw at the Coalition was that it failed to plan municipal enterprises. In its election address in 1936 it claimed of the Coalition

> They part with land cheaply which should be retained. They have entered into commitments that must force up expenditure, and then borrow, the full weight of which is reserved for tomorrow. They do not plan. They wait upon events.[17]

Much of the planning was needed to overcome the financial problems that could follow from increased municipal enterprise. Some members of the Labour Party had a positive horror of borrowing; T.J. Harris, the first Labour Mayor of Coventry could seldom be restrained from preaching against its evils. His views were not shared by all his colleagues, though he was an influential spokesman for Labour throughout the inter-war period. A fear of borrowing could be a great handicap to a Council that needed to spend money. Labour hoped that planning and intervention could get round the problem. Shortly after it came to power Labour devised a five-year plan for capital expenditure. Instead of rushing to spend, it decided on a long term approach, which is why it had little impact on the city in the 19 months it was in power before the outbreak of the war. In opposition it had suggested the establishment of a Stabilised Fund; money would regularly be put aside in order to abolish the city's debts and establish a fund that could finance the schools, roads and other desirable items. Unfortunately, it was pointed out that this would take centuries to achieve. Labour had opposed all Coalition attempts to sell off land. Money should be raised by using the land to establish new municipal concerns such as a bank and printing department. Even before Labour came to power Hodgkinson was urging the Council to 'look forward to the day when central property would be required by the Corporation for laying out the centre of the city on the lines followed by Continental cities'.[18] Such planning was not only for a better city; it was an investment that would yield funds for social spending.

Shortly after its successful election, Labour set out its programme. It contained a commitment to increased spending on housing and education, a minimum wage for council employees, better use of municipal undertakings, and an attempt to provide council tenants with information about their rights. This was overshadowed by the establishment of the Policy Advisory Committee, an attempt to work out long term policy for the city. Because so much emphasis was put on the work of this Committee, and because it produced little before the war, it is not possible to assess the work of Labour in its pre-war control of the city. It is clear, however, that Labour's relations with the unions were not all sweetness and light. Its decision to increase the wages of its lower paid staff led to demarcation troubles, and to the Joint Negotiating Committee complaining bitterly. An attempt to introduce worker participation on buses and trams fell apart, leaving Hodgkinson musing on the problem of the lack of trade union idealism:

> Were we to be the milch cow for the trade unions and to what

> extent would they share the responsibility of government? In a city of militant trade unionism and with the fighting spirit in our own blood how could we comport the clashing forces? The Labour Party had power in its hands, it had socialist aims, but could it be said that our affiliates had socialism in their hearts, and were we to be activated by "divine discontent" or a scramble for a penny bun?[19]

This view of Labour as the upholder of socialist values against materialist trade unions was very far from the links between socialism and workplace action that left-wingers had tried to create after the first war, and was a reflection of how far Labour had come. To trace this change it is necessary to look at the crucial post-war period.

Labour and revolutionary socialism.

Prior to the First World War, the dominant labour movement body in the city was the Trades and Labour Council. It had been established a decade before the Labour Party, it had more affiliations from trade union branches, and it took up local issues on behalf of the trade unions. During the war, Coventry's trade unions, mostly of recent foundation, grew rapidly and took part in major strikes, particularly over shop stewards' recognition in 1917 and the embargo on the use of skilled workers in 1918. As Coventry did not have a long tradition as an engineering centre—the craft unions arrived in the city only a few years before the Workers' Union—craft exclusiveness did not reach the levels of other centres. It was possible for the Coventry Engineering Joint Committee to achieve an uneasy ascendency over the trade union movement in the city, and unite skilled and unskilled in the campaign for a shop stewards' movement. The Coventry Shop Stewards and Workers Committee Movement had been set up as a radical alternative to existing unions, on the basis of one union for all workers, and this had some influence in 1917 particularly at the Hotchkiss works. It remained on the sidelines for most of the war, however, as many radicals saw the official Joint Committee as the best body to unite workers in the factories. The focus of labour and socialist activity remained in the workplaces and in the arguments over reforming the unions and supporting the Bolshevik revolution. The Labour Party, in common with the other municipal parties, gave up most of its activity during the war, and consequently played no part in the industrial action. Social protests, such as complaints about bad housing and high food prices, were mostly led by the trade unions.

Despite its eclipse by the unions, Labour, as the only working class political party, benefited from the radicalism and spread of trade unionism of the war years. In the election in December 1918 Labour stood for the first time, and although there was a split between pro-war and anti-war socialists the Labour candidate came a respectable second, behind the Conservative, but ahead of a demoralised Liberal vote that had also been split. This success was carried through to the municipal election in 1919. There was still confusion as to who were official Labour candidates, but the Party picked up half the seats. (Prior to the war it had only elected three councillors). This electoral success did not reflect a growth in membership of the Party, nor a major commitment to concentration on municipal power. In the post-war years Labour's relations with the unions were unclear, and the Party lacked specific goals. As the radicalism of the war years died down, it lost ground in the electoral field, and saw its political authority challenged by workshop-based politics. Most of the Labour councillors who won seats in 1919 lost them three years later, and for most of the 1920s Labour's representation on the Council was down to pre-war levels, and with the exception of Alice Arnold, its councillors were described in the Tory press as 'moderates'. One was so moderate that the Coalition did not stand against him. In 1921 Labour was only able to contest half of the municipal seats.

In contrast to its poor results in the local elections, Labour benefited from a recovery in the Liberal vote to narrowly win the general election seat in a tight three-cornered conflict in 1923. It lost it next year. The local press sought to claim that Labour's poor showing was due to close identification with trade union militants, but the reality was that Labour was on the sidelines during the industrial struggles that occurred in the city in the early 1920s.

The post-war years in Coventry were marked by an economic boom which stopped dead in the autumn of 1920, and was followed by an economic crisis, particularly in the motor industry. They were also marked by a volatile political climate, mass politics on the streets, and a determined attempt by the small Communist party to win working class support away from Labour.

The small group of Socialist Labour Party members and Workers Committee supporters who founded the Coventry Communist Party in 1920, were mostly unemployed, and put much of their activity into setting up a local unemployed workers' movement. Initially rejecting all elections as a sham, they sought to organise workers into self-activity that would have revolutionary potential. Their partial success in the period up to 1923 throws light on the way the Labour Party approached working people.

For a period of two years from the autumn of 1920, unemployment in Coventry was at a very high level. It eventually declined as the motor industry stabilised itself, and for much of the 1920s Coventry was in a favourable position compared to most of the country. However, the newly formed Communist Party was able to seize the opportunity created by heavy unemployment after several years of full employment, and establish a Coventry Unemployed Workers Committee. This claimed to have been elected at a mass meeting, and that all its major decisions were taken at mass meetings; these were indeed a feature of the movement but in reality the body was from the beginning under Communist leadership. Its aim was uncompromising:

> The Committee is determined not to lead the Workers into side issues, but insist upon the overthrow of capitalism as the only solution for unemployment and all the grievances of the workers which arise from their status as wage slaves ...[20]

Initially the C.U.W.C. put much store on marches and open air meetings, but as time went by effort had to be put into negotiating with Boards of Guardians and the Council. In Foleshill the Board of Guardians was particularly strict in their interpretation of the Poor Laws, and the fact that this area included the council estate at Stoke Heath meant that there was very quickly an Unemployed Workers Committee in action, and several clashes with the police took place. Most of the work was not of a spectacular nature, and led to complaints that local Labour councillors should be doing it.

The parading of thousands of unemployed men round the city was a public coup for the Communist Party. It led to the Anglican church establishing an alternative movement, that did not last long, and to the A.E.U. setting up a movement for its own members. To complement its work with the unemployed, the Communist Party had set up a Workers Committee as a focus for reforming trade unionism around the shop stewards' movement. Although it achieved some recognition in the local trade union movement, its leaders, men like Tom Dingley, who had been imprisoned for his union activities in the war, were mostly unemployed, and it was therefore mainly a propaganda vehicle. It helped to bring Communist and Labour activists together, as did the Council of Action in 1919 and 1920, which opposed British intervention in Russia. It was clear that sympathy for the Bolshevik revolution, and for ideas of direct action, workers' control and soviets went beyond the ranks of the Communist Party, and attracted many in the Labour Party. It was still possible at the time to belong to both parties, though Coventry Communists were very critical of the Labour Party.

In many parts of the country the Independent Labour Party played an important part in building up the individual membership of the Labour Party, and in providing activists for leadership. In Coventry, the I.L.P. was comparatively weak, and in a well-organised coup, the majority voted to join the C.P. This led to a court case over ownership of the I.L.P. buildings, and contributed to bad feelings locally between the Labour and Communist parties. Coventry was one of the few places in the country where this happened. It did not appear to lead to any permanent strengthening of the C.P. which remained small for all of this period, but it weakened the Labour Party, as the I.L.P. never really became a force in the city.

The success of the Communists in organising an unemployed movement led to a special effort being made by the C.P. to establish Coventry as one of its centres. Jack Leckie, who had been active in the war in the shop stewards movement in Scotland was sent into the city to be the C.P. candidate in the next general election. This was a bold choice, as Leckie, like many other Coventry Communists, came from an anti-parliamentary tradition. One (admiring) description of him was a 'a physical force Anarchist and ardent anti-Parliamentarian, who breathes dynamite and talks red armies!'[21] Unemployment and unrest in the factories, combined with a lack of a tradition of Labour politics, created ideal conditions for the C.P. from the autumn of 1921. Basil Thompson, who reported to the Cabinet on the red menace in Britain appeared to be helped by a police agent in the small ranks of the Coventry Communist Party, and many of their activities were blown up out of all proportion in his reports to the Cabinet. But in early 1922 Thompson was consistently sounding the alarm:

> Violent speeches, by Tom Dingley, Leonard Jackson, and other local agitators, which are now of almost daily occurrence, take place entirely unchecked, and it is generally thought that the seeds of serious trouble are being sown in the city. Twelve months ago these extremists had a comparatively small following in Coventry. They were discredited by the great majority of the workers, and there was very little sympathy for them when they were prosecuted. The large amount of prolonged unemployment amongst the engineering

> workers of this centre, however, has made fertile soil for the Communist propaganda, and revolutionary doctrines are gaining much support of late. The national leaders of the Communist movement make a special mark of Coventry, and such men as James Stewart, Jack Leckie, ex-Colonel Malon, George Ebury, William Gee, and William Gallacher, are so well known here that they are almost regarded as local men. There is no doubt that a great deal will be heard of these men during Leckie's electioneering campaign. I wish to point out the urgent need for counter propaganda in Coventry at the present time.[22]

The Communist challenge reached its peak in the spring of 1922 when industrial conflict coincided with social and political struggle. The engineering lockout gave an impetus to the unemployed movement, and gave the Communists the chance to show an alternative, revolutionary model to that of the Labour Party. For a few extraordinary months a public battle for the leadership of the Labour movement took place in the city. The C.U.W.C. decided to contest the elections for the Coventry Board of Guardians for the first time in the spring, and this meant standing against Labour as well as the Coalition. Attacks were made on the C.U.W.C. as a Communist front, but the C.U.W.C. felt that as it had done the hard work in fighting the Guardians, it represented the unemployed much more directly than did the Labour candidates. Indeed, there was a contrast between the engineering workers, all male, who stood for the C.U.W.C. and the women and retired men who stood for the Labour Party, who had little involvement in industry, but knew more about the Poor Laws. In the event the C.U.W.C. candidates all came bottom of the poll, though they took enough votes to ensure that Labour had no successes. As a result of their intervention, participation in the election went from 12 per cent in 1921 to 50 per cent in 1922.

The Communists used the C.U.W.C. as the base to obtain recognition in the local labour movement, and as a core of support for Jack Leckie's campaign for the next general election. Some opponents claimed that people had to declare support for Leckie in order to be allowed to join the C.U.W.C.; whether true or not, it is clear that quite a lot wanted to join. Persuading trade union branches to adopt Leckie was more difficult. The competition had been made more interesting by the fact that Labour had selected as its candidate the leader of the Transport Workers, Bob Williams, recently expelled from the Communist Party for his part in 'Black Friday'.[23] At one meeting called to endorse Williams as candidate, a delegate from the C.U.W.C. made frequent interjections, and the local official of the Vehicle Builders' Union was unfortunate enough to be heard exclaiming 'Bugger the unemployed!' When he refused to apologise, demonstrators appeared at his home and work. He took out a summons against the leaders of the demonstration. In court they refused to give sureties for their behaviour, and were joined by Wal Hannington who was himself in court that day for a speech he had made a month earlier. Ever alert to publicity, Hannington changed his plea and refused to be bound over. All six were sent to Winson Green jail. That night, thousands held a torchlight procession in Coventry, a Free Speech Committee was formed (an act of unconscious irony in view of the cause of the incident) and a picket of the N.U.V.B. offices took place. After a somewhat ungracious apology from the official, the six agreed to be bound over, and returned immediately to the city. The incident was trivial in itself, but occurring during the lockout, and centring on relations between Communist and Labour, it gives an indication of the extraordinary atmosphere at the time.

The 'managerial functions' dispute was a national conflict over a range of workplace issues. To management it was a question of who managed the workplaces; to unions it was the right to apply overtime restrictions, reduce the number of young workers in the factories, and protect the rights of skilled workers to the exclusive use of some work and machines. In Coventry, with a weak tradition of craft unionism, and with some of the most advanced engineering machinery in the country, questions of manning and demarcation tended to have a greater degree of flexibility than in other centres.

The dispute marked a turning point in the history of the unions in the city. The radicalism of the shop stewards movement made its last stand. (Most stewards had been sacked well before the dispute began). It was the first time the engineering unions had been in an all out stoppage, and their disastrous defeat set back the labour movement in the city for over a decade. It destroyed Communist pretensions to leadership and pushed the Labour Party away from workshop politics. It began quietly with just the A.E.U. coming out on strike. The C.D.E.E.A. had gone to great efforts to identify each member of the A.E.U. in their workplaces, and those that did not want to go (a small number) were pushed. For most of the dispute it was a lockout.

For the first two months of the dispute, the A.E.U., by far the largest union in the city, were out on their own, before all the other engineering unions were locked out as well. Everything was quiet for the first five weeks, much to the frustration of the C.U.W.C. It had many ex-union members in its ranks, and was keen to play a major part in picketing the workplaces. It won the support of the A.E.U. Unemployed Committee, but was kept at arm's length by the A.E.U. District Committee. This body, remote from the workshops, found that it could not mobilise its own members, a sad comment on the decline of the shop stewards. After about five weeks of the dispute, the first signs of cracks in the union appeared, and there were reports of groups of men returning to work. The C.U.W.C. had hundreds of potential pickets at its command, the support of the A.E.U. Unemployed Committee, and a clear indication of the A.E.U.'s District Committee's inability to mobilise the membership. Leckie was invited to speak to the District Committee and told them bluntly that the left was going to take over the dispute in the city. He accused the D.C. of splitting ranks, and said,

> they were now determined to fix up an unofficial committee to take control of the Lockout. The Rank and File were disgusted with the position in Coventry and he gave 24 hours ultimatum to link up with the Central Unemployed Committee. They had between 12 and 13 hundred members and would know what to do.[24]

The D.C. refused to come to an agreement, and their next meeting was broken up for a time by a group of members insisting on a settlement with the C.U.W.C. The same meeting, when it resumed, heard further reports of men returning to work and the lack of union response. It was forced to give way. That evening Jack Leckie spoke at an A.E.U. meeting alongside the full time officials, and details of the new Joint Council of Trade Unions and Unemployed was given. Almost at once the character of the dispute changed, and became much more public. The same evening, 2,000 people descended on the Hotchkiss works, where men had gone back. Windows were broken, blacklegs attacked, the works were invaded and only cleared when Leckie persuaded the men to leave. For the next few weeks the lockout dominated the city, with daily demonstrations and mass picketing.

The new arrangement in effect put the Communist Party in the leadership of the dispute, by far the largest seen in the city since 1860. It also linked the industrial conflict with the unemployed issue, and was used by the Party to create support for their Parliamentary campaign. The Party's hour had come, and it was determined to seize the opportunity with both hands. In reality, the local branch of the Communist Party never had more than a couple of dozen active members. The Party was able to have this brief flowering as its policy of linking industrial with political struggle meant that in the crisis facing trade unionists it could put forward coherent policies while the trade union leadership failed to rise to the new situation, and the Labour Party remained ineffective. Many trade unionists, Labour supporters, threw in their lot with the C.U.W.C. as they were seen to be organising and fighting.

After eight weeks of the lockout, the other engineering unions were locked out as well. In an engineering centre like Coventry, the dispute took on the flavour of a general stoppage, though the non-federated firms were not involved. Leckie and the C.U.W.C., as the mass movement, continued to run the dispute in the public way they had used in the past. On 3 May the factories were opened to all workers prepared to accept the new conditions of work. The local paper reported picketing at every factory, and 'the locked-out men and the unemployed had their headquarters on the Pool Meadow from which there was directed a stream of scouts on motor bicycles and push cycles, who reported periodically as to the situation at the different works.[25]

In the early morning there were incidents at a small engineering company where workers had not come out. Two of the Communist leaders of the C.U.W.C. had led a crowd to occupy the building, there had been fighting, a police baton charge and the arrest of the leaders. When the news reached Pool Meadow, the crowd, several thousand strong, 'a mass of singing and marching men and women' marched to the Town Hall and surrounded it and the Police Station. Leckie and union officials managed to persuade the police to release the men uncharged; the Red Flag was sung and the crowd returned to Pool Meadow. No industrial dispute since the strike of 1860 when homeworkers marched round the factories had had such an impact on the city. The mass picketing and demonstrations carried on for several weeks, and was a feature of the lockout in Coventry. In most other engineering centres the lockout was a quiet affair. In Coventry, thanks to the role of the C.U.W.C., 'blacklegs' were followed home from work by crowds, and groups of cycle pickets were despatched from the city to Rugby, Nuneaton, and other nearby centres. The C.D.E.E.A. protested strongly to the Council about the 'intimidation' and eventually persuaded it to draft in extra police.

Wherever there was a mass picket, there too was Jack Leckie. Bob Williams, the Labour candidate, in contrast took no part in the dispute other than writing a letter to the local paper accusing Leckie of using the dispute to develop an anti-capitalist movement, and of driving people away from the struggle. At the time it seemed like sour grapes, but Williams could comfort himself with the thought that the end of the dispute would bring the end of Leckie's moment of glory.

In fact Leckie dropped out of the conflict before it was over, as he was injured in a motor cycle accident while returning from picketing in Nuneaton. Without him, and without Dingley who was arrested and imprisoned for seditious speeches, the picketing began to flag, particularly after the Birmingham police arrived. The long dispute also had an effect on morale. The Communists had been able to run the struggle in Coventry, but had no influence on national negotiations. Under promptings from Leckie, the District Committees of the fifteen unions involved agreed to stand together until a solution was reached that was acceptable to all, but when a national agreement was reached Coventry trade unionists returned to work at the same time as the rest of the country.

The national settlement was a climb-down for the unions, and the A.E.U. and two other unions refused to accept it, until a ballot had been taken. Although up to this point comparatively few A.E.U. members had broken ranks, it was clear that the lockout had been lost, and in the last few days of the dispute many A.E.U. members returned to work. Some went back in confusion, seeing members of other unions returning, some went back in panic, as employers stated they would not sack the blackleg staff they had taken on. Despite all the previous demonstrations and mass picketing, the virtual collapse of the strike in the last few days and the scramble to return was another feature peculiar to Coventry; perhaps a further indication of the lack of experience of most Coventry trade unionists. The A.E.U. District Committee, disgusted with this conclusion to the dispute, and feeling betrayed by the settlement, decided to impose a series of fines and exclusions on all members who went back early. This turned out to be a disastrous mistake. After 13 weeks of lockout and a humiliating settlement men were in no mood to pay a fine to their union. In many cases union branch officials had gone back as well, regarding the ballot as a formality. The result was that thousands of union members, including many branch secretaries, refused to pay the fines and either lapsed from the union or were expelled. Moreover, having expelled so many for non-payment of fines, the District Committee was unable to recruit them again unless they were prepared to pay their fines. The District Committee action turned defeat into a rout, and put an obstacle to union recruitment for the next decade. This, combined with a well-organised attempt by employers to penalise activists, led to a rapid decline in A.E.U. membership in Coventry. By the end of 1922 more than half its members had left; whole branches and their records disappeared, the shop stewards movement ceased to function, and many workshops became virtually non-union. Without stewards, and without the prospect of success on workplace issues, union membership continued to decline in 1923 and subsequent years. By the time of the general strike union membership was down to a quarter of the 1920 figure; the reality was worse, as membership figures included retired members. The fact was that most departments in most factories became non-union. Although union membership declined throughout the country, the rapid decline in Coventry was a peculiar local feature. While mainly caused by misjudgement on the part of the A.E.U., the very intensity of the struggle in Coventry may have contributed to the intensity of the defeat.

The defeat of the unions pricked the revolutionary bubble of the Communist Party. In the interests of unity (and due to a change of line) it was decided not to contest Coventry in the next general election after all, and Leckie departed for a Party job in London. The low morale of the leadership, combined with rising fortunes in the vehicle industry led to a collapse of the C.U.W.C. in 1923. As part of the change of line more emphasis was put on unity, and a new body linking unions with the unemployed was established under the auspices of the Trades Council. But the vital ingredient of mass action was missing. In the spring of 1923, Jack Preece, one of the leaders of the C.U.W.C., complained about Coventry: 'A one-time centre of revolutionary activity, but today a back-wash of deadly apathy and indifference'.[26]

Although the lockout had seemed to bring the industrial and political struggle together, and provide the Communist Party with a great opportunity of leadership, the Party required mass activity to sustain its challenge, and could not survive the defeats of the early 1920s. Its core had been the industrial militants of the war, and by the end of the lockout many had been worn out by unrelenting activity and poverty. Its decline had been precipitated by its political adventurism; most of the Coventry Communists came from the anti-Parliamentary movement that had no time for the Labour Party. After the lockout a rather half hearted attempt was made to join forces with the left in the Labour Party, and a few active Communists such as Bert Cresswell were active inside the Labour Party, a Labour Party also greatly influenced by the events of 1922.

Both before and during the war there had developed the tendency on the part of trade unions to see the Labour Party as the electoral wing of the trade unions, but quite separate and distinct from unions in terms of activity and sphere of influence. The post-war struggles opened up to many Labour activists the vista of linking workplace struggle with political activity, and many welcomed the formation of the Communist Party, and were prepared to work with it. But as it soon became clear that the Communist Party wanted to replace both the trade union leadership and the Labour Party it became easier for Labour to withdraw from any industrial activity and accuse the Communist Party of subverting the proper role of the unions. Many of the members of the Coventry Labour Party had the same aspirations as the Communists, but accepted that there was no alternative but to stand aside from the struggles around the lockout and wait for the Communist challenge to fail.

In denouncing the Communists' revolutionary strategy, Labour was helping to clarify its own. One of the lessons of the 1922 defeat was that the tide of revolution in the country had turned, and that the Parliamentary and municipal road was the only way forward. Labour's municipal achievements had been disappointing to date but the collapse of the alternative had shown the need to concentrate on electoral politics.

The defeat of the trade union movement also suggested to the Labour Party the need to move away from the unions, at least organisationally. A trade union movement in decline would drag down Labour unless it could stand on its own feet. The defeat of the unions was therefore shortly followed by an attempt to establish Labour with its own clear identity.

The decline of the unions and the collapse of the Communist Party also shut a number of doors for working class activists. For the next decade there was little opportunity for choice between the industrial field of action or the political field. The workshops became non-political. In October 1922 the A.E.U. District Committee resolved 'that we revert to the old system of shop stewards and appoint such from the membership in the various shops, without in any way notifying the employers upon the matter'.[27] The return to secrecy meant that many socialists, denied an active role in the trade unions, looked to the Labour Party for their expression.

Early in 1923 George Hodgkinson took over the post of secretary of the Labour Party, initially on a part-time basis but full time after Labour won the General Election. He claimed that he and the I.L.P. took the initiative to take Labour from under the shadow of the Trades Council and the Tenants Defence League (an off-shoot of the Trades Council) and that a new Labour Party was created in 1923. It seems more likely that his appointment reflected the determination to cut away from the rapidly declining organs of the Trades Council, and the desire to establish the Party in its own right. Prior to 1923 its activities had been ill-defined, its membership neglected and its councillors unorganised. In beginning the change, Labour was rejecting the synthesis of workshop and municipal politics that had seemed possible in the excitement of the post-war years. In rejecting the revolutionary road and discovering its own municipal road, Labour was also moving away from concepts of mass action, workshop practice and rank and file movements that had flourished briefly in these years. Furthermore, while stressing its independence from the trade union movement at a time when it was in decline, Labour was initiating a process of establishing the priority of municipal socialism over other forms of working class action.

The Decline of the Unions and the Rise of Labour.

The rapid rise of the engineering industry in Coventry, and in particular the rapid development of large scale production, involving some of the newest technology in the country made it difficult for the engineering unions to establish a firm hold on the consciousness of engineering workers in the city. These long established unions recruited exclusively skilled men for many years, men who saw themselves as an elite, and who were expected to prove themselves by taking individual action if need be to establish the district rate of pay at their workplace, or run the risk of expulsion from the union. In the face of large numbers of workers being signed up to do engineering work who had no or little training it was easy to retreat to a position of craft defensiveness which could be allied to socialist rhetoric, particularly if emphasis was put on workshop practice. In Coventry this defence was never very convincing. The new machinery was designed to make skills interchangeable and to greatly increase the proportion of unskilled to skilled workers needed in the factories. The task therefore was to articulate the needs of the semi- and unskilled workers. This the Workers Union had done, when it had flourished briefly just before and during the war. In the post-war recession its own generous benefit rates helped to bankrupt it when so many of its members were out of work. It was unable to achieve pay improvements at a time when the employers were insisting on major cuts, and it faced a continual attack from the skilled unions in the city, which while uncomfortable at the prospect of having to recruit the unskilled, were hostile to another union taking them and threatening their position.

The rapid decline of the Workers Union in the post war years points to the other side of the coin of the war-time radicalism of the unions. The ease with which both skilled and unskilled union members deserted their unions was a reflection of the shallowness of union consciousness. It was this sort of consciousness that allowed the Communists to flourish for a time, but could not sustain a revolutionary movement. Up to the 1922 lockout the engineering unions in the city had never faced a major challenge. The war strikes had been widespread, but the peculiar conditions of the time ensured that Government intervention one way or the other would soon come. Other strikes had also been partial or limited. The strikers in 1922 had to overcome a lack of experience, a craft tradition that left it up to the workers themselves to organise their own pickets, and a skin deep trade unionism in a city of young, inexperienced workers who cared little for the principles of 'mutuality' and job restriction on which the strike appeared to be based. In 1921 the average age of people in Coventry was only 29, and in Foleshill 26. Young people, with only a few years' industrial experience were not ready to be treated as disciplined craftsmen.

The decline in trade union membership begun in 1920 was greatly accelerated after the lockout, and continued for several more years. It then remained at an extremely low level until the mid 1930s when recruitment again began on a substantial scale. It was not until 1939 that union membership figures reached those of 1920, and this was after the rapid spread of armaments factories, and in a much larger population. For about fifteen years employers in advanced engineering factories had a workforce that was mostly union-free, and little or no opposition to changes in work and payments that were introduced. As a result, when trade unionism did re-emerge, it was very difficult for the unions to move on from struggles about bonus and piece work to challenge employers' control of work.

Prior to the lockout, the shop stewards' movement had mediated between union district committees and workers. With the virtual eclipse of stewards, district committees became isolated from workers. What struggles with employers that did take place were conducted in local conferences between employers' officials and union officials. There were many issues which the unions could not negotiate about simply because there was no one on the shop floor willing to initiate the procedure. This isolation pushed the District Committee into a corner. It felt that semi-skilled men were cooperating with employers to dilute jobs, and showed little interest in recruiting them. Right up to the war the District Committee consisted entirely of skilled members. Even recruitment of skilled members was difficult when the District Committee could not accept them into membership until they had paid the fines that had been imposed after the lockout. This proviso was dropped a few years after the lockout under pressure from the union head office. Even in the mid 1930s, when people were joining unions the District Committee refused to allow in workers who were not already getting the district rate. This made little sense in Coventry when semi-skilled workers could get below the district rate but through piecework earn more than skilled workers on only the district rate.

From about 1923, conditions for the motor industry picked up. Although it remained seasonal, and a high risk industry with several major companies going bankrupt in the 1930s, there was no doubt of many employers' ability to pay, and large groups of Coventry workers saw their standard of living steadily rising. The focus of struggle moved from the way work was organised to the price of the job; disputes over pay were therefore likely to be small, even individual, and the extent of piecework bargaining can only be guessed at. Employers, in general, were content to increase pay if productivity was also increasing, and piecework had the added attraction to them of encouraging workers to establish their own disciplines and speed of work. Surveys undertaken by the A.E.U. District Committee showed that most factories were relatively free of harsh discipline.[28]

Many workers did not entirely desert Labour when they deserted the unions. In 1923 the Labour vote increased in the General Election, and Labour won the seat for the first time. The response to the General Strike in 1926 also showed the willingness of many workers to identify with trade unionism in general, but not with unions in particular. In contrast to 1922, the strike in the city was a quiet affair, with no great demonstrations, little picketing, and no trouble with the police. The strike was conducted mainly by union officials acting through the Trades Council, supported by Labour Party activists. The transport and print workers came out as instructed, but a feature of the dispute in the city was a left initiative within the A.E.U. to class workers in car factories as transport workers, and insist that they come out too. Car companies were engaged in the finishing and despatching of vehicles, and some companies were hiring fleets of cars to avoid the problems caused by a lack of buses and trains, although there is no evidence of this happening in Coventry. This excuse for calling out all car workers was a bit thin, but the N.U.V.B., Coppersmiths, and Sheet Metal Workers all came out on the first day, and this put pressure on the A.E.U. to follow on the third day. Its call got a good response from its members, but to the surprise of unions and employers alike, thousands of ex-A.E.U. members struck as well, and remained out till the end of the strike.

It is not known how many non-unionists stopped work, but over 500 signed the A.E.U. vacancy book.[29] As they stood absolutely no chance of getting benefit, this appears to have been done out of habit, and only a small portion of the strikers did it. A further surprise to the A.E.U. was that after the strike very few rejoined the union. Membership increased by only 51, and this gain was lost in the next couple of months. Even those who made the unnecessary journey to sign the union book refrained from rejoining the union. It would appear that many workers found that Coventry trade unions had little to offer them except rhetoric and policies that were outdated or irrelevant, and therefore there was no incentive to join. However, an identity with the broad labour and trade union movement remained. The General Strike showed the potential of an appeal based on emotion and solidarity, one that could not be sustained on a day to day basis in the city.

While the General Strike remained the most dramatic indication of the hard contrast between working class potential and trade union actuality, this was also shown in the fortunes of the Labour Party in the city. In the 1920s Labour's success in the General Election contrasted with its failures in the local elections, but from 1928 there were signs of improvement. As a result of the boundary changes in that year all the Council seats were elected, and Labour won 11, a dramatic change as the most they had picked up in any one year between 1919 and 1928 was two. The Coalition won the remaining 34 seats, so there was still a long way to go, but from this time Labour had an effective and vocal team on the Council. The next year Labour won a majority of the seats contested. Labour hoped for political power early in the 1930s, but subsequent progress, though steady, was slow. Its final victory was through very gradually strengthening its vote at a time when the Coalition was in decay. Interestingly for most of this period the increase in the Labour vote was not reflected in increasing strength in the trade union movement.

Labour relied heavily on the unions for finance and support in elections. It did not rely heavily on individual members. When Hodgkinson began building the Labour Party in 1923 and 1924 he was able to establish ward organisation and a women's section, and this led to a recruitment drive. By September 1925 the Party had recruited its thousandth member. This impetus was not sustained; by the end of the decade membership was down to half this figure, and although it improved in the mid 1930s it declined again after Labour won the Council. Its membership in 1938 was below that of 1925; for most of the 1930s Labour Party membership was higher in Nuneaton than in Coventry, and after 1937 it was higher in Rugby.[30]

It is possible that Hodgkinson's election to the Council in 1928 had something to do with low membership, for inevitably the focus switched to Council politics. It is also possible that the phenomenon of Labour advance and union decline indicated passive support for Labour and a lack of a union campaign to sign people up.

Labour was successful in drawing together a team of spokesmen and women who could handle municipal politics. More time and effort was required to prepare for municipal power, and Labour slowly came to attract people who were not active in their union or working in factories. Of the 31 Labour councillors and aldermen whose occupations can be identified in 1936-38, only seven were, or had close links with, manual workers, and only four had close links with engineering workers. There were a number of middle class activists, including clergymen, a number of women recorded as housewives, and about one third were Co-op employees. Compared to early post-war figures, this represents a shift away from trade union activists, but this has to be treated with caution, as a number of Labour activists got jobs with Coventry Co-op either because they couldn't get a job in the engineering industry, or because they couldn't get a job that would allow time off to carry out Council business. The Co-op, the only Labour source of patronage, was thus a refuge for Labour activists. However, it is clear that Labour in the 1930s was able to attract some non-working class support, while its leadership remained as leaders because they had severed many of their links with the trade unions.

The danger of a local study is of an overemphasis on special local conditions and the playing down of national politics. Throughout most of the inter-war years, notwithstanding some remarkable vicissitudes, Labour established itself as a major Parliamentary force, and for a few years, a Party of Government. The habit of voting Labour gradually spread among working people and no doubt national developments affected voting patterns in Coventry in a similar way as they did in other parts of the country. What is of interest in Coventry was that for a number of years the number of people voting Labour greatly outnumbered the number of people joining trade unions, just as the response to the General Strike went beyond the trade union movement. The result of this was to reinforce the lesson that Labour learnt in the city in 1922; that Labour and the unions had their own separate concerns with their own momentum and to an increasing extent their own separate personnel. A second result was for Labour to place its struggle on a higher plane than that of the unions. Increasingly the unions were concerned with money, while Labour was concerned with social justice for all. The irony of course was that the decision by Labour to concentrate on municipal politics made it more likely that workplace politics in turn would become narrower in focus.

From about 1934 onwards, trade union membership began to improve, very slowly at first but speeding up from 1937. The vehicle industry and the aircraft industry did well for most of the 1930s, higher pay was given to piece workers, and this stimulated many craft workers to rejoin their unions to try to overtake the pieceworkers. In the late 1930s the A.E.U. at last began recruiting semi- and unskilled workers, most of whom accepted management control over the nature of work and the use of excessive overtime. Because of the lack of challenge over basic control issues there was little resistance to the spread of trade unionism again in the engineering factories. Employers who were in the C.D.E.E.A. were in theory committed to recognising unions, and it was felt that they posed less threat than they had done in the past.

There were a number of clashes over the rights of newly-elected shop stewards, but these were mostly short and local. A feature of the unionism of the 1930s was the non-appearance of the workshop committees that had flourished in the war and post-war years, but instead the development of a system of convenors in a number of large factories. These were often acceptable to the managers, as it made contact with the workers easier, and to the union District Committee for the same reason, and because it was easier to control a convenor than a committee. The need for convenors to organise and co-ordinate the stewards was also an indication of the needs of semi-skilled workers to have someone to negotiate for them; in contrast to the principle of skilled workers looking after themselves.

The new trade union revival still offered scope for radical politics, and the hardening of the divide between workplace politics and municipal and Labour politics once again made it possible for the Communist Party to spread its influence. It had survived the lean years by going through a period of decline and sectarianism, but the prospect of war brought a change of policy and even before the war the Party had again made progress in the Trades Council and the A.E.U. This time it too was shaped by the new situation. It now owed much of its trade union strength not to workshop committees but to its capturing key union posts and influence on the A.E.U. District Committee. During the war it was once again ready to try to link workplace politics to more wider political action, but not in a way that sought to openly challenge either the capitalist system or Labour's political role within that system. The rapid spread of its influence in workshops during the war again showed what

Labour was losing in its neglect of workplace politics, and how the potential of the trade union movement was not being harnessed for political change. By the outbreak of the war the gulf between workshop and municipal politics was such that the growing power of Labour in the Council was not challenged by the growing power of the Communist Party in the unions; each had established areas of influence.

Conclusion

A militant shop steward in the first world war, George Hodgkinson, a key figure in labour's winning council power, concluded, on the basis of a couple of years in office that 'Despite Labour rule a municipal boss was no different from any other kind, the worker a wage earner with no other end in view than the bottom line in the pay packet'.[31] In fact the resurgence of workshop radicalism in the second world war pointed to Hodgkinson's overstatement, but the inter-war period did see a shift from socialism based on workshop power to socialism as a municipal enterprise.

A key factor in this shift was the existence of two distinct ruling groups within Coventry, the manufacturers and the Coalition. The Coalition, with its hands on a number of economic and social levers of power, with its narrow-mindedness and its neglect of municipal duties was an obvious target for the Labour Party. But in taking on this enemy Labour was challenging only the weaker of the ruling groups. Moreover its concentration on attacking the Coalition, and its comparatively weak links with the trade union movement meant that it over-emphasised the road to socialism through municipal planning.

Coventry had quickly become a city whose economic life was dominated by large factories. Inevitably factory life was important in shaping social and cultural attitudes in the city. Labour policies had no impact on factory experiences; Labour's appeal was based on a form of idealism rather than on tangible improvement in most people's working lives. The Labour approach was to take a passive working class as a fact. After 1922 even the trade unions found it hard to involve and motivate working people, at least for a number of years. Labour therefore developed a socialist programme that meant acting on behalf of working people rather than bringing them into power. Its retreat from the workshops, necessary in order to clearly establish its own identity, left a gulf in working class politics that the Communist Party sought, in vain, to fill.

The Labour Party, while still fully committed to the replacement of capitalism with a socialist vision, lacked a strategy for working class power. It therefore came to see its programme of municipal reform as leading to socialism, and itself as the true repository of socialist ideals. A victory for Labour was seen as a victory for the working class, and a victory for socialism. The reality was more complicated than that.

Notes to Chapter 6

The research on which this chapter was based was originally done for a Ph.D. thesis, 'Engineering Workers and the Rise of Labour in Coventry 1914-1939' (University of Warwick, 1979).

1. P. Searby, Weavers and Freemen in Coventry, 1820-1861' (University of Warwick, Ph.D. thesis, 1972).
2. J. Prest, *The Industrial Revolution in Coventry* (1960), 118.
3. Coventry Permanent Economic Building Society, *Annual Report*, 1915. See also Martin Davis, *Every Man His Own Landlord. A History of Coventry Building Society* (Coventry 1985).
4. F. Smith, *Coventry, Six Hundred Years of Municipal Life* (1945).
5. *Midland Daily Telegraph*, 14 January, 28 February, 1919.
6. *Coventry Herald*, 3 January, 1925.
7. *Coventry Standard*, 3, 4 February, 1933.
8. PRO ED 35/6327 Letter from the Director of Education, 31 October 1933.
9. PRO ED 97/609 Memorandum 30 November, 1928.
10. J.B. Priestley, *English Journey* (1934), 69-70.
11. *Midland Daily Telegraph*, 30 January, 1936.
12. *Ibid.*, 6 November, 1936.
13. *Ibid.*, 28 July, 1937.
14. *Ibid.*, 24 November, 1937.
15. George Hodgkinson, *Sent to Coventry* (1970), 129.
16. *Coventry Searchlight*, November 1937.
17. *Midland Daily Telegraph*, 28 October, 1936.
18. *Ibid.*, 27 January, 1937.
19. Hodgkinson, *op.cit.*, 140.
20. *The Communist*, 28 October, 1920.
21. *The Socialist*, 7 October, 1920.
22. PRO. Cab., GT/24 *Reports*, 9 February, 1922.
23. This was the name often given to Friday, 15 April, 1921 when the rail and transport unions decided to call off sympathy strikes for the miners who had been locked out over a wage reduction.
24. A.E.U. District Committee *Minutes*, 21 April, 1922.
25. *Midland Daily Telegraph*, 3 May, 1922.
26. *Out of Work*, 1, 55 (April 1923).
27. A.E.U. District Committee *Minutes*, 3 October, 1922.
28. A.E.U. District Committee *Minutes*; a survey of nine workshops

was taken some time in 1925.

29. *Ibid.*, 12 May, 1926.
30. Labour Party, *Annual Report of Conferences*, 1929-1939.
31. Hodgkinson, *op.cit.*, 142.

1. *Coventry's most famous citizen. Lady Godiva, her part taken by an actress, 1907.*

2. *Craftsmen in the car industry. 1. Maudsley Erecting Shop 1910. Coventry and Warwickshire Collection.*

Craftsmen in the car industry. 2. Standard Machine Shop 949. Coventry and Warwickshire Collection.

Hollywood Triumph. Edward Turner, Rita Hayworth and a Coventry Triumph 1950s. Ivor Davies, It's a Triumph (Haynes 980).

5. *Factory Work for Women. 1. GEC Wire and Lathe Section 1936.* The Loudspeaker, *April 1936.*

6. *Factory Work for Women. 2. Courtaulds Reeling into Skeins 1930s. Courtaulds Ltd.*

7. *Factory Work for Women. 3. GEC Extruding Ebonite Rods 1937.* The Loudspeaker, *September, 1937.t*

8. *Almost the last of a long line. Fred Lee & Co's Dover Street Watch Jewel Makers 1946. Coventry and Warwickshire Collection.*

9. *Assembling Standard Sports Cars on the longest sports car track in the world in 1961. The workers called it the Burma Road.* Coventry Evening Telegraph.

10. *Waiting for the traffic or waiting for the hooter? GEC workers raring to go in 1936.* The Loudspeaker, *May 1936.*

11. Was it the competition or just the taking part? Fitters v Machinists at Alfred Herberts about 1903. Alfred Herbert News, *July 1927.*

12. Some very solid citizens at the Daimler Staff Dinner of 1912. Coventry and Warwickshire Collection.

13. *Just ordinary blokes. A Rate-Fixer's day out in 1929.* Alfred Herbert News, *July 1929.*

14. *The GEC ballroom was one of the wonders of Coventry before 1939. This was the New Year's Eve Dance in 1930.* The Loudspeaker, *January 1931.*

15. Some things don't change. Waiting for treatment in the new out-patients department at the Coventry and Warwickshire Hospital 1913. Coventry and Warwickshire Collection.

16. This was Jordan Well not in 1937 but 1957 before it got developed.

17. It could be the blitz but it is actually the demolition of Butchers Row 1936. Coventry and Warwickshire Collection.

18. The real blitz not only demolished houses but water mains. An unidentified Coventry street November 1940. Coventry and Warwickshire Collection.

19. The remains of the City Centre. Broadgate and the Market Hall Tower looking west 1941-42. Coventry and Warwickshire Collection.

20. The precinct was new but contained a lot of old favourites. Coventry and Warwickshire Collection.

21. Even the picturesque requires constant attention. This was Spon Street, Court 38, North side, about 1957. Coventry and Warwickshire Collection.

22. War and prosperity both contributed to Coventry's housing shortage. This was an unlicensed caravan site in Little Park Street 1953.

?. *And this was one of the solutions to the housing problem.* *'illenhall Estate in its early days. Coventry and Warwickshire* *ɔllection.*

. *Should car owners strike or affluence was a good thing but* *ere were limits .... The Standard Strike of 1956 as seen by the* *ɔventry* Evening Telegraph *of April 30.*

STRIKERS AT THEIR MASS MEETING

Standard Company strikers at to-day's mass meeting on Hearsall Common.

. . . And These Are Their Cars

Chapter 7

High Tide and After: Coventry Engineering Workers and Shopfloor Bargaining, 1945-80

Stephen Tolliday

In the boom of the 1930s, migrant labour flooded into Coventry's fast-growing factories to trade sweat for cash. The money was good, but conditions were poor and management had an undisputed command of the shopfloor. The motor firms were a Trade Union desert. The craft unions and, for a brief period, the Workers' Union had made significant headway in Coventry engineering before and during the First World War, but they were wrecked by slump and lock-out in the 1920s, and thereafter had only the barest toeholds in some sheltered sections of the industry until renewed opportunities presented themselves in the Second World War.[1] From 1939 until the mid 1970s, however, the tide flowed strongly in favour of Coventry's workers. But the late 1970s and early 1980s brought industrial decline and a new reassertion of management control. This essay reconsiders this 'golden age of shopfloor bargaining' from the vantage point of the mid 1980s and assesses the strength, achievement and durability of workplace organisation and shopfloor bargaining in Coventry engineering. What were its causes and consequences? What were the limitations and advantages of the system to labour and management respectively? What brought about its demise?

★ ★ ★

The period between 1945 and 1970 was the high tide of piecework bargaining in Coventry. Wages were high, labour was in short supply and output was climbing. The motor industry was visibly making money and car workers wanted their share. It was the world of the stereotype 'I'm all right, Jack' shop steward and the 'keeping up with the Joneses' working class family. Aggression over money spilled over into controls on the way work was done. Management's first priority was output and they were often prepared to trade off cost control to achieve this. Shop floor supervision was neglected, the foreman often became a marginal figure, and it was the shop stewards themselves who, in pursuit of high levels of output and earnings, often took on quasi-managerial functions.

At the same time, they came under close and continuous scrutiny from their members and argued hard and often for better wages and conditions. The focus of activity was primitive direct democracy on the shopfloor and trade union officials became largely irrelevant to the bargaining process.

Coventry motor workers became a classic example of the 'affluent worker' with high earnings, rising consumption and new aspirations.[2] By the 1960s some 60 per cent were home owners. Door-to-door H.P. salesmen plied a flourishing trade in fridges, TVs, washing machines and vacuum cleaners. There were the new pleasures of foreign holidays, going out to dinner and liqueurs on the sideboard. Manual workers might be rather disdainful of their former 'betters', the white collar workers who now often earned less than they did. But there remained a price to be paid in intense effort, fatigue and the monotony of motor factory work, along with the less often noted anxieties of fluctuating earnings associated with the short-time, waiting-time, interruptions of production and lay-offs that continued to dog the motor industry even through its boom years. As Graham Turner tellingly described it, 'This new blue-collar bourgeoisie is middle class only on the strength of overtime earnings'.[3]

These were also the years when, according to one much-voiced version of history, irresponsible piecework bargaining 'ruined' the motor industry: aggressive, often politically motivated trade unionism it was alleged, resulted in near anarchy on the shop floor and crippled production. More serious accounts, however, have given a rather different picture. Detailed studies by Brown and Batstone, Boraston and Frenkel at the Warwick I.R.R.U.[4] showed that much of the apparent conflict of piecework bargaining was in fact more functional and cooperative than it appeared. The inquiry by Turner, Clack and Roberts[5] into the relative strike-proneness of the motor industry in the 1960s repudiated the notion that bloody-minded shop floor militancy was the major cause of strikes and instead argued that the relatively high level of strikes was due to certain economic and historical features of the industry, notably its cyclical and seasonal irregularities of employment, its high but unstable earnings, and the 'obsolescence' of its collective bargaining institutions with multi-employer bargaining, multi-unionism and cumbersome procedures. More recently, Friedman[6] has argued that the pattern of bargaining should be understood as a 'managerial strategy' to cede control of work to the shop floor and leave the payment system to pace production. Only when this strategy ceased to be workable as competition increased and the need to control costs at all levels intensified in the 1970s, was there a managerial shift towards direct control of the production process.

These were valuable and important studies but they mostly lacked a developed historical dimension. The Warwick studies were dense reconstructions of the inner workings of workplace bargaining at particular moments. Turner, Clack and Roberts focussed on strikes as both the fundamental problem and the key symptom of workplace disorder, and was deeply embedded in the quest for prescriptions for 'orderly' industrial relations that culminated in the Donovan Report.[7] Their diagnosis was an important influence in the Report's advocacy of company and plant bargaining, simplified procedures and more centralised unions which became the established orthodoxy in both government and managerial circles in the 1970s. Although much of their detailed argument remains robust, the prescriptive element now appears seriously flawed: the Donovan formula was probably more thoroughly implemented in the motor industry than anywhere else in the 1970s, yet it proved to have remarkably little impact on the strike-proneness of the industry or the fundamentals of workplace conflict. Friedman's approach was more historical but it depended heavily on relating long-term shifts in the product market to broad shifts in payment systems and work organisation. It provided an illuminating historical typology, but tended also to overstate the strategic coherence of management, to generalise too much from the model case of Standard Motors, and had little to say about the internal dynamics of the systems it described.

In contrast, this essay is explicitly historical and comparative in approach. In the first part it presents case studies of the development and operation of shopfloor bargaining in four major Coventry engineering firms: the motor manufacturers Standard Motors, Rootes, and Jaguar and the leading machine tool firm Alfred Herbert which together accounted for over a third of engineering employment in Coventry in the mid 1960s. It looks at the similarities and differences between the firms to illuminate the dynamics of the system. The second part of the essay builds on this to reconsider the overall working of piecework systems in Coventry, and their consequences for both labour and management, and the reasons for their abandonment in the 1970s.

Before discussing the internal workings of these firms, however, it is important to stress one thing that they all had in common in relation to the external labour market. The labour forces under consideration were all overwhelmingly white and male. The lines of segregation in the Coventry labour market were clearly defined and well-known. In Federated vehicle-building firms less than four per cent of manual workers were women in 1967: Morris Engines employed only 44 (one per cent), Standard Motors 186 (2.3 per cent). The picture in aircraft manufacturing was the same: the biggest firm, Bristol-Siddeley, employed 91 women (1.8 per cent). The only place that featured women in motor firms was in the trim shops where most of the 385 (6.4 per cent) at Rootes and 403 (6.9 per cent) at Jaguar worked. Mechanical engineering followed a similar pattern: Herberts employed eight per cent women. Women's employment in engineering was almost wholly concentrated in electrical engineering: 56 per cent of G.E.C. workers were women.[8]

Similarly, though there are no comparably exact statistics, black workers were excluded from high-paying engineering jobs. Even on the less well-paid buses the unions operated a colour bar more or less openly until 1960 when Morris Minta, a Jamaican, became the first coloured busman.[9] The only inroads they made into engineering were in the lowest-paying and dirtiest end of the trade, particularly the foundries. Even there they were confined to the lowliest jobs by a tacit consensus of management and workers. At Sterling Metals in 1951, for example, management, under union pressure, stated at Works Conference that 'it was their main desire to recruit white labour', agreed to keep black and white gangs segregated and gave white labourers guarantees against the upgrading of Indians.[10] At Herberts in 1953 the A.E.U. Chief Steward threatened strike action if Indians were upgraded from labourers to machines and management gave them informal reassurances.[11] Trade union officials began to be more and more critical of such attitudes as time went on, but they rarely took a firm stand. Overt discrimination within the workplace, however, was comparatively rare: most blacks never got inside the factory gates. Recruitment practices at the major firms were often a sufficient barrier in themselves. Hiring through union offices gave advantages to local and experienced engineering workers; and, as a recent report by the Commission for Racial Equality on the big Banner Lane tractor plant showed, the other main mode of hiring through informal networks of friends, relatives and personal links with foremen effectively kept out black workers who lacked access to these channels of information and influence.[12]

There is no space here to consider the causes and consequences of this labour market segmentation: further aspects of the issue are discussed in other essays in this volume. The point here is only to locate the workers we are discussing in relation to the wider Coventry labour force. It would be wrong to see Coventry engineering workers as an elite or labour aristocracy: men were pouring into the industry all the time from other districts or occupations and few of them acquired distinctive or transferrable skills. But the labour force did have its hierarchies and the workers we are considering were at or near the top of the tree.

Standard Motors: Apogee of the Gang System.[13]

The Standard 'big gang' system, which flourished between 1945 and 1974, was the most developed form of shopfloor control in any British motor firm of its time. For many years the firm stood clearly at the head of the Coventry wages league and was known in the city as 'The Klondyke' or 'The Mint'. It had a powerful shop steward organisation that also played a dominant role on lay district bodies of the A.E.U./A.U.E.W. and T.G.W.U., and, in the factory itself, supervision was cut to the bone and it was the stewards and the gangs themselves which undertook the most significant role in the organisation of production. The Standard system has attracted a fair degree of myth and idealisation, particularly in the work of Seymour Melman,[14] an American sociologist who wrote on the factory in the 1950s and who saw in the system a harbinger of forms of work organisation that could transcend the modern hierarchical factory system, and of Dwight Rayton,[15] a former Standard steward and activist in the Industrial Common Ownership movement, who saw it as a pre-figuration of a labour-managed enterprise. Their uncritical accounts have been incorporated wholesale into later works such as that of Friedman, and generalised there to describe shop floor bargaining throughout Coventry engineering. In fact, Standard was very much a special case, though an immensely important one, and both its achievements and its weaknesses are of the greatest interest.

Before the Second World War, Standard was a largely non-unionised firm, swarming with youth and raw migrant labour and known as 'Boystown'. It was run by the autocratic John Black, who was linked by marriage to the other great motor grandees of Coventry, the Rootes family. The war transformed the firm. The new shops for the building of Bristol and later Mosquito aircraft became the nucleus for rapid union expansion. A number of experienced militants got in at the beginning of the war and recruited rapidly as new labour came in. The aircraft jobs were new and hard to time, and, as was generally the case with aircraft assembly, organised on a 'large gang' system, whereby large work groups were given a price for a whole group of operations and then divided this lump sum within the gang on the basis of the gradings of its members. New wartime jobs were flung at Standard management and they had to work out how to organise them as they went along. The result was very loose prices and some spectacularly flying earnings. The unions were able to utilise the pressing demand for labour to push its own nominees into these shops. Jack Jones, the T.G.W.U. District Secretary, saw it—as the largest works in the city—as the key area for union development and he pushed likely looking people in there with the assistance of sympathetic local wartime labour officers.

Recruitment spread out from the new to the older machine shops. Here progress was less spectacular and it proved harder to push up earnings. Nevertheless, overall, by the end of the war, Standard was 80-90 per cent organised. Black had become sympathetic to working in cooperation with the unions to maximise output and keep control in the works and was working closely with Jones to 'win the war'. With cost-plus contracts, wages were only a minor consideration and during the period 1940-45 Standard, along with Armstrong Whitworth Aircraft, was one of the most strike-free and highest paying firms in Coventry.[16]

The most crucial divergence between Standard and the other Coventry engineering firms, however, came at the end of the War. Then most of them sought to roll back wartime union gains and re-establish pre-war wages and conditions as far as possible, though in practice with little success. Black's strategy was in complete contrast. He foresaw an acute shortage of labour and an insatiable market for cars and opted to continue the high wage/high output pattern into peacetime as a springboard to lift Standard into the big league of mass producers. His initiative was eagerly taken up by Jack Jones and the Confed officials. But his maverick go-it-alone tactics conjured up the spectre of competitive bidding for labour among Coventry employers and resulted in a clash with the Coventry District Engineering Employers Association (C.D.E.E.A.) and Standard's expulsion from the Engineering Employers Federation (E.E.F.). Black believed that his policy was one that all other Coventry employers would be forced to follow but that he could steal a march on them by getting in first. In practice he was proved wrong. Standard did not prove able to achieve a qualitative leap in their share of the market and scale of production, and other firms found that they did not have to follow his lead in order to get the labour that they required. Over the next ten years Standard wage levels slowly fell back towards the more normal high wages of the other Coventry motor manufacturers.

The 1945 Agreement which initiated this system cut hours to 42.1/2 per week against the Federated firms 44 and instituted a minimum bonus of 100 per cent at a time when the Federation had a 27.1/2 per cent target and a 60 per cent average settlement. But it took two and a half years of further negotiations before the comprehensive Standard Agreement of

1948 covering the organisation of production as well as payment, was concluded. In the course of the negotiations, the management had raised the question of organising the whole firm in a single gang with a bonus on output and a company union. This was rejected, but the final agreement provided for reducing the previous 104 small gangs to 15 large gangs in the main plant at Canley and one giant gang at the Banner Lane engine plant. The previous 68 job grades were cut down to eight basic rates. Bonus was to be paid on gang output and prices were to be negotiated with the gangs. There was to be an average 20 per cent wage increase and a guaranteed £5 per week for all adult male workers. In addition, all labour would, it was understood, be hired through the union office, thus ensuring a *de facto* closed shop.

This was quite a remarkable agreement. Not only did it concede high wages, but it also institutionalised large gangs as powerful bargaining units. The new wage structure cut down differentials between grades and a considerable proportion of the highest grades took a cut in wages, though the lowest grades, who were disproportionately represented in the T.G.W.U., the majority union and the driving force behind the agreement on the union side, benefitted considerably. Some of the old gangs had been earning as much as 9s. an hour and the average of the plant was 6s.5.1/2d. The new scheme produced a much more evenly dispersed high average of 6s.1d. compared to a Coventry average of 4s.4d. and the highest rate of a Coventry Federated firm of 4s.9d. Both Confed officials and the leading stewards were consciously trying to mitigate sectionalism and create the basis for united action within the plant by reducing differentials. As far as Sir John Black was concerned, the object was to devise a self-running incentive system with a close relation between effort, output and rewards and then leave the system to very much run itself. But the price in loss of traditional managerial control was high. The stewards enjoyed a great deal of on the job control: stopwatches were banned in the shops, and all final prices had to be agreed with stewards and gangs. The union controlled hiring of labour and the amount of overtime to be worked. Consultation with stewards was at exceptional levels, and while the company was riding the crest of a wave between 1948 and 1954 there was a very real feeling that the shop stewards 'ran the company'.

Even so, it would be wrong to idealise the Standard system. Self-regulation within an incentive structure created its own divisive pressures, both within and between gangs. Take the example of control of deployment of labour and manning levels. Under a Measured Daywork System this would be the essence of job control, but under payment by results it very much threw the ball into the unions' court and was very ambiguous in its effects. Thus there was a standing temptation to de-man gangs and push up the intensity of effort so as to increase income, or to discriminate against members of gangs, since, for instance, by having more members on lower grades within the gang the proportion of the bonus taken by the higher grades was greatly raised. The result, as Eddie McGarry a one time T.G.W.U. Convener, described it was:

> If someone wasn't doing their corner, "Hey, hey come on Jim, it's time you done a bit here. You're getting part of the money so we want you to put your part of it in". There was no skim shanking like that. I would say that the bonus system was the best foreman we ever had. The best form of supervision we ever had was the bonus system itself.

Once the system had been in motion for a few years, these sorts of pressures created the conditions for internal divisions and rivalries. Different gangs might both lay claim to a lucrative new job because they wanted to get it within the boundaries of their own gang to raise their bonus. Or it could have more serious deleterious effects in terms of workers' toleration of exploitation. One of the principal managerial policies pursued by Standard, for example, was contracting work out and sweating their sub-contractors. Now, the biggest job done by women on Gang 13 was hoods and sidescreens. In 1955 the firm decided to sub-contract the job out unless the women agreed to accept a price at the level they could get it done by sub-contractors. The gang, however, decided not to defend the women, but instead, to avoid the new low priced job pulling average gang earnings down, they reached agreement with management to kick the women out of the gang and create a new sewing machinists gang. This position of internal friction is well described by one worker who started at the Standard in 1952.

> The Standard, when I started there was all little empires, every shop was a little empire, all getting different bonuses, all earning different money, and all "You ain't coming on to our gang" or "We ain't getting enough bonus. We got to get some off our gang on to their gang" and all that business, at the Standard. Although it was union it was all different empires. It weren't like I always thought the union was, you know, all brothers together. They were all brothers in their own little circles. (Alf Brogan: No. 3 Machine Shop Gang).

Two other weaknesses of the system should be noted. Firstly, though the system was very well adapted for pushing up earnings, it was unable to maintain the closure of differentials that was one of the original aims. Price-fixing developed on a ratchet system. When a new job came in, the demand was for the price to yield the average earnings of existing work. Then, once the gang got the hang of the job and improved efficiency, the earnings moved ahead. But some sections might not get a new job for several years and gangs working on the oldest vintages had the lowest earnings and those on newest the most. Once a new job came in it was very often possible to leapfrog to the top of the wages hierarchy. In the meantime, however, despite the unions' bargaining strength, large inequities were tolerated for long periods. In fact, in contrast to the relatively stable relativities on individual piecework in non-Coventry firms like Austin, the Standard system had very erratic fluctuations.

The second weakness arose from union control of hiring. This was something very new to the T.G.W.U. and A.E.U. in Coventry. In contrast to the Sheet Metal Workers, the T.G.W.U. had no developed procedures, rotas or criteria to get on the Vacant Book List for Standard. With Standard's very high wages and the tremendous pressure to get in there among Coventry workers, they ran into enormous problems over favouritism and 'backstage work' to get in, which finally resulted in the demise of the system in the aftermath of a scandal. Nevertheless, control of hiring was one of the key means by which the unions maintained their strong position at the Standard in these years, and also by which the T.G.W.U. maintained its dominance in the new plant with around 60 per cent of the membership against 25 per cent for the A.U.E.W.

The power of shop floor organisation at the Standard was therefore more internally contradictory than earlier accounts have pictured it. In addition, the heyday was a rather short period based on particular circumstances, notably the idiosyncratic management of Sir John Black and the relative prosperity of the company. Standard were able to make large profits based on high output in the late 1940s, but by the 1950s they were already suffering from their lack of size in competition with B.M.C. and Ford and were often short of capital to develop new models. By the 1950s, 70 per cent of their profits were coming from their tractor operations and they were anxiously seeking merger partners to give them greater volume and economies of scale.

Black's handling of the firm was coming under heavy boardroom pressure in the early 1950s. Black himself was becoming more and more erratic and according to some of his colleagues was almost schizophrenic. In January 1954 he was ousted in a boardroom coup by another whizz-kid,[17] Alec Dick and from then on there were much more conflictual relations with the unions that soon built up to a head in 1956. Even before Black's departure there had been attempts to remove some of the union controls. In 1950 Black had tried to get back control of hiring, sub-contracting had been used against high-priced gangs, and on two occasions the company tried to enforce redundancies but were forced by shop floor action to introduce work sharing instead. Once Dick was in office, the assaults became frontal. The T.G.W.U. convenor, Gordon Wright, was sacked and then reinstated after a strike, and then caught in a technical 'gross industrial misconduct' and sacked again on an issue where it was hard to mobilise a fight. The 1956 recession, made sharper at the Standard because it coincided with the introduction of a whole new range of transfer machines, produced massive redundancies. An attempt to enforce work sharing succeeded partially, but the size of the drop in output was too great and redundancies followed. A strike won limited monetary compensation for redundancy — a great precedent in the industry—but in the aftermath the management were able to victimise large numbers of more militant stewards and to use the political divisions within the Joint Shop Stewards Committee (J.S.S.C.) to ensure that there would be no real fight for their reinstatement.

The origins of the Standard policy had lain in the distinctive view taken by management of the labour and product market which had been rejected by the C.D.E.E.A. From 1945-57 Standard pursued their policy outside the Federation and their readmission to the fold in 1957 symptomised their desire to work more closely along the normal lines of managerial policy. In practice, however, it proved to be an extremely long-term task to realign the conditions developed at Standard with those elsewhere in the industry. From 1956 Standard was continually pressing to introduce smaller gangs and to relate them more to work groups, both to weaken their bargaining power and to relate incentives more directly to effort. Despite strong resistance in the workplace, the powerful 640 strong engine gang was split into four gangs after the strike. In the next four years the company were able to break up all the gangs larger than 500 and by 1961 there were some 100 gangs at Canley. This was far more than the 20 there had been in 1956, but still meant that Standard had far larger gangs than any other firm in Coventry. The stewards and gang organisation remained powerful. In 1959-60 they were able to resist attempts to use the introduction of the Herald and a new assembly hall to break up the organisation of work and payment based on 'historic gang membership', and in the 1960-61 slump the stewards were able to hold the company to work-sharing while other motor companies nearly all introduced lay-offs and redundancies.

Throughout the 1960s stewards and gangs maintained a high level of shop floor control, though as the firm's economic decline continued their ability to push piecework earnings forward on a broad front was seriously diminished. When Jack Scamp investigated the company for the government-backed Motor Industry Joint Labour Council in 1966, he found that the company were heavily dependent on stewards for their information about the booking of work and the scheduling and flow of production, and often for the necessary information for job timings. In many cases the company feared to open up the question of job times because they had little idea of what the answer would or should be. Even so, as the company declined the workforce were no longer able to maintain their position as pace setters for Coventry. By the mid 1960s Standard wages were comparable with those of other leading Coventry firms and many gangs fell below the District average. In June 1966 Standard as a whole fell below the District average for the first time. The gangs were still ready to increase earnings by increasing output without a proportionate increase in manning, but as the gap with other firms narrowed there became much more stress on the absolute level of increases. More importantly, the company had managed to curb the number and scope of retimings and increased the number of 'sticky' prices whenever gangs failed to take the initiative to force retimes whenever there was the slightest opportunity. On the Mark 1 engine, for example, despite the fact that the job was more or less transformed by continuous small modifications between 1954 and 1965, the price remained unchanged. Also after 1956, the unions had ceded the link between indirect workers bonuses and piecework that had made Standard day workers the highest paid in Coventry. Once the link was broken they steadily fell back and by the mid 1960s the widening disparities of earnings were becoming a serious source of discontent.

By the late 1960s the high wage/high labour productivity/low overheads system had already degenerated considerably. The demise of pace setting wages and internal equity left a form of works organisation where management depended heavily on the cooperation of the workforce but had little to offer in return. Scamp recommended a move to Measured Day Work, but it was not until 1974, when the company had sunk still further and had come under B.L. management, that this shift was made.

In the early years of the Standard system, Black's unique managerial strategy had linked up with a nascent union organisation and each had strengthened the other. The dominance of the T.G.W.U. and the unusually strong links between their shop stewards and the authoritative T.G.W.U. District Secretary Jack Jones, undoubtedly allowed for an unparalleled strategic coherence on the union side. The Agreement raised wages, compressed differentials and linked work organisation and union organisation through the gang bargaining units. The very large gangs ensured significant devolution of job control, though the question of self-exploitation remained unresolved. But the system was geared to expansionism and a leap into the front rank of mass producers that never materialised. By the early 1950s the internal stresses of the system were already apparent. Thereafter they steadily grew worse.

Rootes: Management by Abdication.[18]

At the Rootes assembly plant at Ryton and their engine plant at Stoke, a significant shop floor organisation dated only from the war. But, unlike Standard it only flourished after a bitter attempt by management to roll back union gains between 1944 and 1946. The company attempted to tighten works discipline and push piecework prices down to pre-war levels using redundancies and victimisations of leading stewards. The Works Manager, Horace Pryor, treated stewards and union officials, in Jack Jones' phrase as 'something the cat has just brought in'. The offensive was harsh and at times almost deliberately provocative. The tea urns were caged and padlocked and disabled workers were cleared out: Pryor told the protesting stewards: 'If I wanted my foremen to act as wet-nurses I'd have given them udders'. The unions responded by refusing to negotiate with Pryor present and conducting a series of go-slows and strikes.

After a long struggle culminating in a major strike in 1946 union organisation held the line. The strike victory owed something to the intervention of the Ministry of Labour who suspended half the redundancy notices, but more to widespread district support from other factories and union branches who realised the strategic significance of the Rootes strike—despite the rather half-hearted attitudes of the National Executives of both T.G.W.U. and A.E.U. Management backed down: but they did not immediately reconcile themselves to the union presence. In 1947 the Rootes brothers decided on a frontal assault on what they regarded as the 'Communist troublemakers' of the N.U.V.B., and sacked 60 Trim shop workers including the leading N.U.V.B. stewards in the plant. To their surprise the N.U.V.B. Executive made the resulting strike official and made it a lengthy affair before letting Rootes off the hook with a compromise settlement that agreed to allow half the sackings to stand as long as the other half along with Sam Peers, the leading *non*-Communist steward, were reinstated. This was perhaps more directed at ridding the company of its most militant stewards than at driving out the unions completely, but it was also to be the last time that Rootes placed themselves in the front ranks of aggressive management in Coventry. Thereafter they retreated into quietism and adopted a markedly conciliatory style.

By 1950 Rootes' Coventry factories were 99 per cent unionised and until the end of the 1960s they were one of Coventry's highest paying firms. Consultation with stewards was good, with regular Friday night meetings between management and senior stewards and the strike record was modest and limited to small strikes. There was an unusually small number of conflicts over managerial arrangements or union rights and more serious conflict was more or less confined to issues of wages, redundancies and short-time. With hindsight Rootes managers characterised this period as one of 'management by abdication'. Management regularly gave in on small issues to keep production going and Rootes were notoriously prone to *ad hoc* settlements which the E.E.F. severely criticised as dangerous precedents. At shop floor level, little attention was given to supervision which was poorly paid and had little or erratic backing from senior management. By the early 1960s Rootes were looking to recoup this position by directing negotiations more towards full-time trade union officers and away from the stewards in the hope that this would result in them tightening up discipline over their members and enforcing agreements. The other side of the coin of Rootes' timid attitude at shop floor level turned out to be an aggressive position in Federation politics in the early 1960s where they led the faction arguing for the government to introduce the legal enforceability of agreements.

The unions were able to press their advantages home. In the early 1950s the gangs won the right to elect gang leaders rather than have them appointed by management and thereafter gangs exerted tight control over the booking in of work and the pace of work to ensure the maintenance of good piecework prices, and were prepared to take disciplinary action against any groups or individuals who infringed these practices. Hiring was through the union office, and the extent and allocation of overtime was by agreement with stewards. By the mid 1960s there was also a growing tendency to expand bargaining opportunities creatively by inventing restrictive practices and then 'selling' them to management. At Ryton, where the largest gangs worked on the Assembly tracks, stewards had fairly effective control of labour loading and speed of the track, and there is some truth in Richardson's description of the Ryton stewards in the 1960s as 'something like a self-governing republic'.[19] Yet steward control operated primarily to enhance production and the stewards themselves stressed that the system was both highly productive and low on managerial overheads. For much of the time there was a strong coincidence between many steward and managerial goals, but at times their interests could go in different directions. On manning levels, for instance, in periods of expansion stewards were keen to keep down manning and thus boost earnings; but in slumps they would resist the shedding of labour and thus heighten problems of cyclical production.

This pattern was something like a more casual and unplanned version of the Standard system. But in contrast, the strength of shop floor bargaining at Rootes was never mirrored by a similar coherence of union organisation. In the 1950s in particular, union organisation was marred by severe conflicts between the A.E.U. and the T.G.W.U. The A.E.U. believed that the T.G.W.U. were 'making a determined effort to control the factory' and in 1952 withdrew from the J.S.S.C. in protest. This partly stemmed from the T.G.W.U.'s unwillingness to accept what it regarded as the A.E.U.'s anachronistic claims to exclusive organising rights. Thus the T.G.W.U. consistently fought to establish skilled rates for their members: but when they succeeded the A.E.U. persistently demanded the right to recruit these skilled workers. This was the basis of much of the conflict, but it was also exacerbated by political conflicts within the steward ranks associated with pro- and anti-Communist factions. On the sections there was little cross-union steward representation and the J.S.S.C. was not revived until the 1960s. Overall, the A.E.U. upheld its leading role in the factory. It dominated the direct labour force with some 55 per cent membership against the T.G.W.U. 30 per cent and N.U.V.B. seven per cent, though the position was reversed in the indirects where the T.G.W.U. had 62 per cent to the A.E.U.'s 31 per cent by 1967. However, the really powerful sections like the main assembly line at Ryton was 80 per cent A.E.U. A.E.U. dominance meant less stress on 'levelling up' than at Standard and the divided steward ranks were less likely to develop a coherent plant wide approach.

In the light of this, it is perhaps not surprising that gang sectionalism was sometimes prone to cut across wider union interests. For example, in the mid and late 1950s, the A.E.U. found themselves unable to enforce their policy of equable sharing of work and overtime restrictions on their members in some of the most powerful Ryton gangs. In a period of stop-go and intermittent short-time the A.E.U. branches and stewards wanted to ban overtime while short-time was being worked in the factory, to operate strict rotas on lay-offs and to insist on work-sharing rather than redundancies. At Standard the stewards got this to stick. But at Ryton powerful sections like the Minx track insisted on working overtime to make up earnings they had lost on short-time. The Minx tracks stewards declared that the track was 'saturated with labour' and refused to absorb more labour from other sections as the District Committee wanted, because it would reduce their earnings below their current 'top of the league' 485 per cent. They rejected appeals to union brotherhood and got away with it despite the fact that the majority of Ryton stewards condemned their action as selfishness. Power remained in the sections and it is striking that in such a highly organised factory the fund to subsidise the earnings of senior stewards on union business collapsed in the mid 1950s because of an inability to raise sufficient contributions from the shop floor.

Rootes was the first Coventry company to decide to break with piecework: the decision was made in 1966, confirmed by Chrysler when they took over the company in the following year and Measured Day Work (M.D.W.) was forced in by 1969. At the time, Rootes/Chrysler stressed the high level of disputes and the low productivity of piecework. Yet Stoke had very few disputes and Ryton also had a very good record relative to other firms before the spate of disputes that was generated by the attempt to abolish the system: in contrast, Rootes' Linwood plant in Scotland which had been on a form of M.D.W. since its inception in 1961 had a much higher strike-rate. The company also alleged that their Coventry plants required 50 per cent more man-hours than their European competitors to produce a car in 1968: but this was highly misleading since Rootes methods were deliberately labour intensive and they were one of the lowest ranked companies in Europe in terms of their fixed assets per employee. The real roots of their desire for change lay in the general crisis of the firm at the time and the desire to increase managerial control at *all* levels, of which the shop floor was perhaps the easiest and most obvious target.

In the early 1960s growing competition pushed Rootes to shift from their traditional 'quality' image into the cheap mass production sector. By 1966 they had become 90 per cent dependent on two cheap volume cars, the Minx and the Imp. The Minx was pitched directly against the Cortina and 1100 but attained only a fraction of their sales while the Imp was a 'come-lately' Mini. Their real problems were inadequate models, a disjointed range with big holes in key segments, severe under-utilisation of capacity and an inability to achieve economies of scale. They had gone badly astray in sacrificing their traditional up-market position to compete head-on with the mass-producers. The 'crisis of piecework' in the firm was really only a symptom of the wider business crisis which had them collapsing into the arms of Chrysler. American management naturally confirmed the decision to reform a payments system they did not understand as part of the process of taking command of the company.

Between 1966-69 the company was able to rid itself of piecework through a mixture of carrot and stick, though only after stiff resistance and a campaign of go-slows and stoppages, and only at the price of conceding a rather hybrid form of 'bargained' M.D.W. with considerable continuities from the old system. Unlike Standard, the systems of payment, work organisation and union organisation were never so tightly interlocked and it proved easier for Rootes to pick off factories and even sections individually to bring in M.D.W. At the same time, the sectional power of stewards based on mutuality was very little disturbed and remained intact under the new system.

Jaguar: Conflict and Cooperation.[20]

Before the Second World War, Jaguar too had been a bitterly anti-union firm. The founder and owner, Sir William Lyons, finally formally recognised the unions in 1946, but the hostility lingered on. Between 1946 and 1951 the firm continued to try to dislodge the unions but failed mainly because of the strategic strength of skilled N.U.V.B. workers in the Body and Trim shops. Jaguar were still making pre-war quality models by pre-war methods in a pre-war factory and they were heavily dependent on scarce craft skills in these departments. Despite periodic clashes, including an eight-week strike over the sacking of two leading N.U.V.B. stewards in 1951, the N.U.V.B. held firm. After this dispute, however, Jaguar accepted the permanence of the unions and between 1952 and 1958 there were only a handful of small disputes as output rose rapidly. In the late 1940s recurrent short-time and lay-offs, mainly due to component shortages and restricted steel allocations, had been the main cause of conflict, but during the 1950s the stability of demand in Jaguar's market segment meant that even in 1956 there were no redundancies, while the large profit margins on Jaguar cars enabled the firm to pay some of the highest wages in Coventry. The stable model range meant that there was relatively little shop floor bargaining, and until 1957 there was very little delegation of authority from higher management: questions of prices and work organisation tended to be dealt with by senior managers. But continuing expansion finally resulted in a decision to decentralise authority and give supervisors more scope in these areas for the first time.

The period of industrial peace was, however, interrupted between 1959 and 1963 when the introduction of new models produced new stresses for shop floor management and the old payment system. 1959 saw the introduction of the Mark 2, followed by the E-Type and the Mark Ten in 1960-61. These were major innovations which required substantial work reorganisation. At the same time, management consciously decided to produce the Mark 2 and its successors with lower profit margins than their predecessors as a response to increased competition. The change in pricing policy made the firm newly cost conscious. In addition, Jaguar remained highly dependent on U.S. sales and one of their major fears was that a failure to meet tight delivery dates might jeopardise their position in this market. One consequence was that Jaguar demand was becoming *increasingly* seasonal and the firm highly sensitive to possible losses of output in the key spring and early summer months. The mainly small internal disputes that did occur often threatened problems here, though in practice they rarely did much damage. The more serious losses in this period were occasioned by stoppages at their suppliers, notably at Smiths and S.U. Carburettors in 1961. Nevertheless these new pressures heightened managerial concern about the operations of shop floor bargaining.

The largest category of the numerous small strikes that occurred in this period were concerned with piecework prices and payments structures for the new models which caused many difficulties in a factory with a wide variety of individual piecework and small gangs, and with very poorly developed supervision. Most of the disputes were short lived and often spontaneous and against the advice of shop stewards: lost production was recouped fairly easily through subsequent overtime. Nevertheless the existing state of affairs was a drain on managerial time and nerves and in 1961-62 they called in Urwick, Orr and Partners to devise a Work Study system which they hoped would restore order to their shop floor bargaining. The report that resulted found that the labour force in general exhibited very cooperative attitudes but that despite this both entrenched customary practices and certain objective problems of production organisation made it hard to introduce reforms. Firstly, the process of high quality production, particularly in body, trim and trim assembly necessitated considerable variations and made work inconsistent and hard to evaluate. Secondly there was considerable resistance to change in customary methods. The N.U.V.B. areas in particular had developed a practice of refusing to allow the use of a stopwatch during price negotiations. Among the metal finishers, saw-mill machinists and on the white metal lines it was absolutely excluded and it was little used elsewhere. Following the report the company took certain steps to introduce work study but with little effect at first. Work study engineers were introduced, but they were soon allowed to be assimilated back into more traditional roles as rate-fixers and effort bargainers.

After 1963 this turbulence was replaced by a period of relative quiet, and the period 1963-72 was perhaps above all marked by the growing slackness and lack of direction and management. Until 1963 the old 'Blackpool' managers and their practices had reigned undisturbed for over thirty years since the firm's move to Coventry. After that there was a wholesale retirement of the old generation without any smooth managerial succession. These difficulties were compounded by the 1966 take-over of Jaguar by B.M.C. It was a considerable time before management was taken in hand by the new rather overstretched combine and in the meantime matters continued on a business as usual basis. On the personnel side, until the mid 1960s, there continued to be no senior manager with specialised responsibility for industrial relations which continued to be handled by the Works Manager as one part of his wider functions. The main change was the decision to appoint a more junior industrial relations manager in 1963 when the company simply appointed Harry Adey, the Chairman of the J.S.S.C., to the post and got him to move from one side of the negotiating table to the other.

At Rootes and Standard, management had been fairly content to let the piecework systems pace production: Jaguar, however, were less willing to pursue this course. Rather than allowing the same number of men to boost their earnings by handling more work as output rose, Jaguar wanted to put more men on the lines to deal with increased output so as to safeguard quality. Stewards, therefore, were regularly protesting against the recruitment of extra labour which kept their earnings down and seeking an extension of their rights to negotiate over labour loading. Jaguar stewards therefore never developed the same quasi-managerial roles and remained rather more oppositional. Meanwhile the piecework system was unsatisfactory in many respects to both labour and management. While Jaguar kept their wages high, both because of shop floor bargaining and because they wanted to attract the highest quality of labour, they became very unstable in the mid 1960s. The take-home pay of a track worker could vary from over £30 in one week to £15 in the next. Alongside this there were countless sectional anomalies based on little more than historic bargaining opportunities. These problems were not acute while the system was in constant motion, but they became more so as work study made creeping inroads in the late 1960s and pacemaking piecework bargaining opportunities became scarcer.

Weak management and unsystematic work organisation had its counterpart in a 'structurally untidy and administratively amateurish' union organisation. Organisation was extensive, fairly open and democratic and was a classic case of the Turner, Clack and Roberts generalisation that to the worker 'the shop steward was his union'. Union officials rarely had much to do with the factory and the J.S.S.C. was never able to develop an effective co-ordinating role. This was not because of the sort of inter-union hostility that occurred at Rootes: instead inter-union conflicts were generally settled or contained by agreements and understandings after a difficult period in the late 1950s and early 1960s when the T.G.W.U. staked a claim to and won acceptance as an equal of the N.U.V.B. in the plant. In 1950 the N.U.V.B. had had 50 per cent of the factory stewards but by 1965-66 this had fallen to 33 per cent, while T.G.W.U. recruitment on the tracks had carried them to an equal figure. Concern about the inter-union balance of recruitment to sections at a time of continuous new hiring had been dealt with through a widespread practice of recognising certain shops as the prerogative of particular unions. The Toolroom was A.E.U., paint was T.G.W.U., trim the N.U.V.B. The tracks were mixed, but there were often trends for mixed shops to move towards single-unionism. For instance, the N.U.V.B. had 'closed' one Assembly line: the T.G.W.U. had 'closed' a section of the final line.

Inter-union accommodation was, therefore, fairly effective, but on factory wide issues the senior stewards made little headway in developing a strategic approach of any sort. The mid 1960s found them struggling to devise appropriate responses as problems over lay-offs squeezed them between shop floor discontents and management actions. Erratic and recurring periods of waiting-time in many shops were being used by management as a way of regulating production levels without lay-offs. The response in the shops was the frequent use of 'downers' (short sharp protest strikes). Many stewards felt, however, that this in effect aided management who wanted less production anyway. The Body Shop stewards, therefore, decided on a 'reprisal' strike to stop the whole of the department rather than just those sections involved in waiting-time. The J.S.S.C. opposed their action since it inevitably led to the lay-off of track workers. But their opposition was ineffective, the Body Shop went ahead, and once the track workers were laid off, the whole matter escalated into a factory-wide strike that the J.S.S.C. neither wanted nor thought appropriate. On this and several other occasions in the mid 1960s, the unions got involved in rapidly escalating actions on fairly minor issues and ended up being wrong-footed and forced to back down. As a result, the position of the senior conveners became seriously weakened at this time.

Despite these weaknesses, piecework bargaining saw Jaguar workers sitting fairly near the top of the Coventry earnings league and able to use their bargaining opportunities to keep themselves there. As a classic high wage piecework factory it was in some ways a test-case for B.L.'s ability to force the introduction of M.D.W. in the early 1970s. Resistance at Jaguar was the most powerful B.L. encountered anywhere, with a ten-week long strike in 1972. Unlike other B.L. plants, the introduction of M.D.W. offered no levelling-up trade-off and threatened to submerge the workforce's advantage of bargaining in a prosperous and up-market firm. The coincidence of the M.D.W. strike with the launch of the XJ12 gave the strikers a powerful card, but in the end B.L.'s determination held out and the strikers went back because, as one striker put it, they 'had so many bills behind the clock on the mantlepiece that one more would push it off'.[21] The B.L. buy-out of piecework in the end gave them a flat rate of £44, a substantial increase: three weeks later, however, Longbridge was bought out at a higher rate and temporarily at least, came from behind to supersede Jaguar at the top of the earnings league.

For the rest of the 1970s, M.D.W. and the loss of peak earnings went hand in hand with the loss of corporate identity within the B.L. group. B.L.'s offensive against shop floor bargaining had *also* been an offensive against Jaguar's independent identity. Piecework had sealed a link between the prosperity of the company and the high earnings of the workers. M.D.W. now submerged the former and constrained the latter. The company's relative prosperity was submerged within B.L.'s wider crisis in the late 1970s and the company was starved of cash, development resources and planning. When Jaguar's fortunes also took a dive in 1980, the workers were faced with Edwardes' company-wide offensive on working practices to bring them into line with the more intense factory regime of the mass production plants. The result was a prolonged and bitter clash. The defence of Jaguar's distinctive grading structure reflected both wage grievances and feelings of loss of identity within the larger company. When John Egan, the new Managing Director, set out after the strike to re-establish the Jaguar marque, he was, therefore, able to draw on large reserves of goodwill from the workforce, and was effectively able to call for a shop floor/management alliance in the reconstruction of the company.

Standard had seen advantages to be gained from devolving control to stewards and gangs: Rootes had found it convenient to abdicate control. Jaguar never went that far. Indeed,in so far as they believed that the higher quality of their product necessitated direct control of the production process as well as mere pacing, they were resistant to such policies. Yet their management was generally simply too weak to develop alternative methods, despite an underlying strain of workforce cooperativeness that was to be found under Lyons, under Geoffrey Robinson in the 1970s and again under John Egan in the 1980s. Instead loose management and fragmented unions remained at arms length with a low level of conflict endemic but major conflict only sporadic and largely confined to periods of major product changes or upheavals in payment systems.

Alfred Herbert: Shop Stewards on the Defensive.[22]

Workplace relations at Alfred Herbert, the leading machine tool firm in Coventry, present a sharp contrast to these three motor firms. Despite prosperity and high levels of demand, unions remained marginal until the late 1960s and Herbert's stood low on the Coventry wages ladder. Management, products and payment systems changed only slowly and represented a distinctive 'Herbert' tradition. When changes did come in the 1960s, the reform of corporate organisation, the introduction of new payment systems and the development of trade unionism all moved forward together.

As John Davies has shown elsewhere in this volume, Herbert's before the Second World War was a classic anti-union paternalist shop. Many of these elements were also to be found in the motor firms in those years, yet the Herbert system came through the war and post-war boom more or less intact. Unionism developed considerably during the war, but it did so largely on the basis of a female membership that was almost entirely excluded from the factory once the war ended. Even during the war, union organisation lacked self-confidence and tended to rely on arbitration rather than exerting direct pressure in the shops. After the war unions were tolerated but they had almost no bargaining rights and were only consulted on a few limited issues such as pensions.

The defining characteristics of Herbert's were its management style and its idiosyncratic payments system. Management was based on the personal authority and paternalist style of Sir Alfred Herbert and what one trade union official called 'Herbert's Sunday-school teacher type of management'. Sir Alfred was reluctant to delegate authority and clung to power until his death in 1957 at the age of 91. At upper corporate levels this was a disaster and an unreformed blurred management structure lingered on for ten years after his death in increasing turmoil and confusion. At the time of the government rescue of the company in 1974, this period was described as 'a particularly startling example of lack of control'. Yet paradoxically, while the more vigorous Rootes and Jaguar managements lost control of the workplace, this was the one area where Herbert's did keep firm control.

In contrast to the motor firms, foremen and supervisors retained an important and authoritative role on the shop floor. Partly this was because Herbert's paternalist tradition of works discipline meant that supervision received resolute support from higher management. But it was also linked to their important continuing role in shop floor bargaining. From an early date Herbert's had operated a gang piecework system, or perhaps more properly a small-group piecework system since many of the gangs had only two members. The centre piece of this was that job prices were *not* negotiated but were settled by the rate-fixer directly with chargehands. The latter were gang leaders, but contrary to the practice in motor firms where they were elected by the gangs, at Herbert's they were directly appointed by management, usually by the foreman. The chargehand remained an ordinary manual worker and had no right to hire and fire, but he did play an important supervisory role in allocating work. The company refused to disclose to gang members the 'time allowed' for various parts of overall gang prices, thus effectively excluding gang members from any discussion on prices. During the war the unions had challenged this system at the National Arbitration Tribunal on the grounds that it infringed mutuality, but they lost the case. Apart from Herbert's, only small firms in the forging industry had similar systems of fixing prices with appointed chargehands. Not until 1966 did gangs win the right to have a member present alongside the chargehand and rate-fixer during price-fixing.

The opaqueness of gang earning was compounded by the complex grading system. For example, in 1967 there were 660 different wage grades for a total of 1040 direct workers employed on gang piecework. This grading system was the result of what Williams called an accumulation of 'petrified elements of bygone states of affairs'. A typical wage would include seven elements, including two different types of merit pay, two different types of 'Alfred Herbert Award' and a 'Special Alfred Herbert Award', each of which formed the basis of further complex piecework additions. Thus, despite its 'gang' character, final payments remained obscure and individualised and workers doing the same job could often receive widely differing payments. The main beneficiaries seem to have been the chargehands and the skilled workers who together made up one-third of the manual labour force and who did relatively well from a system that invisibly and differentially allocated gang earnings.

Such a pay system had little to do with incentives, and Williams 1967 investigation found a relatively low level of effort and stability as the primary aim of management. He concluded that Herbert workers were 'satisficers' rather than 'maximisers' since Herbert's did not lose their labour to other firms. In March 1965 the Herbert piecework average was 10s.9d. against a Coventry average of 12s. 4.3/4d and a higher figure for other Coventry machine tool firms, a difference that amounted to a hefty £3 per week. The motor producers offered high but somewhat erratic earnings. But Herbert's rather different product market meant that they could offer something rather different. Producing a bewildering variety of unstandardised machine tools and selling to a wide range of customers, they were relatively immune to sharp fluctuations. In addition, their unadventurous approach to product innovation meant that the product range changed only slowly and most of the piecework prices were historically based—the sort of job price that proved notoriously 'sticky' even in motor factories.

The emergence of unions as significant actors at Edgwick was delayed until the onset of the crisis of the company in the late 1960s. In 1968-69 under the guidance of the management consultants Higher Productivity Ltd., Herbert's belatedly introduced a wholesale reorganisation of corporate structure and corporate strategy. As part of this, they urged the introduction of work study and insisted to management that this could only be smoothly introduced if it was carried through in discussion with shop stewards. As a result, Herbert's for the first time grudgingly extended facilities such as phones and time off to stewards and began sending them on courses to learn about M.D.W. Senior stewards were allowed into new centralised negotiations and a 'closed-shop' agreement was concluded at Edgwick.

These reforms, however, failed to stem the decline of the company and the unions arrived on the scene too late to achieve much. The stewards' first major negotiation and first major 'success' was actually the negotiation of 'voluntary severance pay' at Edgwick when the hourly workforce was cut from 2,321 to 1,305 between 1970 and 1972. It was only with the collapse of the firm and the intervention of the National Enterprise Board that Herbert's became 'a test-bed for Tony Benn's theories of worker participation'. The Rescue Plan was tied to extensive participation machinery but the unions were quickly overwhelmed by their 'responsibility' for solving the crisis, the urgency of the situation and the imperatives of commercial confidentiality. The new centralised steward organisation found themselves in the lap of management, throwing their support behind any management team that might save the company. It was the frustrations of this situation that brought about the first-ever significant strike at Herbert's in 1975 and a sit-in against closure in 1980. Both ended in confusion and failure as the company was cut down to a mere rump.

The Herbert's case highlights significant contrasts with the motor firms and emphasises the indeterminacy of the outcome of shop floor bargaining even in the boom in Coventry. Until the late 1960s the Herbert system held up to exclude any effective shop floor bargaining. At one level this appears to be a functionally interlocking system of authoritarian/paternal management, divisive and inhibiting payment systems, a distinctive labour tradition and a slowly changing production base not subject to the pressures of seasonal or cyclical fluctuations. It appears almost as inevitable that shop floor bargaining would *not* flourish at Herberts as it appeared inevitable that it *would* flourish at the motor firms. But viewed in another light, Herbert's record appears very contingent. Herbert's are generally regarded as being excessively conservative in their product strategy in this period: yet if they had been innovators, it would have thrown their payment system based on stability and historically legitimated prices into chaos. If, as nearly occurred, the shop stewards had wrested the principal of mutuality from management during the Second World War, they might well have made mincemeat of a pay system fraught with so many indefensible anomalies. Under these circumstances the paternalist Herbert image could easily have backfired to become a provocative symbol of arbitrary authority.

Trade Unions and the Limits of Piecework Bargaining.

The case studies stress the variety of shop floor bargaining in Coventry. Among the motor firms there are many similarities in the extent and nature of job control and bargaining. But it must be stressed that there is nothing in the motor industry itself which automatically generated this pattern. Until the early 1960s Coventry stood in a different league of union organisation and bargaining power to the biggest motor manufacturers such as Morris, Austin, Ford and Vauxhall where the unions were very much weaker.[23] The district conditions of Coventry clearly provided a favourable environment for union development, especially the pressing demand for labour, the drive for high output and the relatively slack cost constraints on products before the 1960s. But as the case of Herbert's shows, even these conditions were not sufficient in themselves for the development of strong trade unionism.

Over and above general structural conditions, the actions of both managements and unions were often decisive. At Ford, Vauxhall and Morris, management determinedly set themselves to restrict the role of unions with considerable success: the case of Herbert's shows that such dogged resistance was probably not out of the question in Coventry either. However, at Standard management opted positively to promote certain aspects of union organisation in pursuit of wider business goals, while Rootes and Jaguar both found it convenient to abdicate large areas of traditional managerial control and allow the piecework system to act as a rough proxy for works management. On the other hand, the drive and vigour of unions themselves played a key role. The inroads made by the unions, and particularly the T.G.W.U., during the war were greater in Coventry than anywhere else, partly because of some brilliant opportunism by stewards and officials like Jack Jones. Elsewhere, in Luton, Oxford or Dagenham, wartime union development was very patchy and there remained a long hard slog in the post-war years before the unions achieved critical mass. Effective resistance to the post-war employers' offensive was of great importance, and here the militancy of the shop floor workers proved decisive, though the role of Standard management in breaking the employers' ranks should not be underestimated. It has often been argued that the gang system itself was a root cause of union growth, but it must be emphasised that although the big gangs at Standard and Ryton were undoubtedly potent bargaining units, the more common smaller gangs at Stoke, Jaguar and Herbert's never exerted the same muscle. Moreover, the Standard 'big gang' system in its classic form was as much a symptom of union successes as a first cause.

Often the almost invisible role of individual activists on the shop floor was vital. Factory micro-histories invariably reveal a handful of now almost mythical figures who took it on their shoulders to 'go union mad' and go out and throw themselves head first into recruiting *en masse* at key moments and making potential membership real. In this role, Communists often played a part disproportionate to their numbers. Less is known, however, about the sociology of the various shop floors and their labour traditions that may have made such catalytic action possible. We do not know, for instance, if Herbert's had a recruitment pattern distinct from that of the motor firms. Were 'Herbert' workers born or made? High wages made motor firms a magnet of attraction for semi-skilled workers and against a background of general shortages of engineering labour there was still intensive competition to get these jobs. What sort of workers won out in this competition and why? We have already seen that there were very definite bars to the entry of women and blacks. Those who got to these firms often climbed a ladder of jobs, moving from firm to firm and playing the labour market, often with a paid-up union card as an ace. On the other hand there were also periodic intakes of 'green' labour that could cut across this. One example was the 1971 large-scale intake at Ryton where recruitment coincided with a slump in the nearby Hinckley hosiery trade. The result was an influx of 'woollybacks' and 'knickerstitchers' who, nevertheless, seem to have been quickly absorbed into the industrial relations traditions of the plant.[24] In the mid 1960s, even in a firm like Jaguar, 50 per cent of the labour force had less than five years service. It is possible only to raise these questions here. A fuller assessment must await further research.

These factors shed some light on the causes of union growth and the rise of shop floor bargaining, but what were its consequences? We have paid much attention to the loss of managerial control on the shop floor, but this was not the same thing as the existence of union control. In fact, as we have seen, the shop steward system under piecework was fraught with inequity, lack of security, constant haggling and divisiveness. The results of sectional, fragmented bargaining were only partly satisfactory to stewards. They recognised the bargaining advantages of piecework but were also critical of the system as dog-eat-dog and as vicious in dividing and driving the workers. One result of prolonged piecework bargaining was a chaotic and wide spread of differentials with neither a managerial nor a union rationality behind them. The unions were able to disrupt the managerial rationality of differentials, but not to impose their own. Relativities tended to be quite unique in each plant and their movements depended almost solely on domestic factors. Workers within the same grades had widely different earnings within the *same* plant. It was common for a job to be lowly rated within one plant's hierarchy but highly rated in another. Jobs that were easy to rate-study were often on 'tight' prices and had below average earnings, while jobs requiring no more skill or effort might have high earnings simply because they were hard to assess. While differentials in the American automobile industry had become highly compressed by the 1960s they remained very wide in Britain.[25] Moreover there was no tendency within the piecework system to change this: indeed, steward bargaining seems to have adjusted itself to them and bargaining often took place in relation to maintaining those differentials even among semi-skilled workers. Workers on individual piecework were ready to tolerate surprisingly wide differentials between similar jobs.[26]

It is arguable, in fact, that stewards had more influence over the internal plant hierarchy of wages than over the absolute levels of earnings of the plant as a whole. While there was much leapfrogging within plants, disputes over parity *between* plants were rare. Concern to preserve and use differentials as levers meant that stewards never challenged the overall payments *structures* of plants. Such a leap remained outside the conceptual and political horizons of most steward organisations. In practice, they respected very large areas of unilateral management control and the 'right to manage', especially over issues such as hire and fire, plant closures and information disclosure, and efforts to curb the use of overtime and short-time to cover fluctuations of production were less systematic than they might have been. Steward organisations, with the partial exception of Standard, were at their weakest in mitigating job insecurity and instability of earnings and it was weakness on these issues that gave management a particular leverage in the introduction of M.D.W. when they could offer increased stability of earnings as a trade-off for the loss of continuous bargaining rights.

Stewards were generally unable to develop broader strategic goals. Much of their bargaining advantage in the shops derived from astute manipulation of custom and practice. This, however, should not be confused with unilateral regulation of conditions in the workshops. The rule of custom arose primarily in areas where managerial decisions had hitherto been absent. Its effects were necessarily fairly random, and it could work both ways since both stewards and managers were liable to give ground unwittingly to each other on this terrain since the implications of particular decisions were often not clear. More importantly, the random nature of such gains from shop floor opportunism meant that stewards could not push these gains in any planned direction or generalise them and higgledy-piggledy actions over obscure grievances could sap collective strength. This lack of unity within firms was rarely offset by effective company-wide J.S.S.C.s, which were often unable to overcome inter-union rivalries or develop coherent policies. Over and above the factory level, steward combine organisation remained skeletal throughout the 1960s.[27]

How effective was shop floor bargaining in raising earnings and what impact did it have on the economic performance of the firms concerned? There is a general correspondence between high wages and high levels of shop floor bargaining, but there is an unresolved question of cause and effect. The product market, for instance, may have been at least as important as bargaining in determining wage drift and the wages league. In the mid 1960s, the Coventry firms with the highest levels of pay and with the greatest wages drift were not the motor firms, but Alvis which largely depended on government military contracts and Bristol-Siddeley, with their multi-million pound aviation contracts, and neither had such vigorous shop floor bargaining records.[28] Standard was the best organised firm in Coventry when it strode ahead of the pack on wages as the company expanded in the 1940s and early 1950s: but it was *still* the best organised when its wages fell back towards the district average under the impact of economic decline. Nor did the onset of powerful shop floor bargaining in the motor industry nationally result in car workers outstripping the wages of workers in other manufacturing industries. In Coventry unions consolidated their position in the late 1940s, but workers in Ford, Morris, Austin and Vauxhall were poorly organised until the late 1950s. One might therefore expect the extension of union organisation to have a marked effect in pushing forward relative earnings. On the contrary, however, average weekly earnings in motors were 21 per cent higher than the national industrial average in the period 1949-59; but this rose only to 24 per cent between 1959 and 1963 and then fell back to 16 per cent 1964-68 and 19 per cent in 1968-73.[29] Given that motor industry productivity growth was above average and that union density was increasing in motors from the 1940s to the 1960s more quickly than in the manufacturing sector as a whole, this could be an indicator that shop floor bargaining did not have a decisive impact.[30] Certainly, even in the mid 1960s when wage drift was at its peak between 1964-67, average hourly earnings were moving up less fast (19.2 per cent) in motors than in chemicals (19.7 per cent), all-engineering (20 per cent) and shipbuilding (27.1 per cent).[31] It is notoriously difficult to separate out the impact of bargaining from that of other factors such as rising productivity or tight labour markets, but it does seem that the *prima facie* case that bargaining was a key determinant of motor industry wage levels is a weak one.

What then was the major impact of shop floor bargaining on the performance of firms? The proliferation of bargaining meant numerous short stoppages, but in most cases lost production could be relatively easily recouped through overtime or revised schedules afterwards. Even where this was not the case, most stoppages would only slightly lengthen buyers' waiting lists in ways that did not lose sales. Rising output was generally accompanied by a pattern of small short strikes, but the really significant increases in striker-days corresponded closely to *downturns* in production. According to Turner, Clack and Roberts, in the period 1945-65 there was 'a strong, direct but *inverse* connection between striker-days and production',[32] while in seasonal terms 'striker days are generally highest in months when production is below peak level and tail off as output rises through the year's last quarter, reaching their nadir in December. Three production peaks—in March, September and December—also coincide exactly with three striker-day troughs'.[33] There was, they concluded, clear evidence that motor manufacturers used strikes as a way of regulating output. When demand was not pressing 'negotiations in the car plants appear to drag unnecessarily, or are often allowed to drift into open stoppages of work'.[34] Small dispersed stoppages had little impact on production and larger stoppages tended to be associated with recessions. By the 1960s, the Coventry manufacturers' main problem was not inadequate volumes of production but being able to sell the cars they made at a profit and 'beneficial strikes' could avoid the pile-up of unsaleable cars.

Interruptions of production due to disputes do not seem to have had very serious effects on car makers' performance. The other common charge is that union controls on the shop floor inhibited labour productivity. As the crises of Rootes/Chrysler and Standard deepened in the 1960s, both firms made allegations about low labour productivity based on the low average of cars per man per year as compared with their European competitors. But since British manufacturers had opted for a labour intensive form of production such figures tell us very little. Under piecework the pace and intensity of work were generally high, and, as Thomas and Williams have argued,[35] rather than high pay resulting in expensive cars it may be better to regard it as a case of relatively low pay and labour intensive methods making it less attractive to invest in capital intensive methods and encouraging technical stagnation in the industry. It is becoming increasingly apparent that the long-run decline of the British motor industry was due not to strike-proneness, excessive earnings and low productivity, but a failure to produce the right models for the right markets at the right time, resulting in loss of scale economies and falling profits which in turn made remedial investment and development much harder. Broader managerial failures outweighed the rather overstated adverse effects of shop floor bargaining. Why, therefore, as the crisis of the industry intensified in the 1960s did management see the elimination of piecework bargaining as a vital step in reversing their declining fortunes? At each of the major Coventry firms, employers faced up to major confrontations with their workforces and offered tempting wage increases as sticks and carrots to get rid of piecework in favour of Measured Day Work. Why?

Management and the End of Piecework.

By the mid 1960s Coventry engineering employers felt that they had effectively lost control of their payments systems. Work measurement and performance standards did not exist and prices were negotiated almost solely in relation to earnings levels rather than in relation to work or time values involved. They could not determine differentials and the relationship between incentive payments and effort had become a sham or mere 'horse-trading'. Piecework prices varied according to the intensity and frequency of bargaining and drained management time and nerves through endless day to day bargains and arguments. Prices revolved around ingenious debates over the subjective assessment of jobs and it was hard to refute workers' claims with either logical or rational arguments. The stewards had learnt to outmanoeuvre rate-fixers on all sorts of grey areas of job evaluation such as fatigue-relaxation allowances, the method itself, materials allowances, the learning process, contingencies, the product mix or increases or decreases in continuity. As a C.D.E.E.A. report concluded in 1968, 'It is this absence of standards that slowly and surely wrests from management an area of control that is essentially a management function'.[36]

As a result the costs of most operations were uncertain and unpredictable and the process of production was itself opaque to management. Workers could, if they wished, control the level of output according to their earnings requirements, or their desired level of labour loading, and management possessed no independent yardstick by which to check this. Without any 'objective' performance standards, shortfalls in services and materials were not shown up for corrective action and management had to rely for effective utilisation of plants and machines on the gangs and the stewards. Stewards and gangs were very often cooperative in these processes, but the degree of their dependence on such cooperation was something that was becoming very disturbing to management.

Coventry managers recognised that the labour content of total costs was relatively small, but they increasingly saw it as a vital competitive margin as competitive pressure intensified in the 1960s. Several wider developments served to increase their unhappiness. Firstly, wage drift was beginning to spread to staff salaries as DATA and ASSET unionised and began to use comparability arguments. In what in retrospect was a very naive diagnosis, the engineering employers came to believe that scrapping piecework would 'deal appreciably with the growing problems posed by staff unions in seeking to achieve and maintain a certain parity'.[37] In fact, under M.D.W. the range of comparisons that staff unions utilised were to become far wider and more visible. Secondly, the vogue for company wide package deals and productivity bargains posed a threat that big settlements or buy-outs could force up piecework targets throughout Coventry. Thirdly, there were growing government pressures for the engineering employers to put their house in order and to develop more 'orderly' collective bargaining, partly because of government concern with the inflationary risks of payment by results and partly because the engineering employers had presented themselves as the champions of reform before Donovan and felt called on to show willing themselves.

These issues rather blinded them to many of the ongoing advantages they derived from piecework. Even wage drift had its benefits. As the C.D.E.E.A. themselves noted in 1968, it 'allowed management to have a flexible wage system which could readily and unobtrusively be manipulated in order to improve wage levels to attract or retain labour':[38] though they also noted that it was hard to manipulate it in a controlled fashion. Secondly, though attention was usually focussed on loose rates as a cause of drift it also arose from increases in output and productivity and management never sought or was able to evaluate the relative contributions of these two aspects. Thirdly, the unions' near obsessive focus on sectional earnings meant that employers escaped from serious bargaining pressures on wider issues such as status, overtime pay, holidays, sick pay, pensions and fringe benefits at local levels.

Moreover, though the employers were sensitive to the possible spread of comparability bargaining to staff, they largely ignored the fact that, through the Coventry Toolroom Agreement (C.T.A.) skilled workers had been virtually removed from the front-line of bargaining for almost thirty years. The C.T.A. was introduced in January 1941 to base Toolmakers' earnings on the average earnings of skilled fitters, turners and machinists in Coventry Federated firms. The main aim was to prevent the migration of Toolmakers to the highest paying firms and eliminate the opportunity for skilled workers to 'play the market'. As a result there was very little labour turnover in the Toolrooms—especially since the only way to get 'extras' was through merit payments which usually depended on long service. Toolmakers relied for their pay increases not on bargaining but on the automatic operation of the C.T.A. and in many firms the organisation of Toolmakers became weak and quietistic. The highest paying piecework firms paid their Toolmakers much less than their pieceworkers but came under almost no pressure to remedy this. Yet consideration of the C.T.A. usually focussed not on its effect in the Toolrooms but on the role played by the regularly published figure of average earnings on which the Toolroom rate was based, and which became used as a pace-setter and bargaining target for pieceworkers. It is true that this publicly available average rate was a useful bargaining point for shop floor bargainers, but it would be foolish to think that if it were removed, unions would not find other target figures. When the C.D.E.E.A. considered terminating the agreement in 1965 many senior managers were reluctant to get rid of it for this reason and argued that in fact it was a stabilising element that averted comparisons with *peak* earnings. Despite frequent complaints about it in public, they decided that it was really a symptom rather than a cause of wage drift and decided to keep it.[39]

After much heart-searching they finally decided to scrap the C.T.A. in 1972. They still saw abolition as very much a leap in the dark. In the end the decision was made under the impetus of three growing pressures. Firstly, the imminent withdrawal of B.L. from the Federation would narrow and destabilise the base on which the rate was calculated. Secondly, it seemed that wider restructuring of payment systems in the District would be hampered by its continuity. And thirdly there was strong direct pressure from the Department of Employment and Productivity to get rid of it as an anti-inflationary measure.

The working of Coventry piecework was illogical, inelegant and erratic: but it was not rampant. Weak piecework systems were themselves symptoms of what the C.D.E.E.A. called 'a wider derogation of managerial control'. For over twenty five years, management had paid almost no attention to control of the labour process, integration of production engineering and workshop organisation, the flow and scheduling of production in the workshops and front-line supervision. The role of the foreman had shrunk, sunk in status, and was regarded disdainfully by pieceworkers who often earned more than those who supervised them. Management had come to believe that it was not worth wasting resources on training supervisors. Ford who had always employed day-work, had a ratio of one supervisor to 20 workers: but at Rootes it was 1:50 and in the mid 1960s the Coventry average was 1:45.[40] Instead management relied on payment incentives to do the job for them. By the late 1960s they were realising that the haphazard operation of loosely controlled incentives were a poor substitute for a managed workplace. But they did not fully realise the extent of the managerial tasks that would face them if they abolished piecework. They wanted to replace an incentive by a coercive system where they would establish and implement their own norms. But they almost completely lacked the personnel, knowledge and techniques to do so and they were only slowly to acquire them over the next decade—by which time the Coventry engineering and motor industries were no more than shadows of their former selves.

Measured Day Work and Industrial Decline.

The record of Measured Day Work (M.D.W.) has been so bound up with the precipitate decline of the motor and engineering industries in Coventry in the 1970s that it is difficult to make a strict comparison between it and piecework as bargaining systems. At the biggest B.L. factories of Longbridge and Cowley where car production has survived at fairly high levels, there were clearly two phases of M.D.W.: a period of 'leisured' day work and weak management control following the buy-out of piecework, followed eventually by a dramatic second phase under Michael Edwardes when the screws of the system were drastically tightened in the early 1980s. But at Standard the business collapsed before this second stage was ever reached, and at Ryton it came only after control had passed from Rootes to Chrysler to Talbot and the business had become so depleted as to become unrecognisable. Herbert's was collapsing even before the reform of the payment system began in earnest. Only Jaguar might provide better scope for comparisons, but there, unfortunately, we have little data on recent developments.

However, there are certain broad comparisons which can be made which throw further light on the operations of piecework. Firstly, both stewards and management believed that M.D.W. would destroy the bargaining power of the shop floor. They envisaged plant and group negotiations being centralised in the hands of management and union officials thus curbing sectional activities. In the long run, something like this has certainly occurred at Longbridge and Cowley, though the senior stewards have forced themselves into a continuing major role in plant and group bargaining alongside the officials. But it would be wrong to attribute these developments solely to the shift in bargaining system. They have to be placed in the context of the depth of the B.L. crisis in the late 1970s and early 1980s, the shift in political climate, internal shifts in power within the unions, and the wholesale transformation of B.L. management and the modernisation of production. In the shorter term, it is more remarkable how little the simple change in wage systems accomplished.

For instance, at Chrysler and Standard the stewards continued to find plenty of bargaining opportunities through mutuality on work study and manning. At both plants the companies conceded mutuality on operational times and backed down on full work study. There was no proper introduction of job evaluation to accompany M.D.W. but instead a mix of negotiations, parity, custom and practice and work study. The stewards in particular used their sectional strength to control labour loading. By refusing overtime they increased manning whenever production went up and then resisted de-manning when it went down. At the same time, M.D.W. triggered a new wave of company-wide comparability struggles (notably Linwood's demands for parity with Ryton) and created a new focus in claims for increased lay-off pay. Shop floor conflict increased significantly between 1970 and 1973 and strikes at Chrysler rose to record levels.[41]

At the same time, the intensity of effort and the pacing role of piecework fell away. The Coventry companies found themselves unable to get continuous sustained effort without incentives. Stewards ceased to attempt to correct production problems as they occurred or chase up materials, and more 'bad' work was allowed to go down the lines since this no longer had any impact on earnings. Instead of the focus of bargaining being almost exclusively on pay, it shifted towards effort, conditions and security of earnings. Extra labour was now welcomed on the sections to ease effort rather than shunned because it reduced earnings. M.D.W. had been hastily established with little method or time study and no thorough reform of supervision. It put the responsibility for maintaining the continuity and quality of production and the flow of materials squarely on to management's shoulders: but management was not equipped for these new tasks. It was only after a gap of several years that employers began to integrate their new payments systems with restructuring of work organisation and managerial systems, and to follow through the extensive implications that the new system had for stock and quality control, buying and production programming, and production engineering and job design.

The elimination of piecework clearly curbed classic wage drift, but it also opened up new patterns of differential and comparability bargaining. Most notably, inter-plant differentials became more visible and Ryton wage levels in particular became the target for parity claims at Linwood and other Chrysler plants. One result was a 'concertina effect' with claims for parity succeeded by claims to re-establish differentials and then by claims for parity again. At the same time anomalies and differentials became an intense focus of conflict, especially for craft groups and toolmakers who now reappeared on the bargaining scene after many years of relying on the C.T.A. In the early 1970s these groups were involved in a string of strikes that were disproportionately costly to the numbers involved as they sought to reposition themselves in the wages table and achieve status and bargaining rights. These struggles were crucially exacerbated by being caught up in the restrictions of government pay restraints which seriously hampered the development of more 'rational' pay structures. In the long run, however, the hierarchy of differentials was significantly rearranged in the decade following the introduction of M.D.W. The dominance of production workers was eroded. On the one hand, their advantage over indirect and unskilled workers was eroded by the redistributive effects of incomes policies, notably threshold agreements and equal pay legislation which brought significant catching up by the lower paid. On the other hand, after 1975, vigorous workplace bargaining by skilled workers finally successfully re-established skill differentials and took them to the top of the tree.[42]

As we have noted, steward bargaining continued to thrive through a late Indian summer through the early years of M.D.W. More recently it has suffered some severe setbacks, especially at Cowley and Longbridge, though it is as yet too early to say whether this managerial offensive has been decisive. Elsewhere, however, as at Jaguar, sectional bargaining has been superseded not by the destruction of stewards but by a new institutionalisation of powerful senior stewards and conveners in close 'bargaining relationships' with management. Even in crises, many managements have preferred to enhance the authority of these groups and deal with formal hierarchical steward organisations than attempt to demolish them. As a result the scope of bargaining has often widened. Undoubtedly this has occurred at the cost of day-to-day responsiveness of steward organisation and workplace democracy, but it is the economic crisis and political climate rather than changes in bargaining structures that are primarily responsible for the stifling of sectional militancy.

In the post-war boom, Coventry engineering workers pushed shop floor bargaining further than any other comparable group of workers. Energetic sectional bargaining and direct workplace democracy won significant gains, though shop floor bargaining was always more cooperative and less confrontational than has often been argued and many aspects of workers' lives received scant bargaining attention. Bargaining remained primarily opportunistic and weak on coordination and strategy. In many ways it depended on a weakness of management that was unlikely to persist. M.D.W. was just one part of a slow but important restructuring of management which has accelerated rapidly in recent years. Unions in the 1980s now need to find new and more appropriate forms of bargaining linking workplace democracy and militancy to factory and group level strategy in face of more highly developed management control. One tragedy of the current recession is that the workers of Coventry's ravaged motor and engineering industries have little chance of once again playing a front line role in such developments.

Notes to Chapter 7

1. On the inter-war years, see: S.W. Tolliday, 'Militancy and organisation: Women workers and Trade Unions in the motor trades in the 1930s', *Oral History*, 11, 2, Autumn 1983; S.W. Tolliday, 'Trade Unions and shop floor organisation in the British motor industry, 1910-39', *Bulletin*, Society for the Study of Labour History, Winter 1983; S.W. Tolliday, 'The failure of mass production unionism: the motor industry in the inter-war years', in C. Wrigley (ed.), *A History of British Industrial Relations. Vol. 2. 1918-39* (forthcoming). For other views see: J. Zeitlin, 'The emergence of shop steward organisation and job control in the British motor industry', *History Workshop*, 10, Autumn 1980; and the reply by D. Lyddon in *History Workshop*, 15 and the rejoinder by Zeitlin in *History Workshop*, 16.
2. See J.H. Goldthorpe, D. Lockwood, F. Beckhofer and J. Platt, *The Affluent Worker: Industrial attitudes and behaviour* (1968).
3. G. Turner, *The Car Makers* (1964), 239-40.
4. E. Batstone, I. Boraston and S. Frenkel, *Shop Stewards in Action* (1977); W.A. Brown, *Piecework Bargaining* (1973); W.A. Brown, 'A consideration of "Custom and Practice"', *British Journal of Industrial Relations*, X, 1972, 42-61; W.A. Brown and K.F. Sisson, 'The use of comparisons in workplace wage determination', *British Journal of Industrial Relations*, XIII, (1975), 23-51.
5. H.A. Turner, G. Clack and G. Roberts, *Labour Relations in the Motor Industry: A study of industrial unrest and an international comparison* (1967); G. Clack, *Industrial Relations in a British Car Factory* (1967).
6. A. Friedman, *Industry and Labour: Class struggle and Monopoly Capitalism* (1977).
7. *Royal Commission on Trade Unions and Employers Organisations. Report* (1968).
8. C.D.E.E.A. Numbers employed 20 January, 1967. Coventry Record Office.
9. S.W.C. Winchester, 'Spatial structure and social activity: a social geography of Coventry' (D. Phil. thesis, University of Oxford, 1975).
10. Works Conference Notes, 14 August, 1951.
11. Works Conference Notes, 18 June, 1953.
12. Report of an inquiry by the Commission for Racial Equality into

recruitment practices at the Banner Lane factory, 1982.

13. In each of the case studies that follows the basic sources are the following: (1) Records of the E.E.F. and C.D.E.E.A. to 1959. (2) Works and Local Conference notes deposited at the Modern Records Centre, University of Warwick. (3) C.D.E.E.A. papers in the Coventry Record Office. (4) Minutes of the District Committees of the A.E.U./A.U.E.W., T.G.W.U., N.U.V.B., Sheet Metal Workers. N.U.V.B. Head Office Correspondence in the City Record Office. (5) Newspaper files, especially the *Times* and the *Coventry Evening Telegraph*. (6) Extensive interviews with workers, stewards, officials and managers. I would like to thank all of these people for their cooperation, though I have only cited them by name when I have quoted them directly.
    In addition, for the Standard case I have used the deposit of Standard Papers at the M.R.C. and the Standard Joint Shop Stewards Committee Minute Books for the 1950s.
    See also: G. Robson and R. Langworth, *Triumph. The Complete 75-year History* (1977).
14. S. Melman, *Decision making and productivity* (1957).
15. D. Rayton, *Shopfloor Democracy in Action* (1972).
16. R. Croucher, 'Communist politics and shop stewards in engineering, 1935-46' (Ph.D.thesis, University of Warwick, 1978).
17. G. Turner, *The Leyland Papers* (1971).
18. In addition to sources in Note 13 I have also used: A.E.U. Humber Shop Stewards Committee Minute Books for the 1950s and N.U.V.B. files on Ryton in the Coventry Record office. See also Ministry of Labour files in the P.R.O. LAB 10 for the events of 1944-46.
    See also: S. Young and N. Hood, *Chrysler U.K. A Corporation in Transition* (1977); 8th Report of the Expenditure Committee, Public Expenditure on Chrysler U.K. Session 1975-76. (1976); G. Foster, 'Rough Road for Rootes', *Management Today*, (1969), 93.
19. K. Richardson, *Twentieth Century Coventry* (1972).
20. In addition to sources in note 13 see A. Whyte, *Jaguar, the history of a great British car* (1980); Clack, 'Industrial relations', *op.cit.* I am grateful to Paul Worm for his assistance in researching newspaper files on the company.
21. David Craddock, Assembly worker, quoted in the *Times*, 6 September, 1972.
22. Again, see sources in note 13. In addition see R. Williams report on Herbert's to the N.B.P.I.: for the changes of the late 1960s I am particularly grateful to Ken Grainger for allowing me to draw on

unpublished material for his forthcoming Warwick thesis. On the 1970s see: Coventry Trades Council *et. al., State Intervention in Industry: a workers' inquiry* (1980).

23. S.W. Tolliday, 'Government, employers and shopfloor organisation in the British Motor Industry, 1939–69', in S.W. Tolliday and J. Zeitlin, (eds.) *Shopfloor Bargaining and the State: Historical and Comparative Perspectives* (Cambridge 1985).
24. P. Jones, 'Politics and the Shopfloor', *International Socialism*, (1973).
25. S.W. Tolliday and J. Zeitlin, 'Shopfloor bargaining, contract unionism and job control: an Anglo-American comparison', in N. Lichtenstein and S. Meyer (eds.), *The American Automobile Industry: a social history* (University of Wisconsin press, forthcoming).
26. W.A. Brown, 'Piecework Bargaining', *op.cit., passim.*
27. S. W. Lerner and J. Bescoby, 'Shop steward combine committees in the British Engineering Industry', *British Journal of Industrial Relations* (1966).
28. C.D.E.E.A., 'Wage drift, work measurment and payment systems,' unpublished paper (1968).
29. J. Durcan, W.E.J. MacCarthy *et. al., Strikes in Post War Britain, 1946–73* (1983), 333.
30. C.D.E.E.A., 'Wage drift'.
31. Turner, *et al.*, 'Labour relations', 113.
32. *Ibid.*, 124.
33. *Ibid.*, 127.
34. K. Williams, J. Williams and D. Thomas, *Why are the British bad at manufacturing?* (1983), Ch. 3.
35. *Ibid.*
36. C.D.E.E.A., 'Wage drift'.
37. *Ibid.*
38. *Ibid.*
39. C.D.E.E.A., Sub committee reports to the Management Board on the advantages and disadvantages of the C.T.A., 4 November to 14 December, 1965.
40. C.D.E.E.A., Report on requirements for supervisory training, 1968.
41. See Young and Hood, 'Chrysler'.
42. W. Brown, 'Incomes policy and pay differentials: the impact of incomes policy upon workplace wage determination in the

engineering industry , 1972-75', *Oxford Bulletin of Economics and Statistics*, 38 (1976); W.A. Brown, 'Engineering wages and the Social Contract', *ibid.*, (1978).

Chapter 8

Domestic Life in Coventry 1920–1939

Peter Lynam

People produce other people. Family life is central to this process of social reproduction. The cycle of infancy, childhood, adolescence and adulthood takes place and is endlessly repeated in the family setting. The family is one of the major contexts of personal and social experience. Yet it is a difficult subject to investigate, especially for the historian. Most families leave behind them no written records. This means that oral testimony is going to be the crucial source of both information about and attitudes towards family life in the past. But the difficulties do not end with the obtaining of that testimony. The material used in this chapter is drawn from interviews with Coventry people and in this case the problem is to isolate what is unique to Coventry about the experiences and attitudes described. In many respects the interviewees might be speaking for the members of working class families of any industrial town in twentieth century Britain. Work on the family of the Coventry car worker continues. Moreover other studies of twentieth-century working class family life in other places are beginning to appear, most notable so far, Elizabeth Roberts on Barrow. It should soon be possible to see how far the people in our study are speaking for Coventry, how far for a wider national experience.

Any book which attempts to analyse and describe the life and labour in a particular place during a particular period will not want to neglect the voices of those who underwent the experience. History is partly made by people and partly by the historian: in this chapter that co-operation becomes more visible. The historian has framed the questions but the answers come from some of the people of Coventry.

The material in this chapter broadly covers the period 1920-39 and is drawn from a wider study of Coventry car workers based on 60 coupled interviews over three generations. Because the focus in this chapter is on home life most of the evidence has been drawn from the talks with women who, apart from relatively short periods at work either just before marriage or during the war, spent most of their time on the domestic front.

It should be remembered that many people now resident in Coventry, some for decades, spent their formative years in other towns and regions. Even for those proud to have been born in the city it often transpired that a parent or grandparent had come from outside. Marjorie Clark remarked of her own parents, for example:

> Mother was a cook in service in Cheshire. And dad was an engineer, a toolroom man, in Altrincham ... Dad came first, got a job in Coventry and got into lodgings. Then mother followed and, of course, being in Coventry, as cook-housekeeper. And then they got married in Coventry and stayed afterwards ... They must have come to Coventry about 1906-1907, married about 1909 ...
> Lack of work in Altrincham. The toolroom trade ... was very slack and they were appealing in the Altrincham newspapers for qualified engineers to come to Coventry. And my dad cycled ... 90 odd miles, and six of them cycled, engineers from Altrincham to Coventry and got jobs ... Well, he went to the Ordnance when he first came to Coventry, he worked at the Chain, but it was at the Ordnance when he first came to Coventry, because it was just before coming up to the 14-18 War ... He was a universal miller.

There were a few who, on being asked about parents and grandparents, could list employment in what were the Coventry trades of the late 19th century: weavers, watchmakers, and cycle makers. Family fortunes had fluctuated according to the state of trade; all had known depression, slump. My sample being divided into three generations made it more likely that those in the third generation would have a parent who had been employed in Coventry's motor industry before they were born. Often, uncles and aunts in the city were similarly employed.

June Bream came as a very young child to Coventry in the early 1920s. Her background displayed the peculiar characteristic shared by the families of tradesmen working in the motor industry at an early stage of its development:

> I was born in Liverpool, in Wavertree, West Derby ... My grandma had a boarding house in Southport and my father worked in. Before I was born my father worked in Scotland and my eldest brother was born in Scotland. My sister was born in Manchester and my other brother and myself were born in Liverpool ... My father was an old coach-builder and in those days they had to travel to where the work was. So they had a big tool box and the man was known by his tool

> box whether he was a good tradesman or not. And then after I was born my father moved down to Coventry, looking. You know they used to travel all over the country for work. And he came down to Coventry and then after he'd been down here a couple of years then the family moved down with him.

Kath Smith, on the other hand, had not had to come as far as had June. Born when the city was smaller but important as a munitions centre, Kath too represents the natives' experience:

> I was born in Raglan Street ... the old Singer works that was one of our playgrounds almost when we were children ... I suppose it would come into Hillfields now but it, then it wasn't. It was not far from Pool Meadow actually, so I was right in the centre of the town almost.

Housing was always a problem for working people but as other essays have emphasised, the flood of migrants into Coventry produced a housing shortage which lasted almost thirty years. Moreover much of the housing was small and lacking in conveniences, prompting frequent attempts to find something better. It was unusual for those born in one house still to be living there a decade later. Indeed the family would move from rented accommodation according to the price charged for it and the space it provided, taking into account growing families or children leaving home on marriage, thus making payment for unused space an extravagence. Family accommodation was a function of family life-cycle, and could be taken as an index of family fortunes. Irregular employment or unforeseen adversity could prompt a move to more restricted but cheaper living space. Such a process, experienced by so many was touched on by Lillian Rowney who although leaving the parental home when she married in 1941 had already had several homes:

> I was born in Coventry, in Melbourne Road, just around the corner, 147 ... We moved, we moved. And we went to live in Craven Street, not very far away. Then from Craven Street we went into Lord Street, and that's where I lived when we got married ... Yes, well we were growing up and we wanted more room in the house. The house wasn't very big you know, and we wanted more room, so we went in a bit bigger house in Craven Street ... then from Craven Street we went into Lord

> Street ... Well, by that time my sisters were getting married. I had two sisters, one brother was already married. So then we moved again... into Lord Street, which was a nicer house as well.

And what would be a 'nicer house' in the mid-1930s? Marjorie Clark said:

> We lived in a house in Kingston Road without a bathroom, just a two up, two down. Mother and dad wanted a house with a bathroom and we had a chance to move into a slightly larger house. That was the reason we moved into Queensland Avenue.

Two up, two down was the most common form of accommodation, even though families were larger. Some older members of the sample lived in the old weavers' or watchmakers' houses with large windows and an extra floor that was one large room. Harry Petch, sharing one such large bedroom with the other boys in the family also had to contend with his grandfather's pigeons flying in and out of the big window. The *Midland Daily Telegraph* in 1919 was calling for three bedroom houses to be built as young families would soon grow and need more space. As it was, families with a number of children slept several to a bed, with a curtain dividing boys from girls in the back bedroom and parents in the front bedroom with a baby's cot if necessary. Very large families had older boys and girls sleeping in the downstairs back living room. This was the time of the posh front room, rarely used. Furniture consisted of large cupboard (for crockery, etc.), table and set of chairs. There were few radios and obviously no television. A front room might have a piano and not just for show.

The home was the mother's domain. She did the cooking, washing and mending. Sometimes other family members—daughters especially—helped with the cooking and cleaning. Young children were often assigned domestic tasks like swilling out the yard, polishing the fireplace, dusting mantelpieces, polishing the hall lino. Such tasks included some real jobs that took time to complete, but some seemed simply to give children the chance to show willing. Older girls in a family of boys might have more involved domestic tasks; it was a form of socialisation, learning a future role they would play as adults. In other families, girls and boys learnt about domestic chores. A woman's work was particularly laborious. Washing clothes could take the best part of a day; in the 'courts', Stanley Young remembered, women did their washing within earshot of each other. Labour-saving devices — vacuum cleaner, washing machine, spin-dryer—were the exception in the late 1930s. Preparing meals also took time. There were larger families, more mouths to feed. There were evening meals to prepare, but also midday meals for men and young workers in the family often returned from workplaces to eat at home, along with children of school age. So they would not be long out of the house, morning or afternoon, before their next meal was having to be planned.

That 'home was mother's domain' was the expression used by June Bream when she recalled her childhood years. Her mother was confined to bed after losing a baby:

> She was very poorly and for the last 12 months of my school life I didn't go to school ... and in those days we used to have the school board man come, as they called him, and if you didn't go to school they used to come and see why you didn't go. So I think I'd been off some time when he came round and he said, "Oh, but you must go to school". And I was looking after my mother ill in bed, and my father and two brothers and sister, and I was only 13.
> So what I had to do ... one week I used to go mornings and then the next week I used to go afternoons and then I had to fit my duty at home in between. And dad used to come home on a Friday night, you know, and when my father came home mother always used to have a clean pinny on, you see. It was always the thing that you always had, because it was wages day ... And I was going to take over because my sister was working, you see, I was the only one that could do it. And I can remember my father coming home and he said, "Where's your clean pinny?" And he says, "Go and get it on", so I went and put my pinny on and came back again. And he says, "Here you are" and he threw his wage packet in. And I was only 13 you know ... "You're the mother in the house", he says, "till your mother's well now".

Although June missed some school because of domestic responsibilities, and this was no unique experience, the notion of the woman's place being in the home was strongly reinforced by the education that was given. June would normally have had lessons in sewing, cooking, and laundry, as did other girls at school. At senior school there was one teacher:

> She used to teach you to be a housewife, a mother. They used to have this part where it used to be like a house and you used to have the old grates in it, you know, and gas stoves where they were all black-leaded, and of course you had to do all that. And you had to, you had special times, and it was either cookery or washing and ironing, you know, or housework. And when you went in here, and you had to go in every room, you had a kitchen and a living room and a bedroom. And if you were doing cookery ... you had to cook the meal in the morning and then the teacher and the rest of the class, or some of the class, used to stop for dinner and you used to have to wait on table. They showed you how to set the table.

Most women stopped paid employment on marriage, as Census figures for 1921 and 1931 bear witness, although as Josie Castle shows in this book, GEC provided the opportunity for some exceptions. For women, the home became the focus of work. Imelda Wintle remembered her mother's working hours with appreciation, and is typical of the sample in this respect:

> She used to describe herself as a "poor old slave", you know, with the family and that. I mean she was on the go all the time. She used to do her own decorating and things like that, and cutting down clothes, you know, and making do ...
> Well, I was supposed to keep my own bedroom clean and tidy. And brother used to get the coal and chop the wood and help with the washing up. And, of course, as we got older we got more jobs to do.

Within the family such chores might well be the justification for pocket money when children completed tasks. But there is a more serious blindspot when the Census is referred to, namely that housewives might well be engaged in economic activity which made an important contribution to the family budget. One woman recalled:

> ... When we were little, you know, and money wasn't quite so good, I've seen my mother take in washing, and she's washed it and ironed it and, when we were kiddies, take it back the same night.

It was common for wedding presents to include a sewing machine; a useful gift and a piece of capital equipment. It was used for mending clothes and often for making them, particularly for children. Much effort would be spent on immediate family needs but there was evidence of local networks whereby women supposedly not 'at work' could make some money. Of childhood clothing, Marjorie Clark said:

> Usually, I believe, we had them made. In those days, dressmakers were more common than they are today. Very few clothes were bought off-the-peg. And I believe mother used to make them a lot herself and probably someone she knew ran them up as well, you know, a local dressmaker. That was the thing in those days, there were quite a lot of little dressmakers. You could go to a local one and have things made ... that would be in the houses ... You'd know someone who could make a blouse or a shirt ... That's where most of our things came from ... Of course, my father would go ... to a tailor's for a suit, but there again, it wouldn't be off-the-peg, it would be tailored. And coats and hats, of course, we would buy those. But most of the things were either made at home or made by someone we knew who was a dressmaker or tailor.

Women made preserves, like jams and pickles. Bread was made sometimes once or twice a week but that practice quickly died out with the availability of cheap bread from city bakeries. If women prepared the food, the men often grew it in a back garden or on an allotment. Growing vegetables and fruit occupied many hours for men in spring and summer evenings and weekends. The boys would be involved—like the girls they too were being socialised—digging the garden or weeding, carrying implements and produce, perhaps spreading fertiliser. (Horse-drawn vehicles provided enterprising small boys with pocket money as they sold horse dung to those growing fruit or vegetables). Such gardening was both recreation and contribution to the domestic economy. It combined hobby with necessity when money wages might be irregular because of lay-offs and seasonal unemployment common in the city's motor industry. A small minority of the older section of the sample worked neither garden nor allotment. The build-up of Coventry reduced available land, but houses with gardens had room, and neighbours and relatives swapped produce for variety or payment in kind. Gardens held livestock—laying hens, chickens, rabbits—which might be regarded in the late 20th century as a throwback to the image of the rural background of migrants. In fact, it supplemented the family diet with eggs and meat. Living in the city made poaching nearly impossible; none of the sample regarded it as a moral question.

Sunday dinner was the best meal of the week come what may. Children running errands for food did so only for the simple, cheap items. The expense of this meal meant mother went personally to the butcher, knowing what to look for. It was the occasion for a ritual unity of the family and taken seriously. The week's meals followed a pattern, with variations according to each family's routine, but Kath Smith put it well:

> Sundays we had roast, always had roast, always had roast meat, a roast dinner Sunday and of course we had the cold meat on Monday. And we always had the meat and potato pie on Tuesday. I suppose it could have been sausage, or something, on a Wednesday or Thursday. It was always fish on Friday and it was always a makeshift dinner on Saturday. It may be sometimes on a Saturday we would have fish and chips instead of faggots and peas. But when you come to think that fish and chips then was thre'pence, tu'penny fish and a penny worth of chips ... and on Sundays for tea we'd always have salmon and fruit and cream ... but when you think a tin of salmon was eleven pence ha'penny and a tin of pineapple was five pence ha'penny ...

The pattern here was determined by domestic tasks—like Tuesday being washday which meant the stew could be doing and finished off with the pastry—and the family's financial circumstances. Pay-day was at the end of the week, hence the Sunday feast, while the days immediately before pay-day called for ingenuity to keep the family fed on shrinking resources. The breadwinner had to be preserved and the children fed. Imelda Wintle and Eva Shilton made their respective comments on this:

> I've seen her eat bread and mustard, and she'd eat a sandwich of cabbage and things like that. Since, later on in life, I've mentioned it to her she said "Well I couldn't see you lot go without". And she'd make do, she was a typical mother, you know, heart and soul for her children ... He would have larger helpings than ... the children, but I've never known him have anything extra. Like he was the same as mother, you know, he used to get pleasure out of seeing us alright, but he was a good eater and he never left anything. She didn't like cooking but she would always cook for my dad because he liked the things we didn't. He loved oxtail stews, anything in that line ... She

> did always look after him, there was no doubt about that at all ... I think with him having so much ill-health, when he was well she would look after him to keep him well.

What were the lives of the children like in the homes of Coventry's working people? How did they get on with their parents? Judging by the sample, fathers were respected, but mothers particularly were held in affection. We might ascribe this to children seeing what mothers did around the home and appreciating the effort spent on their well-being. Fathers' work held more mystique; located some distance from the family home and outside the child's universe. Fathers left early for work, perhaps returning briefly for a midday meal. They might work hours of overtime at short notice—not unusual in the motor industry—and children saw less of them. In both World Wars men were away for months or worked very long hours. We can only speculate on the effect of this absence on children growing up in the years 1914-18 and 1939-45; not all would have experienced it but many must have done.

Children may have realised there were emotional or financial problems but parents did not worry them with such concerns. Perhaps the eldest child would be confided in, but usually only when they had reached adolescence. Children were also protected from the emotional trauma of death. Brothers, sisters, grandparents died but children seem rarely to have attended any funerals. However, the death of a parent was a dreadful experience for young children especially. But a father's death meant, in addition, the loss of the main breadwinner. The family was in trouble unless older children were already in paid employment, still single and resident in the parental home, so that funds could be pooled for family maintenance. It often meant a move to cheaper accommodation and the mother's quest for work: perhaps cleaning work, taking in washing, or factory work, none of it likely to be well-paid. The loss of a mother had its emotional impact and needed older members of the family to rally round. Vera Langford's fiance was confronted with such a situation:

> His mum had died and he had a job in London. And then when his mum died he came back and sort of helped look after the younger ones. Because there were quite a few young ones, and him and his dad and his elder brother sort of brought them up between them.

Census records for the inter-war period show the vast majority of women in employment to have been spinsters or widows. Recurrent illness suffered by a male breadwinner meant a wife's search for paid employment also. The questions about 'women's two roles' in home and workplace really take root from the 1950s.

Parents influenced children's behaviour more than did any other family relative. Very occasionally a neighbour or close friend of parents might have made their impression, but insufficient to rival that of the parents. Teachers were strict for the most part and in this respect had some influence. Teachers encouraged good behaviour but so did parents, who probably had more stake in children's behaviour, for it reflected on the family. Children did not live under fierce parental discipline but it was firm.

> Well, we always classed ourselves as being respectable. "And don't bring trouble home" and that kind of thing. I think if we had've done we would never have been able to enter the house again ... my mother was like that ... she meant it. She just wanted us all to be happy and respectable and live a decent life ... and that was what we did; no-one ever brought trouble to her ...

That was how Lillian Rowney summed up what was expected of her, and it was echoed by others like Kath Smith:

> I suppose they just wanted us to grow up to be honest, hard-working citizens. I suppose they would have liked to give us the moon and liked to see us make our way in the world.

There was respect for parents not just in school years but extending through the early years of work when son or daughter could be more independent as a wage-earner. Respect remained but with family life-cycle having reached the stage of minors in paid employment living in the parental home, it was clear that relationships must change with altered circumstances. Insistence on being home by a set hour was adhered to, however, although that rule might be bent when courtship began.

Despite limited finances, children's birthdays were celebrated within the family, or might include a couple of friends from the locality. Money and space prevented many or the more boisterous from attending. Mothers baked cakes for such events and provided food for what was as ritualistic as the Sunday dinner. Fathers made an effort to mark such occasions, internal to the family, also. Such occasions as the celebration of birthdays were times when the family marked the changes to which its members were subject. That passage of time had its inexorable effect on family roles and relationships.

Family entertainment has undergone marked changes in this century and such changes were evident when the sample was asked about this aspect of their lives. In a number of those posh front rooms stood a piano or some such musical instrument. One family member could usually play the instrument in question, although families rarely sang together. Perhaps at Christmas when members of the wider family would be present would there be such musical participation. Such traditions lasted until radio and later television came into more families' lives as forms of cheap entertainment. June Bream and her family entertained themselves in this way:

> Of course there was no television or anything in those days, you know ... My father used to play the violin and my eldest brother he used to play the violin and after he got married his eldest daughter played the piano. And we were never great singers but everybody used to sing. But before my brother got married ... there were just the two violins and very often on a Sunday, you know, they'd just sit there and that was your Sunday, listening to their violins, and singing.

Family games were played on Sundays or during festivals like Christmas —when there might be little else to occupy time and energy—and when relatives or family friends came visiting.

Television was a novelty for some years, taking some getting used to for older people, but children in the 1950s were the first generation to experience it in their most formative years. One woman recalled family entertainment in the post-war years:

> We started off with an old radio and then we gradually worked our way. I think my daughter was about three when we had our first television set, a little tiny nine inch one. We did buy the first one, I think we bought the second one, and then we've been renting one now for about 10-12 years. They weren't expensive, not in those days.

The effects of television are still argued about, and are not our concern here, but its arrival was a landmark in family entertainment.

Reading was a family activity which used up the recreation time of young and old alike. Children joined the library during school years, being attracted by subject matter that ranged from hobbies to adventure stories and books about foreign lands. It reflected a curiosity about the outside world when there was little opportunity or money to see it for themselves. Reading was popular and there were a few avid readers. But not all parents encouraged reading: a few were hostile, seeing it as evidence of idleness or the source of 'fancy ideas'. There were children with the time to read but not the inclination. Comics were popular, being exchanged within and between families of children. Every stage of the life cycle and each family role seemed to have reading material aimed at it. Children's comics, women's magazines and popular daily papers all had mass markets in Coventry.

Autodidacts were also in evidence. Their reading habits cultivated intellect, sharpened critical faculties so essential to the city's working class organisations. Such people exercised a leadership function where opinions were being formed. Encyclopaedias, novels, the classics, anything to stimulate thought and imagination, attracted them; and they encouraged their not always willing children to tread the same path. In the sample it was the exception for there to be a number of books or no books at all.

In a migrant family, relatives were not likely to be near at hand. In such circumstances, a family wedding was a major event. For native Coventrians, however, the city's 20th century growth had provided little reason to move and find work elsewhere, so families of this type gathered easily for wedding celebrations. Weddings and marriage were approached in practical fashion. In this respect Vera Langford speaks for many of her generation when asked what her wedding was like:

> Registry Office. We hadn't got any money for a big 'do'. What we had got we kept, you know, we sort of spent on necessities ... Just family.

Many started married life in inauspicious circumstances. The city's motor industry provided many with a living, as many as it provided with spells of unemployment. With a number of other women, Marjorie Clark was made redundant from Standard Motors just six weeks before her wedding. Nonetheless preparations for it had been going on for some time and the celebrations were determined.

> We got engaged on New Year's Day in 1937 and got married on New Year's Day, 1938 ... We saved enough for the deposit

> on the house, that was £50, that was a lot of money then! Oh yes, we saved very hard ... Yes, mother helped me in a lot of ways, even if it was only with a bottom drawer, that sort of thing. And for the year that I was engaged she had no money from me for my keep. I kept all my money ... and saved every penny of it for the wedding and everything like that ...
> It was a white wedding at an Anglican church and ... it was bitterly cold ... It was a very happy wedding ... There was no reception, no photographer, no honeymoon because I was out of work and my husband was on short time ... So my mother saved the turkey from Christmas, cooked it and we had that for the reception ... at home. There was about 20 in the house, quite a crowd there ... My mother's brother came from Anglesey and my dad's sister came from Manchester. They were the only two actual relatives at the wedding, apart from my sister and her husband.

For Bertha King, her wedding brought an additional surprise:

> If you'd got a job then you'd got to hang on to your job ... the day we got married he'd had his redundancy notice the night before, but he didn't tell me. So when we started married life, he'd had his redundancy.

A honeymoon for a newly married couple in the inter-war years might well have been their first trip away from Coventry for more than a single day. 'Family holidays' are a commonplace now but earlier in the century they were limited by lack of time, money and transport. Families did visit relatives in the city, Sundays being popular for tea. Migrants to Coventry were less likely to enjoy this kind of family contact as it could involve a long journey to Lancashire, Yorkshire, London or wherever, and an overnight stay. Thus it was unusual for whole families to travel any distance. Only if relatives lived in the countryside could such family travel acquire the label 'holiday', offering space for children to play, plus the benefits of fresh air and exercise. Similarly could country cousins—in ones or twos—enjoy a city stay at minimum expense, a facility called on when looking for work in Coventry. Rarely did fathers holiday with the family, unless holiday pay had been negotiated in the workplace. The 1938 legislation marked a turning point in provision of holiday time with pay, but war the following year delayed families enjoying the change they had anticipated. Charlie Evans speaks for many in the inter-war years when he was asked about family holidays at the seaside: 'Nobody ever saw the sea in them days, only them who lived by it!'

Families did use the bank holidays for day outings. Resorts like Blackpool were popular with day-trippers, but annual holidays for whole families were unusual. By 1939, Coventry car ownership was surpassed only by that of London. This increased mobility opened up new possibilities for travel. Cycles, motor cycles and sidecars were used particularly by young workers for travel some distance from the city with boy friends or girl friends. This was the heyday of rambles in the countryside and camping, an ideal break for youngsters with money and families who could afford it.

Sundays, like weddings, were traditional and ritualised. The Sunday dinner we have already noticed. Sunday walks were also popular with families, 'leafy Warwickshire' being all around. But of course for some it meant religious observance and Coventry's churches and chapels provide ample evidence of religious activity, the diversity of which seems a natural corollary of mass migration from numerous points of origin with attendant religious traditions. All children attended Sunday school, with parental encouragement, either to get them out of the house or to get that religious instruction which even agnostic guardians seem to have regarded as a positive stage in constructing a morality for their children. For children it was enjoyable; there were stories, and outings once or twice a year. 'A bun and a ha'penny' attracted any waverers. Also, it provided companionship on an otherwise quiet day for boisterous young children. But family observance was a minority feature of Coventry Sundays. Families, generally, did not pray together or say grace. A minority of families attended church or chapel regularly, perhaps sang in the choir, so that for those children Sunday school was only one of several religious events they might participate in on a Sunday.

It is often difficult to discover parental interests outside the family. Children saw parents in that role alone, but it is reasonable to assume parents had other, external interests. As most of the sample remembered it, however, women often confined themselves to the home, and they recalled mothers who rarely went out when the children were young. Mothers spent recreation time in the evening either sewing, knitting, making clothes, listening to the radio or reading. All this went on in the living room, keeping an eye on children not yet in bed. And of course male breadwinners faced long working hours also as Derek Coss recalled of his father:

> When he wasn't working overtime, he would be home at

> quarter to, ten to six. The hours were eight 'til half past five, with one hour for lunch. And on a Wednesday night, they would finish at six o'clock, so he'd get home ... at quarter past six. But of course there would be four hours on a Saturday morning from eight 'til 12, that made it 47 hours a week.

It was common for such male breadwinners to work in garden or allotment in spring and summer until bad light prevented them. There were always pubs near at hand for socialising and drink, and men were certainly attracted to them. But only a minority of men drank to excess as a way of life. A number were teetotal and many made do with the occasional pint. In a migrant city, however, pubs were the natural rendezvous for single men, as were the many clubs in Coventry. Public houses have long been the marketplace of the working class and when work was erratic the companionship could well lead to employment. Matt Nelson, from a north-east coalmining community, remembered women hardly ever in a pub up there. In Coventry, however, wives might join husbands in pubs or clubs, meeting others from the locality.

In general, men had more interests outside the home, whether pubs, sports activities, union meetings, hobbies or whatever. Men and women did attend cinemas and theatres when such forms of mass entertainment flourished. Mothers were known to go to afternoon film shows with friends occasionally; there were social circles organised through local churches, which provided companions for women otherwise tied to the home but mothers seemed to have little time to themselves: their 'recreation' was often homebased and spent on the welfare of the family, making clothes, baking cakes, and so on.

Mothers were not remembered for their participation in sports in the way that some fathers were, for men were actively involved before marriage or while the family was still young. Age was a key factor in sports participation, giving way to a spectator interest. The eldest children recalled their fathers as young men in this respect. Memories depended on the sequence of child birth in the family. According to family life cycle, if the eldest remembered their fathers as active players, the youngest children remembered them doing no more than reading the sports pages while sitting in their favourite armchairs. Children experience their parents in different ways.

Outside the family was always the wider community, of which the family was part. Family members were not confined to family relationships alone, but mixed with others in the streets, schools and other workplaces that together made up the city. The most insular could only be so with difficulty. Few people were not linked into their local neighbourhood.

Earlier in the century, Coventry was much smaller, but bursting out of its mediaeval confines. There was an intimacy in the old city, as Vera Langford from Hillfields remembered:

> ... there used to be a lady in the street. If anybody had a baby, she would come and look after the mums, because all the babies were born at home in those days. She'd come and look after the mum and feed the children and get a meal for the husband. She used to be paid very little money because there wasn't a lot of money about, and there was one lady down in Berry Street who used to do that ... I was 15 when my youngest brother was born and I remember at the time that I'd got a little job and this lady used to come in ... and get our meals ready for us in the evening.

Others had similar memories but stressed that such work was limited to those who could afford that little extra, particularly where regular cleaning and washing was concerned. During a confinement, however, such help was appreciated. We can imagine how news travelled on the grapevine. Similarly when parents suffered illness there was help offered with care of children, and neighbours 'looked in' at regular intervals. Old photographs of street scenes show numerous children and women on doorsteps watching their children at play. Larger families, smaller homes and no motorised transport to prevent it, made such scenes quite understandable. Local school with limited catchment areas reinforced neighbourhood cohesion.

In Coventry, the streets and districts reflected the migration of labour. George Stockford's experience was typical of so many in the late 1930s:

> When we were growing up it was a complete cosmopolitan area. Coventry was expanding like the devil, and even the house I live in I can remember being built as a child. There was scaffolding up everywhere, there was building going on everywhere, and they were literally flooding in ... Just going up from our house there was old Coventrians next door. The people next door come from the North. The people next door come from Liverpool. The people next door to them came from Lancashire, Blackpool. The people next door to them were Irish, and there were Irish again; there were Scotch next door to them. And going back the other way again, they were

> Reading people; the next lot came from Scotland. The next lot come from Derbyshire, the others I don't know where, the next one was a Dutchman come from Holland. They were a complete mixture. They had come for work and the houses were, it was £25 for the key and 11 bob a week if you were paying for it yourself, or it was 15 bob rent and rates if you were renting.

Those near neighbours had different trades and occupations: machinist, turnsaw, draughtsman, fireman, gas meter reader, builder, market trader, skilled engineer. A similar diversity occurred in other streets and areas, it was recalled. And yet certain areas were to contain concentrations of Welsh and Scottish, for example.

Those older people interviewed for this study knew the hard times of the 1920s and 1930s and for them, even today, life is much better than they could have imagined. Life is more comfortable, life expectancy extended, a result of better living standards from the late 1930s on. The danger for that generation is that the attitudes they have to the past and present can prevent them acknowledging how hard life has become once again for those raising families or seeking work.

It is in the details of domestic life that the real facts of poverty and prosperity become clear. Even in an economy as buoyant as Coventry's, seasonal lay-offs and unemployment, together with large families, could rapidly turn a comfortable situation into an anxious one. On the other hand, as many other essays in this book show, Coventry was, certainly from the 1930s on, a stronghold of the affluent worker. The roast every Sunday, the buying of your own house, early TV and car ownership all bear witness to rising living standards. From 1945 expansion and optimism were widespread. Not everyone experienced the improvement in quite the same way or to the same degree, but enough did for it to constitute a trend. Children had more space, perhaps a bedroom each. They were better educated, there was a national health service, and a welfare system. Youngsters seeking work could choose between a fairly well-paid job and a better paid job. More people could afford labour-saving devices in the home, houses had bathrooms, families could afford holidays together, abroad too. If not often in paid employment before the war, married women after the war found there were jobs to go to. Women might have two roles, but they provided the family with two wage packets, allowing many to enjoy the period of affluence while it lasted. The question we are left with, however, is how families with no wage to depend on will survive through what remains of the 20th century?

Chapter 9

Recreation in Coventry Between the Wars

Jeremy Crump

While many other economic activities stagnated, the popular culture of the inter-war years was marked by the further growth of commercial forms of leisure. By 1935, there were 4,448 cinemas in Britain, against 3,500 twenty years before, catering for 907 million attendances. The opening of the Hammersmith Palais de Danse in 1919 marked the beginning of the first of two dance crazes based on large, public halls. Established spectator sports, such as football and cricket flourished while new ones, speedway and greyhound racing, were well suited to speculative investment by promoters. Gambling on football pools attracted ten million punters in 1938. The development of motor transport facilitated the growth of driving for pleasure for two million private car owners by 1939 as well as the popularity of seaside holidays.

Paid annual holidays had been extended to 11 million workers by the end of the period, and popular residential holidays were coming to rival day trips and weekend excursions to the main resorts. Even outdoor activities such as cycling, camping and hiking required capital investment if taken at all seriously. The dynamism of certain sectors of the economy, rather than the depression of the traditional industrial areas, underpinned these changes. It was not blighted areas such as the North East or South Wales which set fashions in leisure pursuits—in the latter, rugby and choral singing sank to miserable levels compared with their Edwardian splendour—but new industrial areas, especially London, with its domination of the production and distribution of newspapers, radio broadcasts, films and records. The light engineering and electrical industries whose factories lined the arterial roads of North and West London were those whose products, wages and industrial relations most adequately provided for a consumer-led boom of the type enjoyed by many Americans in the 1920s, with their cars and washing machines, radios and gramophones. The glossy world of the cinema and dance hall was attractive not only as a colourful escape from the grimness of closed-down factories—it also represented the culture of the most dynamic parts of the economy. Likewise, in Coventry, cinemas, dance halls and social clubs increased in number and size in response to the vitality of the local economy, not its weakness.[1]

By the 1920s, much of England had long shared in a national popular culture sharing common values in sport, theatre and drinking habits, differentiated by class, albeit subtly, rather than geography. This had been brought about from the mid-nineteenth century as railway communications facilitated the growth of music hall and theatre circuits, national sporting competitions and a popular press which set common agendas for enthusiasts throughout the country. Entrepreneurs did not exploit such opportunities equally rapidly in all fields, and local capital could resist for a time the advance of the entertainment empires of men such as Oswald Stoll, the music hall magnate, just as the local press did not at once fall into the hands of a small number of combines. Nineteenth century legislation had done much to encourage local authorities to enforce common standards of policing and public order, while drink legislation and the Gambling Act of 1884 further encouraged conformity. During the decades before the First World War, local authorities enlisted the support of large capitalist enterprises in their efforts to regulate popular recreation, as was the case in London's music halls and Birmingham's pubs.[2]

Against this background of commercialised leisure already national in character, the present study aims to examine how the particular circumstances of Coventry's economic and social development between the wars mediated broader trends. Two features emerge strongly. Population growth, due to immigration, and the town's prosperity, stimulated the development of commercially-run facilities for leisure, yet penetration by national capital was limited. Meanwhile, the larger firms and their workers promoted provision of works' social clubs, so that by 1939, many of the town's best sports facilities, dance halls and concert rooms were on the premises of firms such as G.E.C., Alfred Herbert, Courtaulds and Standard Motors.

The development of commercial leisure

While attention inevitably focuses on new developments, the persistance of older forms of recreation should not be overlooked. The Easter Pleasure Fair was still held on Pool Meadow for a week in 1922, featuring P. Collins' amusements. Circuses and travelling shows, for all their modern equipment, preserved a form of amusement largely unchanged since the time of Sanger and Barnum. By contrast, religious organisations still provided centres for many people's spare-time activities, as well as their religious needs. The inhabitants of Red Lane recalled the Saturday night dances and whist drives at St. Barnabas Church Hall, built in 1933, and at the 'tin mission' which preceded it.

The Bible Class Football League could still challenge the Coventry and District League to a representative match in 1920. A survey carried out by the Coventry Sports and Social Association into the city's leisure facilities in 1943 found that, even before the bombing, Church halls had provided the only accommodation for cultural activities in several suburbs and new housing estates. By 1943, 26 such halls were fully used for religious and recreational purposes. This reflected the circumstances of wartime, but also indicated the continued role of religious organisations in the inter-war years. It is quite possible, however, that the actual religious content of what went on in the halls was somewhat attenuated.[3]

In 1919, the city's chief constable noted with disapprobation how quickly the pre-war level of arrests for drunkenness had returned.[4] There are the usual difficulties involved in the use of such statistics, given varying intensity of police activity, but the figures in Table 9.1c may suggest a correlation between economic well being and drunkenness, and the increased incidence of arrests in the late 1930s is striking. Nevertheless, Coventry should not be viewed as a violent Klondike where wealthy migrants drowned their feelings of anomie in drink. In 1926, the rate of arrests was 12th highest among large towns, far below that of Newcastle, Liverpool, and Salford, less too than neighbouring Birmingham. In common with the rest of the country, the interwar years in Coventry saw a slight decline in the total number of pubs, quite marked when related to population growth. New pubs were often larger than those whose licence they took over. J.B. Priestley commented in 1934 on

> whole new quarters, where the mechanics and fitters and turners and furnace men live in neat brick rows, and drink their beer in gigantic new public houses and take their wives to gigantic new picture theatres.[5]

Contrast, for example, 1930s Tudor pubs such as The Newlins, Tile Hill Lane and the Maudsley, Allesley Old Road, or the art deco Tollgate, Holyhead Road, with old city centre pubs which still survive, such as Ma Brown's (The Old Windmill), Spon Street, and the Nurseryman Tavern in Chapelfields.

While facilities for drinking in pubs declined, especially for those on new estates, licensed clubs kept up with population growth.[6] (Table 9.1b, 9.1c). Coventry's oldest C.I.U.-affiliated club was that in Cox Street, the Coventry Working Men's Club, founded in 1860 before the

C.I.U. itself (f.1862), but Coventry had no extensive working men's club tradition in 1918. All but a handful of the licensed clubs then in existence were profit-making drinking clubs, or the social branches of friendly societies, political parties or other voluntary organisations. During the 1930s, migrants from areas where club life was strong gave renewed impetus to the C.I.U. in Coventry. Scots miners dominated the Binley Colliery Club, while the Hen Lane Club (f. 1934) was known locally as the Little Rhondda Club. North-easterners were to be found among the officials of most clubs. At the same time, the growth of skilled employment led to the formation of trade union based clubs such as the A.E.U. club in Foleshill Road and the Coachbuilders' Club in King Street.

Working men's clubs were not the large organisations with high turnovers from drink sales, augmented by takings from bingo and fruit machines, which many have become, and which were encouraged by the council's allocation of sites for new clubs, such as the Canley Club, in new suburbs after the war. Very few had full-time stewards, and breweries were not interested in investing in the club trade. The Birmingham Brewers' Association blocked their deliveries to Coventry clubs after the Stoney Stanton Road Club had had difficulties paying bills, and the clubs were forced to turn instead to the Midlands Club Brewery, a cooperative venture in Leicester, and to the Hook Norton Brewery.

As well as drink, the clubs still offered activities which had been their staple in the nineteenth century. Educational work was still important, and most clubs possessed libraries. Alongside performances by professional entertainers were free and easies, presided over by concert secretaries who were chosen according to their ability to keep order. Club life remained exclusively for adult males—women were admitted only on specific occasions, nor was there any articulate protest to such subordination. As well as a refuge, or bolt-hole, from domestic life, the clubs were centres for social relations away from the workplace. Their facilities could not compare with those of the big works' clubs, but they provided a sense of independence which was not to be found in the public house either. The C.I.U. was avowedly non-political, but individual clubs preserved ties with a radical past. The 1925 Club, for example, grew out of the British Socialist Club.

The years immediately following the First World War saw Coventry's major sports teams, amateur and professional, more securely established than they had been for some time, with grounds which could accommodate large numbers of enthusiastic spectators. Like other

Midland towns, such as Leicester and Nottingham, Coventry had a strong indigenous rugby tradition. The sport was taught in elementary schools and was further strengthened by immigrants from South Wales and Salford in the twenties and thirties. Coventry Rugby Football Club, established in 1874, moved to Coundon Road in 1921, having acquired a supporters' association in the 1920s. Coventry and North Warwickshire Cricket Club (f. 1851) merged with the Coventry and District Club in 1919, and able to return to its Binley Road ground, asserted itself as the city's principal club, a model for other teams. Denied first class cricket for most of the period, the Binley Road ground was at times host to the Warwickshire Second XI, but strong amateur teams were also able to attract good crowds. Coventry City F.C. had long since abandoned its links with the Singer Company, and in 1905-06 had been taken over by a syndicate of local businessmen. Successful play and large crowds in the war years allowed the club to leave the Southern League for the Football League Division II in 1919, their application for membership signed by the Mayor and the city's M.P. Its success was greeted with rejoicing throughout the town. Almost parallel to the economy, the post-war boom, with crowds over 20,000 in the first season, gave way to the slump into the third division south in 1924-25, and transfer to the third division north the following year. The thirties saw the advent of Harry Storer as manager and the period when fans shouted 'Come on the Old Five' to encourage the team week after week to put five past the visitors. Over a hundred goals were scored in 1931-32, 1932-33, 1933-34 and 1935-36. Coventry's generous defence meant that promotion was not achieved until 1936, when over 40,000 watched the crucial promotion game against Wolves. Big crowds continued to follow the team as they finished fourth in Division II in 1937-38 and 1938-39. Such form was not to be repeated after the war. It is clear though that the popularity of football as a spectator sport in Coventry depended on the team's success. There was strong identification with the team when results were good in the thirties, but bad play in the twenties and early fifties suggested that such loyalty had to be earned.[7]

There is little indication that the popularity of spectator sports seriously interfered with interest in participation. The Coventry and District Football League increased the number of its divisions to four in 1936-37 to ease the burden of postponed fixtures and allow players more chance to go to watch newly promoted Coventry City. The growth of the League was parallel to that of sport in the city as a whole. Revived by nine clubs in 1919, the League overcame problems of unfulfilled fixtures and from 1928 had more applicants for membership each year than vacancies. It was strong enough to survive the withdrawal of the major works teams in 1934, and by 1939 had 60 teams in five divisions.

As elsewhere, cinema was firmly established in Coventry before 1914 (see Table 9.2), but was transformed during the interwar years by technological changes and the growth of audiences.[8] The first films were exhibited at travelling shows, and were soon among the attractions on offer at the Hippodrome and Opera House, both of which were licensed for films in 1910. The same year, T. Clement's Salerooms were licensed as the first building in Coventry to be given over solely to that purpose. Later known as the Electric Theatre, then as the Star, it was typical of an early generation of cinemas whose small size made them unable to compete for long in a crowded market. The Coronet in Payne's Lane, for example, seated 125. Nevertheless, some of the earliest buildings survived throughout the period, either by their managements' willingness to modernise and innovate, as at the Royal (f. 1911), and the Scala (f. 1913), which showed Coventry's first talkies in 1929, or on the basis of a neighbourhood audience's support. The Prince of Wales (f.1910) was affectionately known as 'the bug and flea pit' by Red Lane inhabitants. The second period of cinema development, between 1926 and 1938, included the building of suburban cinemas, such as the Savoy in Radford Road (1938) and a series of increasingly large and luxurious super-cinemas, culminating in 1937 with the Rex, which could accommodate 2,500 people, and afforded among its attractions a dance floor, a restaurant overlooking Corporation Street, an aviary with tropical birds and the only genuine Wurlitzer in Coventry.

The growth of the cinema was largely carried out by local capital. Coventry did not diverge from the provincial pattern in this respect. Chains with ten or more cinemas owned only 27.5 per cent of the country's cinemas in 1935, and the trend towards concentration was strongest in the London area. Deutch and Noakes owned the Crown for a short time after 1925, but Odeon cinemas only came to Coventry in 1940-41 when the need to develop bomb-damaged sites provided an opportunity. Previously, Gaumont-British had bought the Coliseum in 1928 and reopened it as the Gaumont, the city's first super cinema, in 1931, while the A.B.P.C. chain outbid local interests in buying the Empire after the fire there in 1931. But the biggest chain in Coventry was that owned by Charles Orr, an Irish building contractor who had built several of the early cinemas. In partnership with H.T.A. Philpot, Orr's '5 star' circuit, which actually included six cinemas, dominated local exhibition between 1930 and 1934, when Philpot left to set up a rival company. Philpot drew attention at the opening of the Rex to the fact that

> It is, perhaps, somewhat significant, in these days of huge combines that my brother and myself, as a Coventry concern, should have augmented our existing circuit by providing a Theatre of this calibre for the public and Coventry ...[9]

The same interests were behind the city's limited number of commercial dance halls. F.H. Turner had intended to develop a leisure complex, with shops, ballroom and cinema at the Coliseum in Jordan Well, but sold out to Gaumont in 1928, unable to finance the project. More successful was Orr's Rialto development in Moseley Avenue, which began as a silent cinema in 1928 and was extended in 1936 to include the Rialto Casino Ballroom, one of Coventry's major dance halls.

High wages and the local concentration of the car industry made for high levels of car ownership in Coventry from an early date. *The Times* in January 1916 compared it with Detroit, and observed that

> It is the motor city. One sees more women driving motor-cars in the streets than anywhere else. Many of them own their own cars, and the well-to-do middle-class woman learns to drive her own car as naturally as her sister in the south learns to play hockey. The people travel.[10]

At this stage private car ownership was still very much a middle class phenomenon, but by 1939, nearly one person in five was a car owner, indicating a much wider social spread. By national standards the figure is remarkably high, anticipating a level of ownership not attained nationally until the 1960s (see Table 9.1).

By the late thirties, Coventry had a large number of relatively wealthy, young, mobile workers who provided a ready market for leisure industries. Ventures such as the Rialto Casino and the Rex, as well as the level of car ownership, indicate that entrepreneurs were beginning to exploit the situation. Yet it is striking that commercial development remained limited in scope and mostly small-scale. New spectator sports, such as speedway (f.1928) may have been more commercially orientated than football and cricket, but there was no attempt at any infusion of modern business methods comparable to that of the Sky Blue revolution of 1960-61 at Coventry City F.C. The city's boom was too rapid and too insecurely founded for national enterprises to show an unusual amount of interest in this Midland town. By 1939, according to the C.S.S.A. report, recreational facilities were 'totally inadequate to meet the requirements of the population'. Market forces, constrained by licensing laws, had provided large pubs and cinemas but little else for the suburbs while the cinemas, dance halls and pubs in the city centre were overcrowded, and little had been done to accommodate drama groups, music and art, what the report called in Arnoldian terms 'the more intellectual and cultural activities'. Municipal provision of recreational facilities, seems to have been modest. Library and museum provision depended heavily on the pre-1914 benefaction of Carnegie and more recent gifts from Alfred Herbert.[11] By contrast, the larger firms offered a wide range of social facilities to their employees.

Works' Social Clubs

In November 1935, the editor of the G.E.C. magazine, *The Loudspeaker*, drew the readership's attention to the wide range of social events promoted by the firm's Magnet Club during the forthcoming month. He reported that

> In addition to outdoor sports the programme includes a wide variety of indoor functions. Swimming, table tennis, chess and billiards are attracting more members than ever before, whilst the weekly attendance at the regular Wednesday and Saturday dances and whist drives exceeds 1,400. On November 4th the G.E.C. Legion Orchestra hold their second Popular Concert of the season; at the first the audience numbered 1,000. The following day, November 5th, you are invited to the annual bonfire in the playing fields ... From Monday, November 11th to Saturday, November 16th, the Photographic Society hold their annual exhibition in the club... Looking further ahead the display of Christmas goods will be opened December 5th ... The Dramatic Society will present their first play of the season on December 10th. On December 19th will be held the Annual Partner Drive ...[12]

By this time, the club's outdoor sports included angling, football, rugby, men's and women's hockey, and in summer, cycling, cricket, motoring, bowls and golf, as well as the annual gala, which attracted as many as 1,200 spectators. The club had a membership of c.4,000 in 1935 and an annual turnover in 1938 of £33,000. While the size of the club, renamed the G.E.C. (Coventry) Social Club in 1936, its facilities and range of activities put it to the fore of such organisations, there were many comparable clubs in Coventry between the wars. No fewer than 25 were represented at the inaugural meeting of the Coventry Works' Sports Association in 1934 (Table IV), representing all the main sectors of Coventry's industry. At the outset, though, it is worth bearing in mind the C.S.S.A.'s qualification that 'in certain cases these facilities are excellent but in others they consist merely of a glorified "canteen atmosphere"...'.

The practice of employers sponsoring their workers' leisure, whether in the form of annual outings or more frequent activities, was rooted far back in the nineteenth century, often as an element of work discipline and cultural regulation. J.J. Cash, ribbon weavers, and one of the few Coventry firms to survive from the mid-nineteenth century, had established a cricket club before the 1880s and by 1914 had fostered an active community life at Kingfield, with nursery and adult schools, canteens and welfare work supervised by Sidney Cash. Like other firms which showed an early interest in industrial welfare, such as Cadbury's and Pilkington's, Cash's were Quakers. Alfred Herbert established an institute in the Butts in 1907 and encouraged his employees to play team games as part of the family firm paternalism which he sought to foster. Other firms had sports teams and outings before the First World War, and in the case of the cycle manufacturers, Rudge-Whitworth Ltd. promoted an annual sports day (f.1897), open to all comers, and a cycle club for employees (f.1882) which served to advertise the product as well as stimulate the workers' interest in cycles.

Yet the social clubs of the interwar years were for the most part not in this older paternalistic tradition. Few were closely linked to the Industrial Welfare movement, although many were related to broader welfare schemes within individual firms.[13] Most of them received financial help from owners, especially in the early stages and with grounds and buildings, but were to a large extent self-financing thereafter. Cash's gave their employees a sports ground in 1919, just as Courtaulds built a new club house for theirs in 1936. The new pavilion at G.E.C., opened in 1938, cost £9,000 of which the firm paid £5,000. Herberts were unusual in distributing their magazine, *The Alfred Herbert News*, free to employees. Most charged for them, and while they may not have covered costs, and certainly not the editor's salary, straightforward paternalism was avoided. Coventry Chain appointed a fulltime social organiser in 1919, but he seems to have lacked success and respect. Far more typical were men such as George Radford, a van driver at the London Laundry who became general secretary of the social club as a voluntary duty in 1936, or Fred Hopewell, organising secretary of the Magnet Club, who was paid by the club itself.

Some features of the old style survived, most notably at Herberts where Sir Alfred and Lady Herbert played the role of aristocratic patrons at Sports Days and presentations. G.E.C.'s local manager, Sir William Noble, fulfilled a similar function, but most firms lacked titled leaders, and municipal dignitaries were invited to do the honours. Even the most established set-piece for patronage, the works outing, was more often paid for by the workers themselves after the war, and top management did not accompany the trips. There were exceptions, but outings after 1918 tended to reinforce structures of authority less fundamental to the firms' existence. Thus foremen's outings aimed to assert the solidarity of a particular stratum within the workforce, while departmental outings, which replaced works trips at G.E.C. in 1931, acknowledged the effective range of contacts within a large factory. Even so, Herberts achieved a curious mixture of old and new forms in 1939 when the annual all-works outing went to Butlin's at Skegness, then in its third year of opening.

Despite the cultivated survival of such archaic features of social relations within the firm, works' social activities in the interwar years were encouraged by employers as a response to fairly precise problems of management, although there was no certainty that initiatives would be received in the spirit in which they were intended to be received. Courtaulds had already seen the possibility of using philanthropy to improve labour relations and the company's public image in the early years of the century. Following complaints about carbon disulphide emission in 1906, the company was the subject of local authority proceedings, inquiries by the Labour press and questions in the House from Arthur Henderson, none of which made recruitment of female employees or negotiations over wages and conditions any easier. The local manager, Harry Johnson, informed the board in London that

> several of the larger firms in Coventry take an active and direct interest in ... outings of their employees, and it may be undesirable to be behind them. The recent attacks on the company and the attempts to create dissatisfaction among its employees may render it even more desirable that we should fall into line.[14]

The influx of migrant workers and dilutees in the First World War led to an intensification of social activities, much of which survived the war, and was boosted by employers anxious to combat the threat of further challenges by organised labour to their authority over their own workforce. For some firms, recreation and welfare provisions represented the soft end of a campaign to reassert the primacy of management which culminated in the 1922 engineers' lock-out. In this spirit, Coventry Chain set up a Welfare and Recreation Committee in December 1918 and a workers' representation committee in 1919, when they also began to publish a magazine, *The Link*, which was atypical in its propensity to preach to the workforce, as when the January 1920 issue printed a nine-item 'Industrial Creed', advocating the mutual interests of capital and labour and the need for harmony and cooperation. A Herbert employee later recalled that in 1922 the recreation ground had been much used during the lock-out, 'many of the men spending hours at games, which time might have been employed less profitably elsewhere'.[15]

Once the revolution scare of the early post-war years was dispelled, recreation and welfare were seen less as solutions to present labour problems, rather in more general terms as means to increased productivity and identification with the firm. Non-union firms such as Courtaulds before 1938 no doubt hoped to achieve placid labour relations this way, but a more pressing problem, especially from 1934 onwards, was the need to recruit and keep skilled labour. An effect of the Magnet Club had been to help socialise G.E.C.'s skilled technical employees, who were male and mostly migrated with the firm from Salford in 1921. It is no coincidence that many of the committee members and club stalwarts described in the pages of the *Loudspeaker* were from Manchester, nor that emphasis on sport in this and other clubs would appeal chiefly to young male workers. In 1937, the *Loudspeaker* recommended the club programme to new employees, with activities

> to enable them to fill their hours of recreation and leisure with health-giving sports, and to endeavour to prevent that feeling of loneliness which so often besets the stranger in a strange city ...[16]

From the various works' magazines, some impression may be gained of the cultural milieu of these clubs. The magazines themselves exude an in-group chumminess and contain worthy educational articles about the firms' products and other branches and on safety at work. They were not always accepted without demure. A letter published in the *A.H. News* in 1931 maintained that 'the high-toned articles may look nice to the heads of the firm but this journal is not written for them but for the workpeople'.[17] The correspondent wanted more humour, notices of the programmes at the '5 star' cinemas and articles about Jack Payne and Jack Hilton, rather than the 'Masters of Music' featured hitherto. But such criticism was rarely aired, and, on this occasion was heavily put down by another correspondent, a department secretary in the drawing office, whose favourite items were Sir Alfred's editorials, and who asserted the importance of promoting team spirit through the magazine. He regretted that the previous writer 'appears to expect a low type of comic paper, that would appeal to the less intelligent workers only'.

Educational activities had small followings, although many young people availed themselves of free technical college places administered by the clubs. The G.E.C. Telephone Society (f.1924) attracted small numbers of those who wanted to improve their knowledge of developments in electronics, and functioned as in-service training for technical staff. Exclusivity was fostered by separate clubs for staff and works. Staff clubs enabled the upper echelons of large firms to socialise with their own ranks, freed from the formality and crowded facilities they had to endure at works events. Annual staff dinners were common occurrences, and several firms had separate staff organising committees for dances and outings. The G.E.C. employees were especially fortunate in that the Peel-Connor estate, 'The Grange', covered 140 acres, of which 14 acres was used by the works, 10 acres by the Magnet Club and 40 acres for the Grange Golf and Social Club. The Grange Club offered not only the wholly exclusive sport of golf and largely middle class tennis, but also separate facilities for billiards, dining and dancing—indeed, all the facilities of a country club. It hosted many inter-firm golf competitions between the wars, including the Oscar Harmer Challenge trophy, presented by Herbert's second in command and competed for by the managers and staff of Coventry's leading firms.

Other sports tended in varying degrees to class exclusivity, although not always with the approval of club committees. Membership of a motor club demanded ownership of a car, or motorcycle, and the income to run one on jaunts across the Midlands, but table tennis, which rose to popularity in the 1930s, made no such material demands. The A.H. Recreation Club were dismayed that in 1936 a misunderstanding existed that the new table tennis section was solely for the benefit of the staff.

The clubs as a whole attracted large numbers of employees. In part this was because membership gave access to lunchtime canteen and recreational facilities, and total membership exaggerates participation in out-of-work activities. Nevertheless, attendance at functions was often large, and facilities came under increasing pressure of numbers towards the end of the 1930s. Clubs reported difficulties in the worst of the depression, and some sections were forced to close as their members became unemployed. Much the same had occurred in 1921. But by the end of the 1930s, new building was undertaken at G.E.C., Herberts and Courtaulds to extend changing and canteen facilities as firms took on more workers.

Sizeable as the numbers involved were, many did not join their firm's social club, or did not make much use of the facilities. The General Secretary of the A.H. Recreation Club, E. Thomas, observed in 1939 that 'The Recreation facilities at our disposal already cater for a fairly large number of employees, but there are many for whom the present activities have little or no appeal'.[18]

He noted in particular the relatively small number of women involved in club activities. The nature of women's recreation at this period is not clear. Certainly they constituted at least half of dancers, a large part, even a majority, of cinema-goers and, at least in inner-city areas, a sizeable proportion of pub-goers. For many married working class women their domestic role must have left them with little opportunity for leisure outside the home or immediate neighbourhood, and the practice of leaving work on marriage excluded them from works' clubs unless in the company of their husbands. Married women are occasionally named in works magazines in various contexts, but it is not stated whether they were widows or childless or whether they were in some way challenging the convention of ceasing to work on marriage. The involvement of unmarried women in works' activities presented a real problem to employers, and particularly to those like G.E.C., Courtaulds and London Laundry for whom recruitment and labour discipline among female employees was central to business efficiency.

Women were given little control over the use of leisure facilities. The A.H. Recreation Club had no female members on its management committee until 1940 and the Magnet Club committee welcomed women only as representatives of all women's sections such as women's hockey. In part this reflected the lack of women belonging to the ranks of foremen and technical workers from which the personnel of committees were drawn, but it is noticeable that activities which were evenly mixed, such as cycling and swimming, were never represented by women. Firms' magazines were almost without exception patronising towards women, and cartoons, jokes and the presentation of women in pen-portraits cast them in predictably subordinate roles. Women's pages were domestic in focus and rarely successful. For the most part, they did not celebrate the achievements of individual women workers or their collective activities, and so lacked the appeal that team news had for male workers. Nor can they have hoped to rival commercially produced women's magazines.[19]

Firms and clubs showed intermittent bursts of enthusiasm for encouraging women's participation. The London Laundry's social club, formed in 1936, was exclusive to men, despite the four to one numerical dominance of women at the works. Women there were unable to enjoy certain benefits such as membership of the Christmas fund. Many firms tried to promote keep-fit exercise from the mid-1930s on, often under the auspices of the Women's League of Health and Beauty (f.1930). It had the attraction of providing women employees with discipline and exercise at the same time, at little cost and in large numbers. Instructresses pointed out how it helped girls to 'enjoy life and work much better than before' and that it was consistent with the belief that 'the success of the mass depends entirely on the individual'. The League of Health and Beauty's similarity to the German Strength Through Joy movement may have had roots in the eugenicist beliefs of their founders, but there is no evidence that the League's aim of 'the achievement of racial health and beauty by natural means' was taken too seriously in Coventry.

Such initiatives met with varying success. The London Laundry branch of the Everywoman's Health Movement folded after just over a year in 1939 through lack of support. It had never achieved a membership of more than 25. The G.E.C. Ladies' Physical Culture Club, affiliated to the League of Health and Beauty, had over 200 members in 1937 in two classes, and survived until the war, but with diminishing enthusiasm despite displays in Coventry, Birmingham and London.

Not all women's activities were doomed to failure though, and there are several examples of autonomous women's sections and activities providing sociability for employees over long periods. Women's sports, even women's soccer, had been common during the First World War, and continued until the ending of munitions work and the dispersal of the hostel labour force in 1918-19. By 1930, the Magnet Club ran two women's cricket teams and seven departmental teams, although these came in for a certain amount of ridicule in *The Loudspeaker*. In 1932, there was the first of a series of women's cycling camps. The fashion for departmental outings had meant that trips such as that of the coil-winders and the assembly section were virtually all-women affairs, and women began holding their own annual dinners in 1928. It is not apparent though how such occasions related to women's prospects of advancement at work or their status within the organisation, unlike the complex rituals of competitive display at full staff dances.

A prevalent myth concerning works' teams is that companies were able to exert a semi-feudal pressure on employees to play for their own team. It is likely that there were cases in which people were spoken for and accepted on account of their abilities as footballers rather than fitters. The Keresley Colliery Company employed two former members of the Yorkshire 2nd XI to strengthen its cricket team in the 1930s.[20] But in the light of the shortage of skilled labour, works teams had less control over their players than they wished. In the days before the foundation of the Magnet Club, G.E.C. had a football team which won the second division of the Coventry and North Warwickshire League and three knock-out competitions in 1921-22. The failure of the management of the team to seek election to a higher division led most of the players to look for other teams. Throughout the period, a common response of club secretaries to poor results or difficulty in raising teams was to appeal to employees to play for their own firm. The Magnet R.F.C. secretary lamented that G.E.C. workers were playing rugby for teams such as Coventry R.F.C., Trinity Guild R.F.C., and Technical College Old Boys, and similar complaints were heard in all sports. Particularly galling must have been occasions on which players who had started with works teams achieved a higher standard and went on to play for established Coventry sides—or worse still, other works teams. Successful teams and clubs could expect the opposite to happen. The Alfred Herbert Bowls team was the strongest in the area during the late twenties, and could attract players from elsewhere. Indeed, the A.H. Cycling Club attracted so many non-Herbert employees that it disaffiliated from Herberts in 1936 and merged with the Coventry Road Club. The A.H. Recreation Club eventually found the contradiction between the pursuit of sporting excellence and furtherance of the Herbert Spirit too much and banned non-employees from representative teams in 1939.[21] Other firms did not follow the example.

The to-ing and fro-ing among sportsmen between clubs suggests that, whatever the interests of patrons and club secretaries, many workers saw the provision of sports facilities in instrumental terms, and valued a high standard of sport above allegiance to the firm, lessening the intended impact of recreational provision on control of the labour force. But the extent of such instrumentality should not be exaggerated. For most employees there was no chance to be poached, even if they had wanted to foresake the company of their workmates. The weakness of some sections as a result of redundancies in 1920 and 1932 indicates that most did not continue their association with the works club once they had lost their job there. Work and leisure represented related aspects of life for such people.

As the C.S.S.A. report noted, the facilities owned by the big firms were among the best in Coventry, and had considerable attractions to non-employees. Under some circumstances, recreation clubs were pleased to open their facilities to others. The use of a football pitch as a neutral ground for the Midland Daily Telegraph cup final brought status and publicity, and confirmed the club's influence with the local football authorities. Regular dances were open to the general public on a commercial basis, although employees could get tickets in advance. The larger the receipts, the better the position of the club's funds. At other times, there were forces making for exclusivity, well illustrated by the formation of the Coventry Works Sports Association.

The Association was formed at a meeting in the G.E.C. ballroom in October 1934. At its 21st anniversary celebration, F.E. Higham, of the Sales Division of Standard Motors spoke of its starting 'in a small way with great visions'.[22] Certainly one can accept his assertion that it was by then the biggest association of its kind anywhere, but its beginnings were hardly small, nor its aims visionary. With 25 founder members, the association had no difficulty in its first year in establishing viable leagues, with thousands of playing members in 30 football and swimming teams, 17 cricket teams, nine snooker and billiard teams and sections for tennis and rugby. The Mayor, Alderman Friswell, and the city's M.P., W.F. Strickland, gave the proceedings at the first annual presentation the stamp of municipal approval. While the association's primary aim was to promote sporting activities among industrial workers, its formation was prompted by the frustrations of works teams competing in city competitions. Their grievances were the inability of local teams to fulfil their fixtures and the poor dressing room facilities of such clubs. They were not necessarily disappointed with the standard of play since works teams continued to enter local leagues. The Coventry and District Cricket League changed its rules to allow clubs with teams in other leagues to participate, and G.E.C. entered their first team in that league and their second XI in the C.W.S.A. Division I.

The partial withdrawal of works' social clubs from participation in the sporting life of the towns was reversed during the war. The C.W.S.A. had ceased to operate on the outbreak of war, but was revived by 14 clubs in April 1940. The bombing of November 1940 closed the association down again. The shortage of recreational facilities was a source of concern to the Ministry of Labour and their local Welfare Officer, John Walter, who sought to co-ordinate what facilities had survived the bombing and requisitioning. The department, together with the Mayor, convened a meeting in January 1942 when it was decided not to revive the C.W.S.A., but to broaden its scope, making works' facilities open to the general public under the regulation of the C.S.S.A.[23] The latter body was under the chairmanship of Harry Storer, formerly of Coventry City F.C. and now social secretary of Humber-Hillman. With the aid of a gift of £95,000 from the U.S.-British War Relief fund, the Association opened a social centre which it was to advocate as a model for community centres, intended as the foci of post-war recreational planning. The firms were not so enthusiastic about the experiment. Herberts were least willing to participate. Sir Alfred Herbert declined to respond to the mayor's invitation to the meeting at which the C.S.S.A. was set up and the Recreation Club tried to keep its distance from the new body. The secretary wrote in June 1943 that the club had affiliated 'on the understanding that we do not necessarily conform to all your rules, in particular, we cannot agree to any non-employee becoming a member of our club, or to use our sports ground...'.[24] When the war finished, the Education Committee were not interested in supporting Community Associations, and the C.S.S.A. centre was bought by B.T.H. Ltd., as a social club. The C.W.S.A. resumed its activities, and survived until 1980, when it was thought superfluous since the constituent sections were now strong enough to look after their own affairs.

Dancing

The relationship between works social clubs and the recreation of the town as a whole was at its closest, and most beneficial to both parties, in the regular dances which were held on factory premises. Dances were already being put on by the Armstrong Siddeley Athletic Club, Daimler, Humber and the Ordnance Factory as early as 1921. In the absence of commercial ballrooms, other than the Gaumont and the Rialto, the factories provided the main alternative to church hall dances, and were far grander. Church halls lacked the sprung floors favoured by dancing enthusiasts.[25]

Dancing was enjoyed by all classes of society, from the city's bourgeoisie who could pay 15s.0d. for a ticket to attend the Coventry and Warwickshire Hospital Annual Ball at the Drapers' Hall to the clientele of the Red House in Red Lane, of whose open-air dances on summer evenings Vic O'Brien recalls that 'We did waltzes, tangos, quick step ... We had to pay 2d., and if we had a few extra coppers you'd have some bottles of pop'.[26]

But the dance craze seems to have been strongest among skilled manual and clerical workers, people who had served their time and could afford to pay 1s.6d. to 2s.6d. for admission. For them, the refined, formalised ritual of the dance halls provided an appropriate setting for courtship and social aspiration. The halls banned drink, and although men would go to pubs first, the doors were closed at 9.30 with the purpose of excluding those who had drunk too much. Dance halls provided regular rendezvous for groups of friends—questions would be asked about absent members of the group—and keen dancers could attend as often as cinema-goers since there were dances every night except Sunday, with the biggest on Fridays and Saturdays.

The dance halls offered a number of attractions. Courtship no doubt provided the basic motivation. Toolroom employees met few women at work, and none from the class of office and shop girls they were most likely to marry into. The standards of behaviour current among dancers were formal. Young women, who arrived first at about 8.00p.m. and danced together to start with, would not tolerate men whose breath revealed where they had spent the intervening time before they entered the dance hall. Men were expected to carry a second handkerchief for their right hand so that they didn't soil their partner's dresses—or touch any exposed skin.

Dancing per se was probably enjoyed most by the women, who spent time at home and work trying out steps with sisters and friends, often to the radio or gramophone. The complexity of the dances of the 1930s, foxtrot, waltzes, quickstep and tango, required tuition, and men needed to be confident of their dancing before they could be among the first to venture onto the floor.[27] Ability to dance was therefore an asset in successful courtship, and while many learnt from their sisters or other female acquaintances, others went to one of the city's many dancing schools, such as Orme's, Professor Daniels's or Patterson's. There were beginners' nights at the Liberal Club and at the major ballrooms.

The dance halls also offered cameraderie. Groups from different areas of town would frequent set pitches in each dance hall where friends could expect to meet. Courting couples were left to other areas of the dance floor where they could try to be—literally—lost to the group. Despite such territoriality, there is no evidence of group violence at dances, and fights were very rare, perhaps due to the control of alcohol, but also a reflection of the respectable style of the proceedings and of dancers. There were no doubt some for whom the attraction of a particular hall lay in its resident dance band. While big London bands might play at the Drill Hall or the Ritz, often after playing at the Hippodrome earlier in the evening, most halls had local bands, some of whom, such as the

Gaiety Dance Band and Billy Monk's New Rhythm Band achieved a wider reputation in the Midlands and went on to broadcast and occasionally to record. Bands were admired for their general musicianship and arrangements, rather than solo flare. Instrumental solos were rare, and more attention was given to vocalists. American jazz had its enthusiasts in the Coventry Rhythm Club, the 106th such club in Britain, formed in 1936-37 with the encouragement of the *Melody Maker*, which had a regular column of news from clubs around the country. Billy Monk, a former Oxford University student, was present and he and his band performed at the club's dances, held in church halls, and jam sessions. There were also record concerts, to which members brought along their favourite records. Other Rhythm Clubs had a speakeasy atmosphere; the Bolton Rhythm Club was raided in May 1937 resulting in 285 summonses for illegal drinking and dancing.

The commercial halls and the biggest firms' halls, by contrast, offered their customers something of an all-enveloping experience, in which crowds of well-dressed youths danced decorously—as far as space permitted—to carefully arranged music played from scenically decorated bandstands under increasingly sophisticated lighting. Already enticing before the war, the halls were to be like Aladdin's caves at the time of the blackout.

The biggest firms' hall, which most effectively escaped the canteen atmosphere and rivalled purpose-built commercial halls, was the G.E.C. ballroom, often referred to as 'The Connor'. Attendances were large, already averaging 450 in 1924. By 1936, the average was over 600. Special occasions, in particular the New Year's Eve dances, drew massive audiences, as many as 1,350 in 1930. Numbers were limited to 800 in 1937, and a second dance was run on January 1, 1938, to accommodate the 750 unsuccessful applicants. The Magnet Club prided itself on the standard of the floor and facilities, claiming it to be 'the City Hall' in 1930 when they hosted the Civic Ball. The ballroom was redecorated in 1926, 1930, 1932, 1935 and 1936-37, and acquired during the course of the 1930s tip-up seating, an illuminated fountain, a soda and ice-cream buffet, a Hammond organ and a lighting system with fourteen programmes which could be set to provide sequences for various dances. The waltz programme, in pastel shades, lasted for over half an hour. G.E.C. took other opportunities to impress with their own contributions to the technology of leisure, as when the chimes of Big Ben were relayed through large G.E.C. loudspeakers to the New Year's Eve Ball of 1929.

The G.E.C. ballroom was regarded as one of the best gigs in Coventry by musicians. The Gaiety Dance Band beat Reg Adams and his band to it in the mid-1920s, and were not succeeded until 1937, when the Billy Monk Band, who played there until 1958, played the Wednesday date. The Saturdays alternated between two bands who had broadcast for the B.B.C., Tony Linnell's and Vincent Ladbrook's.

Conclusion

Coventry's rapid economic growth in the later 1930s was the base for the development of a wide range of popular recreation with some distinctive local features. While the activities were much the same as those elsewhere, in Coventry the pattern of ownership and promotion was distinctive. It reflected a booming local capitalism, and catered principally for skilled and semi-skilled workers in the large firms. These people, with good wages, had access to the leading sports and social clubs, with their new pavilions and refurbished ballrooms, to the super-cinemas and to commercial dance halls.

Leisure in Coventry in the late 1930s was typified by brash, glossy, mass activities. Leading Coventry firms, the car manufacturers and G.E.C. had a direct interest in the expansion of these technology-intensive recreational pursuits. The trend throughout is of increasing scale, bigger cinemas, growing membership of social clubs, bigger crowds at Highfield Road, reflecting larger, more regular incomes. The wartime experience pointed to the limited access which the rest of the population had to such cultural goods, and to the relative lack of encouragement of liberal values such as creativity in the arts. Yet the war tended to confirm the attraction of pre-war forms, especially the cinema and the dance hall.

With reconstruction and further prosperity in the 1950s, decline set in for established forms of leisure. Increasing domesticity and greater personal mobility did not affect participation in sport, or drinking, but the great crowds of inter-war and wartime cinema and sport, both professional and amateur, were to become rareties in the face of television and motoring. The alternative offered by the C.S.S.A. was not explored, and while the arts and adult education have received encouragement since the war from local government, they have not come to play the integrative social role envisaged by exponents of community associations in the 1940s. But nor has the bid of large firms for cultural leadership produced the intimate association of workers and employers which they had initially hoped for.

Table 9.1. Drinking places and drunkenness

1a. *On-Licences*

	No.	*per 000*	*Index* (1922=100)
1919	236	1.74	96.7
1924	228	1.72	95.6
1929*	241	1.40	77.8
1934*	250	1.35	75.0
1938	242	1.10	61.1

1b. *Licensed Clubs*

	No.	*per 000*	*Index* (1922=100)
1919	42	0.36	64
1924	61	0.46	98
1929*	73	0.42	89
1934*	83	0.45	96
1938	100	0.45	96

1c. *Proceedings for drunkenness per thousand*

	Coventry	*England and Wales*
1919	1.10	2.66
1924	1.25	2.18
1929*	0.90	1.48
1934*	0.90	1.11
1938	1.24	na

* indicates that a boundary extension had taken place.

Sources: City of Coventry Chief Constable's reports.
Population figures are from City Medical Officer of Health Reports.
G.B. Wilson, *Alcohol and the Nation* (1940).

Table 9.2. Cinemas

	No. opening	*No. closed*
1901-5	1	-
1906-10	4	-
1911-15	11	-
1916-20	2	-
1921-25	1	1
1926-30	5	2
1931-35	3	1
1936-40	3	-
1941-45	-	4
1946-50	-	-
1951-55	-	-
1956-60	-	6
1961-65	-	5
1966-70	-	1

Source: D. Janes (unpublished typescript).

Table 9.3. Private Cars

Private Cars per thousand population.

	Coventry	*G.B.*
1921	(12.6)	
1922	17.2	
1923	27.5	
1924	na	11.3
1925	na	
1926	50.1	
1927	58.4	
1928	61.3	
1929	72.8	
1930	85.2	
1931	(89.9)	
1932	82.2	
1933	91.8	
1934	105.2	29.2
1935	117.8	
1936	138.1	
1937	152.4	
1938	170.5	
1939	184.1	
1940	160.3	

Sources: City of Coventry Chief Constable's reports, 1919-23.
City of Coventry Abstract of Accounts, 1926-40.
Medical Officer of Health *Reports* (for population estimates except in census years).
A. Halsey, *Trends in British Society since 1900* (1972) Tables 2.1 and 9.9. (Population figures for GB from census years.)

Table 9.4. Founder Members of the Coventry Works Sports Association, 1934.

Alvis Engineering Co.	Alfred Herbert
Armstrong Siddeley	Lockheed Borg & Beck
BTH	Morris Motors
British Piston Rings	Pattison and Hobourn
J.J. Cash	Rover Sports Club
Courtaulds	Riley Sports Club
GEC	Rudge-Whitworth
Climax	Renold Chain
Coventry Gas	Shanks and Son
Dunlop	Standard Motors
Fozel Castings	Singer
General Auto Panels	Triumph
Humber-Hillman	

Source: *Loudspeaker*

Notes to Chapter 9

1. For general accounts of leisure between the wars, see A. Howkins & J. Lowerson, *Trends in Leisure, 1919-39* (1979); Chris Cook and John Stevenson, *The Slump* (1977), pp. 24-28, and James Walvin, *Leisure and Society 1830-1950* (1979). *The Long Weekend* by Robert Graves and Alan Hodge (1940) gives a more impressionistic account of the more visible trends. Another local study is Paul Wild, 'Recreation in Rochdale 1900-40' in John Clarke, Chas Critcher and Richard Johnson (eds.), *Working class Culture* (1979). Gareth W. Williams, 'From Grand Slam to Great Slump: Economy, Society and Rugby Football in Wales during the Depression', *Welsh History Review*, June 1983 describes the effects of unemployment on the popular culture of S. Wales. On holidays see J.A.R. Pimlott, *The Englishman's Holiday* (1947) and J.K. Walton, *The Blackpool Landlady: a Social History* (1978). Holidays with pay are dealt with by S.G. Jones, 'Labour and Recreation' (Ph.D. thesis, University of Manchester, 1983).
2. On the growth of commercial leisure, see Peter Bailey, *Leisure and Class in Victorian England* (1978). Licensing laws and their local administration in the 19th century are discussed by Brian Harrison, *Drink and the Victorians* (1971); Penny Summerfield, 'The Effingham Arms and the Empire: deliberate selection in the evolution of music hall in London' in Eileen and Stephen Yeo (eds.), *Popular Culture and Class Conflict, 1590-1914* (1981) and A. Crawford and R. Thorne, *Birmingham Pubs 1880-1939,* (1975). Drinking habits are discussed in Mass Observation, *The Pub and the People* (1943), a study of Bolton in 1936-39.
3. Red Lane Old Residents' Association, *Red Lane Reminiscences* (1983), Coventry and District Football League *Minute Books* (1912-1974), CRO 617, Coventry Sports and Social Association, *A War Time Social Survey* (1943) CRO 240.
4. *Police Reports*, 1919-37.
5. J.B. Priestley, *An English Journey* (1934) 71.
6. I am grateful to Mr. J.F. Cooke, secretary of the Canley Social Club and Institute, for much of the information on club life. See also CRO 545, Coventry Working Men's Club 1927-60.
7. The records of Coventry City FC were largely destroyed by fire in 1967. The club's history is recounted by Derek Henderson, *The*

Sky Blues (1968) and Neville Foulger, *Coventry. The Complete History of the Club* (1979). G. Dalton's *Making a Century* (1951) describes the development of the Coventry and North Warwickshire Cricket Club whose *Minute Books* 1919-1950 are kept at the Coventry Record Office, CRO 549. Details of major sports clubs are given in *Victoria County History of Warwickshire*, Vol. IV. On Coventry's rugby-playing tradition, especially the sport's strong roots in local schools, see Kenneth Richardson, *Twentieth Century Coventry* (1972).

8. Derek Janes of the Herbert Art Gallery provided a list of Coventry cinemas (unpublished typescript). For early cinema programmes see *What's On in Coventry and District* 1921-22. Details of the Rex come from its *Souvenir Programme*, 1937, in the CRO local records department. On cinema nationally, see Michael Chanon, *The Dream that Kicks* (1980) and James Curran and Vincent Porter (eds.), *British Cinema History* (1983).
9. Rex Cinema, *op.cit.*
10. *Times*, 21 January 1916.
11. Richardson, *op.cit.*, 270-71.
12. This section is largely based on material from works' magazines held at the CRO:
    The Alfred Herbert News 1927-40.
    The Limit, 1918-21 (White and Poppe).
    The Link, 1919-21 (Coventry Chain Co.).
    London Laundry News, 1938-39.
    The Loudspeaker, 1924-38 (GEC Telephones).
    The Rayoneer, 1938-39 (Courtaulds).
    The Rudge Record, 1908-20.
    Further information was gathered from records of J.J. Cash and the London Laundry in the CRO. For Courtaulds, D.C. Coleman's *Courtaulds: an economic and social history* (1965) was valuable.
13. *Loudspeaker*, 123, November 1935.
14. On industrial welfare, see Helen Jones 'Employers' Welfare Schemes and Industrial Relations in Interwar Britain' in *Business History* 1983 and Elizabeth Sydney, *The Industrial Society* (1960). Older traditions of paternalism are discussed by Patrick Joyce, *Work, Society and Politics* (1980). On labour relations at the end of the First World War in Coventry, see James Hinton, *The First Shop Stewards' Movement* (1973).
15. Coleman, *op.cit.*, 162.
16. *A.H.News*, November 1929.

17. *Loudspeaker*, 139, April 1937.
18. *A.H. News*, May 1931.
19. On Women's recreation and the reinforcement of its domestic orientation in the period, see Howkins and Lowerson, *op.cit.*, 15-16; Ann Oakley, *Sociology of Housework* (1974) 92-95. On Women's magazines, see Cynthia L. White, *Women's Magazines* (1970).
20. Information from Mr. J. Bott, present member of the club.
21. *A.H. News*, May 1939.
22. CRO 847, Coventry Works Sports Association records 1953-80. Earlier material comes from the *Loudspeaker* and the local press.
23. CRO 240, Coventry Sports and Social Association Records, 1943-53.
24. CRO 240/2/9.
25. This section is based largely on an interview with Mr. John Spencer of Cannon Park, Coventry, who was a fitter at Standard Motors and Cornercroft in the late thirties and during the war. He is currently editing and publishing a part-work, *Dance Band Days*, which contains musicians' accounts of their own careers and photographs of the bands. Mr. Sid Howe gave additional information about the Billy Monk band, in which he was the pianist. Information about the early twenties comes from *What's On in Coventry*, and that about the Rhythm Club from the *Melody Maker*, 1937. Details about the GEC Ballroom are from *The Loudspeaker*.
26. *Red Lane Reminiscences*, 95.
27. By this time, the so-called 'jazz dances' of the 1920s — shimmy, Charleston and Black Bottom were no longer danced. Frances Rust, *Dance in Society*, (1969), chs. XI and XII draws a distinction between the vigorous, often controversial dances of the twenties with the sedate character of most ballroom dancing in the thirties (97-98). In the midst of the uproar about the Charleston, the Bishop of Coventry is said to have called it 'a very nice dance'. *Ibid.*, 90.

Chapter 10

Changing Concepts of Secondary Education: Coventry's Comprehensive Schools

Robert G. Burgess

Since the end of the Second World War the citizens of Coventry have not needed to examine financial statements and educational statistics to know that education is big business in their city. For the changing landscape in Coventry has included much new educational building: primary schools on housing estates, comprehensive schools around the perimeter of the city, two new colleges of further education, a college of technology (later to become a polytechnic) and a college of education that has subsequently become part of the new University of Warwick. All these institutions have been established in the last thirty years. The citizens of Coventry therefore have primary, secondary, further and higher education available to them within the city boundary. Indeed, the local education authority is responsible for all educational institutions apart from the university, although representatives from the Authority are members of the university court and university council.

Alongside this massive building programme a number of new educational developments have taken place, especially in the sector of secondary education. Among educationalists Coventry has become synonymous not only with educational change in general but with comprehensive education in particular. Many other local education authorities have seen Coventry as a centre of educational experiment and new ideas. Indeed, the physical structure of Coventry's comprehensive schools has been adopted and adapted in many other English secondary schools where the House system for pastoral care is a feature of the educational scene. In addition, the authority has also created several community colleges in the secondary sector and has recently considered ways in which its comprehensive schools and the comprehensive principle can be further developed. Accordingly, just as experiment and change were key concepts at a time of educational expansion in a developing city so they are still on the agenda at a time when the city's secondary schools are experiencing falling rolls. The focus of this chapter will therefore be upon the changing concepts of secondary education in Coventry since 1945. In particular, we shall examine how members of the local authority have defined the term 'comprehensive' and how they have developed comprehensive education in the last forty years. However, comprehensive schools, in common with other organisations are products of the past and of the social context in which they are located. Accordingly, we turn first to a brief examination of the development of secondary education in the city before 1945.

The Education Act of 1902 gave powers to county councils and county borough councils to establish elementary and secondary schools, technical colleges and evening classes and to provide teacher training places. Before that time secondary education had been provided in endowed grammar schools that had given pupils an academic education. Indeed, it was this type of school that the 1902 Act envisaged as local authorities could now establish secondary schools for pupils aged eleven to sixteen who would be given an academic education.

Coventry had two endowed grammar schools: King Henry VIII School and Bablake School for boys but no provision for the education of girls at the secondary level apart from a Pupil Teacher Centre. However, the majority of places that were offered at these schools were for fee payers as the Authority showed relatively little interest in providing free places or selective places. Indeed, in a report to the Higher Education Sub-Committee in 1905 the Secretary made some attempt to assess the secondary school places that were required in a city that had a population of 72,000. On the basis of the evidence provided it appeared that Coventry needed to provide 812 places for boys and 580 places for girls. However, the Secretary recommended that fewer places should be provided as in his view Coventry did not contain a middle class population. In 1905 King Henry VIII School had accommodation for 160 boys while Bablake could house 425 boys. In addition, the Education Committee agreed to establish a girls school at Barr's Hill for 250 to 300 girls.

Accordingly, the secondary school accommodation was somewhat short of the estimated requirements and the provision of free places was even lower. It was only from 1908 that the Authority provided 15 junior scholarships for three years to boys, 15 intermediate scholarships for two years to boys and 30 junior scholarships for girls. However, many parents paid for pupils to attend these schools with the result that by 1916 there was considerable overcrowding in the city's three secondary schools where numbers on the roll outstripped accommodation. Such a situation appeared to call into question the recommendations that had been given to the Higher Education Sub-Committee about the population of Coventry and their attitude to education. Indeed, such was the demand from parents that further premises were acquired to establish Stoke Park

Grammar School for girls.

By 1918 the authority faced problems concerning school accommodation and the need to discharge the new obligations that were being placed upon it by the Education Act of that year. Under this Act each authority was obliged:

> to make, or otherwise secure, adequate and suitable provision by means of central schools, central or special classes or otherwise:
> (1) for including in the curriculum of public elementary schools, at appropriate stages, practical instruction suitable to the ages, abilities and requirements of the children: and
> (2) for organising in public elementary schools courses for advanced instruction for older or more intelligent children in attendance at such schools including children who stay at such schools beyond the age of fourteen.[1]

To make provision for these requirements the Coventry Authority converted one elementary school into a central school and created 'higher tops' or advanced classes in four elementary schools. Pupils who wished to gain admission to these schools were required to pass a highly competitive double examination. Indeed, in 1925 the examination results indicated that 328 pupils could profit from secondary education, but the Authority only provided sixteen scholarship places for boys and thirty six places for girls. The result was that many parents paid for their children to attend secondary schools with the consequence that there was further overcrowding.

By 1925 it was clear that the Authority had not provided sufficient places for pupils, especially in secondary schools. A report to the Education Committee in that year revealed a deficiency of 3,427 elementary school places and showed that 91 out of 123 senior classes contained more than 40 children. The city's secondary school accommodation was totally inadequate as there was a deficiency of 1,400 secondary school places.

Further problems arose for Coventry, in common with other local authorities, when the Hadow Committee reported in 1926.[2] Among this Committee's principal recommendations for school reorganisation was the suggestion that education up to the age of 11+ should be known as Primary Education and after the age of 11 as Secondary Education. If separate schools could not be provided, it suggested separate departments or classes in public elementary schools which would provide post elementary education in senior classes.[3] There was also a proposal for the provision of different kinds of secondary schools: grammar schools with a literary or scientific curriculum and modern schools that would offer four year courses which were to be 'realistic' and practical.

These recommendations gave Authorities an opportunity to reconsider the provisions that they made for different types of education. In addition to meeting the demands of Hadow, Coventry had to cater for increases in the school population caused by migration and extensions to the city boundaries in 1928 and 1932. Coventry experienced a 39 per cent increase in population between 1921 and 1931 (see chapter 2). Boundary extensions brought in a further 2,717 pupils in 1928 and 1,331 pupils in 1932. Such increases magnified Coventry's problems of finding suitable school accommodation. The Authority established a building programme which included seven new schools containing nine separate departments of which five would be for senior pupils. In addition, all central and advanced courses were extended to four years and the senior schools were asked to provide a three year course for pupils aged 11-14. Between 1930 and 1933 plans were drawn up for four new schools containing eight separate departments and practical facilities were to be provided in a further four schools. Courses in technical subjects, art and commercial subjects were provided for pupils aged 13+ to 15+ in a Junior Technical School, a Junior Art Department opened in 1930 and a Junior Commercial School opened in 1936. The number of 'scholarship' places were also increased. After 1935 all places in the girls' secondary schools were available as special place awards and the number of places purchased at the boys' secondary schools were increased to thirty.

The Authority was, therefore, attempting to provide more secondary school accommodation for its pupils but at the outbreak of the Second World War, it still had overcrowded schools and school reorganisation under the Hadow recommendations was far from complete in the secondary sector. Such a situation made the Authority ripe for change in the post-war years and it is therefore in this context that the move to comprehensive education has to be viewed.

At the start of the Second World War, Coventry was in the midst of a programme of educational development which aimed to overcome problems of school accommodation. The Authority's plans included new Elementary and Secondary schools, a School of Art and some extensions to its Technical College. In addition, the Authority had acquired seventeen building sites on the outskirts of the city.

At a meeting devoted to 'Planning and Education' in May 1940, the

Director of Education indicated that the Authority had already started to consider ways in which to structure its schools. Reports in *The Coventry Standard* revealed that the Director was principally concerned with the location and provision of secondary schools. He wanted new secondary schools to be erected around the outskirts of the city on ten acre sites where they could accommodate 500 children. These schools were to be similar to the secondary schools provided for 'scholarship' pupils as the newspaper reported him saying,

> There was no reason why children between 11 and 15 years of age in a senior elementary school should have less good amenities, less good provision from the educational point of view and less playing fields and special subject rooms than children between 11 and 16 years of age who happened to be in a secondary school. "We have got to get away from that false distinction which has really originated from old class distinction and which is now getting out of date" he said. "Children of a nation as a whole must be looked at as a whole".[4]

Such a statement highlights how the Director and the Authority were considering ways of promoting educational opportunity within the city. In particular, Coventry was considering building large schools which would have parity with grammar schools and would at least narrow, if not end, the inequalities in provision among the Authority's secondary schools. It was some of these ideas that figured in the post-war plans for comprehensive schools.

However, in 1940 the comprehensive school was highly controversial. Two years earlier the Spens Committee had rejected the idea of a single school and favoured the idea of separate secondary schools.[5] The only support that the Spens Committee were prepared to give the common school was on an experimental basis. Meanwhile, as Barker has shown, the Labour Party only gradually took up the idea of comprehensive education.[6] Barker argues that Labour Party policy in education was not based on socialist principles but was closely related to the educational experiences of its members. Certainly, it was not until 1942 that the Labour Party conference resolved in favour of multilateral schools, a forerunner of the comprehensive school. Even then, the Labour Party was not united in favour of multilateral schools but the internal debates did keep the idea before the public.[7] Coventry's plans for future developments in education were affected by the war, when the city was

Table 10.1. School Places Lost in Coventry 1939-1942.

Accommodation lost through occupation by other services	2,716
Accommodation lost through use as air raid shelters	1,284
Accommodation lost by destruction, by enemy action (and not recoverable without rebuilding)	4,187
Total	8,187

Source: G.C. Firth, *Comprehensive Schools in Coventry and Elsewhere* (Coventry 1963), 11.

heavily bombed. During the air raids many schools were damaged and several were lost. Coventry's pre-war problems of insufficient school places and suitable school buildings were magnified. The number of school places lost by the end of 1942 are shown in Table 10.1.

With such a severe shortage of school places, it was evident that Coventry would have to undertake a major rebuilding programme. In July 1943 the Board of Education issued a White Paper on Educational Reconstruction which reiterated the Spens model of secondary education but stressed that flexible transfer could take place between schools and could be combined on a single site or in a single building. Indeed, R.A. Butler (President of the Board of Education) declared in the House of Commons:

> I would say to those idealists who want to see more than one form of secondary education in the same school—sometimes called multilateral school—that I hope that more than one type of secondary education may from time to time be amalgamated under one roof and that we may judge from experiments what is the best arrangement.[8]

However, such ideas were left for Local Authorities to consider. In Coventry, the Director of Education responded to the White Paper in a *Report on Educational Reconstruction in Coventry* which was presented to the Education Committee in December 1943.

In this report the Authority 'took stock' of its educational problems while responding to the White Paper. Among the main problems were shortage of school accommodation and teaching staff, inadequate buildings, and a number of schools that had not been reorganised under the Hadow recommendations. Much space in the report was devoted to long term plans for the reorganisation of schools. The Director repeated his call for equality for all in secondary education when he stated:

> Any new secondary schools to be erected should be planned with a view to the ultimate reconstruction of secondary education for all and as regards buildings, equipment and amenities should be on a parity with other types of secondary schools. It will be necessary, therefore, to take early steps to plan and obtain estimates for any such new schools required.

The Education Committee was, therefore, encouraged to think about the provision of new secondary schools within the city and was reminded that the Authority had already purchased large sites for school construction which could be more effectively used if different types of secondary schools were in one building or on the same site. In this respect, the officers of the Authority suggested to the Committee that multilateral schools should be established.

In formal terms, the report exercised caution by keeping within the tripartite framework for secondary schooling. Accordingly, it suggested that the total number of schools required in the city would be 4 Grammar schools of 450+ pupils, 8 Technical schools of 450 pupils and 18 Modern schools of 450 pupils. On this basis no further grammar schools were required, but there were to be more technical schools as the Education Committee considered that these were more suitable for Coventry's industrial population. However, tripartitism (grammar, technical and modern schools) and multilateralism (schools divided into different courses) were to co-exist. Finally, it was indicated that decisions would have to be reached on the structure of multilateral schools, co-educational schools, the distribution of advanced courses, the allocation of pupils and their transfer between schools at a later date. The Authority had, therefore, laid plans that could be seen as an early stage on the road to comprehensive education in the city.

In the following year, many of the proposals in the White Paper became law in the 1944 Education Act. This Act made it the duty of Local Education Authorities to provide free secondary education when it stated:

> The statutory system of public education shall be organised in three progressive stages to be known as primary education, secondary education and further education; and it shall be the duty of the local education authority for every area, so far as their powers extend to contribute towards the spiritual, moral, mental and physical development of the community by securing that efficient education throughout those stages shall

Table 10.2. The 1946 Development Plan Proposals for Coventry Schools.

No. and Type of Schools	*Total No. of Places*
10 Multilateral	12,500
2 Boarding (1 boys, 1 girls)	600
3 Voluntary Modern (2 Roman Catholic, 1 Church of England)	1,440
2 Independent Grammar Boys	1,000
Total	15,540

Source: Coventry Development Plan 1946.

> be available to meet the needs of the population of their area.[9]

While this Act made it the duty of each Local Education Authority to provide free secondary education, it made no mention of specific types of secondary school. Indeed, as Archer has commented:

> What the 1944 Act did do was to create the necessary but not the sufficient conditions for imposing a tripartite, or any other organizational scheme on the [educational] system ...[10]

The 1944 Act gave Local authorities a framework within which to make their post-war plans. Each local Education Authority was, therefore, required to produce a 'Development Plan' to indicate their intentions to the Ministry.

The first Development Plan for Coventry, prepared in June 1946, revealed that Coventry had a school age population of 30,000. The Authority traced its problems back to the 1920s and 1930s when a rapid growth in population resulted in insufficient school accommodation. The war time destruction and devastation of school buildings had exaggerated the accommodation difficulties even further. The Authority indicated that if it was to comply with the requirements of the 1944 Education Act, it not only had to rebuild and repair war damaged schools, but it also had to complete the Hadow reorganisation of its schools which was started before the war. Only when this had been completed could it commence new developments in secondary education.

Despite the Ministry's inclination towards tripartitism Coventry proposed multilateral schools. The 1946 Development Plan contained the proposal outlined in Table 10.2. This proposal was controversial. The Authority argued that its special problems warranted a new form of secondary school but the Ministry of Education had practical criticisms. First, they thought the Development Plan under-estimated the size of the city's school population and the future needs for schools. Secondly, they considered the proposed eight form entry multilateral schools were not sufficiently large and should be increased to ten form entry. Here, the question of the size of a multilateral school was considered in tripartite terms as the main consideration was how many pupils were required in such schools to produce a viable academic sixth form.

After considering the Ministry's comments, the Authority submitted a revised plan in which some of the Ministry's main objections were met. However, the question of school size remained unsettled. Furthermore, the Authority indicated that it was now uncertain about the character of its proposed secondary schools:

> The final decision on the nature of the proposed new secondary schools has not yet been made. There is a body of opinion that inclines to the view that the schools shall be comprehensive and they have been so described in the Plan. This must not be taken as an indication that the multilateral idea has been abandoned ... the provision of these schools in instalments will provide an opportunity of studying the advantages of the multilateral school and a final decision will be made, in the light of the experience gained.[11]

The debate had shifted. The terms multilateral (a school divided into particular courses) and a comprehensive (a common-curriculum secondary school) were used interchangeably. The idea of providing multilateral types of schooling on the same site meant that Coventry's secondary schools also would incorporate aspects of the tripartite system.

The Director appointed a special advisory group consisting of the President and Vice-President of the Coventry Teachers' Association, the two joint secretaries of the local Teachers' Association and eleven local teachers to consider the Authority's ideas for a comprehensive school system. In addition, members of the Authority held numerous discussions with officers of the London County Council and the Ministry of Education in order that evidence could be gathered on principles associated with school size and school design.

By the early part of 1949 the Authority had decided in favour of comprehensive schools. This idea was applauded by the local press in March when a reporter stated:

> Coventry is to be one of the first authorities to build a new school of the "comprehensive" type. The idea is one favoured

> by the Ministry of Education. It has been brought forward because of the pressure on school accommodation now and to come. In Coventry the shortage is chronic, and any scheme that will provide more and better classrooms is welcomed.[12]

Contemporary accounts of the reality of conditions in Coventry's schools are provided in the reports of His Majesty's Inspectors (H.M.I.). On the basis of a survey by the Ministry of Education in the Authority's schools in 1948 it was estimated that only 80 per cent of the classrooms in use were in permanent or good temporary buildings, while the remainder were in poor hutting or hired accommodation or makeshift premises. In addition, it was thought that 26 per cent of secondary school classes contained more than 40 pupils, a situation that the H.M.I. regarded as 'a most unsatisfactory position both for the children and the teachers'. Reports written on individual schools add colour to the general picture. In 1950 an H.M.I.'s report on Frederick Bird County Secondary School (Boys' Department) commented:

> The boys have the use of eight permanent classrooms, two H.O.R.S.A. classrooms and a dilapidated wooden hut which provides two class spaces. About a quarter of a mile away is an annexe consisting of two small classes in an individual hut which has been hired by the Authority. It is a poor, ill-lit building without playing space and nothing but the present critical emergency would justify its use.

This situation was not untypical as an H.M.I.'s report on Broadway Secondary School concluded:

> In common with other Secondary Modern Schools in the area it [the school] is faced with an acute accommodation problem which is likely to become increasingly serious before the building of new schools brings permanent relief in this part of the city.

There was, in fact, universal agreement that Coventry required new secondary schools. Indeed, a local headmaster who was a member of the special advisory group has subsequently commented that even if there had been no education act in 1944, Coventry needed to develop new schools as much of the pre-war provision was inadequate.[13] Coventry's move towards comprehensive schools can, therefore, be attributed to

Table 10.3. The 1953 Development Plan Proposals for Coventry Schools.

No. and type of schools	*Total number of places*
10 or 11 comprehensive (10-12 form entry)	18,000 +
2 Roman Catholic campus sites	2,400
2 Church of England comprehensive (6 form entry)	900
2 Independent Grammar Schools	1,050
2 Boarding schools (1 girls, 1 boys)	600
Total	22,950 +

Source: Coventry Development Plan 1953.

several factors relating to post-war accommodation, overcrowding, the poor quality of the buildings and the demand for secondary school places from the local population. The Authority could claim, unlike other Authorities, that the special circumstances which it faced, forced it to develop a comprehensive school system. This situation allowed the Coventry Authority some room for manoeuvre in its negotiations with what was by now a Conservative government about establishing new secondary schools. In 1953 a pattern of secondary school provision was recommended in the Development Plan as shown in Table 10.3.

Although this scheme was approved by the Ministry of Education a variety of terms and conditions were imposed on the Authority's plans and it is these that are important. The comprehensive schools that were to be established had to be experimental and capable of being turned back into separate grammar, technical and modern schools. The comprehensive schools that were built had, therefore, to be constructed with the tripartite system in mind. These schools that were to be established, therefore, carried a comprehensive label whilst containing structural elements that were associated with tripartitism.

Certain elements of the Coventry comprehensive story have passed into educational mythology as the Authority is named in numerous books on the development of English education and comprehensive education[14] as a pioneer in the comprehensive movement, a champion of the cause of revolutionising the English school system. Yet, we might ask, how was 'comprehensive' defined in Coventry? What was the pattern of comprehensive schooling? How has the comprehensive principle been established and developed in the Authority's schools?

Until the early 1950s comprehensive education was only an idea in the English school system. There were no school buildings to visit or schools that could be seen in operation. Contemporary writing indicates there was no agreement about what constituted a comprehensive school.

Accordingly, we need to consider the ways in which local administrators, architects, councillors and teachers attempted to translate a set of abstract ideas into educational practice, and to see the ways in which they developed comprehensive schools in the city.

The first point to make is that Coventry's comprehensive system developed very slowly. Coventry was among the first authorities to construct comprehensive schools and when the city's first two comprehensives opened their doors in 1954 there were only eleven similar schools in existence in the whole of the country. However, it is important to remember that while the Authority is generally said to have 'gone comprehensive' in 1954 this only involved two boys' schools with a total of 1,852 pupils on their rolls. Another twenty one years were to elapse before all secondary schools maintained by the Authority were to be comprehensive.

There was a gradual movement to comprehensive education as, first selective schools and some secondary modern schools and eventually the remaining secondary modern schools and the two girls grammar schools were replaced by or reorganised as comprehensive schools. The early comprehensive schools that were established in the 1950s involved amalgamating selective and non-selective schools (see table 10.4). The initial intake to the city's first comprehensive schools contained selective pupils, that is pupils who had on the basis of the eleven plus selection examination been given selective secondary school places. Coventry continued to operate the eleven plus selection examination alongside its comprehensive schools and pupils from areas of the city without comprehensive schools were allocated 'selective' places within the comprehensive schools that existed. This was done to offer equality of educational opportunity across the city. Accordingly, for the Woodlands School it was estimated that 60 selective places could be given to boys residing in the catchment area and 30 selective places to boys who resided in other parts of the city. As a result for each entry of 300 pupils the intake comprised 90 'selective' pupils and 210 'non-selective' pupils. The latter all lived in the school's catchment area. Similar schemes were also in operation for other schools with the consequence that secondary school selection which was originally devised to determine grammar school entrance was used to decide the intake of the city's comprehensive schools.

The first comprehensive schools not only involved a core of pupils from the selective schools but also teaching staff. The headteachers of the former selective schools were chosen to lead the new comprehensive schools: Mr. F. West of the Technical Secondary School became the first

Table 10.4. The Initial Intake of Coventry's First Four Comprehensive Schools.

School	No. transferred from Selective School	No. transferred from Secondary Modern Schools	No. of new entrants	Total on Roll at opening
The Woodlands Boys' School	390 (Former Technical secondary pupils)	398 (Former Templars Secondary Modern pupils)	290	1078
Caludon Castle Boys' School	421 (Former John Gulson pupils)	90 (Former Stoke Boys' Secondary Modern pupils)	263	774
Lyng Hall Girls' School	380 (Former Priory High pupils)	187 (Former Stoke and Frederick Bird Secondary Modern Girls)	185	752
Whitley Abbey School (co-educational)	383 (Former Churchfield High pupils)	230 (Former Cheylesmore Boys and Girls Secondary Modern)	229	842

Source: Derived from Table 15, G.C. Firth, *Comprehensive Schools in Coventry and Elsewhere* (Coventry 1963), 69.

head of Woodlands, Mr. H. Tilley of John Gulson became the head of Caludon Castle, Miss L. Ims who had been head of Priory High became head of Lyng Hall and Mr. F. Lewis who had been head of Churchfield High took up the headship of Whitley Abbey School.

Many of these developments mirrored the patterns associated with the establishment of comprehensive schools in other authorities, for as Firth indicates, the early comprehensives which were developed in England,

> were established as extensions of former grammar schools, and most people will appreciate readily that their traditions helped considerably in setting standards of tone and discipline, as well as allaying the apprehensions of some parents.

Meanwhile, he continues

> The same degree of confidence may not be so apparent, in the initial stages when the comprehensive schools have emanated from secondary modern schools, and, consequently, a few years must elapse before strong fifth and sixth forms can emerge.[15]

The Coventry Authority used the selective system to establish most of its initial comprehensive schools as, of the schools that opened in the 1950s, only Binley Park began with a predominantly secondary modern intake.[16] Such evidence suggests that these Coventry schools were developed very much on traditional, selective school lines. Indeed, the first head of Woodlands speaking to Rotarians in 1954 remarked that, 'The comprehensive school is not revolutionary. All the things have been tried time and time again. We have only brought them together'.[17] If this was the understanding of one of the first heads what was the understanding of councillors and in particular those councillors who chaired the Education Committee during the formative period of comprehensive school development?

In the early 1950s great play was made of the variety of courses that could be offered in these new schools. For example, in 1954 Alderman B.H. Gardiner, the Chairman of the Education Committee, was reported as saying that Coventry had decided to build schools where a variety of courses could be provided rather than building a number of different schools.[18] However, it could not be denied that Coventry continued to provide secondary education in a variety of different schools alongside its comprehensives: secondary modern schools, two selective grammar schools for girls, and a boarding school for boys. In addition it also purchased places for boys to attend the two Direct Grant Grammar (later Independent) schools in the city. The main forms of local authority provision over the years are summarised in Table 10:5 which shows that comprehensive education was only fully established in the 1970s; first in the voluntary sector when the Catholic schools became fully comprehensive in 1970 and subsequently in 1975 when no further selective places were available for girls and the Authority no longer purchased places outside the maintained sector for boys. The development of comprehensive education was as slow in Coventry as in many other authorities. Indeed, although the authority could claim it was among the first to build comprehensive schools, it took twenty one years to fully establish its comprehensive schools. For Coventry, like many other authorities who had not 'gone comprehensive', was still operating secondary school selection and was concerned about grammar schools and grammar school courses.

In the 1960s, it was not unusual for comprehensive schools to be compared with grammar schools. Indeed, leading members of the Labour Party, including Hugh Gaitskell and Harold Wilson referred to comprehensive schools as 'grammar schools for all', a strategy that was designed to overcome the fears of the general public, especially parents who resented the abolition of the grammar school. A similar strategy was used locally by Alderman Callow, who chaired the Education Committee between 1958 and 1961, and who compared Coventry's comprehensive schools with grammar schools when writing in the *Coventry Evening Telegraph*. Having commented on the provision of secondary modern schools and grammar schools he went on to remark that comprehensive schools

> are both grammar schools and secondary modern schools. All eight of these [in the city] provide the same courses as those provided in grammar schools but in addition offer all the courses available in secondary modern schools and the additional advantage of the possibility of changing from one type of course to another within the same school as aptitudes develop.[19]

Such remarks indicate that at least for him the comprehensive school was little more than one school that combined all the courses that were available in different schools. Like West some years before, he saw the Coventry comprehensive as bringing together all courses under one roof.

Table 10.5. Secondary Schools Maintained by Coventry L.E.A. 1960-1975.

	No. of schools			*No. of pupils on roll*		
Type of School	*1960*	*1971*	*1975*	*1960*	*1971*	*1975*
L.E.A. Comprehensive	8	11	16	8532	13240	22297
L.E.A. Selective (Girls)	2	2	0	1123	1155	-
L.E.A. Secondary Modern	17	8	0	7760	4157	-
L.E.A. Boarding	1	1	1	172	178	168
Roman Catholic Grammar	2	0	0	576	-	-
Roman Catholic Secondary Modern	4	0	0	2222	-	-
Roman Catholic Comprehensive	0	4	4	-	4487	5193
Church of England Comprehensive	0	1	1	-	517	886
Total	34	27	22	20385	23734	28538

Source: Derived from Tables 42, 43 and 44 in G.C. Firth, *Seventy Five Years of Service to Education* (Coventry, 1977), 154-5.

A similar theme was touched upon six years later by Alderman Sidney Stringer in his capacity as Chairman of the Education Committee when he stated that the Authority was 'bringing into existence many more schools which are equal to grammar schools. They will not be called grammar schools but comprehensive schools'.[20] On this basis the term comprehensive appeared to many leading councillors who chaired the Education Committee to be little more than a label to describe an institution that was equal to a grammar school and which provided grammar school courses in order that pupils could maximise their intellectual ability.[21]

Certainly, in the 1960s grammar schools and selection still held a significant place in the heartland of the Coventry 'comprehensive revolution'. The city still operated a selection examination at eleven, provided places at the Direct Grant schools for boys, maintained two grammar schools for girls as well as allocating selective places within the comprehensive schools. Accordingly, the early 1960s witnessed some criticism from headteachers. The headmaster of Caludon Castle School commented in his speech day address in 1960 that 'A truly comprehensive school hasn't even been brought into existence ... though Coventry has created comprehensive buildings it was still without a single comprehensive school because the schools' incomplete intake prevented their becoming what their names, size and cost proclaimed them to be'.[22] Further criticism followed from other headteachers as in 1964 the head of Whitley Abbey School concluded that Coventry now needed to choose between returning to a grammar and secondary modern school system or go fully comprehensive. He thought that if the

Authority continued to abolish secondary modern schools while retaining grammar schools it would result in a situation whereby the comprehensive schools would be little more than secondary modern schools within a selective secondary system.

By 1965 a Labour government had taken office and had issued Circular 10/65 which requested that local authorities should provide details of their plans for secondary education with a view to ending selection at the age of eleven and introducing comprehensive schools.[23] At this time Coventry had a working party in existence which was considering the pattern of secondary education in the city. It was the work of this group which resulted in a shift in emphasis in the city's plans. While in the 1962 Development Plan the girls' grammar schools were to be retained, by September 1966 the mood had changed. The Education Committee decided to move towards a fully comprehensive school system which involved the abolition of the two girls' grammar schools and the disappearance of secondary modern schools. However, these proposals were challenged when the Conservatives gained control of the City Council in the local elections of May 1967. The result was that plans for secondary education were changed once more. During the period in which the Conservatives controlled Coventry, secondary modern schools were still being phased out, a further comprehensive school was opened, and building programmes for comprehensive schools continued. Yet the girls grammar schools were retained and the Authority continued to purchase places at the direct grant grammar school for boys.

This situation continued until 1972 when Labour took control of the City Council once more. The Labour group had, during their period out of office, made it clear that they would develop the fully comprehensive school system they had advocated in 1966. Accordingly, the autumn of 1972 witnessed a battle between the two main political parties concerning the future development of secondary education in the city. Broadly speaking the Conservatives accepted the demand for comprehensive education but argued that if some parents wanted their children to be educated in a grammar school their rights should be respected, while the Labour group wished to end selection, bring the two girls' grammar schools into the comprehensive system and end the purchase of grammar school places for boys. At this stage these proposals to end selection were supported by eighteen petitions from various groups including the local branch of the National Union of Teachers whose Executive welcomed the proposal for a fully comprehensive system and the abolition of the eleven plus examination.

The Labour proposal was approved by the Council and subsequently by the government with the result that Coventry City Council would no longer purchase selective places in the direct grant schools, would reorganise the girls' grammar schools into the comprehensive system, would end selection at the age of eleven and would develop the city's comprehensive schools as community schools serving each neighbourhood, a recommendation which had emanated from a working party that had reported on youth and community services in the city.[24] It is this proposal that has formed a basis for planning the pattern of secondary education in the city in the 1970s and set the tone for discussions about comprehensive education in Coventry in the latter part of the twentieth century.

One significant feature that occurred in the 1970s has been the establishment of community colleges. Holroyde indicates that these schools owe their existence in no small measure to the initiative of Robert Aitken who was appointed Director of Education in 1969 and who has written widely on the extension of educational provision through the development of community colleges.[25] The first community colleges were opened in the academic year 1972-73 in the city centre (Sidney Stringer School and Community College) and on an estate on the outskirts of the city (Ernesford Grange School and Community College). Subsequently they have been joined by four other comprehensive schools and in October 1983 three further schools including a Roman Catholic comprehensive were designated community colleges. According to Aitken the policy of developing community colleges involves translating the schools into community centres which are open for 48 or 50 weeks a year, six days a week for twelve to sixteen hours each day, providing a variety of additional buildings, equipment and recreational facilities.

Coventry's secondary education sector now consists of twenty-one comprehensive schools including nine community colleges. The basic pattern of schools and community colleges are summarised in Table 10:6. Although the first comprehensive schools were established in the early fifties it was not until the 1970s that the city was completely served by a network of these schools in all areas. Indeed, it was only in 1975 that the city could be described as fully comprehensive. Furthermore, as Table 10:6 indicates, many of these purpose built schools took several years to complete as building by instalments was a part of the educational scene. Such a scheme allowed the Authority to develop particular features in its comprehensive schools which have influenced the activities that have occurred. It is, therefore, to an examination of some of the distinctive features of Coventry's comprehensive schools which have attracted much interest beyond the city that we now turn.

In many ways there is great diversity among Coventry's comprehensive schools: some exist on the outskirts of the city, while others blend into the landscape of the inner city, many are purpose built, while others have been adapted from former grammar schools or campus schools, many are co-educational while others are single sex, some are schools and community colleges and some are within the voluntary sector. Nevertheless, within this diversity some common features can be identified. First, the 'traditional' purpose built comprehensive school that contained physical houses to support a pastoral system and second, the community college. Each of these features of comprehensive schooling in Coventry will be examined in turn.

When members of the Coventry Authority were developing comprehensive schools in the early 1950s they were informed by the Ministry of Education that these schools had to be large enough to sustain a sixth form. On this basis they needed to think in terms of ten form entry schools that could cater for 1500 pupils. Plans for developing schools of this size needed to take into account ways of breaking the institutions down into small manageable units.

Walter Chinn, Director of Education at that time, was a member of the governing body of a Quaker Boarding School where he had seen the advantages of the House system in breaking the large school down into smaller, more manageable units. Here, Chinn saw an opportunity of utilising this approach in the state system. Accordingly, he rejected other systems for subdividing the large school[26] and instead advocated the House system which he argued was the method 'traditionally used by Boarding Schools ... where children live in Houses presided over by a Housemaster who has responsibility for the moral welfare of those in his care as well as exercising some control over their educational progress'.[27] In these terms, Chinn made it clear that the establishment of a House system had been modelled directly on the independent sector. Indeed, it had originally been his intention to have Houses established on the Independent School model (including facilities for pupils to be in residence for short periods) and also to appoint House staff in the same manner as Independent Schools whereby senior teachers would take responsibility for Houses as well as leading academic departments. However, in Coventry such a scheme was thwarted by the Teachers Advisory Group who were consulted on the Authority's plans for comprehensive schooling. This group objected to Chinn's scheme of academic staff being responsible for Houses as they thought it would result in all senior positions in the schools being allocated to teachers who had selective school experience, a situation that would leave senior

Table 10.6. Coventry's Comprehensive Schools and Community Colleges

Name of School	*Year of opening as a comprehensive*	*Completion to planned size*
Alderman Callow *	1974	1978-79
Barrs Hill *	1975	1978
Binley Park	1959	1969
Caludon Castle	1954	1958
Coundon Court *	1956	1975
Ernesford Grange *	1972-73	1974
Finham Park	1970	1971
Foxford	1956	1973
Lyng Hall	1955	1969
President Kennedy *	1966	1972
Sidney Stringer *	1972	1973
Stoke Park *	1975	1977
Tile Hill Wood	1957	1973
Whitley Abbey	1955	1970
Woodlands	1954	1956
Woodway Park *	1968	1975
Blue Coat Church of England	1963	1973
Roman Catholic Schools		
Bishop Ullathorne R.C. +	1969	1964
Cardinal Newman R.C. *	1969	1975
Cardinal Wiseman Boys R.C.	1970	1972
Cardinal Wiseman Girls R.C.	1970	1970

Notes: * Schools that are also community colleges.
+ Bishop Ullathorne along with the Wiseman Schools was originally a campus school offering selective education.

Source: Derived and updated version of Table 70 in G.C. Firth, *Seventy Five Years of Service to Education* (Coventry, 1977), 252.

secondary modern school teachers with little chance of obtaining senior positions in developing comprehensive schools. Accordingly, they suggested that separate positions should be created in Houses and departments in order to give secondary modern school teachers an opportunity to obtain senior posts. It was this suggestion that was adopted by the Authority.

Of all the elements of Coventry's comprehensive schools it is the House system that is best known, having been taken up and used in several other authorities and referred to in countless books as the distinctive feature of the Coventry comprehensive school.[28] Physical house units have been a key feature of the building stock in all the early schools but different types of houses were constructed. For example, in Caludon Castle School the House blocks also included teaching areas, while in the Woodlands School, Houses were originally planned as social accommodation that was devoid of teaching space. However, as Arthur Ling, the City Architect, explained, these House units posed a particular architectural as well as educational problem as they were additional to the normal teaching areas but had to be provided at no extra cost compared with the cost of places in smaller secondary schools.[29] He summed up the problem of designing a House unit in a day school by comparing it to a boarding school when he commented:

> With the house system in a boarding school there are sufficient residential activities to make the house an almost continually active unit, but with a day school the amount of time outside the basic teaching curriculum that can be devoted to house activities is considerably less and therefore there is an advantage in associating some of the basic teaching activities of the school with the house.[30]

Accordingly, the basic structure of the House blocks in many Coventry schools has been a two storey unit with House accommodation on the ground floor and teaching rooms on the first floor. In general, the House accommodation has consisted of space for two Houses with House Heads' studies, a staff room (common to both Houses), toilets and cloakrooms for pupils and staff and a large hall that can be used for assemblies, teaching and dining as kitchen units are attached to each block.

This physical plant has had considerable influence on the internal organisation of schools. In a survey conducted in 1962 Firth found that all the comprehensive schools used the physical House organised on a vertical basis; that is each House contained a cross-section of the whole school in terms of age and ability apart from Caludon Castle School where the Houses were divided into lower and upper schools.[31] Meanwhile, in a further survey in 1976 he found that a number of adaptations had been made. Although vertically grouped houses were still predominant (in ten out of sixteen schools), there was also a shift towards horizontal Houses organised on a year basis until the fifth year or divisions into Lower, Middle and Upper School in the first and second, third and fourth, and fifth and sixth years respectively.[32] However, no matter what approach is used, it is often associated with the physical House unit which is a central feature of the purpose built Coventry comprehensive school. In the 1980s when the population of Coventry's secondary schools are in marked decline with schools that were formerly ten form entry coming down to an annual intake of six forms, problems abound concerning the use of space and the organisation of pastoral care. House bases are, therefore, a central focus of the debate on horizontal and vertical systems. Many schools have had to modify their pastoral arrangements taking into account the physical structure of the purpose built House block.

The importance of the pastoral system is evident in many schools today given the space that is devoted to a description of the arrangements for pastoral care that is discussed in many of the school prospectuses in Coventry. Certainly, the two schools that were originally constructed in this way still see the House as an important part of school organisation and as a way of breaking down the large unit. The prospectus for Caludon Castle school in 1982-83 states:

> The comprehensive school is a large unit but that does not mean it has to be uncaring or impersonal. It is the purpose of our well defined House system to see that there are knowledgeable, firm, yet caring adults directly responsible to ensure each pupil's welfare.[33]

Similarly at the Woodlands School for boys the importance of the House system is outlined in a four page section of the school prospectus in 1982-83. It begins by stating:

> The physical house system, operating under the guidance of a Housemaster, constitutes a decisive influence on the development of the pupils during the whole of their school career. Such a system enables one to care for, to keep an eye on, get to know, nurture, admonish, encourage, discipline and educate, in the widest sense, the individual child in a way that would probably not be possible under an alternative form of organisation. In other words, to carry out the 'needle and thread' work necessary to ensure the proper development of the individual child and to ensure that his problems and difficulties, his ideals and aspirations, do not pass unnoticed.[34]

Among the advantages that are claimed for the House system is that it establishes a sense of 'community' within the large school. Yet it is still the subject of much criticism. In particular, Firth[35] points to the way in which it creates some tension with the academic organisation of the school; a situation that was confirmed by Bazalgette[36] in his study of a Coventry comprehensive school where he found a strict subdivision between the pastoral and academic organisation which he argued was created by the House system.[37] Nevertheless, the schools are committed to some form of pastoral care which forms a central part of the school curriculum. Furthermore, a recent decision by the local authority to create pastoral bases which incorporate the careers service and facilities for the sixteen to nineteen age group underlines the point that Coventry comprehensive schools are still involved in extending the frontiers of comprehensive education, a situation that is also represented by the development of comprehensive schools as community colleges.

Community colleges have been developed in Coventry since the early 1970s. The first to be established was the Sidney Stringer School and Community College in the city centre. Coventry has since developed five other secondary schools as community colleges, designated three further schools as community colleges and is committed to developing the remaining secondary schools in this way.[38]

The development of secondary schools as community colleges is officially intended to respond to the social and educational 'needs' of the areas in which they are located,[39] although there is some doubt as to whether the 'community' that the schools supposedly serve can ever be identified.[40] Such schools are transformed into community centres which are open twelve to sixteen hours each day, both within and beyond the traditional school term and provide facilities that cover a range of activities and organisations with playgroups, pensioners, parents and children coming together on one site.

While the community college concept has been developed from Henry Morris's idea of the village college,[41] in Coventry it has been applied to an urban context where schools have been given additional resources to provide equipment and staff to service their locality. In addition, Robert Aitken has argued that the community dimension can also be extended to the day school where it can enhance the education of pupils by overcoming the culture clash between home and school, and develop pupils' self-respect by utilising the skills of parents and teachers.

Of all the schools and community colleges that have been developed it is the Sidney Stringer School whose aims, objectives and practices have been carefully documented by its first head Geoffrey Holroyde,[42] by Arfon Jones,[43] its second head, by other teaching staff[44] and by the evaluation of those outside the school.[45] The school population is approximately 50 per cent Asian, 40 per cent English and European, and ten per cent West Indian. It opened in August 1972 with an intake of 1900 pupils, 140 teaching and community staff and 70 non-teaching staff. Among the distinctive features of the school is its mode of government, its House system and its curriculum.

As Jones has remarked one of the key aims of this school was to raise the consciousness of the people in the area and to develop a mode of democratic control.[46] In these terms, the Local Education Authority decided to delegate authority and accountability to local people through the governing bodies of the community colleges. Accordingly, an attempt was made to shift away from the traditional governing body by combining the statutory responsibilities of a school governing body with the strengths of a Community Association. Under this system the Association elects a Council, some of whose members represent it on the Governing Body. As a consequence the Governing Body involves pupils, parents, staff, local residents and LEA representatives in equal numbers. It is this group that is supposed to determine the policy for the school and college and who have responsibility for the plant, for finance and for community development. However, it is widely known that such a scheme does not work in the way in which it was originally envisaged despite the descriptions provided by the two headteachers. Accordingly, community colleges are attempting to devise ways in which the community association might be broadly representative of the community.

As far as school structure was concerned it was the House system and position of House Head which was utilised at Sidney Stringer School. However, the principles involved were adapted and extended. As in the 'traditional' comprehensive school the House Head was responsible for a group of 120 pupils but with a much greater responsibility for making home contacts. Each House Head was to be involved in 'at least one face to face contact each year with the parents or guardians of every pupil in the House, either by inviting parents to school or by visiting homes'.[47] In terms of home visits these were to be *positive* so as to encourage communication between home and school and to promote educational ideas. Such work carried with it implications for the role of the pastoral staff which shifted towards community action, adult education and some elements of social work.

Such work is seen as a central element in developing the aims of Sidney Stringer School. The 1982-83 school prospectus outlines what the institution hopes to achieve before going on to explain how they attempt to make it work through the House system:

> Each year 240 young people are divided into two Houses, each House under the control of a House Head.
> The House Head is the key member of staff.
> The House Head starts with 120 eleven year old children and takes them through until they leave school at 16.[48]

By developing such a system Jones has argued, it allows for a two way interchange to occur between the family and the institution so that the values of the community can be transmitted to the institution and plans for curriculum development can be transmitted to the parents.[49] In turn the pastoral base with the careers service and provision for sixteen to nineteen year olds has the potential to deal with the young unemployed. However, as with all new schemes some evaluation is demanded.

Certainly at Sidney Stringer School several developments have taken place. The school has an acknowledged commitment to mixed ability grouping and team teaching arrangements. In addition, it has also engaged in curriculum development in multi-cultural education (resulting in a curriculum which was singled out for praise by the Rampton Committee[50]) and in the field of social education. While this demonstrates something of the diversity involved, the developments that have taken place in the field of social education demonstrate some of the conflicts involved in producing a common curriculum for members of a comprehensive school.[51]

When the school opened the humanities faculty planned a social education programme for pupils in years four, five and six which looked at issues such as women in society, welfare rights and related areas of interest. During the first year of its existence this programme was optional with the result that it was only taken by pupils who were not taking examinations, a situation that would have status implications for the option.[52] To broaden the intake to this course the humanities team persuaded the head to make this course compulsory in the upper school—a situation that was agreed subject to the programme containing an element of careers education. Despite the compulsory nature of the course Richards reports that the team considered that it still lacked status without an examination.[53] As a consequence they entered into negotiations for the course to become examined as a Mode 3 C.S.E. subject which resulted in changes to the content of the curriculum and to a change in title from social education to social studies. In turn, negotiations were also carried out to examine the subject at G.C.E. 'O' level. As a result it was argued that status was achieved, but no longer was the course 'education' oriented as the teachers could not define the

Table 10.7. Secondary and Primary School Pupil Numbers 1971-1982 in Coventry.

	Nos. on roll in September		
	Primary Schools	*Secondary Schools*	*Total*
1971	40,829	23,734	64,563
1972	41,006	24,803	65,809
1973	40,992	27,247	68,239
1974	40,205	27,995	68,200
1975	39,214	28,538	67,752
1976	38,360	28,945	67,305
1977	37,007	28,842	65,849
1978	35,299	28,702	64,001
1979	33,379	28,364	61,743
1980	31,347	27,944	59,291
1981	29,586	27,210	56,796
1982	27,780	26,779	54,559

Source: Coventry Education Committee, *Comprehensive Education for Life: A Consultative Document* (Coventry, 1983), 16.

curriculum and teach material on community action because they were constrained by examination requirements. Such an account contains a salutary story about the comprehensive school curriculum and the pressure of the examination system. If the achievements of the comprehensive school are to be 'measured' in terms of examination performance we might ask what kind of future is there for comprehensive schools in Coventry?

Since the mid 1970s Coventry in common with many other cities throughout the United Kingdom has experienced a fall in its pupil population (see table 10.7). Such trends have resulted in school closures in the primary sector and the redeployment of teachers among schools across the city. In turn, the Authority has also considered the education of 11—19 year olds and issued a consultative document on this topic in 1981.[54] In his introduction to this document the Director of Education remarked:

> We are ... fundamentally looking for a strategy to educate 11 to 19 year olds into the 21st century. There are a variety of approaches available, some of which are more radical than others ... the only approach not open to us is to do nothing.

This consultative document (later known as the first consultative document) outlined the kinds of courses that could be made available and the type of organisations in which they could be located. On the basis of receiving evidence, examining published material and looking at the approaches adopted in other local education authorities a working party on post primary education in the city issued a second consultative document entitled *Comprehensive Education for Life.*[55]

This document received wide press coverage both locally and nationally.[56] On the basis of the decline in the birth rate, rising unemployment among school leavers and an assessment of the 'needs' of the community, various proposals were outlined concerning the development of comprehensive education in the city for the remainder of the twentieth century. A major feature of the proposal concerned the use of Coventry's current resources in secondary schools. Accordingly, while other local education authorities thought in terms of closing schools the Coventry Authority proposed developing all its comprehensive schools as community colleges; a development which it argued would make best use of the building resources, and allow for the development of new approaches to courses for 14 to 18 year olds including education, training and work experience. Furthermore, it argued that by developing all schools as community colleges it made their resources available to the whole 'community' and resulted in education being available throughout life. While this proposal was a natural extension of comprehensive education and a radical move in comparison with the plans of other authorities, it was shortlived as within two years of issuing *Comprehensive Education for Life* further proposals were issued by the authority which included plans to close three secondary schools (two of which were community colleges). Clearly the Coventry rhetoric has not matched the reality once more.

The initial scheme had more to say about physical resources rather than curriculum content. We might therefore ask: what plans were made for developing the curriculum? In the *Comprehensive Education for Life* document it was maintained that the educational programme would need to be developed 'to include life, social, personal welfare and learning skills as well as vocational skills and the pursuance of competence and excellence'.[57] Accordingly, it was argued that a programme based on experience alongside academic learning was essential. There was some discussion of schemes used in other countries and particular emphasis was placed upon the modular scheme developed in Ontario's secondary schools, which it was maintained, could be adopted in Coventry's secondary schools with modules not only being offered in 'traditional' subjects, but also in areas of study such as 'Practical aspects of everyday life', 'Enjoyment of life' (art, craft, music, games, literature and film), pre-vocational and work experience and a personal status programme. Such curriculum development not only implied change in curriculum content but also in the status of the learner, in the role of the teacher and in the interaction and pattern of relationships between teacher and taught. However, the document also raised a further problem in terms of the assessment and validation of these courses which it suggested should be linked to traditional modes of examining in the first instance, a situation that Webster[58] has argued creates real problems for developing the scheme. Indeed, it had a mixed reception among local teachers. While some leading representatives of the local branches of the National Union of Teachers (NUT) and National Association of Schoolmasters/Union of Women Teachers were reported as being broadly in favour of the scheme because it appeared to retain schools and save teachers' jobs, others were suspicious.[59] In particular, some Executive members of the local branch of the NUT claimed that the document should neither be endorsed nor rejected as it failed to deal satisfactorily with such issues as the modular curriculum, the examination system and equal opportunities, yet started to consider the value of what is taught and attempted to specify curriculum objectives while discussing education as a life long experience. Some local teachers have questioned the validity of this proposal which they felt contained a deficit model of the 'customers' in Coventry's schools and colleges and disregarded the contribution of primary education in the life long learning process. Furthermore, it was feared that these course proposals may result in a hierarchical system with more than a hint of bilateralism within the comprehensive system.

In some respects their fears are justified in a city where headteachers still talk in terms of examinations passed, Advanced levels and entrance to university as measures of the success of their institutions. Even a brief glance at any Coventry secondary school prospectus confirms this picture where several pages are devoted to examinations passed at Advanced and Ordinary levels of the G.C.E. and at C.S.E. To pupils and parents who receive these documents the message is clear: examinations count and are as much a central feature of Coventry's comprehensive school system as they are elsewhere. Certainly, Robert Aitken is correct to argue that *Comprehensive Education for Life* contained a plan to be developed in an evolutionary way for the 21st century as there is much to be done in breaking down conventional attitudes to education not only among teachers and pupils but also among the educational establishment and the citizens of Coventry. The question that remains is whether the Coventry Authority have identified a way forward and whether it can bring about radical educational change and development at a time when redeployment and redundancy are items on the local labour market agenda for teachers as well as school leavers.

Coventry's education service has often been identified with educational expansion, innovation and change in the post second world war period. Yet this oversimplifies matters as the economic and political context has to be taken into account. From the early 1950s to the mid 1970s was a period of economic expansion and demographic growth which helped to fuel educational development in England in general and in Coventry in particular. However, the subsequent economic decline, the recession, unemployment (especially among young people) and a dramatic fall in school rolls have posed many problems about the use of resources in the English educational system and here Coventry has not been an exception. Throughout the last forty years the city's Directors of Education have, in different ways, helped to pioneer different forms of comprehensive schooling and comprehensive education. Indeed, in the educational imagination Coventry is synonymous with comprehensive schools and educational change. Yet the evidence suggests that while Coventry was among the first authorities to build comprehensive schools it is, in common with many other authorities, still in the process of developing the principles of comprehensive education in relation to a variety of different age groups.

Certainly, its chief officers have planned boldly and introduced new ideas into the city's education service. Yet such ideas have to be seen in the context of the schools on the one hand, and the educational system and the society on the other. As a consequence, there have been comprehensive schools built in the city but whether comprehensive education has been achieved is open to question. It is, therefore, important for the citizens of Coventry to engage in debate with politicians, administrators, teachers and students if comprehensive education is to be achieved by the end of the twentieth century.

Notes to Chapter 10

1. *Education Act, 1918*, London, HMSO, section 2(1), 1.
2. W.H. Hadow, *The Education of the Adolescent* (1926).
3. *Ibid.*, 95-6, 172-188.
4. 'Address on Educational Training', *Coventry Standard*, 11 May, 1940.
5. W. Spens, *Report of the Consultative Committee on Secondary Education with Special Reference to Grammar Schools* (1938).
6. R. Barker, *Education and Politics 1900-1951* (Oxford, 1972).
7. Even when Labour took office Ellen Wilkinson showed some ambivalence towards multilateral and comprehensive schools, having herself gained educational success through the grammar school. See B.D. Vernon, *Ellen Wilkinson 1891-1947* (1982), esp. 201-230.
8. *Hansard*, London, HMSO 1943; col. 1829.
9. *Education Act, 1944*, London, HMSO; section 7, 4.
10. M.S. Archer, *The Social Origins of Educational Systems* (1979), 583.
11. City of Coventry, *Primary and Secondary Education Development* as revised in 1948.
12. 'Coventry Experiment in Education', *Coventry Evening Telegraph*, 12 March, 1949.
13. F. West, 'A comprehensive school built on a house basis', in National Union of Teachers, *Inside the Comprehensive School* (1958), 84-87.
14. See for example, Archer, *op.cit.*; C. Benn and B. Simon, *Half Way There* (Harmondsworth, 1972); G.C. Firth, *Comprehensive Schools in Coventry and Elsewhere* (Coventry, 1963); G.C. Firth, *Seventy Five Years of Service to Education* (Coventry, 1977); R. Pedley, *The Comprehensive School* (3rd edn., Harmondsworth, 1978); D. Rubinstein and B. Simon, *The Evolution of the Comprehensive School* (2nd edn., 1972).
15. Firth, *Seventy Five Years*, *op.cit.*, 256.
16. For the implications that this model has had on the organisation and the curriculum of comprehensive schools, see, for example, D.H. Hargreaves, *The Challenge for the Comprehensive School* (1982).
17. 'Comprehensive Schools Solve Problem', *Coventry Evening Telegraph*, 28 September, 1954.
18. 'The New Schools Offer a Great Opportunity', *Coventry Evening*

Telegraph, 10 June, 1954.
19. W. Callow, 'Schools: What the city plan means', *Coventry Evening Telegraph*, 22 March, 1960.
20. 'Plea for Historic Grammar Schools in Coventry', *Coventry Evening Telegraph*, 10 September, 1966.
21. This level of understanding can be compared with the position that existed nationally in the Labour Party. See Barker, *op.cit.*, and Vernon, *op.cit.*
22. 'Speech day address', *Coventry Evening Telegraph*, 2 December, 1960.
23. See Department of Education and Science, *The Organization of Secondary Education* (Circular 10/65), (1965), which indicates that there was no clear idea about comprehensive education or comprehensive schools as six different ways of organizing a comprehensive school were suggested.
24. Coventry Education Committee, *Youth and Community Services* (Coventry Education Working Party Report, 1972).
25. For a discussion of Robert Aitken's style as a director of education, see T. Bush and M. Kogan, *Directors of Education* (1982).
26. Other methods of decentralising large schools included divisions into year groups or the subdivision of schools into Lower, Middle and Upper School units. For a summary of the approaches that can be used see E. Halsall, *The Comprehensive School* (Oxford, 1972).
27. Address by Walter Chinn to the Housemasters and Housemistresses Meeting, 1958.
28. See, for example, Benn and Simon, *op.cit.*, Pedley, *op.cit*
29. A. Ling, 'Comprehensive Schools', *Times Educational Supplement*, 11 March, 1960.
30. *Ibid.*
31. Firth, *Comprehensive Schools.*
32. Firth, *Seventy Five Years.*
33. *Caludon Castle School Prospectus for 1982-3* (Coventry, 1982).
34. *The Woodlands School Prospectus for 1982-3* (Coventry, 1982).
35. Firth, *Seventy Five Years.*
36. J. Bazalgette, *School Life and Work Life* (1978).
37. For further criticism of the House system in comprehensive schools, see, for example, Pedley, *op.cit.*
38. For a discussion of this proposal see Coventry Education Committee, *Comprehensive Education for Life: A Consultative Document* (Coventry 1983).

39. Fur further discussion see R. Aitken, 'Combating loneliness in the big city', *Education,* 23 May, 1975, 574–5.
40. See, for example, M. Merson and R.J. Campbell, 'Community education: instruction for inequality', *Education for Teaching,* Spring, 1974, 43-9.
41. For a further discussion of this approach see C. Fletcher and N. Thompson (eds.), *Issues in Community Education*, (Lewes, 1980) especially the paper by C. Fletcher, 'Developments in Community Education: a current account', 5-10 and by H. Morris, 'Architecture, Humanism and the Local Community', 11-19; the latter being originally presented in 1956.
42. See, for example, G. Holroyde, 'Effective Management' in J.E.C. MacBeath (ed.), *A Question of Schooling* (1975) and G. Holroyde, 'The Sidney Stringer School and Community College' (Case Study Materials) in R. McHugh with E. Milner and O. Boyd-Barrett, *A Case Study in Management: Sidney Stringer School and Community College,* (Milton Keynes, 1976), 18–44.
43. See A. Jones, 'Sidney Stringer School and Community College', in Fletcher and Thompson, *op.cit.* 79-85 and A. Jones, 'Sidney Stringer School and Community College' in B. Moon (ed.), *Comprehensive Schools: Challenge and Change,* (Windsor, 1983), 85–97.
44. See, for example, J.K. Richards, 'A Cautionary tale', *Times Educational Supplement*, 26 August, 1977.
45. See Equal Opportunities Commission, *Formal Investigation Report: Sidney Stringer School and Community College* (Manchester).
46. Jones, *op.cit.*
47. Holroyde, *Case Study*, 30.
48. *Sidney Stringer School Prospectus for 1982-83* (Coventry, 1982).
49. Jones, *op.cit.*
50. A. Rampton, *West Indian Children in Our Schools* (1981).
51. For discussions of the difficulties of introducing a common curriculum into the comprehensive school see D. Lawton, *Class, Culture and the Curriculum* (1975); M. Hold, *The Common Curriculum: Its Structure and Style in the Comprehensive School* (1978); and Hargreaves, *op.cit.*
52. For further discussions on the status implications of school subjects see M.F.D. Young (ed.), *Knowledge and Control: New Directions for the Sociology of Education* (1971); J. Rex, 'Aims and Objectives', in M. Craft (ed.), *Teaching in a Multicultural Society* (Lewes, 1981), 36-52; I. Goodson, *School Subjects and Curriculum Change* (1982); I.

Goodson and S. Ball (eds.), *Defining the Curriculum* (Lewes, 1984).

53. See Richards, *op.cit.*, and for similar arguments see Goodson, *op.cit.*, on the teaching of rural studies.
54. Coventry Education Committee, *The Education of 11 to 19 Year Olds: A Consultative Document* (Coventry, 1981).
55. Coventry Education Committee, *Comprehensive Education.*
56. See, for example, J. Cross, 'The Coventry anti-climax', *Times Educational Supplement*, 22 April, 1983; H. Webster, 'Comprehensive Education for Life: a consultative document', *Community Education Network*, vol. 3, no. 4, (April) and for special features see the *Coventry Evening Telegraph*, 28 and 29 April, 1983.
57. Coventry Education Committee, *Comprehensive Education*, 59.
58. Webster, *op.cit.*
59. Cross, *op.cit.*

Chapter 11

Looking Back on the Blitz

Tony Mason

The purpose of this chapter is threefold. First, to recall the German air raids on Coventry during the second world war, to summarise what happened and to assess the major effects. Second, to take a fresh look at what have been identified by historians as controversial episodes during the blitz and to examine some important features of the experience which previous writers have either ignored or touched on only in passing. The final and longest section will attempt to trace how the bombing of Coventry has been interpreted and used by individuals and groups in the local community over the past forty years. Time is not merely a great healer: it alters the vantage point from which past events are seen and may both underline their importance for later generations or remove them from the area of contemporary concern.

As a centre of munitions production and, with Birmingham, the place where the bulk of Britain's fighter planes were made, it was obvious that Coventry would be subject to air attack in war. It was even chosen as the location for a laboratory experiment by two scientists employed by the Government in an attempt to forecast the results of a raid by 500 bombers on a typical English town.[1] When the German Air Force turned its attention to civilian targets in the late summer of 1940 Coventry was bound to be high on their list.

The first raid was on 18 August. Fourteen bombs fell in Canley Road and Cannon Hill Road. The first raid in which people were killed took place ten days later when thirteen bombs were dropped on the Hillfields district. Sixteen people died and three hundred houses were damaged. Between 18 August and 12 November Coventry was attacked on twenty-four occasions. Few parts of the city escaped some damage and a total of one hundred and eighty-nine people were killed and two hundred and fifty-nine seriously injured. On the night of 14/15 November, 449 bombers raided the city for almost eleven hours. Five hundred and sixty-eight people were killed and eight hundred and sixty-three seriously injured.[2] Two thirds of the mediaeval city centre was either completely destroyed or badly damaged. The cathedral, Owen Owen's, the Empire Theatre and the Market Hall were among the more important buildings destroyed. One hundred and eleven out of the one hundred and eighty principal factories sustained some damage and particularly badly hit were the Daimler factory at Radford, G.E.C. in Whitefriars Street and British Thomson Houston in Alma Street. Even more damaging, electricity, gas, telephone, transport and water services were all severely disrupted.[3] About twelve per cent of the city's houses were rendered uninhabitable or destroyed.

There were eighteen more raids to come of which two were particularly serious and approached the destruction of November 1940. They took place within forty-eight hours of each other in April 1941. On the night of 8/9 April two hundred and eighty-one people were killed and five hundred and seventy seriously injured while on the night of 9/10 April one hundred and seventy were killed and one hundred and fifty-three seriously hurt. The first raid lasted for over five hours and the second for almost four and a half. These raids saw the destruction of Coventry and Warwickshire Hospital, St. Mary's Hall and King Henry's School with direct hits on the Council House, Central Police Station and L.M.S. Goods Office, as well as to forty-two factories of which four were seriously damaged. Thirty thousand houses were also damaged and public services again seriously curtailed.[4]

The first response to the city centre devastation was one of shock. It did not seem that recovery from such a blow was possible. Eighteen hundred troops were called in after the November raid and they spent a month helping civilian labour to patch up property and restore essential services. Housing the homeless and finding billets for the emergency labour brought in from outside were both serious immediate problems. Lack of electricity, gas and water supplies were largely responsible for around 12,000 workers being made unemployed on the morning of 15 November, but within two weeks eighty per cent of them were back at work. Similarly after the April raids 108 factories were deprived of their normal gas supplies but half had had them restored within ten days and the rest in just under another week. One fact that aided industrial recovery was that damage to buildings was greater than damage to the machinery inside them. Coventry showed that even the most intensive bombing would not, of itself, bring about permanent damage to a city's economic life.[5]

There are four main issues concerning the bombing of Coventry which remain the subject of argument, or in one case, silence. First, was Coventry 'sacrificed' to keep the Enigma secret? During the 1970s a story developed about the November Raid. It followed the publication of a series of accounts of how Allied cryptographers had, early in the war, broken many of the German military codes. The essence of this new theory was that the raid could have been prevented or, if not prevented, its impact limited by counter measures because it was known in advance that Coventry was to be the target on November 14. The reason that nothing was done and nobody was warned, so this story goes, was that the Government did not want to do anything which might suggest to the Germans that their codes had been breached. Coventry people add their own gloss: that Churchill himself decided that the city must be sacrificed.

The reality, however, was very different. As a centre of British aircraft production, Coventry had already attracted the attention of the Luftwaffe and would clearly do so again. Its defences had therefore been strengthened earlier that November but it was not expected that they would be tested so seriously so soon. On 11 November, Air Intelligence had learned, via Enigma, that the German Air Force was about to launch a large scale night raid led by the pathfinder squadron Kg100 using target finding radio beams. The operation was to be called Moonlight Sonata which suggested a three stage raid at or near the time of the full moon. Unfortunately only target numbers were given, together with the name Korn which meant nothing to British Intelligence. A captured German airman had also mentioned the raid and named the target as either Birmingham or Coventry. His evidence was ignored because a captured map pointed to targets around London. Also filed away was some further Enigma information, collected between 12—14 November, which gave the radio beam bearings for three targets, Birmingham, Coventry and Wolverhampton. Similar signals associated with German experimental beam transmissions had been going on for two months unaccompanied by raids and it was thought that these were part of the same experiments. London was still thought to be the target although the Air Ministry told Churchill that if further intelligence came in they 'hoped to get instructions out in time'.

Events moved rapidly on Thursday 14 November. By 1 p.m. the German Air Force beam tunings showed that a raid was to take place that night and at 3 p.m. it was seen that the beams intersected over Coventry. Jamming attempts failed owing to a technical error and the night fighters which went up to take on the Germans just could not find them. The anti-aircraft batteries also had a bad night. A terrible combination of operational inadequacy, intelligence uncertainty and bad luck ensured that the bombs fell on Coventry largely unhindered. But there was no conspiracy. The identity of the target had been known for four hours and not two days.[6]

Second, the performance of the emergency services. How far did they fail to meet the challenge of the heavy raids? How far were such failures a local or central government responsibility? Third, did the local population panic? How far was the trekking out of the city a common sense reaction to enable tired factory workers to obtain much needed rest—how far a spontaneous reflex of fear and hopelessness? Finally, although historians have largely ignored it, there was looting in the city after the raids. How much was there, who was involved and how important was it?

Tom Harrisson in his book *Living Through the Blitz* felt that the emergency services had not been well enough prepared. In particular the treatment of the shocked but otherwise uninjured majority left much to be desired. Facilities such as mobile canteens were urgently required and in particular information was needed about a whole host of things from how to obtain emergency ration books and financial compensation for war damaged buildings to the local and national news. More voluntary social workers were required to disseminate personal information with the cups of tea. Rest Centres should have been established on the edge of the town to take those made homeless. One reason why some of these things had not been done was hinted at by the Report of the Coventry Reconstruction Co-ordinating Committee of 31 December, 1940. The committee, in agreeing that the existence and whereabouts of organisations that can give help must be publicised, said 'We are aware of the risk that knowledge that help is available may sap the self-reliance of the individual...'. But the risk had now to be taken. Too late for Coventry and many other places too.

O'Brien, the official historian of Civil Defence, also thought that the services in Coventry responded sluggishly and he emphasised the relative failure of cooperation between those services not under the general direction of the Ministry of Home Security, namely public health, food, industrial production, information, housing and repairs to gas and water services.[7]

George Hodgkinson complained that the Ministry of Home Security's forward planning was far too sketchy to deal with such a situation as the November bombing inflicted on Coventry. 'All the normal services of the local authority were shattered. The Town Clerk could not at first be found and only two members of the War Emergency Committee, conscientious objectors in the 1914-18 war, reported for duty'. The Minister of Home Security proposed putting the city under martial law but the idea was vigorously and successfully opposed. There was mistrust of the local authority from Whitehall. Even before the November raid the Ministry of Labour's welfare officer had characterised the local council as one which would 'talk and talk but put off action to a future time ... there are obstructionists and muddlers with no imagination' and she claimed that the billeting of industrial workers had been botched by the Town Clerk's department. Similarly after the April attacks, the Deputy Regional Commissioner drew attention to the 'party influences and personal jealousies and animosities' existing in local councils which could often obstruct the national interest.

None of this can have helped the efficient functioning of the emergency services which were particularly defective in two areas. Munition workers had threatened a strike in the autumn of 1940 because of the difficulties they were experiencing in getting to and from work. Bus and tram conductors were in particularly short supply and the Ministry of Labour refused to release female factory workers to take over. The tramway system was put out of action by the November bombing as was almost half the fleet of buses but the problem was made worse by the failure of many of the drivers to report for duty. The Reconstruction Co-ordinating Committee recommended after the November blitz that the police should have the power to stop every private car leaving the city in rush hours and insist that every seat was filled. They were also in favour of disciplining drivers who did not turn up and suggested that efforts should be made to induce workers to acquire bicycles. This issue resurfaced after the raids of 8/9 and 10/11 April when driver absenteeism caused serious problems with still twenty per cent absent from work on 15 April.[8]

But perhaps the most costly inadequacies were in the fire fighting service. The *Midland Daily Telegraph* ran a couple of articles on the lessons which might be drawn from the Blitz in December 1940 which placed particular emphasis on the unnecessary difficulties encountered by the valiant firemen. There was a plan for mutual assistance between local brigades. But the forces had never exercised together and when brigades from other towns in the area arrived to give their help on the night of 14/15 November 'the couplings of the equipment did not marry up, the hoses and nozzles were dissimilar and in consequence the city had to burn for lack of water and almost criminal neglect'. More fire watchers might also have helped damp down the fires in the early stages; it is well known that the Cathedral was destroyed. What is often not realised is that the Holy Trinity church next to it survived due to the foresight and organisation of the vicar who placed teams of firewatchers on each of the nine lead roofs, all connected by telephone to the North Porch where he and his two sons co-ordinated activities. A fire engine stood ready in the church and the Archdeacon's court was converted into a static water tank. Only one incendiary penetrated the roof. The problem of recruiting sufficient fire watchers was not really solved until after the worst raids were over. There was also some criticism of those people who were leaving the town each evening in order to sleep the more soundly somewhere in the surrounding countryside.[9]

Some local authorities did better. Shoreditch, in London, and Clydeside towns, according to one account. The Germans did better too. They already had a national fire service in 1939 and most small towns and villages had volunteer fire corps which could be combined to go to help local towns which were the victims of heavy raids. The Luftwaffe had fifty-three motorised fire fighting battalions and sixty-three small towns had mobile units of fire protection police who could be moved quickly to the districts being heavily attacked.[10]

It is difficult at this distance to disentangle entirely responsibility for the errors, largely of omission and preparation, that were made. It is not clear that central government would have done any better if it could have ignored the local representatives of the people. But what does appear clear is that neither local nor central government held a high opinion of each other and this undoubtedly hindered the work of dealing with an emergency. Moreover, the uncertainty as to who was responsible for what may have had more serious implications than the confusion over the order for twenty miles of flexible jointed piping which the Staveley Coal and Iron Company worked all of one weekend to produce for Coventry at a cost of £20,000. No one knew who had ordered it. It certainly wasn't needed and the final surplus was not disposed of until 1944.[11]

In May 1972 a young historian, trying his hand at journalism in the *Sunday Times Magazine*, said of the big raid of 14/15 November, 'the first blitz on Coventry produced mass panic; thousands fled the town'. Survivors of the experience, both those who had held official positions and those who had merely anonymously done their bit, wrote to the *Coventry Evening Telegraph* to say that the young man had got it wrong. There had been no panic although of course there was shock and horror at the extent of the damage. Once the initial impact had been absorbed, most people 'got on with the job'. Now of course it all depends what you mean by panic.

Leaving the city after work to sleep in the towns and villages nearby was common during the air raids of 1940-41 in many provincial towns. It is not clear when it began in Coventry but it was certainly taking place before the heavy raid of 14/15 November as the following advertisement from the *Coventry Standard* of 12 November, 1940, indicated.

> Comfortable, private, pleasantly situated country home; safe, Coventry buses pass daily, 20 miles, two or three adults,

moderate terms, Braunston near Rugby.

Many people marked 'SO' on their front gates to indicate that they were 'sleeping out'. Almost a year later, in early October 1941, the Friends' Ambulance Unit carried out an enquiry on the nightly exodus from Coventry and their eight page report lies in the Public Record Office.[12] No one to whom they talked could offer anything like precise numbers of the people involved. In fact estimates varied hugely. The Coventry police, for example, estimated that 100,000 people were sleeping out during the main raids, that, out of a total population registered for food rationing of 194,000.[13] The Deputy A.R.P. Officer, on the other hand, thought that 70,000 were sleeping out during the raids and said that he thought it was still 50,000 in October 1941. The local Medical Officer of Health agreed. Another A.R.P. officer thought that the number sleeping out in the autumn of 1941 was 24,000. The Midland Red bus company said they carried 5,000 more people into Coventry before 9 a.m. each morning than they had done before the blitz. On the other hand only about 6,900 were accommodated in Warwickshire Rest Centres after the November raids and 2,700 after the April ones. By October 1941 the largest group of nightly evacuees was thought to be car owners who could afford to pay for accommodation as the market took over from pity in determining what was offered by whom. One informant claimed that over half of the residents of Cannon Hill, a prosperous district about two miles from the city centre, still slept out. The report concluded that the numbers leaving the city at the time of the raids was probably between 70 and 100,000 and that at the time the report was compiled, October 1941, had fallen to 15-20,000. Another raid on Coventry would send it up to 50,000 and the large scale exodus would be repeated if really heavy bombing returned.

Whatever one thinks about these figures all seem agreed that they were large. Moreover as we saw earlier in this chapter, by the eve of the November raid, Coventry had suffered twenty-four attacks and undoubtedly people were nervous. Further, if you were hard at work in a munitions factory all day you needed your sleep at night. Sleeping out might be a sensible way of getting it. Ritchie Calder, in a report on Air Raid Morale for the Foreign Office in 1941 noted that the raids on Coventry did not produce a single case of neurosis. It is also interesting that 2,200 workers appeared before the local Labour Supply Committee asking for a transfer shortly after the November raid but that 2,000 were persuaded to stay. There was however some lack of enthusiasm in some quarters for restarting the nightshift. After the April raids the Deputy

Regional Commissioner went out of his way to praise the morale of Coventry people. 'There was no panic and nothing in the nature of a general trek from the city'. Tom Harrisson, in *Living Through the Blitz*, was of the opinion that trekking was only a temporary device in Coventry and not the 'way of life' it was in some other places, such as Southampton.

Well it may have become a 'way of life' for some people in Coventry too. The Chief Constable thought that Coventry people were 'easily shaken' as late as March 1942 and offered as evidence a recent night alert which prompted 'large numbers' of people to leave the city both by car and on foot.[14] Clearly some people did rush away from the disaster with little thought of where they were going nor when they would come back and that was probably more the case after the November raid than at any other time. Jobs and homes, of course, were strong pulls to bring them back again. Panic may well be the right word to describe the behaviour of some of the people in those November days but it will hardly do as a label for them all.[15]

It is impossible to be certain how much of a problem looting was in Coventry during the blitz but what is clear is that the authorities took a serious view of it in spite of Tom Harrisson's assertion that no record exists.[16] The Chief Constable's report for 1940 listed five hundred and fifty-eight cases of looting of which 408 were from meters and machines. Five hundred and twenty cases, again, coincidentally, 408 thefts from meters, were noted in 1941 but after that the category disppears from his annual survey of offences for the city. Of course the circumstances were ideal. Ruined properties everywhere, owners and residents absent for one reason or another; the forces of law and order in part distracted by other more pressing matters all amounted to maximum opportunity and therefore maximum temptation. Breaking open meters seems to have been particularly common amongst youths and children. In November 1940 three seventeen year olds, a fifteen year old and a twenty-one year old trooper were charged with stealing from meters in evacuated houses. Other offences were taken into account, there was one previous conviction and sentences of three months hard labour for three, six months for one and probation for the juvenile were meted out. With the shopping centre so badly damaged the remains of the stocks in many shops were a standing temptation, especially easily consumed or marketable items like cigarettes which Coventry workers often claimed were in short supply. Three Salford Auxiliary Fire Service men received six months hard labour for stealing cigarettes from a shop while a female shop assistant got twenty-eight days for the same offence. Several soldiers imported into the city to help with demolition work were also convicted of looting. Contemporaries thought that there had been a rapid increase in petty crime among children. Looting, of course, was not an offence which appealed to magistrates, one of whom suggested it should be met by corporal punishment. Another suggested that looters should be shot. The fact that they weren't seems both testimony to Britain's liberal values, a general social responsibility and the fact that an outbreak never became an epidemic. Nevertheless it was a problem against which citizens and authority had to be on their guard after every raid.[17]

How a person looks back at the blitz will depend on several factors. But in particular it will almost certainly have something to do with whether you or yours were bombed, played a role in rescue, lost friends or relatives. Even the way in which those experiences are interpreted will probably change over time. The worst blows are often cushioned by the passage of time. You may look back with pride on your own part in an obviously historical experience even if that part was the bit one of simply being there. You may place it in the wider context of shared community involvement in which everyone appears, at least in retrospect, to have been pulling together in pursuit of a common goal. Each new generation will see the blitz as an historical moment and what it means for them will depend on their own immediate circumstances and ideas.

The immediate survivors had the most urgent job of trying to make sense of it. Tom Harrisson thought that it did not take the people of Coventry long to find their bearings. 'Out of the rubble began to grow local pride ... no one had ever suffered more. It was a wonder to have endured at all'. By the Saturday morning, with no repeat performance in the previous twenty-four hours, people began to feel rather more optimistic.[18] One important prop to recovery was the fact that Coventry was the first provincial town to receive such intense treatment. Unlike rambling London, Coventry was a relatively small city and the destruction of its centre was all the more impressive. Moreover the destruction of the Cathedral became a very important symbol which, via some adroit Government propaganda yet to be seriously studied, gripped the imagination of the world. In the fight against fascism the destruction of Coventry took an early and prominent symbolic position.[19] With the dawn came fame. As the Mayor told the City Council on 3 December,

> for some days after the raid, most of us were cut off from the ordinary sources of news and hence we did not realise how famous Coventry had suddenly become. It was, I think on the Monday that telegrams and messages from all over the

> country, and indeed, the world, began to pour in, and we learned what a deep impression had been produced by the manner in which Coventry had stood up to its ordeal.

£35,000 had come in without asking! The high and mighty certainly descended upon the city, Sir John Reith, Herbert Morrison, Wendell Wilkie, Robert Menzies but above all, the King, all came to see for themselves and to help Coventry people to take it.[20]

This fame has, so far at least, not been lost. As the President of the Coventry Free Church Council said in November 1957,

> wherever you travel, not only in this country but across the world, you will find, when you tell people you come from Coventry, that it is a name they have come to know and respect. It is a proud thing to be able to say that about one's own city.[21]

In a sense Coventry's renown is permanently institutionalised in the relationship with towns like St. Etienne, Lidice, Dresden and Stalingrad. It is no accident that George Hodgkinson became the first Englishman to be made a freeman of the city of Sarajevo and in general Coventry's civic dignitaries have never been short of invitations from abroad. On the other hand it is doubtful whether any of the other badly bombed British cities could have mustered so distinguished a turnout for the fortieth anniversary Mayor's luncheon in 1980 which was attended not only by representatives from the twin cities but from the main London embassies, M.P.s including Edward Heath, councillors and many of the organisations which had been active in the blitz. As the Czech Ambassador said in 1958, the war record of Coventry was well known in his country.[22]

And of course Coventry's fame was partly linked to the rebuilding of both City and Cathedral in a modern style. The idea of reconstruction and rebirth and the image of the phoenix was inescapable. Much of the responsibility for that must go to Donald Gibson, the City's first architect. The dust had hardly settled before the *Coventry Standard*, out of action for two weeks, the only time it failed to publish from its inception in 1741, gave Mr. Gibson a public platform from which he proclaimed his vision of a planned city, with every street designed in relation to the rest. As the *Standard* said, while the effect of the raid must be deplored 'it has cleared the way for a replanning of Coventry which would never have been possible in peace time'. As the long years of rebuilding began after the war Coventry's name was kept before a world wide public. This was particularly true in relation to the new Cathedral.

Immediately after the war the slogan was 'Everyman's Cathedral needs everybody's help'. And almost every man did seem to be contributing. Although much of the first £100,000 came from large donations such as the £25,000 from the owners of the *Coventry Evening Telegraph* and the £10,000 from Standard Motors, over half of the money was made up of gifts of a guinea or less. Anyone who gave a pound could be numbered among the founders of the new cathedral. The Church itself tried to exploit the situation by linking it with the movement for church unity. The local headlines proclaimed 'Coventry Again Makes History' and asserted that the hallowing of the Chapel of Unity was 'the most significant event of modern times in English Church History'.[23] This theme of spiritual alliance with physical renewal has never been completely lost and is the emphasis of the school textbook *Reconciling the World: Ruin and Revival* which was published in 1970.[24] But such high hopes could not be realised. By the time of the tenth anniversary of the Cathedral's consecration in May 1972, although much was made of it with visits by the Berlin Philharmonic, a performance of Britten's War Requiem, a Lubeck week and an international conference on Social Planning and Tomorrow's City 'a cynic might say that this only showed how the heart of man will go out to any symbol of hope if sufficiently glamourised and presented with enough jazzed up publicity'. The £1.1/4 million building had already attracted ten million tourists. By 1972 the blitzed sites which had been very much in evidence in 1945 had been replaced by a modern city in which unemployment was at five per cent and car ownership the highest for the city's size in Britain. The Church was back in its twentieth century backseat.[25]

If the blitz provided opportunities for politicians, churchmen and architects, what of the ordinary Coventrian? What does it mean to ordinary people? The anniversary of the November raid has been celebrated every year since although its closeness to the traditional Armistice Day observance probably did not help it to establish itself firmly in the city's litany. Several hundred members of the public attended a service at the communal grave in 1951 and the Mayor of that year said that it stood out from all the other engagements of the Mayoral year. But it soon disappeared from the front page of the local newspaper and attendances were nearly always small although individuals would occasionally write to the *Evening Telegraph* saying that they were remembering people whom they had known who had died in the bombing, but quietly and privately.[26]

The local British Legion tried to persuade the Council to organise the event towards the end of the 1950s and were in part successful in that in 1960, for the twentieth anniversary, it was made a civic occasion and linked with Armistice Day. But by the 1970s little notice was being taken of it again and few members of the public were taking part.

On the twentieth anniversary of the November raid, the *Coventry Standard* went out and asked people both what their memories of the blitz were and whether or not those events should be forgotten or remembered. A fairly predictable range of opinions resulted. Elderly people either did not want to talk about it, disliked the new Coventry or felt that the younger generation ought to be made aware of what their elders had had to put up with. Younger people in general seemed to think it ought to be remembered and the paper claimed that that was the view of 'an increasingly large percentage of Coventrians'. Two ladies who had survived the blitz provided more authentic-sounding views. 'Those of us who lost everything in the war will never forget. We don't need anniversaries and war films and books, we just remember...'. And a second lady said 'everything seemed so vast, so much happened, we thought that nothing more could happen. We often believed that things never would come right again'.[27]

Twenty years later still not only could the local paper look back with pride but with nostalgia and humour too. Those were real celebrations with a Blitz Ball at the Rialto. It could even place the Coventry experience in a wider perspective. Although the blitz had come to Coventry first, it had been even more terrible in Dresden and Hamburg, Tokyo, Hiroshima and Nagasaki. In 1980 the reporters could go out into Coventry's streets and ask the people not what they thought about remembering the blitz, but what they thought of the previous evening's television documentary. It made one young lady proud of her city and of the people who died, or survived to tell their terrifying story. It was, she said, a great example of British pluck. 'Please don't let it die Coventry. We managed to survive then when all the odds were against us. We can do it now if we try'.[28]

The *Coventry Evening Telegraph* has always recognised the value of the blitz in helping to underline a political point. In 1949, for example, the editorial used the anniversary to urge Coventry men and women to enrol in the civil defence forces. When sufficient volunteers were not forthcoming, a house to house canvas was organised in anniversary week and the newspaper again took the opportunity to point the citizen in the direction of his and her duty. 'Surely there are sufficient public-minded people in this city who by a little self-sacrifice and training can play their part in trying to ensure that civilians shall be spared another ordeal such as that of 1940'. Similarly in 1980 when the enemy was economic, the blitz was summoned to remind readers that triumph did follow adversity and that Coventry should look ahead. Again, in November 1983, the blitz experience was used as a peg on which to hang support for Cruise missiles.[29]

In one sense the blitz is a shared experience whether we were there or not. If you live in Coventry in particular, it is part of your history and it is always there to be dragged into the present to underline policies, and to point morals. Attention has already been drawn to the use made of the blitz by the local paper in this respect. The lady quoted above by the *Evening Telegraph* was doing something similar. We survived the blitz in the 1940s: we can survive de-industrialisation and unemployment in the 1980s is her exhortation. The emphasis is on endurance in both cases, rather than on prevision and planning. It involves a passive acceptance of circumstances rather than a sense of practical alternative policies. In the long run this ideological impact of the blitz may be as important as the concrete ring roads and shopping precincts. As a Great Moment in the history of both city and nation, the blitz has often been dusted down and brought out into the day's light to serve some purpose or other. That is one good reason for taking a closer look at what actually happened.

Appendix I
Coventry Casualties 1940-1943

Killed	Civil Defence Workers	115
	Others	1,085
Treated in Hospital		*1,859*
		3,059
Buildings	Completely destroyed	
	Houses	4,330
	Shops and Dwellings	273
	Lock-up shops	351
	Offices	121
	Industrial Premises	73
	Warehouses	84
	Hotels	28
	Theatres/Cinemas	14
	Clubs	4
	Hospitals, Nursing Homes	4
	Garages, Filling Stations	80
	Banks	1
	Schools	5
	Public Utilities	7
	Corporation Properties	12
	Miscellaneous	151

50,479 houses were damaged.

Source: *Coventry Standard*, 28 October, 1960 (from the municipal handbook).

Appendix II
A letter from Mrs. Muriel Jones, 13 September, 1981 about the raids of November 1940 and April 1941

The night of the November Blitz, I was on day shift with my sister and two friends. Just as we left work the siren sounded so we ran as fast as we could, hoping to get to our digs or a shelter. One of my friends stopped along the road to say goodbye to her sailor boyfriend, it was their last goodbye, they were never seen again. We made it to one of four shelters, and ours was the only one that escaped the bombs, all the other occupants were killed. About 60 people. After the raid we had to dig ourselves out as best we could, to face all the damage. Around us our digs were gone along with a lot more houses. Our landlady and husband with them, although they were in a garden shelter. We made our way back to work, only to find the section where we worked was out of use having been hit. We were in a state of shock, suffering from torn off finger nails, cuts, bruises. I had a broken big toe and nose, my sister a broken arm, also one of my friends, done in a desperate bid to dig ourselves free from the rubble. We were hungry, tired and very cold. Neither help nor advice was at hand. So passing a shop on Stoney Stanton Road, where we had wandered looking for help I saw bread and tinned soup in the window, through a badly cracked pane. There was no reply to our knocking and shouting, so I took a brick and pushed the window in, helping myself to a loaf of bread and three cans of soup. I punched holes in the tins, we pulled the bread to pieces as best we could manage, very difficult with blood on your hands and face, and damaged finger nails. But our teeth were good and we managed. It was beautiful bread, soup and 'blood'! Then at last we found help, but not before we were sick, throwing up that lovely soup and bread. The wardens on duty took us to a van, and gave us warm tea, then on to a first aid post, where we were crudely patched up. No use going to hospital, as that was in a terrible state. But a doctor did set our broken bones. We were given a ticket for a train journey home or anywhere to get us out of the city. So just as we stood up, in dirty work overalls, absolutely filthy from head to foot, we walked to Bedworth where we found transport to take us to join the evacuation train to the North.

Nearby our present house there was a shelter to protect about ten people ... They were called Anderson Shelters, dug into the ground, made of corrugated metal sheets, reinforced, and covered with about three feet of earth. From the outside, it looked like a mound in the ground, with a stone bench at each side. There were no lights inside and no doors. On this particular night, we claimed our seats (inside the shelter) as quickly as possible along with present neighbours. As we could already see incendiary bombs falling from the planes flying overhead. After about an hour, we started to feel hot and sticky, there seemed to be little if any air. Then we all heard a crackling sound after a light explosion, and having had experience of such bombs we all knew there and then, buildings were set alight around us. It was then panic struck. The enemy had come back to burn what they thought was left of the previous raid or utility works that had built up during that past six months. The crackling getting louder, we really prayed all we had left to do. Then we heard the voice of an air raid warden calling 'Run for your lives. The wood yard is on fire and getting everything going with it'. Out eight of us came all women and girls. The sight and heat were more than we could cope with. On top of this, although the guns around the city were doing their utmost to keep the planes out, it was an almost impossible task, and the planes that got through after dropping their load machine-gunned at random as they made their getaway. The warden told us to crawl along the ground, keeping distance between us, until we reached the nearest public shelter on Foleshill Road. That meant crawling past about 50 houses in rows, then over the main road. In doing so, we had all the skin rubbed off hands and knees, cuts to faces or any exposed part of the body, as we passed over broken glass and hot fragments discharged out of the air. The warden tried to save the life of one old lady 78 years of age by wrapping her in a blanket and dragging her behind him. Her sister had to be left in the shelter as we were almost sure she was already dead. Whether she was or not, I shall never know or with shock or suffocation from the dense fumes seeping in the shelter [sic]. On our way we heard a woman cry for help, it was unbelievable. There she stood outside her burning home with a little bowl in her hand in the hope we could help put the fire out. All we could do was drag her to the ground and say, to hell with your house Mrs., your life first. We eventually made it to a shelter. It was so crammed with so many seeking protection like ourselves. I shall never know how we squeezed in, so much, that two people were already dead standing supported by those around. The little old lady was also dead, that was being dragged along the ground. By the time we reached the shelter, the journey must have taken well over an hour, I don't really know. Time meant nothing. Trying to reach your goal. But one thing that was hard to bear by all, having your mouth and lungs filled with smoke, and not a drink in sight to take dryness and thirst away. And every one in the same position.

Appendix III
The account of W. Ray Turner as published in the Coventry Evening Standard, 18 October, 1963.

He had gone to put out an incendiary when there was a bang. 'I do not wish to inflict details of any wounds I had sustained on the reader, except to state that the major injury was the almost complete severance of my foot at the ankle caused by shrapnel from a ... "high-explosive" incendiary bomb. But what I do want to do is to try and give an impression of the awful experience with which the average Coventry casualty had to contend on and after that awful November night...'.

He crawled and was pushed down and then up the shelter steps and lay on a neighbour's kitchen floor in a pool of blood, swigging brandy. Eventually a small car was brought by a neighbour to take him to the nearest first aid post.

'There was I, lying on my back in the rear seat, holding my foot on to prevent it coming off my leg completely, and every moment causing me untold agony and, of course, all this time it seemed that hell in all its fury had been let loose.

'At length we arrived ... at a first aid post about a mile from home where I was greeted most cordially by the wardens ... and laid out on a first-aid table.'

He was about to have a cup of tea when another big bang was followed by an end wall falling out.

'I found myself in the dark underneath the table on top of which I had been lying'.

Eventually he was taken by ambulance to Coventry Workhouse Infirmary, a vehicle he had helped design.

'I was fortunately on a lower stretcher as the person above me was killed by an ordinary incendiary bomb piercing the roof of the vehicle ... but still worse happened when a bomb was dropped directly in the path of the vehicle and owing apparently to shock, our driver could not pull up in time. The whole load of us dropped sideways into the bomb hole'. He was thrown on top of another person on a stretcher. The girl driver of the ambulance together with a rescue squad eventually got it going again.

'I must here mention the absurdity of the arrangements whereby I and many others who were living almost outside Coventry, were conveyed to hospital in the very centre of the city, which was always the main objective of the German attack'.

He always took down the shelter with him a roll of 25 £1 treasury notes and he was still clutching them when he came out of the anaesthetic. He awoke in a bomb-damaged hospital with no lighting and men in tin hats with lamps, carrying out dead bodies. He thought this was about 11a.m. on the Friday morning after the raid. He was wrapped in a travelling rug and lying on the floor in an 'awful state'.

'From then onwards through the day I prayed to be taken away from that house of death, and yet not a soul came near. Nobody came near to clear up the terrible mess I was gradually getting into and which usually happens following an operation'. He lost consciousness and came round thinking that he saw his wife and heard someone say, 'well if that is him, I am afraid you must now go'.

'To this day I have been unable to find out positively what had happened, but I suppose that I had been thought to be dead, or that I was simply a bundle of blankets. However, there I was, lying in all my filth as everything I had to do I did and indeed I was in a really shocking state.

'Eventually I did manage to attract the attention of someone by pure luck, as the whole ward, owing to its precarious state, had been evacuated. If it had not been for this person seeking some of his belongings I would have soon succumbed'.

He was found at about 11 a.m. on the Saturday morning. Between noon and 2 p.m. he was picked up and carried on a stretcher to a converted omnibus, able to carry 24 live or 100 dead bodies. A woman near him died and he lapsed into unconsciousness .... He was moved to Rugby workhouse where he was placed in a ward with the mentally ill.

'There was I, cooped up in a ward with individuals who were either dying or crazy'. It was a frightening experience. One man died while he was trying to talk with him 'and the ward sister laid him out in front of me who was fully conscious but inarticulate and yet unable to close my eyes for some reason I cannot explain.

'Although I am not going to give details of the next few days and nights I must say I do wish to record this state of affairs as it really was, so that those whose duty it was to see that proper preparations were made can realise the mistakes they made by which many people of Coventry, like myself, were forced to suffer, when, with a little foresight, this anguish could, in part, have been avoided. Since I had been taken from home in the car on that Thursday ... I had seen no one I knew'.

Fortunately an old friend of the family, a Rugby councillor, came on a tour of inspection of the ward on the Sunday and recognised Mr. Turner. The following Monday, his wife and daughter came to see him, 'just before the effects of what was now acute gangrene laid claim to me and accompanied by terrific head noises, I faded into a coma in a manner so awful ... it is almost beyond description'.

Notes to Chapter 11

1. According to R.M. Titmuss, *Problems of Social Policy* (1950) 329, the forecasts were not very useful failing to draw attention to the probable extent of house damage and making no reference to the problem of homeless people.
2. One calculation suggests that you stood a sixty per cent greater chance of being killed or injured that night in Coventry than during the whole of the war anywhere else in Britain. According to George Hodgkinson the local committee of the Ministry of Information was about to publish a morale boosting piece on the long odds against getting hit. *Coventry Standard*, 11 November 1955. Norman Longmate, *Air Raid* (1976), 190.
3. Details of this raid have received their most comprehensive treatment in Norman Longmate, *ibid.*
4. Eleven staff and twenty-three patients were killed at the Coventry and Warwickshire hospital as a result of an undetected delayed action bomb which exploded between seven and eight o'clock on the morning of 9 April. For the detailed report of these raids by the Deputy Regional Commissioner see PRO H.O.207/1068. See also the Report of the Coventry Reconstruction and Co-ordination Committee 1 May, 1941, PRO, H.O.186/603.
5. The lesson of Coventry's rapid economic recovery was not the one which Bomber Command drew from the blitz experiences of 1940-41. The German Air Force failed to push home its attacks. More intensive bombing could win the war. To this end 60,000 people were killed in the blitz on Hamburg, for example, in the summer of 1943 and thirty per cent of its houses destroyed, but within five months it had regained eighty per cent of its former productivity. R.M. Titmuss (1950), 305. See also Tom Harrisson, *Living Through the Blitz* (1976 ed.), 300-01. T.H. O'Brien, *Civil Defence* (1955), 407, 639-42, and Sir Charles Webster and Noble Frankland, *The Strategic Air Offensive Against Germany 1939-45*, Vol. I (1961), 181-2 and Vol. II (1961), 237.
6. This account is largely based on F.H. Hinsley, et.al., *British Intelligence in the Second World War*, Vol. I (1979), 316-18, 528-36.
7. Tom Harrisson, *op.cit.*, 325-37. T.H. O'Brien (1955), 630. The Report of the Coventry Reconstruction Co-ordinating Committee is in H.O.186/603.

8 Tom Harrisson felt that the transport which had brought imported labour, police and army personnel into Coventry might have been used to meet some of the problems as it was not in use for most of the time. See also H.O. 186/603, H.O. 207/1068, H.O. 207/1069. George Hodgkinson, *Sent to Coventry* (1970), 156.
9. George Hodgkinson, *ibid.*, 157-58. *Midland Daily Telegraph*, 11 December, 1940. Booklet on Holy Trinity, Coventry (1979 ed.), 15. The National Fire Service took over responsibility for all brigades from August 1941 and the Civil Defence Duties (Compulsory Enrolment) order was eventually applied to Coventry. Minutes Waterworks and Fire Brigade Committee, Coventry City Council, 27 May, 2 September, 1941. On the difficulties of obtaining fire-watchers for the Cathedral see R.T. Howard, *Ruined and Rebuilt. The Story of Coventry Cathedral 1939-1962* (Coventry 1962), 8-13.
10. See the unpublished M.A. dissertation of Amin Hamid Zein el Abdin, 'Administrative Responses to the Blitz on Coventry, 1940-41', University of Warwick, 1976. See Webster and Frankland (1961), Vol. I, 483 and Vol. II, 238-9. The Germans also had more and deeper shelters and up to 1942 their civil defence machinery worked so well in keeping down the number of deaths compared to the British experience that the British authorities were reluctant to accept the official figures. Webster and Frankland, Vol.I, 488.
11. The Civil Defence Regional Commissioner's Office was philsophical. 'It is impossible now (May 1941) to say exactly who was responsible for ordering this piping but I think we all agree that it was ordered in good faith and was a necessary expense'. H.O. 207/1068.
12. On file H.O. 207/1069.
13. The Air-raid assessment report suggested that the population of Coventry was down to 162,000 following evacuations after the November and April raids. H.O. 192/1657.
14. He was trying to persuade the authorities to camouflage the Swanswell pool which, he felt, would boost local morale. H.O. 207/1069.
15. The *Coventry Standard* of 15 November, 1957 claimed that if more people had been at home, the casualties would have been greater. But as we suggested earlier, there might also then have been more fire watchers.
16. Tom Harrisson, *op.cit.*, 136.
17. Watch Committee Minutes, 29 April, 1941, 31 March, 1942. *Coventry Standard*, 30 November, 7, 28 December, 1940, 11

January, 1941. H.O. 207/1068. The national figures were 646 looters found guilty at Magistrates courts in 1940, and 2,508 in 1941. The Assizes figures were respectively 55 and 255. Criminal Statistics England and Wales 1939-45 Cmd.7227 (1947), 22-25.

18. Tom Harrisson, *op.cit.*, 136-37.
19. Churchill actually agreed to release more information on blitzed towns when it became clear that the unauthorised release of news about the November raid in Coventry had given Britain 'a propaganda coup in America and even in Germany itself'. Ian McLaine, *Ministry of Morale* (1979), 219. Though a propaganda film, 'The Story of Coventry', made for the Ministry of Information by British Paramount News at a cost of £700 and designed for overseas distribution only was objected to by the Air Ministry and the censorship and never distributed at all. PRO. Inf. 6/441.
20. *Coventry Standard*, 7 December, 1940, 8 February, 22 March, 1941.
21. *Coventry Evening Telegraph*, 16 November, 1957.
22. He also said he liked the new buildings and found the Hotel Leofric 'remarkable'. *Coventry Evening Telegraph*, 15 November, 1958, 15 November, 1980. On the Coventry Committee for International Understanding see W.E. Rose, *Sent from Coventry* (1980).
23. *Coventry Evening Telegraph*, 14 November, 1945. The War Damage Commission provided the bulk of the money, over £1,000,000.
24. Marian Would and Dennis Starkings were the authors.
25. *Coventry Evening Telegraph*, 24 May, 1972.
26. See for example, *Coventry Evening Telegraph*, 14 November, 1951, 15,16 November, 1953.
27. *Coventry Standard*, 11 November, 1960.
28. *Coventry Evening Telegraph*, 15 November, 1980.
29. *Coventry Evening Telegraph*, 14 November, 1949, 15 November, 1952, 15 November, 1980 and November 14, 1983.

Chapter 12

Society and Politics in 20th Century Coventry

Bill Lancaster and Tony Mason

In a volume of essays dealing with a range of local topics there is a need for a chapter which sketches in the major developments of the locality's history. This chapter is not an attempt to provide a potted history of Coventry since 1900. Rather its aim is to identify and explore what we consider to be the four major themes which have shaped the Coventry we know today. First, the changes in the built environment, in the form and nature of those streets and buildings which are so often taken for granted by the population. Second the focus on the role played by people but particularly the wielders of power, notably politicians and planners in the reshaping of the city. The broader issues of local politics and trade union activities are also discussed in both their local and national contexts. Finally the essay is concluded by an attempt to sketch in the most recent upheavals in the local economy and to assess the wider social ramifications of the recession.

Economic and social developments during the present century have brought both benefits and problems to Coventry. The city in 1900 presented a curious blend of the ancient and modern. Unlike other major midland towns Coventry had not prospered during the second half of the nineteenth century. Thirty years of economic and relative demographic decline had followed the collapse of silk weaving in the 1860s. There were few signs in Coventry of the confident Victorian architecture that so characterised other cities. Even the High Street, which started in old Broadgate, petered out after a mere hundred yards into an area of courtyards and slum dwellings that boasted the second highest density rates in England.[1] Coventry in 1900 still occupied little more than the site of the mediaeval city. The old staple trades of silk and watches could still be found clinging tenaciously to life in workshops and small factories scattered throughout the town, while the central area was still dominated by three mediaeval spires, a labyrinth of narrow streets and timber framed buildings. Coventry could still find a place on Henry James's checklist of quintessential English towns.[2] But large bicycle factories were already established and the motor car industry was putting down roots. Alfred Herbert's recently formed machine tool company was prospering and Coventry at last appeared to be emerging from half a century of economic stagnation. New terraced housing was being hastily erected by the Newcombe Estate Company in Earlsdon and Stoke to accommodate the growing factory workforce and the city's population showed signs of sustained growth.[3]

By the 1930s the city was widely recognised as one of the national centres of production of the motor car. The cycle trade had long given way to the car which in turn had brought in its train a rapidly expanding machine tool and metallurgical industry. Many other towns in the 1930s would have been glad of just one of those new industries. But Coventry's fortune was compounded by the arrival of two other major manufacturing activities: artificial textiles and electrical equipment. Coventry in the 1930s was no longer seen as being peripheral to the national economy: it was now a bustling, rapidly expanding city. Wages were high; the population, thanks to rapid migration, was young and there was none of the depression that still afflicted other areas. Yet while the quickly growing suburbs of mock Tudor housing and art-deco fronted factories gave the visitor an impression of solid prosperity the central area still retained much of its ancient character. This contrast certainly impressed J.B. Priestley when he visited Coventry in the 1930s. The city of the motor car, he said, could have provided an authentic setting for 'The Meistersingers'. However impressed by the buildings, Priestley noted some grumbles about the locals as one young Daimler worker told him:

> You go into one of these pubs. All right. What do you hear? All about gears and magnetos and suchlike. Honest. That's right. They can't talk about anything else here. Got motor-cars on the brain, they have. I hardly ever go into a pub. I go home and have a read.[4]

This comment pinpoints an important element in twentieth century Coventry—indeed it is impossible to understand the city without being aware of it—Coventry was a city of workers with fewer professionals, managers and bureaucrats than other comparable towns, with perhaps the exceptions of Hull, Stoke and Wolverhampton. And that is still true today. Despite its size and prosperity the city has never been renowned for quality shops. There is an abundance of high street multiples which have successfully catered for prosperous workers but Coventry must be the only city of its size that can boast only one major department store. Coventry has been a city in size and status since 1918 when the diocese of

Coventry was created. But in civic character and cultural institutions it long reflected the small Victorian town it had recently been, more designed for the creation rather than the consumption of wealth. Several factors explain why the city had a small number of middle class citizens. Economic stagnation for much of the nineteenth century undoubtedly set the pattern. There were few substantial family firms in nineteenth century Coventry and no new distinctive large middle class suburbs emerged. This situation was compounded by Coventry's proximity to Birmingham which attracted the regional bureaucracies of both banking and insurance. Moreover it was the county town of Warwick which enjoyed the benefits of an expanding county administrative machine. By the time that Coventry began to enjoy prosperity the city had little appeal to the new breed of factory managers and company directors. Ironically the main basis of Coventry's new prosperity, the motor car, allowed this new social strata to seek accommodation in beautiful rural Warwickshire, many of whose villages were within easy motoring distance.

The narrowness of the local middle class was reflected in local politics. The 'shopocracy', an amalgam of small traders and professionals who governed Coventry for much of the nineteenth century received only a minor transfusion from the first waves of migration during the present century. The new units of production quickly became large but the principals of these firms rarely showed an interest in local affairs. Even Sir Alfred Herbert, one of Coventry's few entrepreneurs to bestow munificence upon the city, conducted much of his business affairs from his Hampshire estate and showed little interest in the city council. Few in number and lacking in leadership, the political power of the middle class was vulnerable to the growth of a determined labour politics. Perhaps it is surprising that the 'shopocracy' clung to the reins of local government for so long but when they lost control of the council in 1937 Coventry became the first major midland manufacturing town to fall to Labour.

The social composition of Coventry during the early twentieth century was also reflected in the dearth of cultural amenities. The city possessed poor library facilities and neither art gallery nor museum. Literary and artistic activity was virtually non-existent. The middle classes were rarely visible apart from the Sunday morning motoring excursion from the small ghettoes of detached dwellings, such as Stoke Park and Earlsdon, to attend service at Holy Trinity, their Rover cars choking the narrow lanes to the north of Broadgate.

Life was certainly better in Coventry for many people than in many other urban areas but it was not without its problems. The surge in population, particularly after the late 1920s, placed the existing local facilities under severe strain. Housing in particular was in especially short supply. The city possessed a relatively small stock of nineteenth century housing. The bicycle boom of the 1890s and early 1900s stimulated new housing development, but even those new streets of red brick and slate failed to meet the demand. The power of building interests in local politics made matters worse when in the post first world war years the local council refused to implement fully the new public housing legislation.[5] The slump in the engineering industry in the early 1920s was accompanied by a decline in housebuilding. By the early 1930s when the local economy was expanding rapidly again, Coventry was faced with a housing crisis.

The problem was not just one of too few homes. Inter-war Coventry was short of space. The series of boundary extensions that had taken place after 1890 had eased some of the strain but even in the 1920s the council was forced to erect one of its few public housing projects in Radford, which was then outside the borough. Negotiations with the Stoneleigh estate eventually secured a large tract of land on the city's southern edge. Rather than see this new resource come under public control with housing apportioned on grounds of need, the land was handed over by the council to the speculative building industry. Of the 23,130 houses erected between 1930 and 1938 only 711 were rented to tenants. Working class home ownership was realised by many in these years and in terms of quality those handsome 1930s dwellings with their double bays and stained glass represent perhaps the highest standard ever in the history of working class housing. Yet it must be remembered that they were usually bought at a high price in terms of the workers' family budget and many other Coventry workers could not afford them. The builders themselves were greatly surprised by the willingness of Coventry workers to buy the new properties. The foreman of the Quinton Road estate in 1935, for example, told a newspaper reporter that he had expected the new estate, as was the pattern elsewhere, to be purchased by small landlords for subsequent letting. To his astonishment not one house on this development was let for rent.[6] We must, however, be careful not to assume that this trend towards working class owner occupation represents the unchanging desire of the British to occupy their own freehold. For most of the new householders in the 1930s it was simply a case of Hobson's choice, though perhaps not a bad one. Home ownership did not apparently affect political allegiance. Coventry, with the highest rates of working class owner occupation for a town of its size, increasingly voted Labour in the 1930s. Furthermore the first point in the Labour Party's 1937 local election manifesto promised an acceleration of council housebuilding. Indeed housing was a key local political issue in the inter-war period. The speculative building boom on the Stoneleigh estate gave the south of the city a face of prosperity, but two miles north families were to be found living in squalor in the Whitmore Park hutments, wooden shacks hastily erected to house migrant munition workers during the first world war.[7]

There were other dimensions to Coventry's unordered prosperity in the inter-war period. The motor, aircraft, electrical and high quality engineering trades paid high wages to nearly 70,000 citizens in 1938. Yet the city's central area had hardly changed since the 1870s when it had to service the needs of a population a sixth of the size. The population of Coventry was now rapidly catching up its old rivals, Nottingham and Leicester but in terms of civic amenities and shopping facilities was way behind both. Some development did take place before the war. Part of the Burges was rebuilt in 1930, and Fleet Street in 1931. The new Cooperative store was erected in West Orchard in the same year. 1934 saw the beginning of the Trinity Street scheme and the building of the new Market Hall. In 1936 Butcher Row and Little Butcher Row, Coventry's oldest streets, were demolished to make way for Trinity Street, while Broadgate was partly reshaped to accommodate Owen Owen's new department store. Finally in March 1939 an area adjacent to the Council House was cleared for the building of a new civic art gallery. Apart from these activities little fundamental change was made in the central area and no expansion was made of its area. Many Coventrians were undoubtedly attached to the old city and were apprehensive about changes. The Trinity Street scheme, for example, was first drawn up in 1904. The original plan envisaged the new shopping mall stretching as far as Primrose Hill Street on the edge of Hillfields. The opposition of shopkeepers and trades people and a public petition against the plan delayed both the implementation and scope of this development.[8] When Butcher Row and Little Butcher Row were finally demolished in 1936 hundreds of citizens crowded the narrow lanes to attend the Mayor's official closing ceremony. On the other hand the forces of change could match those of tradition. A huge crowd attended the official opening of Trinity Street and the construction of Owen Owen's was keenly followed by the local press.

The root of such ambivalence of course lay in the composition of the inhabitants. Between 1901 and 1939 the population of the city had risen by over 160,000 and nearly 47 per cent of this growth was the product of migration. Moreover this demographic process was accelerating during the 1930s. In the eight year period 1931-39 over 42,000 migrants settled in Coventry.[9] Old Coventry may have still presented a quaint, antique prospect to the sensitive visitor, such as J.B. Priestley, but to the majority of those who came to stay, the old buildings were equated with the slums of the depressed areas that they had recently left.

In many ways the local Labour Party during the 1930s articulated the misgivings and aspirations of Coventry's growing army of factory workers and their families. It was not only a matter of housing and shopping facilities. Education and health also presented enormous challenges. Upwards of a thousand children per year were entering the city in the period of most rapid migration. Schools were notoriously overcrowded. The ruling coalition of Conservative and Liberal councillors' were obsessed with 'economism'. In order to control the rates in the mid 1930s the council cut back on education services; new school building was delayed and existing buildings were not maintained; some schools even lacked heating systems and at Red Lane, it was claimed, children were taught while they shuffled in turn in front of an open fire. Such civic parsimony was singularly out of place in booming Coventry.[10] Similarly the local Medical Officer of Health regularly expressed concern during the 1930s over the shortage of hospitals and the city was also bedevilled by transport problems.

What was needed to ensure the smooth functioning of a modern city? The Labour Party said municipal planning, a task for which the fag end of 'shopocracy' rule was particularly ill fitted. Holding back the rates and protecting deeply entrenched interests had always been their prime political concern. It was the Labour Party who had forward looking ideas. It had sprung from the old Independent Labour Party branch, the centrepiece of whose politics had been municipal reform. Under the leadership of George Hodgkinson and Sidney Stringer the Coventry Labour Party in the 1930s welded the old ideas of William Morris and John Ruskin onto the theories of town planning which had recently come to prominence under the influence of Le Corbusier and the garden city movement. This civic idealism was supplemented by a contemporary political mechanism: the Russian notion of the 'Five year plan'. The new administration quickly set about implementing their civic philosophy. A town architect, Donald Gibson was appointed in 1937— one of the first such posts in the country. A five year policy document was issued. The Capital Works Programme envisaged the expenditure of £1,570,000 over the five years. Education was to receive the largest slice of this particular cake and parcels of land were earmarked in various parts of the city for new school building. Sewers were to be rebuilt, a civic airport laid out, parks extended and new streets were to replace the narrow mediaeval lanes. The most innovatory item in the programme, however, was the 'land sterilisation' scheme. This involved spending £300,000, the second largest amount in the plan, on protecting public spaces and tightly controlling development.[11]

The five year plans necessitated the expansion of local government. Funds were allocated to extend the Council House in order to provide room for the force of planners and officials that was needed to implement the scheme. The organisation of activity inside the Council Chamber also underwent fundamental reform. The Policy Advisory Committee, set up in 1937 by the new administration, was a landmark in British local government. Its function was to impose cohesiveness on development policy, including providing guidance for individual council committees. One of the committee's initiators, George Hodgkinson, has stressed the 'advisory' nature of the new committee. But in the world of politics there is 'advice' and 'advice' and Hodgkinson has noted with candour that 'in the light of study and experience the Capital Works Programme and the tempo of capital development came under its [the P.A.C.] supervision'.[12]

Coventry's role as one of the country's most important centres of arms production had been growing since 1935. Indeed most of the expansion which took place in the local economy during the 1930s was dictated by the needs of the national arsenal. Local firms expanded their workforce when the city became the major manufacturer of aircraft engines. Existing capacity could not cope with the multiplying demands of the R.A.F. and new shadow factories had to be built by the government around the edges of the city. These new works were managed by local firms and added greatly to the size of the local workforce.[13] The evacuation of mothers and children was as much a part of early wartime Coventry as elsewhere but the exit of evacuees did not ease the city's housing problem. The continuous influx of workers into the city's factories produced a housing crisis that soon became a Government priority. The National Service Hostel Association, a government agency formed in May 1941, took over the land allotted for school building together with various sites on the adjacent 'green belt' and erected sixteen hostels for the accommodation of over 12,000 factory workers.[14] Yet even the rapid building of these barrack like dwellings was not enough. The bombing of the city in November 1940 and April 1941 also destroyed over 4,300 houses and 600 shops, damaged over 50,000 other houses and destroyed 4,000 school places.

The main impact of these raids was to inflate Coventry's structural problems. The old Capital Works Programme was dwarfed by the enormity of the task of rebuilding the semi-devastated city. On the other hand the events of November and April provided an unexpected opportunity for the realisation of the plan for Coventry so recently shelved by the coming of war. Now a strong case could indeed be made for the wholesale clearance of large tracts of land and the rebuilding of the city along new lines. We have already noted that local labour politicians largely shared the planning ideas of the architect and soon after the November raid the weight of central government was placed behind the movement for large scale redevelopment. Sir John Reith, the Minister of Works, encouraged local politicians to redesign the central area on radical lines. The minister obviously saw the benefit to propaganda and morale of such a scheme and he went so far as to warn the Corporation against piecemeal redevelopment promising in return that sweeping new legislation would provide the legal framework necessary for the plan's implementation.[15]

The first part of the Gibson scheme, Broadgate House, was completed in 1948 but the city plan was not published until 1951. Nevertheless the broad outlines of the new city were presented in model form during the war for citizens to inspect. Indeed Coventrians had been given a preview of Gibson's ideas at an exhibition held in St. Mary's Hall in 1938. The central feature of the design was the traffic free shopping area. Many retailers were extremely apprehensive of such a revolutionary change. The Chamber of Commerce opposed the scheme. They doubted whether the public would take to the precinct concept and they did not like the loss of freehold that was to accompany it. The local 'establishment' were not however united in their opposition. The *Coventry Evening Telegraph* in particular became a keen advocate of the Gibson scheme and the proprietor, Lord Iliffe, financed the building of a large model for a touring exhibition. Thus brave new Coventry with its precinct, ring road and new Cathedral became an early symbol of Britain's post-war rejuvenation. From the Festival of Britain showground to the Pathe newsreel Coventry was presented as a snapshot of life in post-austerity Britain.

Yet modern cities are a complex of social processes as well as streets and buildings. Planning has to be sympathetic to the existing social structure while fulfilling its duty to provide an environment of some style. The planning officer for Exeter, a city which received proportionally equal devastation from enemy bombs during the last war, gave priority to this point in his post-war development scheme. He noted in the preface to the Exeter redevelopment document that 'Cities have personalities and characters as men have: and the planner must try to catch the personality and character of the place before he can plan'.[16] Ancient Exeter with its Georgian and Victorian county town buildings and market town economy presented few problems in terms of discerning its civic character. The end result was an imaginative scheme of infilling between what remained of ancient civic gems and respecting as much as possible the existing street pattern. Coventry presented a different and far more difficult problem. First there were few substantial buildings of character for the architect to respect. Coventry's relative economic stagnation over the two previous centuries had bequeathed little of architectural merit. What remained after the bombs was a hotchpotch of mediaeval wood frame edifices and tatty Victorian infilling. There were no graceful corner structures to build around nor were there many major buildings in the central area, such as Exeter's magnificent market hall, which warranted preservation. If two centuries of economic decline had left little in the way of architectural character what aspects of the citizens' personality warranted the attention of the planner?

From the beginning the reforming local politicians and the new planning department realised the social ramifications of the task which they had set themselves. The problem was that Coventry, in terms of its population, was probably like nowhere else in mid-twentieth century Britain. Nearly half of the local citizens came from elsewhere and a high proportion of the remainder were the children of migrants. In short, the sense of local identity and character among the population was weaker than in other places. How strong their attachment was to what remained of the city and what their feelings were about the redevelopment scheme were points which the planning authorities did not neglect. The plan for wholesale redevelopment of the central area met with considerable local enthusiasm. Droves of Coventrians visited the model exhibition. The transport department ran a special bus tour of the city centre with a planning official on board pointing out the main areas of redevelopment to the passengers. During the dark days of immediate post-war austerity enthusiasm for a new centre of bountiful retail outlets was to be expected in a large predominantly working class city that had recently suffered so much.

But what about the wider aspects of civic development, particularly those major sections of the city which lay beyond the planned ringroad? In broad terms the remainder of the city had two functions: work and housing. Twentieth century economic development has not,in the main, been tightly controlled by the planning authorities. The green belt had been saved by Abercrombie's 1938 Act but industrial development within cities had been allowed without restriction. Coventry was no exception. Large factories could be found in all areas of the city. The shadow factory scheme followed this pattern and new large units were built at Banner Lane, Browns Lane and just outside the city boundary at Ryton. Existing plant at Radford, Canley and Stoke was enlarged. Added to this uncoordinated pattern were the multitude of small firms that had emerged organically along classic nineteenth century lines. Thus even the middle class suburb of Earlsdon was also the home of many minor engineering establishments and small units are still to be found in the back gardens of residential areas. Attempts at zoning have been tried since the 1930s but the persistance of small firms has meant that it has had little impact.

Housing after 1945 presented an even greater challenge. The housing crisis was a national problem in the decade and a half after the war but in Coventry for obvious reasons it was particularly severe. With at times 15,000 families on the waiting list, widespread squatting in old military buildings and an illegal camp site facing the council house in Little Park Street, politicians and planners had to act swiftly.[17] Yet housing never received the same attention as the central area. By the late 1940s central redevelopment had become an *idee fixe* of both politicians and architects. The planning and redevelopment committee thought long and hard over the suitability of shop edifices yet rarely gave their attention to similar questions posed by housing development. The cynic could argue that this inattention seemed to have little effect. The city centre, with the possible exception of the new Cathedral, has no building worthy of note yet Coventry's post-war housing estates are no worse, and no better than elsewhere. By the late 1950s with the worst of the housing crisis over, new developments in public housing took a more imaginative turn. Large estates gave way to smaller units which could be knitted into existing residential areas. The Spon Gate Comprehensive Development Area Scheme, begun in 1961, is the most impressive realisation of this new approach. This small development, a mixture of tower blocks, maisonettes arranged around squares and several rows of low rise flats run by a housing association, was imaginatively landscaped around the River Sherbourne blends easily with older housing stock. This style is now being adopted in the Hillfields area and the result is far superior to the characterless blocks of 'no fines' concrete that disfigure so much of the city's earlier public housing.[18]

What the Spon Gate scheme highlights is that sympathetic design and planning could take many of the rough edges off post war housing. But there have been few Spon Gates. The architects and planners could barely cope with the work of rebuilding the centre let alone give much attention to the rest. Convenience dictated that the housing crisis could be best solved by designing large estates each of which contained between 15 and 20,000 people. Moreover off the shelf designs could be utilised and new building methods employed. Further actual construction could be left in the capable hands of firms such as Messrs. George Wimpey and their pacesetting foremen like Ben Jardine.

We have to register a number of points for and against the steel frame, 'no fines', concrete structures that now grace vast tracts of modern Coventry.[19] On the positive side such housing did provide desperately needed accommodation. These new homes were well equipped with sanitary facilities and the size of the dwellings was adequate, if not generous. On the negative side, however, especially in the 'no fines' concrete dwellings has been the difficulty in heating and the attendant factor of damp. The estates themselves have not had a happy history. In general council estates nationally have been unable to cope with changing working class life styles and continuing social differentiation. The more prosperous sections of the working class have abandoned the estates in pursuit of affluent individuality as owner occupiers, a tradition already established in Coventry. Those who have remained have had to cope with worsening structural problems and an increasing sense of inferiority.

The local planning department must bear its share of the blame. Central government was responsible for the deterioration in building standards especially during the 1950s. But local decision makers designed the overall layout and scale of the developments. The large, so-called 'neighbourhood units' of Canley, Tile Hill, Bell Green and Willenhall were designed to accommodate 15-20,000 residents in decent dwellings and with a 'planned' environment. Several social surveys were conducted by the planners and the University of Birmingham in the late 1940s on behalf of the council. What the authorities wanted to know was the attitude of citizens to this type of estate and the services which the potential tenants required.[20] The planning department survey concluded that the majority of residents had only a thin attachment to their particular community or neighbourhood. The survey revealed that neighbourhood friendship networks were generally narrow, usually confined to immediate and very near neighbours. In terms of facilities, especially shopping, the Coventrians of the late 1940s were unanimous in their desire for a large well equipped central retail area with suburban outlets confined to the provision of everyday essentials. The findings of these surveys tended to reinforce the major thrust of the reconstruction plan and convinced the decision makers that they were providing the people with what they wanted.

Despite widespread approval for the 'Gibson Plan' there remained a few who were not so enthusiastic. Apart from shopkeepers who were apprehensive over changes in property tenure there were also those who were concerned over the quality of post-war housing. As early as December 1940 the local correspondent of the *Daily Worker* noted that 'This talk of rebuilding our cities ... gives me grim memories of what they said in the last war'. This writer went on to point out that during the inter-war period 'hideous estates sprawled themselves over the fields; jerry building reached new heights of technique; new slums replaced old'.[21] Similar fears were presented in a more constructive manner during the immediate post-war period when a group of local people initiated a scheme for a model estate to be built at Binley Woods. This plan was based upon the Peckham community health experiment of the 1930s which combined local health services with sporting and recreational facilities. The Binley Wood scheme was designed to overcome the problems associated with large housing estates.

The plan demanded a considerable commitment from residents as its wide range of services, which included a farm, was to be self-financing. 'Binley Woods' bore many striking resemblances to earlier 'Garden City' schemes and Donald Gibson, George Hodgkinson and K.E. Barlow, a local doctor, were prominent supporters. But the scheme failed to negotiate a series of crucial obstacles. Building material was strictly rationed and difficult to obtain for non-public sector developments. The plan was also hampered by virtue of its site being located just outside the city boundary, which meant that the organisers had to deal with two separate local authorities. The designers of the estate wanted to build nine storey blocks of flats instead of some of the houses, in order to increase the population of the community while conserving land for the community farm. High rise development had many opponents in the late 1940s, including several Labour councillors who had previously given their support to the scheme. They joined forces with opponents from the adjacent authority and the result was a refusal of planning permission, rather ironic in view of subsequent events.[22]

The majority of Coventrians were perfectly willing to accept what the new council planning machine suggested. There were few 'communities' to disrupt and the residents on the new estates could look forward to the provision of new facilities such as ten form entry comprehensive schools, the large health centres and new parades of small shops. Their more important, and regular visits to the new shopping centre, within the ringroad, could be speedily executed thanks to unprecedentedly large car parking facilities. Those who had to rely on the corporation bus service would, it was hoped, soon be spared from this irritant with the provision of a municipal helicopter service from the suburbs on to the proposed heliport roof over Pool Meadow!

The helicopters never came but increased prosperity, on a scale unimaginable in the late 1940s, with its attendant shifts in consumer preference, soon made the new shopping precinct inadequate. Prosperity and a stabilisation of the population during the 1960s also fuelled a reaction against the large neighbourhood system. Life within four 'no fines' concrete walls became somewhat incongruous with the affluent car workers new life style of car ownership and foreign holidays. Similarly the vast monotony and sterility of estate architecture checked the affluent workers' desire for individuality and at the same time worked against the formation of small communities. The corner shop was missing. Although you might get to know your immediate neighbours it was not easy to meet many others. The neighbourhood unit system, did not work because planners in the 1940s made the mistake of assuming that the needs of a housing hungry, unstable population would not change. Indeed, the sociological survey of the 1940s drew attention to problems that were present in the estates from the beginning. Certain new neighbourhoods, for example, were experiencing alarmingly high turnover rates as tenants exchanged dwellings in order to move to a more 'respectable' street. The sociologists also pointed out that neighbourliness was difficult to achieve on the new estates. The main problem here was that people tended to cling closely to friendship networks that were based on regional origin. This was especially the case with migrants from the north, Scotland and Ireland, who it was reported, often found Coventry and Coventrians cold and unfriendly.

The carrying out of the 1951 development plan has to be seen as the realisation of a scheme designed by a new class of professionals, implemented by newcomers for the benefit of a population with shallow roots in the city. The 'shopocracy' had been routed in 1937 and the voice of 'old Coventry' continued to be associated with narrow minded backwardness. The defeat of the old elite was compounded by the support of the *Evening Telegraph* for the reconstruction plan. The isolation of the Chamber of Commerce, the main opponents of the plan, was increased by the tendency of many of Coventry's firms, both retail and manufacturing, to come under the control of outside owners. There was almost an element of irrelevant antiquarian charm in the announcement in 1951 that the new Lord Mayor, Harry Weston, was the first Coventrian to hold this office for eight years. More significantly, 84 per cent of the ruling Labour group of councillors elected between 1945 and 1955, were born outside Coventry.[23]

It is often claimed that the current problems of Coventry, social and economic, stem from the fact that the city has been ruled for three decades by a 'slate of shop stewards'. Engineering workers, particularly trade union activists, have undoubtedly played a prominent role in local Labour politics since 1937. Such a claim implies that it is cultural barbarians who are in charge. It was also often claimed that the Labour Council spent lavishly. Such an analysis seems to be based very largely on myth. Labour were never profligate with ratepayers' cash. The old penny pinching attitude of the 'shopocracy' continued to be applied to many areas of civic expenditure. Libraries and education have taken a smaller share of the civic budget than in other large urban areas. On the other hand the Labour Council has been widely acknowledged for many innovations, such as the reform of the structure of local government and the city's early commitment to comprehensive education. Indeed for decades Coventry's Labour Council considered itself in the van of municipal development—even the fire engines were painted yellow prior to the emergence of the West Midland County Council.

The voters of Coventry continued to support the Labour inspired reconstruction of the city. Local election results between 1945 and 1955 gave Labour an apparently unbreachable majority. In November 1945 thirty Labour councillors were returned to face an opposition of eighteen Progressives—an amalgam of Conservatives and Liberals. Interest in local elections as indicated by turnout, was often not great. In 1945 only 44 per cent of the electorate bothered to vote but discontent over austerity in 1947 pushed the turnout up to 54.5 per cent. The increased vote in 1947, however, had little impact upon the composition of the council with Labour retaining its 2-1 majority. This situation continued in 1949 when the vote dropped again to 44 per cent. The *Evening Telegraph*, in an editorial on the 1949 poll, concluded, perhaps with a note of despair that 'newcomers to Coventry were strengthening the Left'.[24]

The opposition, which was now dominated by Conservatives, found local politics a hard struggle. They criticised some fringe aspects of Labour's municipal policy such as public catering in the local British Restaurants and pressed the need to ease the motorists' lot by speeding up construction of the Ring Road but the Conservatives presented no major policy initiative. In many ways little had changed in the nature of the local opposition to Labour since the 1930s. The Conservative candidates who stood for election in 1951 were an assortment of small businessmen, managers, and retired publicans. They were the champions of small shopkeepers threatened by the planning machine, municipal enterprise and municipal trading.

Ironically the most cogent criticism of Labour's reconstruction policy came from within the party's own ranks. Moreover dissent was expressed not by idealist new recruits but by one of the Party's most senior members. Bill Haliwell came from a background of industrial militancy. In the 1920s he had been a leading activist in the Communist-inspired Minority Movement of left wing trades unionists. By the 1930s he was a leading Labour councillor in Coventry, his seniority being confirmed by his chairmanship of the Policy Advisory Committee and promotion to the Aldermanic bench. His opposition in the 1940s to local Labour policy expressed a fundamental socialist view of the role of Labour in a mixed economy. In particular he protested strongly against his party's near obsession with rebuilding the central area. Haliwell along with Ald. Alice Arnold, another trades union activist of the 1920s, resigned from the party in 1945. He continued to draw attention to the drain on local resources caused by central redevelopment, a policy he claimed that could only result in Labour presenting capitalism with a better environment in which to operate. What he wanted was a basic redirection of council resources away from the precinct and into schools, housing and hospitals. Haliwell's disapproval gave rise to a steady stream of criticism against his former colleagues. His attack on the visit of Labour councillors to Graz in 1948, for example, was enthusiastically recorded in the local press which has since made the adverse reporting of civic junkets a speciality.[25] But Haliwell's critique of Labour had no electoral effect. Apart from the loss of Lower Stoke to the Conservatives in 1953 Labour enjoyed nearly a decade of unopposed rule. Their policies may not have been acceptable to Haliwell but the consistency of the Labour vote tends to confirm the popularity of the socialist programme they put forward. Yet something happened to local Labour politics in post-war Coventry; something which in broad terms can be described as a shift away from the idealism of the 1937 victory and the 1951 structural plan and a turning towards the more mundane practicalities of managing the system. Without more detailed research on such matters as the changing composition of Labour Party members and the structure of ward committees it is difficult to account precisely for this process. There are many scholarly versions of the post-war decline of Labour but none fit the experience of Coventry. Moreover, the key moment in Coventry appears to have been April 1955 rather than in the 1960s.

The local elections of May 1955 were preceded by a month of high controversy. Objections had long been raised in the press and amongst Conservatives against Labour's opposition to the Civil Defence plans of the Government. Hodgkinson in particular had consistently argued the futility of implementing precautionary measures against a nuclear attack. Moreover, his experience of wartime Coventry had convinced him that international fraternity was of more value than defence expenditure. Labour's attitude on Civil Defence had been often criticised but prior to 1955 the issue had been somewhat marginal. This situation changed dramatically in April 1955 when a party of delegates from Stalingrad were invited to Coventry by the council to repay a visit of the previous year. The lavish entertainment of the Russian guests by the councillors was widely reported. An article in the *Coventry Standard* noted that 'mellowed by an eight course dinner at which vodka and five different kinds of wine were served, the 200 people who attended the banquet in St. Mary's Hall ... to mark the end of the Stalingrad delegation spoke affectionately of each other's countries'.[26] This visit, at the height of the cold war, and rising Conservative fortunes nationally proved to be the moment for which local Conservatives had been waiting. The *Standard* informed its readers that the issue at the forthcoming poll was simple, 'It's the Kremlin versus Coventry. It's Conservatism versus Communism'.[27]

The Conservatives entered the local election with the slogan 'Clear out the Reds'. It was pointed out that Coventry Labour Party's view of Civil Defence and the H-bomb was the opposite of national Labour Party policy. For the first time since 1945 the Conservatives entered the local election campaigning on an issue that had both national and local relevance. The *Standard* reported that its own survey of the population revealed that Coventrians were equally divided on the Stalingrad issue. The Conservatives were able to claim that the local Labour Party was dominated by a few extremists who did not represent the views of ordinary Labour voters.

Labour had certainly misjudged the mood of the local population. The city was highly prosperous and was enjoying the fruits of the mixed economy. Moreover many local workers were dependent on the defence industry for their livelihood. The results in May confirmed the Conservatives' optimism. Five seats, Bablake, Godiva, Lower Stoke, Walsgrave and Whoberley were lost by Labour. Most of these wards were relatively affluent and dominated by skilled workers. The local Labour Party was deeply shocked by this setback. Leading Labour councillor Sidney Stringer claimed that the campaign had been 'the most vile in all my years in politics' and blamed the result on the local press.[28]

The Coventry Labour Party appear to have quickly interpreted the electoral message of 1955. Civic adventurism in bricks and mortar was acceptable but taking a firm stance in national and foreign affairs was not. The message from Labour supporters was underlined in the Parliamentary elections that took place in the following month. Not only were Labour majorities reduced in Coventry but the eve of poll ritual march from the major factories to hear the addresses of Labour candidates at Pool Meadow drew scant support.[29]

There is a cruel irony for Labour in the events of 1955. The main energy of the local Party since 1945 had been directed into the rebuilding of the central area. By 1955 the precinct was beginning to take shape and Coventry's affluent workers at last had a shopping centre commensurate with their spending power. Yet the connections between the availability of consumer goods in bright new shops and the ideals of municipal socialism were difficult to make, even amongst the more informed members of the population. When Coventrians did their Saturday shopping few were bothered by whether or not the Corporation held the freehold of the buildings that housed the new emporiums. What mattered more was the availability of money to spend and Coventry's capitalist owned industry was proving an ever bountiful provider. Perhaps Haliwell was right. More attention to housing, health, education and public transport would in the long term have provided a more solid political allegiance for Labour.

The ups and downs of local elections after 1955 closely followed the national trends. The next major threat to Labour's rule was produced by the austerity measures of the Labour Government in 1966. Car production slumped and some local firms declared redundancies. Coventry's long boom appeared to be faltering. Worse was to follow. The incomes policy declared by the government was particularly hard for local workers who had long enjoyed the benefits of free collective bargaining and wage differential leap-frogging. Thus Coventry began to suffer for the first time in many years the twin problems of rising unemployment and stagnant wages. The Conservatives, ably led by Gilbert Richards, seized the opportunity and mounted a vigorous electoral campaign. Apart from criticising the policy of central government the Conservatives fought the 1967 election on four key local issues. The first two, protect the grammar schools and prune the rates were predictable. The third attacked Labour's housing policy and promised council tenants the right to buy their homes. Finally the Conservatives put forward an attractive policy on public transport. They attacked the trend towards higher bus fares and the resulting decline in passenger numbers. Instead they proposed a major reduction in fares which they claimed would produce a greater utilisation of facilities and an improved service, a policy strikingly similar to that currently operated by the Labour councils in South Yorkshire.[30]

This blend of national issues and local Tory populism proved to be decisive. Labour lost control of the council after thirty years continuous rule. Even the defiant singing of the 'Red Flag' by Labour councillors in the mayor's chamber could not disguise the scale of the setback. The overall turnout in 1967 was 48.7 per cent but in some key marginal wards such as Woodlands and Wyken over 60 per cent of the electorate voted.[31] The more thoughtful party members knew all too well that Labour's problems ran deeper than poor electoral performance. Local idealism had been toned down since 1955 and George Hodgkinson had long since ceased to play his inspirational role. Labour by the mid 1960s had become a party of civic administration. Few new ideas were being generated and more worrying the party held little attraction for the young. Richard Crossman confided in his diary in December 1965 after a presentation to mark his twentieth year as M.P.:

> I have tended to get depressed about Coventry. ... I am ... aware of a decline in the Party and a decline in its quality on the council. Mostly it was old people who were there for the presentation; only a handful were young.[32]

This generation gap was to present long term problems for the local party. The lack of new blood in the 1960s and 1970s made the party staid and unadventurous. But more importantly, it rendered the party hierarchy unwilling to adapt and resistant to the ideas of the new, young left politicians who rose to local prominence in the late 1970s. These problems were made worse by the different social background of the factions. The old party establishment had been dominated by engineering workers: the new young activists were white collar workers from the public sector.

The Tories stayed in power for another three years. Apart from a small degree of financial retrenchment, however, there were few new policy initiatives. The man in the street could have been forgiven if he had failed to notice the change in political control. Since 1967 local elections have been broadly in line with national and regional trends and Labour has never been able to recapture the commanding majority it enjoyed in the immediate post-war years. Yet Coventry still remains a distinctly Labour city. The Liberal party, for example, has made little progress.

Similarly Labour holds three of the four local Parliamentary seats. Coventry South West, which contains the city's more affluent suburbs, remained in the early 1980s a key West Midland marginal.

The emergence of Labour as the dominant local party broadly coincided with the establishment of large scale trade unionism in the city's major industries. The workers combinations in the Victorian staples of silk and watches collapsed during the post-1860 period of economic decline. Trade union activity in the new metal industries was, spasmodic prior to 1914. Although the Workers Union, founded by Tom Mann at Foleshill in 1898, had some success in the bicycle factories in the years before the Great War, in general local trade unionism was confined to the more skilled workers.[33] The war radically altered the climate of industrial relations in Coventry. Armaments production was introduced into most of the major local factories and the size of the working population rapidly increased. The Amalgamated Society of Engineers enlarged its membership but the most important development was the growth of organisation amongst semi- and unskilled workers. The Workers Union was the chief beneficiary and soon became the largest trade union in Coventry.[34] High wages and union recognition, particularly of the new shop stewards system were the hallmarks of industrial relations in wartime Coventry.

These gains, however, did not survive the economic recession of the early 1920s. The engineering lockout of 1922 virtually destroyed the Workers Union and reduced the engineers to a rump of its wartime strength. Some former shop stewards abandoned industrial activities choosing instead to concentrate their energies on building up the local Labour Party. Organisation amongst the less skilled workers in the subsequent years of prosperity was virtually non-existent. During most of the inter-war period trade unionism in Coventry factories was restricted to toolroom and similar craft areas.[35]

The return of war in 1939 brought another upsurge in union membership. The A.E.U. saw its fortunes restored to those of pre-lockout days. Again the less skilled workers were able to establish a union branch in most factories. This development was to prove more enduring than the ephemeral presence of the Workers Union two decades earlier. Semi- and unskilled workers were now being organised by the Transport and General Workers Union. This union was far more solidly based nationally than the old Workers Union had been and in Coventry the T.&G.W.U. was controlled by the tough and able Jack Jones. The A.E.U. was also beginning to recruit less skilled operatives, a development which augered well for the prospects of widescale trade union organisation when hostilities ceased.

Despite austerity and material shortages the Coventry economy, as we have seen, continued to grow in the immediate post-war period. Employers did not face the same pressures that were present in the early 1920s. Rather the opposite was the case. Many firms were desperately trying to increase production, particularly of motor cars, for export. Unions which had been perceived by employers as an obstacle to post-war readjustment in 1918 were now seen as essential allies in Coventry's industrial progress. Employers employed and unions recruited workers who were organised on the 'gang system'. This method of workshop control, based on piecework payment, can be traced back to Starley's first bicycle factory and was the standard form of labour organisation in Coventry factories. During the war trade union organisation tended to follow this traditional structure with each gang appointing a shop steward. The stewards had also gradually assumed many of the production functions of the gang leader. Thus as local factories struggled to switch from arms to motor production it became essential to involve the unions in workshop management. Unions were granted recognition, high wage settlements and an element of control over recruitment. Employers on the other hand were assured of a smooth transition to peacetime production with the added bonus of low management overheads. The short term benefits of this labour-management bargain are demonstrated by Coventry's increasing share of the U.K. motor market in the years just after the war. Standard in particular saw its market share rise by 40 per cent.[36] This system of industrial relations remained intact for over two decades but by the mid 1960s, as Coventry manufacturers were being increasingly outpaced by car makers elsewhere, the piecework system and all that it underpinned began to be criticised. Gradually all the major local employers recognised that payment by the day, usually called measured day work, as practised by Ford and General Motors, offered greater control over the labour force. It was increasingly being felt by many Coventry employers that the unions had become the dominant partner in the post-war bargain. Stewards, it was alleged, had become skillful manipulators of piece rate negotiations and were all too willing to turn to strike action to achieve their demands. The system which had helped Coventry to prosper in the 1940s and early 1950s was now seen as the main cause of relatively low productivity and high labour costs.

Wages in Coventry motor firms were undoubtedly higher than elsewhere during the 1950s and 60s. Yet the caricature of the greedy Coventry car worker who worked half as hard as his Dagenham counterpart and was more prone to go on strike is somewhat misleading. As Stephen Tolliday shows in this volume, cooperation with management was the norm. The underlying cause of the demise of piecework was the naive assumptions of management in the years after the war that unions could both serve their members' interests and undertake important responsibilities for production. In short, many local firms prospered in the post-war decades with virtually no structure of junior management.

The recession of the late 1970s and 1980s has brought Coventry full circle. Local staples, especially motor cars, have been routed by foreign competition. The plight of the contemporary Coventry car worker appears very similar to the experience of silk workers in the 1860s. What economic growth is taking place in present day Britain is having little beneficial impact upon Coventry. The city again seems set to become an economic backwater with few signs of growth and an exodus of labour. A range of explanations have been put forward to account for Coventry's remarkably rapid decline. Poor industrial relations, government interference—especially the campaign in the 1950s and 1960s to encourage local firms to expand in depressed areas, and weak investment by local companies have all been cited by a wide range of commentators. Yet other car towns, notably Birmingham, Cowley, Dagenham and Luton have been subjected to similar pressures but have retained the bulk of their manufacturing capacity. The problem peculiar to Coventry is that the local economy was not only overdependent on the motor industry but that virtually all the local automotive firms were, by the 1960s, ill suited because of their size to survive the increasing competitiveness of the international market. It is no accident that what remains of the British motor industry is centred in towns which are dominated by a single large manufacturing plant. The paradox of the last eighty years is that a major reason for Coventry's long boom, the multiplicity of firms in the motor industry, has become the major cause of decline. The only viable motor car establishment to survive the recent recession is Jaguar. Rootes has become a mere assembler of French components, while the once proud Triumph marque continued for a few years in the form of a few badges attached to a Japanese car which was assembled at Cowley.

A qualification however, needs to be made to this depressing tale. The British motor industry, by the late 1970s, had reached an historic crossroads. Entry to the E.E.C. coincided with an unusually weak range of British products. Models were either outdated or bedevilled by quality and reliability problems. European manufacturers soon captured nearly 40 per cent of the home market. The choice facing British manufacturers was varied. Those companies owned by American parents integrated their U.K. operations with their European counterparts. Ford and General Motors are two successful examples of this strategy. Unfortunately for Coventry the Chrysler Corporation were experiencing problems in many parts of their empire and did not possess the resources necessary for the establishment of a high volume European operation. The British-owned Leyland faced a more complex situation. The company produced both high volume and specialist products. The Cowley and Longbridge plants which produced high volume products badly needed investment to keep up with the European companies and the American subsidiaries. The specialist producers, Jaguar, Rover and Triumph, also required a large injection of capital in order to meet the growing competition from such companies as Audi, B.M.W., Alfa Romeo and the Scandinavian manufacturers. The various schemes devised by Ryder and the National Enterprise Board underlined Leyland's commitment to the large and medium volume plants. Some commentators speculated that Leyland would slowly divest itself of the large volume plants and concentrate on the potentially more profitable specialist products.[37] The announcement of the collaborative agreement with Honda in 1979 to produce a new Japanese designed quality saloon at Canley was seen by many as an end to local uncertainty over Leyland's long term commitment to Coventry.

The change of Government in 1979 soon quashed the cautious optimism that had been present in the local car industry. The Conservative economic strategy of high interest rates tended to overvalue the pound, particularly in the U.S.A., the major market for Coventry specialist cars. Demand for Coventry models rapidly declined. Moreover Leyland management embarked upon a new rationalisation plan. The company's production was to be concentrated into two plants, at Cowley and Longbridge. Triumph production was transferred to Cowley along with the Rover models produced at Solihull. The Courthouse Green engine plant was closed and Alvis, Climax and Jaguar sold off to private buyers. In the first three years of the Conservative government the number of Leyland employees in Coventry fell from 27,000 to 8,000. One recent writer has summarised the effects of Conservative policy in these three years as turning a process of 'gentle decline into quickening collapse'.[38] Overall the city's top fifteen manufacturing firms shed

31,000 workers between 1979 and 1982. Well known pillars of Coventry's economic base such as Herberts, Triumph Motors and Renold's disappeared .[39]

The crisis of the Coventry economy was apparent throughout the 1970s. The majority of Coventrians, however, were unaware of the impending industrial collapse. Unemployment in 1979 stood at just over five per cent, exactly the same level as in 1971. There was a noticeable rise in youth unemployment during the late 1970s but this could be explained as part of a national problem rooted in demographic factors. Similarly wages generally in Coventry were no longer higher than in most other manufacturing centres. Again this could be put down to the economic turbulence of the 1970s which had weakened the bargaining position of workers. Given Coventry's still formidable trade union movement optimists saw no reason why this pattern of relative wage decline should continue. Moreover the election of the Conservative government was not considered a harbinger of hard times to come. Coventry had prospered reasonably well during previous Tory administrations. Indeed the last real boom in the local economy had been stimulated by the policies of Mr. Anthony Barber.

Unfortunately economic brakes were applied rather than released by the new government. Monetarist policy was quick to bite local industry. Redundancy lists and closure notices in the local press became as depressingly regular as the obituary column. The biggest surprise, however, was the lack of protest from the local Labour movement. Numbness, bewilderment, and even an element of resignation characterised the city during this period. It was as if all the ominous prophecies of the anti-union editorials that regularly appeared in the *Coventry Evening Telegraph* during previous periods of industrial unrest were finally being realised.

Even defensive strategies were difficult to devise. Michael Edwardes's new tough industrial relations programme had seen the removal of Britain's strongest motor factory trade union leader from Longbridge. He also demonstrated at Speke in Liverpool that he could and would close plants in the face of trade union opposition. Moreover the local Labour movement had little ammunition to try and halt the offensive. Factory occupation, used to such effect by continental trade unionists had, thanks to the Meriden Triumph Motorcycles fiasco, no local currency. The opposition was undoubtedly diminished by redundancy payments which in many cases promised to cushion families for a year or two from the still unrealised effects of the recession.

Young people, particularly school leavers, were the real victims. Job opportunities, especially much prized craft apprenticeships all but vanished. Only 95 apprentices commenced training in 1981. By 1982 only 16 per cent of fifth form school leavers found employment. The early 1980s have been barren years for Coventry youngsters. Even the success of the local pop group 'The Specials', has brought little relief. Parents and politicians had failed to remedy Coventry's plight, but for a brief moment the young had their song. 'Ghost Town' was a success because it gave vent to a phenomenon that was national. The lyric's sombre comparison of boom time and recession express an experience that has been felt only much more sharply in Coventry than elsewhere. 'The Specials' have now broken up and redundancy money is fast running out. Unemployment levels have yet to fall, unlike local population figures. Coventry is now for the first time in one hundred years a net exporter of labour. The main loss appears to be amongst the young skilled and technical management sectors, people that any town can ill afford to lose. Little development work is now taking place in local industry. Talbot's research department at Whitley including many key personnel, for example, was removed to Paris in 1983. Research at Leyland's Canley site is now a service for plants outside the city. The Conservatives promised in 1979 that a restructuring of the economy would be followed by increased investment and employment opportunities but there is no sign that the promise is being realised. Coventry's peculiar dependence on manufacturing and its historically weak tertiary sector has meant that the city is a poor location for the so called high tech industries.

Coventry in the mid 1980s displays none of the confidence in the future that was so apparent in the immediate post-war years. The city, which for four decades was the natural habitat of the affluent industrial worker is finding it difficult to adjust to a situation where the local authority and university rank amongst the largest employers. Coventry's self-image of progressiveness and modernity has all but vanished. The citizens now largely identify themselves and their environment as part of depressed Britain. This is a sad comparison to the chirpily confident soldier and his girlfriend who took part in the 1945 government film 'A City Re-Born'. Viewing Donald Gibson's model of the new Coventry they found difficulty in containing their optimism.

> *Soldier*: "This is a good model, Betty, isn't it—the city'd better be good too, it's where we're going to live."
> *Commentator*: "Coventry is going to be a place to live in where people can believe how pleasant human life can be ...

It must be not every man for himself, but every man for the good and the happiness of all people living ... Every man must believe in the good and happiness that is to be shared ... to be shared, equally".
Girl: "... Goodbye darling ... don't be long".
Soldier: "... Don't worry, darling ... it can't be long now. We'll soon be together in our own little home with a ..."
TRAIN WHISTLES
"... with a nice little garage".
Girl: "... and a nice little nursery".[40]

Notes to Chapter 12

1. H. James, *English Hours* (1981 ed.), 131-133.
2. J.E. Swindelhurst, *Notes on the Expansion of Coventry during the last twelve years* (1912), 6-7.
3. *Ibid.*, 12.
4. J.B. Priestley, *English Journey* (1934), 69, 74.
5. See Frank Carr's essay, chapter 6.
6. *Midland Daily Telegraph*, 15 July, 1936.
7. *Ibid.*, 11 October, 1935.
8. 'Trinity Street', (1937), pamphlet; Local Studies Collection. *Midland Daily Telegraph*, 27 November, 1937. There were 14,000 cars owned by Coventry citizens.
9. See Bill Lancaster's essay, chapter 2.
10. *The Coventry Searchlight*, November 1937.
11. G. Hodgkinson, *Sent to Coventry* (1970), chapter 10, passim.
12. *Ibid.*, 134.
13. For a discussion of the 1930s rearmament programme in Coventry and elsewhere see R. Croucher, *Engineers at War 1939-1945* (1982) chapter I, passim.
14. K. Richardson, *Twentieth Century Coventry* (1972) 93-94.
15. *Architectural Design*, December 1958, 473.
16. T. Sharp, *Exeter Phoenix: A Plan for Rebuilding* (1946), 9.
17. Medical Officer of Health Annual Report, 1948.
18. Spon Gate C.D.A Planning Document 1961.
19. In 'no fines' concrete the sand and cement mixture had been altered in order to produce quicker drying. Building regulations were waived in order to facilitate this, hence, 'no fines'.
20. P. Sargant Florence et.al., *Coventry Sociological Survey 1949-51* (1951).
21. *Daily Worker*, 6 December, 1940.
22. K.E. Barlow, *A Home of Their Own* (1946) ch. VIII *passim*; *The Family Health Club Review*, July 1947; *Coventry Evening Telegraph*, 2 July, 1947; L. Kuper (ed.), *Living in Towns* (1953), 179; *Camera Principis*, 124, n.s. 15, September 1946, 2-3.
23. This information was gleaned from: a) *Coventry Evening Telegraph Year Book*; b) Obituary notices; c) biographical details from George Hodgkinson.
24. *Coventry Evening Telegraph*, 10 May, 1949.

25. *Ibid.*, 12 December, 1945; 18, 19 November, 1948.
26. *Coventry Standard*, 15 April, 1955.
27. *Ibid.*, 7 April, 1955.
28. *Coventry Evening Telegraph*, 3 May, 1955.
29. R. Crossman, Introduction to George Hodgkinson, *op.cit.*, xxv-xxvi.
30. *Coventry Evening Telegraph*, 3 May, 1967.
31. *Ibid.*
32. Richard Crossman, *The Diaries of a Cabinet Minister*, Vol. I, (1975), 416.
33. R. Hyman, *The Workers Union* (1971), 21.
34. James Hinton, *The First Shop Stewards Movement* (1973) 218-221.
35. Frank Carr's essay, chapter 6.
36. P.E.P. Engineering Reports, 2 (1950), 26.
37. K. Bhaskar, *The Future of the U.K. Motor Industry* (1979) chapter 7.
38. S. Taylor, 'De-Industrialisation and Unemployment in the West Midlands', *Political Quarterly*, 52, 1981.
39. City of Coventry Economic Monitor, November 1982. 2,700 former Leyland employees now work for United Scientific and the Kaye Organisations, the companies which took over Leyland's 'Alvis' and 'Climax' operations in Coventry.
40. Ministry of Information, 'A City Re-Born', P.R.O. Inf.6/616.

INDEX